THE TRUTH ABOUT AIDS
(Previous editions)

Many useful facts and opinions about the medical and social aspects of AIDS.

Nursing Times

Should be available to every GP for his own use and for lending to those concerned . . . well referenced yet written with a minimum of technical jargon.

The Physician

A wealth of research and published material from medical and popular sources in a detailed and extensively referenced book.

British Medical Journal

Useful and interesting book that patients will read and benefit from.

Journal of Royal College of General Practitioners

Excellent and thoroughly readable book.

Caring Professions Concern (CICP)

Probably the best single volume of the whole AIDS issue available today. I recommend it to pastors and those with care responsibility as well as others with more general interest.

Restoration

If *Which?* offers a best buy then *The Truth About AIDS* is my choice . . . the tone, suggestions and response seem to mirror exactly what Jesus would require of us all in the current crisis.

Third Way

Personal faith, questions and weaknesses are honestly shared by a Christian doctor who does not regard the finality of death as failure.

Life and Work

About the author

Patrick Dixon is the author of twelve books including *The Truth About AIDS*, *AIDS and You*, *Out of the Ghetto and into the City*, *Signs of Revival*, *The Truth About Drugs*, *The Genetic Revolution*, *The Truth About Westminster*, *The Rising Price of Love* and *Futurewise*.

He trained as a doctor before specialising in the care of those dying of cancer and then of AIDS. Following the first edition of *The Truth About AIDS* he started ACET (AIDS Care Education and Training) in June 1988, as a national and international Christian response to AIDS. Dr Dixon was CEO until 1991 and today helps lead an international network of independent care, prevention and training initiatives known as the ACET International Alliance, active in the UK, Ireland, the Czech Republic, Slovakia, Russia, Ukraine, Croatia, Uganda, Zimbabwe, Nigeria, India, Thailand and in partnership with projects in many other nations. ACET projects work with a wide variety of international agencies, including UNICEF, UNAIDS, Tearfund, Christian AID, Samaritan's Purse, Operation Mobilisation and Action Aid.

Dr Dixon is also Chairman of Global Change Ltd, a consulting and trends forecasting company, a frequent commentator in media around the world and an adviser to many large corporations on issues such as the digital society, new technology, biotech, globalisation, leadership, motivation and corporate values. He is 47 years old, lives in West London, and is married with four children. As a family they are active members of a local church, in partnership with the Evangelical Alliance and Pioneer.

http://www.acet-international.org

The Truth About AIDS

and a practical Christian response

DR PATRICK DIXON

'With God, all things are possible.'
Jesus Christ

ACET INTERNATIONAL ALLIANCE
and
OPERATION MOBILISATION

Previously published by Kingsway 1987, 1990 and 1994

This edition published 2004 by ACET International
Alliance PO Box 46242, London W5 2WG, UK
   (see page 562 for contact details)
In partnership with Operation Mobilisation

0 9547549 0 5

Unless otherwise indicated, biblical quotations are
from the New International Version © 1973, 1978, 1984
by the International Bible Society.

Book design and production for the publisher by
Bookprint Creative Services, P.O. Box 827, BN21 3YJ, England.
Printed in Great Britain.

CONTENTS

ACKNOWLEDGEMENTS

This book was first published in 1987 and led to the creation of ACET (AIDS Care Education and Training) as an international Christian initiative. Today ACET International Alliance is a community or network of many independent AIDS programmes seeking to show Christian unconditional love and to save lives.

This special not-for-profit edition is a partnership between ACET International Alliance, Operation Mobilisation, Tearfund, Africa Inland Church, Emmanuel Hospital Association and World Vision.

I am particularly grateful to Mark Forshaw for Chapter 15, Isabel Carter, Dr Langkham and Marion Derbyshire for contributing appendices, and to all who have helped in different ways to make this project a reality, in particular to the unfailing encouragement of George Verwer, Susie Howe, and Ray and Joy Thomas without whom this would not have happened.

I am also profoundly grateful to the generosity of Operation Mobilisation and other organisations as well as individuals who have helped fund thousands of copies of this resource for those in the poorest nations.

Others who helped along the way include Dr Veronica Moss, John Spencer, Dr Eric Douglas, Peter Scott, Jennifer Oldroyd, Rachel Ashley-Pain, Gerald Coates, Dr Rob George, Caroline Akehurst, Dr George Rutherford, Professor Eric Wilkes, Maurice Adams, Jayne Clemence, David Kabiswa, Colin McPhail, Alan Ellard, all the others who have been part of the international ACET family, many at Ealing Christian Fellowship and Bridge Church. And none of this would have been possible without the love and practical support of Sheila my wife, who continues to play a major role in running ACET International Alliance.

How to use this book

This book is designed to be used as a collection of resources to assist and encourage people in every nation to develop rapidly a wide range of practical and sustainable Christian responses to HIV and AIDS. You may want to read it from the beginning or to use the chapter headings and the Index to locate what you need, to adapt to your own situation and culture.

This book is a general guide and should not be used as a substitute for expert medical advice by those needing care.

Improve this book and encourage us

This work is still in progress. You can help us by telling us ways we can improve it, omissions, inaccuracies, additional examples of best practice and Christian mission or extra useful resources to add. Do tell us of projects you have started as a result of reading this book.

Please email: isdixon@dircon.co.uk

Help us to distribute this book

Free copies of this book are available to Christian organisations. Please help us by emailing us with details of your organisation, how many copies you can use and to whom they will be given. We will do our best to meet every request.

A shorter resource, *AIDS and You*, is also available in English and other languages, including Romanian, Czech, Turkish, Hungarian, Russian, Spanish, French, Urdu and Paite, for church leaders, youth pastors and project workers. It can be ordered in bulk for distribution by Christian organisations in the poorest nations.

Please email: isdixon@dircon.co.uk

BAD NEWS AND GOOD NEWS

A terrible catastrophe has hit many African nations since 1987, when the first edition of this book was published, warning of coming disaster and encouraging urgent Christian action. Uganda reported then just 738 AIDS cases, South Africa only 41. But the writing was on the wall, with rapid spread of HIV across the continent already well underway.

Sadly, many of the book's original predictions have become a tragic reality. Over 85 million people have become infected, and half have already died, leaving tens of millions of orphans. India, China, Russia and many other parts of the world are now on the frontline.

Today, more than ever, we need an urgent, effective response, with life-saving prevention and compassionate care. The good news is that in many of the poorest, hardest-hit nations, the church has now become a major provider of HIV programmes (equalled only by government – and in some countries like Burundi exceeding government). We are in a race against time. We must learn lessons from the past. As we have seen in countries like Uganda, HIV can be beaten, step by step, when we all pull together: church, community organisations, leaders, business, media and government.

The church, however, continues to focus on care and neglect prevention – a warm-hearted, loving response that is shortsighted, foolish, poorly serves the real needs of the community and will lead to disaster. One project I know in Africa spends $350,000 a year caring for children in a sixty-bed unit, yet nothing on preventing millions more children from dying. The same budget would be enough to pay 200 villagers as educators, saving at least 100 lives a year each. That's 20,000 people who are also never going to infect others, 10,000 women whose babies are not at risk, up to 100,000 children who will not be bereaved. We have a moral and urgent duty to ensure we spend as much time, effort and funds on prevention as on care. Caring is the easier option: easy to raise funds, easier to set up, easy to see the impact of what you do, easy to get people motivated. Prevention is the greater challenge.

After an appallingly slow international response, the wealthiest nations have finally woken up to the nightmare before their eyes in poorer nations. International agencies, multi-nationals, foundations and governments are now committing far greater resources to fight spread and improve care. But they are severely handicapped by lack of quality, 'on the ground' community programmes and networks. An example of this is the WHO 3 by 5 programme, with the bold aim of providing free anti-retroviral medicines to at least 3 million people ill from HIV infection, mainly in Africa. On the other hand, the church is the largest organisation in the world, with a proven track record of delivering excellent programmes over many decades. A major challenge is to connect the two movements together: international financial muscle with armies of Christian project workers. Both need each other, hence the huge emphasis today on partnerships, including Faith-Based Organisations (FBOs).

The words of Jesus have been proven true: 'To him who has much, more will be given.' Larger, well-established Christian agencies are set to grow rapidly, but in turn will be limited by capacity unless they form well-established federations with like-minded smaller projects through whom regional and national objectives can be met. I say again: well-organised, quality programmes that are large and able to prove their impact are unlikely to be short of financial resources over the next decade, but we must do all we can to make sure that small organisations also get the help they need to grow, since they provide at least 80% of community support in developing countries.

The problem of AIDS is too great, too urgent, and the shortage of quality partners is an urgent unsolved problem for international agencies. What we need is a global Christian movement. It's already established and growing fast. But we have far to go.

Patrick Dixon, February 2004

CHAPTER ONE

THE EXTENT OF THE NIGHTMARE

It was 1981. In a Los Angeles doctor's office the men sitting in white coats were worried: within a few weeks they had diagnosed their fourth case of a condition so incredibly rare they had hardly expected to see it in their collective professional lifetime. They were baffled by the series of strange pneumonias that got worse despite normal antibiotics. All of the patients were men. All were young. All of them had died.

Three and a half thousand miles to the east, at a hospital in New York, several doctors were faced with similar problems: strange tumours and lethal pneumonias in young men. What was going on?

The cases were all reported to the infectious disease centre. Could this be some sort of epidemic? Were the pneumonias and cancers caused by the same thing? What did the men have in common? Every day new reports of deaths came flooding in. It was becoming clear that most if not all of the deceased were men who had had sex with other men. The disease quickly became labelled 'the gay plague'. How wrong they would turn out to be.

Dozens of strange infections were seen – with all the classic signs of weakened natural defences. The disease was called AIDS – Acquired Immune Deficiency Syndrome. It took some time to discover that the culprit was a tiny virus, called the Human Immunodeficiency Virus or HIV. It is now known that someone can be infected with HIV for ten years or more before developing the illness called AIDS.

Just five years later, by November 1986, 15,345 people had already died, another 12,000 were dying, and a further 30,000 were feeling unwell.

People were concerned that maybe up to a million people in the United States were also infected but were not yet ill. At first the 'experts' predicted only one in ten of those infected would die, then two in ten, then three in ten, then nine out of ten. Now we know that almost everyone with the infection will die as a result.

Most estimates from the early 1980s were exceeded. By April 1990, there were over 126,000 cases reported in the United States. (There were estimates of possibly 200,000 to 300,000 feeling unwell and maybe 700,000 infected, representing up to one in sixty of all men in the United States between the ages of 20 and 50.) In New York, AIDS became the commonest cause of death for men and women aged between 25 and 44, with 100 AIDS deaths every week. One in every sixty-one babies carried HIV. By 1993, more people were dying of AIDS in the United States each year than died in the entire ten-year Vietnam War, compared to 6,000 deaths in the UK. By 2002, over 45,000 American citizens were still being infected every year, despite fifteen years of prevention campaigns.

The number of people already doomed in the United States made the Vietnam tragedy look like a minor skirmish, with one new infection every thirteen minutes. The coffins, if placed end to end, would stretch for 1,000 miles.

Yet while all the attention at first was on America, another similar but far more catastrophic disaster was silently destroying another continent, and no one had noticed.

The African experience

Some years after AIDS was diagnosed in the United States, the first cases were recognised in Africa. We know today that for years thousands had been dying, but their deaths were blamed on tuberculosis and other diseases.

In many towns and cities across Central Africa, up to a third of all young adults are infected. A third of the truck drivers running the main north/south routes, and half the prostitutes in many towns are carrying HIV. One relief agency in the early 1990s talked unofficially about pulling out of Central Africa. What was the point in drilling more wells when most of the people would be dead in a few years?

By 2004, over 45 million Africans were infected, of which more than 30 million were still alive. A further 12 million children had lost one or both of their parents. The effects over the last 15 years have been catastrophic. Seven countries, all in southern Africa, now have prevalence rates higher than 20%: Botswana (38.8%), Lesotho (31%), Namibia (22.5%), South Africa (20.1%), Swaziland (33.4%), Zambia (21.5%) and Zimbabwe (33.7%).

Uganda remains one of the only countries to have subdued a major HIV/AIDS epidemic, with the adult HIV prevalence rate continuing to drop, from 8.3% at the end of 1999 to 5% at the end of 2001. Huge challenges persist, however, such as taking care of the 880,000 Ugandan children who have been orphaned by AIDS. 60% of all adults infected are women.

I have visited villages where grandmothers are looking after their grandchildren because so many young men and women – the parents – have been wiped out by AIDS. Armies of troops in Central Africa are being decimated, not by rockets and machine guns, but by AIDS. Breadwinners for families and providers of the countries' wealth are missing. The educated elite, living in the main towns and cities, have often been worst hit.

In the country, fields are uncultivated and cattle wander aimlessly. One journalist visiting an African country described areas where whole families had been wiped out, and plantations gone back to bush. I have met someone who claims to have satellite photographs of a country in Central Africa, taken two years apart, showing not deforestation, but reforestation as the amount of farming falls. The country is not at war. This is an effect attributed to AIDS.

As early as 1991 I found it hard in a city like Kampala to find a family that was not attending an AIDS funeral on average once a month. Deaths continued to soar over the next decade among young adults. In Africa they called it the 'slim' disease. Some Africans believe if you sleep with only fat women you are safe. 'To be fat is to be healthy.' Uganda has seen a dramatic response to prevention campaigns, but for those already infected it is all too late.

In the early days of the pandemic, officials stood at the doors of some hospitals, selecting the fit ones for treatment. Anyone who looked thin and weak was sent back into the bush: 'Probably got AIDS. Nothing we can do for him.' Many were sent away with perfectly treatable diseases, such as tuberculosis. You cannot tell the difference at the door.

Years and years of careful preventive medicine has been undermined. How do you start educating about a disease which produces no illness for years? Or when nurses are still battling against ingrained habits just to get mothers to give their children a healthy diet?

The children's wards are full of dying children, including babies under one or two years old. Many are not dying of famine, but of AIDS. A terrible tragedy is that a significant number in the 1980s and early 1990s caught the virus, not while in their mothers' wombs, or from their mothers' milk, but from the use of unsterilised needles.

AIDS is not a gay plague; there are millions more women and children infected with HIV throughout the world than there are gay men. It gained this reputation in the United States because gay men were first to be diagnosed, yet 98% of all new infections worldwide are heterosexually acquired – and in the poorest nations.

The global pandemic

We are seeing very rapid spread of HIV in Russia and other former Eastern bloc countries. In Romania, up to one in ten of all children in orphanages became infected before the revolution in 1990, and a similar percentage shortly after. The route was mainly infected needles rather than the widely reported micro-transfusions used as a tonic.

In South East Asia, HIV is spreading so fast that it threatens to dwarf the African problem by the year 2015. However, there is hope that if denial is replaced by openness, and if openness leads to intensive prevention, then the eventual size of the tragedy may be significantly reduced. South East Asia has the advantage of advanced warning – something Africa never had.

In Thailand, many experts predicted a serious AIDS epidemic because of the sex industry and international sex tourism. However, by the time the Thai government was prepared to acknowledge the situation, the epidemic was well under way. In three years, half a million were infected – the great majority heterosexually. But, as with Uganda, a prompt and aggressive health campaign has saved the lives of millions of Thai people.

In Indonesia, the fourth largest population of all countries, infection rates have jumped in a year from 15% to 40% among drug users attending treatment centres in Jakarta.

In India alone there are more sexually active people alive than adults in the whole of sub-Saharan Africa, and by 2001 India had more HIV cases than any other nation. What happens in the East is likely to have a massive impact on the world situation. In Bombay (Mumbai) alone there are an estimated 1,000 new infections every night, just in the huge red light district which attracts over 100,000 young men daily. Some parts of India have HIV infection rates of more than 1%. If that rises as it has done in parts of Africa to more than 15% then we could see four times as many AIDS deaths in India than there have been in the entire world up until 2003.

China, with a fifth of the world's population, registered a rise of more than 67% in reported HIV infections in the first six months of 2001. Although surveillance data is sketchy, at least a million Chinese were living with HIV/AIDS at the end of 2002. Since the early 1990s, tens of thousands of rural villagers (and possibly many more) have become infected in China through unsafe blood donation procedures. Untreated sexually transmitted diseases doubled from 1997 to 2001 and huge population movements within the country are also accelerating spread.

Denial of heterosexual risk

Many have tried to play down the heterosexual problem as a non-issue for white men and women, especially in wealthy nations. This is remarkably short sighted and inaccurate. Heterosexual acts are now the commonest cause of new infections in countries like the UK. You can't place a ring of steel around a country and hope. What happens in one nation affects others. What hits Burundi also affects Rwanda. Infections travel. You can have a great health campaign, but if the epidemic is out of control elsewhere, watch out.

It is clear that heterosexual spread in the US or Europe is far slower than in many developing countries. While viral variation could be the reason, with more virulent strains in some places (see Chapter 2) or some genetic susceptibility (see Chapter 5), the overwhelming evidence is that untreated sex diseases such as gonorrhoea and chancroid facilitate the spread by damaging the protective surface of the genitalia. Differences in the numbers of sexual partners between wealthy and poorer nations are not enough to explain the much slower rates of HIV spread.

The AIDS epidemic worldwide is still in its very earliest stages. And with no vaccine or cure on the horizon, this is an epidemic that threatens our future. But even if a drug was found tomorrow that was as effective against HIV as antibiotics are against TB and syphilis, we have to remember that, despite these effective treatments having been available for 50 years, we have the largest global epidemics of both illnesses today. In other words, even a cheap and widely available cure will not mean the end of AIDS. Effective vaccines are a long way off, and antiretroviral therapy is beyond the reach of most of those with HIV, is toxic and must be taken for life under close medical supervision.

Many churches are experiencing phenomenal growth in different parts of the world. Millions of young people are becoming Christians each year. Often there are spectacular conversions resulting in radical changes in lifestyle. Heroin addicts throw away their needles. Marriages are rebuilt. The results are often permanent, but so is any previous infection. AIDS will damage churches physically, emotionally, psychologically and spiritually, unless they are prepared.

At a conference for church leaders, I met a man who had been a heroin addict before his conversion four or five years previously. He was now leading a church. This kind of success story is happening in many different nations. Some of these people are developing AIDS.

So what do we do? How can we prevent the disease? How can we cure it? How can we cope with it? The rest of this book addresses these four questions. Is AIDS really so different from any other disease, or is it just the mass hysteria and panic associated with it?

What's so special about AIDS?

AIDS is certainly unusual or unique in two respects. First, I do not know of any other illness today where people are beaten up, killed or denied basic medical care just because they happen to have a particular diagnosis.

Secondly, I do not know of any other illness which has generated so much political debate, pressure, campaigning and aggressive activism. Some companies are now saying it is hard to conduct normal medical research in the area of HIV or AIDS because the political pressures threaten to overwhelm and interfere at every level. They are certainly under huge pressure to give away their ownership of any AIDS therapies they create, and that means investors get worried and less money is available for AIDS research, especially into vaccines. One day I hope we will have a vaccine that works, but whoever makes it will face irresistible demands to give it all away 'to save the world'.

Discrimination, prejudice and fear are seen every day in many countries. It is true that some activism has been driven by members of the gay community in developed countries, rather than by drug users, heterosexuals or those with haemophilia, or by those in the poorest nations – a fact which becomes very obvious at the larger international AIDS conferences.

Indeed, global AIDS events are often split by two conflicting interests: first by gay HIV activists who have a particular agenda, and second by far less well-organised and less well-resourced representatives of the vast majority of people with HIV who live in the poorest nations.

AIDS has also attracted the eccentric and the bizarre. I was recently sent literature from an organisation claiming that the US government deliberately made HIV as part of a cunning plot to reduce the world population by 75%. The Mafia and the CIA are said to be deeply involved. Equally bizarre are some of the 'cures', including eating earth and drinking vinegar, or high-cost preparations with no proven value. Other minorities try to persuade people that HIV is harmless and does not even cause AIDS (see Chapter 5 'Questions People Ask').

Yet in another sense there is nothing special about AIDS. It is just the latest in a long series of epidemics spread by sex. Sleeping around has always carried risks to health. Now it can be lethal.

Sex diseases (STDs) are common. Over 30 million people in

the USA are estimated to have genital herpes. Some 56 million, or 20% of all US adults, are estimated to be carrying an STD at any time. 50% of all adults in Mumbai India are carrying an STD. Worldwide there are an estimated 250 million new STD infections each year. With ordinary STDs the damage is usually more obvious, immediate and less serious than with HIV.

More than 300 years ago a plague broke out in Europe and spread across the Western world. Vast numbers died. Early symptoms were mild, the second stage made people very ill, and half of those who developed the third stage died, many with brain damage. It was a terrible disease, and it was spread by sex. It was named 'syphilis'.

Syphilis only stopped being a major threat with the discovery of penicillin at the end of World War II. During the war, United States army recruits were warned that, after Hitler, syphilis was Public Enemy Number One. A famous US Army war poster showed a prostitute walking with Hitler on one arm and the Japanese Emperor on the other. The caption read: 'VD (venereal disease) worst of the three.' Syphilis has not gone away; we are in the middle of a major heterosexual explosion of cases which often produce few or no symptoms and are untreated for a long period.

Gonorrhoea also became a curable sexual disease with penicillin – until the recent advent of penicillin-resistant strains which are now spreading rapidly across the globe and becoming harder and harder to treat. There is an unprecedented epidemic of genital herpes. Highly infectious and appallingly painful blisters prevent sex. There is no cure and it can cause problems throughout a person's life. There is also a big increase in cases of cancer of the neck of the womb (cervix), some of which are associated with a virus infection which is due to sleeping with multiple partners.

There is also the heart-rending problem of infertility. Have you ever wondered about the huge test-tube baby programme in many wealthy nations? The major part of the caseload is women

with badly damaged and scarred fallopian tubes – the thin, delicate tubes which guide the egg from the ovary to the womb. The
cause is an infection called pelvic inflammatory disease (PID),
which can be caused by a tiny organism called chlamydia. There
is no treatment that can undo the damage of pelvic inflammatory disease. One in ten women develop it after being infected
with chlamydia, gonorrhoea, or some other infection. It causes
aches and pains that are chronically disabling, and it gradually
causes the reproductive organs to stick together.

The difference between HIV-related diseases and other
sexual epidemics is that HIV can infect you for years before you
know it, and by the time you do, it may have infected hundreds
of others. The long 'silent' delay between infection and death is
why HIV is so dangerous, not the fact that it kills.

The other difference is that once you develop full-blown
AIDS, which can take many years, you face almost certain death,
unless you die of something else in the meantime. As we have
seen, there is no cure and no vaccine, nor is there likely to be in
the foreseeable future. There are many misleading reports, but no
good results; many expensive and toxic treatments that help
prolong life, but no way to rid the body of infection. However,
some of these treatments can protect those who have recently
been exposed, particularly the unborn or small babies.

A rapidly spreading, silent killer which is difficult to detect,
infectious and lethal causes panic. Radiation disasters are
similar: you cannot hear, see, or touch the enemy, nor feel the
damage it is doing until it is too late – sometimes not for years.
No wonder the Chernobyl nuclear reactor disaster in Russia
caused such terrible pandemonium: false rumours, false scares,
false cures, false hopes abounded. AIDS is the same today.

If a man had sex with a work colleague and three weeks later
was dead, and that was repeated across the country, the impact
would be dramatic. You wouldn't need any health campaign
because the coffins would be the campaign. But with HIV and
AIDS the very long time lag produces a credibility problem: the

only people who really understand what is likely to hit us are the mathematicians. An invisible terror can be ignored. If we have to wait another ten years to see exactly what is happening, we will be too late.

The great cover-up

Why are so few people being honest about the extent of the problem and the risks? AIDS is a hard illness to talk about, especially in Africa and Asia. In Africa there is an added sensitivity: confronted with a tragedy affecting their whole continent (and for once not related to war or famine) in an international atmosphere which they see as racist, many have been extremely unwilling to be honest. They are afraid of anti-black backlash if it is said that the problem started there. They are also afraid of economic ruin due to decisions of multinational companies to pull out, and the collapse of their tourist industries. Many of these countries desperately need foreign currency to prevent total bankruptcy. In addition, it has often been difficult for doctors to be sure of the diagnosis. Testing is expensive, kits are hard to obtain and sometimes hard to use. Indirect methods sometimes have to be used, such as a negative skin reaction to the standard tuberculosis (TB) test. Most AIDS-related deaths seem to be happening out in the bush, unnoticed and unregistered. The wards and clinics see mainly early cases.

So we have a bizarre situation where doctors in some countries have been reeling under an impossible workload, and where even government members or relations of the country's leaders were dying, but the problem was denied, or blamed on other causes, or impossible to assess. Scientists studying the epidemic in Africa and Asia are often there under tolerance. Intensive research is going on to understand the disease, but the results are sometimes censored. A scientist may have to sign an agreement not to disclose publicly what he sees happening.

Information is leaking out all the time, but if it is traced back to a particular person or team the workers may be thrown out of the country or into prison. Fortunately, the situation is changing. It has to. The cover-up has had one appalling consequence which prevents an educational campaign. How can a country embark on mass prevention for a disease it says it does not really have? And there is denial for emotional reasons too, not just economic ones. How can you accept from a mathematician that maybe a third of your entire nation could die?

South Africa has had its own reasons to cover up. It has an enormous problem, especially in the black townships where huge numbers of migrant workers originate from countries further north where AIDS is taking a terrible toll.

In places like Soweto, the town providing labour for the deep mines in Johannesburg, there have been up to 50,000 men living without their wives (officially). In the days of apartheid their wives and children were all meant to stay in homelands like the Transkei. They didn't, of course, and drifted out in search of their husbands to build illegal residences made from corrugated iron, wood and plastic. Every now and then these 'shanty towns' were bulldozed to the ground and the women were trucked back, sometimes more than 1,000 miles away.

Fifty thousand men on their own with a few prostitutes spelt trouble, yet this situation has been common in South Africa. The historic white government had no political will to change anything. For them, a major disease that selectively hit black Africans and offset the birthrate may have been convenient. But the new post-apartheid regime has also found it hard to talk about AIDS. Nelson Mandela fought for recognition of the disease, but when he handed over leadership of the nation the government mood changed to one of confusion and denial.

Life after AIDS

Cover-up or no cover-up, honesty, secrecy, or confusion, one thing is clear: nothing will ever be quite the same again. AIDS is fundamentally altering fashions, behaviour, culture – in fact every fibre of our society. In some places, fat is back in fashion. Who wants to look thin? 'Perhaps he has AIDS.' The Hollywood dinosaur of the movie industry is thrashing its tail and the ground is shaking. Television producers are stepping over each other in their zeal to include AIDS in soap operas, plays and comedies.

Magazines like *Cosmopolitan* say that smart girls carry condoms. They hope that smart girls will not feel like loose girls when they produce the packet. They hope too for a new courage and honesty so that people will always tell of their unfaithfulness and promiscuity or drug addiction. They hope for new security in relationships so that when a girl or boy suggests using a condom, the other will not treat it as a terrible insult or lack of trust.

Whether such hopes will remain hopes or actually get built into a strange harsh reality of rubber-separated sex is unclear. But one thing is almost inevitable: out of the ashes of the crematorium will rise a new sub-culture which will affect a whole generation in many parts of the world. A culture of stable relationships and marriages. A culture where a man and a woman find mutual sexual fulfilment for life. We are seeing the early signs of this in many parts of the world, whether America, where over a million teenagers have signed a pre-marriage abstinence pledge, or in places like Uganda.

The reality is that even an AIDS cure in 2008, or a remarkable vaccine in 2010, will not erase the traumas of a generation, nor eradicate the problem. As we have seen with the resurgence of TB and syphilis, low-cost treatment does not mean the end of the story. The message is burning home: sleeping around has always been unhealthy. Now it can be suicidal. Taking AIDS out still leaves the other epidemics untouched. The mid-twenty-first century will look at the 1980s, 1990s, and the early years of the new century as the 'era of AIDS'. The reasons for its spread, its origins, the apathy of governments, and the mistakes of scientists will be debated by historians for generations.

AIDS is likely to dominate the rest of our adult lives – especially the lives of doctors and nurses, and of young people becoming sexually active today. The question is this: will you be able to hold your head high? Will you be proud of the way you responded when you look back on it all?

Apart from a radical change of lifestyle in our society, which will not help those already infected anyway, our only hope remains in understanding this strange virus so we can fight it. But what exactly *is* a virus?

CHAPTER TWO

WHAT'S SO SPECIAL ABOUT A VIRUS?

All viruses are dead. There is nothing alive in a virus at all. A virus is no more living than a computer game you can buy in the high street. Bacteria are different: bacteria breathe oxygen or carbon dioxide, need warmth to grow, and they grow larger and divide into two. In fact, bacteria behave like cells in your own body.

Some bacteria make poisons, such as the tetanus toxin which causes rapid death. Others live quite happily on every corner of your body, for example in your gut, where bacteria help you to digest food. If you take antibiotics, some of these bacteria die and the result can be diarrhoea. So while some bacteria keep us healthy, others bring disease because of the poisons they make when growing.

You can see bacteria under the microscope. I have taken a swab from a man or woman's genitalia and touched a microscope slide with it. I can see the red gonorrhoea bacteria easily and make an instant diagnosis. In most cases a single large dose of penicillin will kill the bacteria. Penicillin works by weakening the cell wall that holds the little organism together. The bacteria swell, burst, and die. A swab containing syphilis organisms is even more interesting: these creatures swim like little eels, thrashing about on the wet glass slide. Instant diagnosis. Immediate high dose penicillin. Immediate cure in most cases.

But AIDS is caused by a virus (HIV). Thousands of bacteria

can fit inside a cell in your body, but virus particles are so minute that hundreds of thousands of them could fit inside a single bacterium. They are totally invisible under a normal light microscope. Viruses cannot grow and cannot divide. They don't breathe, don't need food, don't live, and never die. All our technology has failed to produce a single non-toxic drug that attacks and destroys a virus as well as antibiotics kill bacteria.

The kiss of death

The only real weapons we have against viruses are natural ones: antibodies, which can also destroy bacteria. These are Y-shaped. The mouth of the antibody is shaped exactly to fit over part of a germ. Thousands of them lock onto a germ so that the tails bristle like a hedgehog. Sometimes that is enough to burst bacteria or to stop viruses from being able to touch a cell. Special white cells in the body stick on to these bristles and eat up the germ. These white cells are those that you find in pus, cleaning up an infected wound. The trouble with antibodies is that the body takes three days to produce the right antibody for the right virus. During this critical three-day period, the body is totally unprotected. Yet only an hour or two after viruses enter the bloodstream they have completely disappeared. You can hunt through the entire body cell by cell, with the best electron-firing microscope, and find nothing.

Why? Because every virus particle has disintegrated. Each one has burst like a soap bubble when it touches the ground.

The virus bag has disintegrated and vanished. And what about the contents? They too have disappeared without trace, but the cell they touched has received the kiss of death.

A virus is a bag containing a short piece of coiled-up 'string'. The string is formed entirely of four different chemicals arranged in an order. When stretched out, it reads like a language:

abbdauaabdacccuabdauccdaaabuaauccdaa

This language is what we call a genetic code. It is the language used by the nucleus (brain) of every cell in your body. A cell of your body under the microscope looks a little like an egg. It has a central round core called a nucleus and a more transparent-looking outer area. The nucleus is black and is packed full of your chromosomes. You have forty-six chromosomes which determined everything from the moment you were conceived, including the length of your arms, whether you have black or brown hair, whether you will be bald by the time you are 30, your height, gender, basic build, the shape of your nose. Everything.

Each of these chromosomes is tightly coiled up like a spring. If we stretched out the message and then typed out the sequence, and put all the messages from all the chromosomes in one cell in your body into a book, that book would be the size of *Encyclopaedia Britannica*.

These instructions program not only your outside appearance, but also every type of cell in your body. Have you ever thought how a skin cell learned it was a skin cell and not a nail- or hair-producing cell? How does a cell know it should produce bone and not hormones? If I cut my hand, how does a skin cell know to divide and go on dividing until the gap is covered and then stop? The answer lies in that vast book of instructions. The amazing thing is that every cell nucleus in your body carries a carbon copy of your entire genetic code.

Life-changing technology

We have already succeeded in altering the genetic code of a bacterium so it contains a small piece of code taken from a human being. This piece of code tells the bacterium not to produce poison but to produce human insulin – previously diabetics were dependent on insulin obtained by crushing the pancreas of a pig or cow. This new strain of bacteria grows and divides for ever, with each new organism containing a perfect set of instructions for making human insulin.

In 2003, over 500,000 genetically mutated animals were born in UK laboratories, each unlike any animal ever seen before. Human genes have been added to pigs to make them grow faster. The 'superbreed' is blind, impotent and suffers from severe arthritis. Human genes have been added to cows, sheep, rabbits, mice, and even fish. Scorpion poison genes have been added to cabbages, spider genes to goats. We urgently need the technology to cure disease and to feed the world, but its abuse to create, say, designer families for tomorrow's parents is just one nightmare possibility for the future.

Various laboratories around the world have now 'decoded' the entire genetic material of a human. This will one day enable us to say that:

ABCADDA = insulin
UBCADDDD = length of nose
UBCCABBA = amount of pigment in hair

The correct bit for any part of a human can then be cut out and transferred, or be reprogrammed and put back into the cell.

It is also possible to map out every single instruction a virus contains and understand precisely what it does in the cell it affects, so why can't all this remarkable technology produce a cure for AIDS? Consider what happens when the virus bubble touches its target cell.

How the virus kills a white cell

The surface of HIV is specially shaped so that it only fits on to a very small range of cells in the body. The flu virus latches on to cells in the nose, while HIV mainly latches on to one particular type of white cell (CD4 + T-lymphocyte), some brain cells, and one or two others.

When HIV touches the cell and the bubble bursts, the genetic code (RNA) is injected into the cell. Within minutes the code is being read by the cell and the message is carried into the cell brain, or nucleus. The message is then added permanently to that cell's 'book of life' as DNA. The process has taken only a few minutes and is complete. The cell looks normal in every way but is now doomed. It may continue to look normal for several years. During this time the white cell continues to travel in the blood looking for invaders while blissfully unaware of the invader within. If the attacked cell divides, the two daughter cells also carry perfect copies of the hidden message. It is likely that the infected cells in semen or vaginal fluids are the main source of HIV transmissions during sex.

Each cell infected by HIV becomes a biological time-bomb travelling in the bloodstream. Millions of them waiting to explode.

One day a particular germ enters the body that this particular cell is geared to deal with. There are thousands of different white cells, all designed to kill different kinds of organisms. It just so happens that out of all the thousands of different infections a person could have caught, this particular one fits the role of this particular cell. It springs into action, programmed by its brain to react. It starts to produce proteins. The cell should help the body turn out finished antibodies that are the exact shape and form to fit the intruding germ and kill it. It's at this point that the effect of the virus is finally revealed. The virus message then overrides the entire cell system and orders a new product to be made: thousands and thousands of HIV messages in genetic code. These are then carried to the outside wall of the cell where each is wrapped and thrown out of the cell. So infected white cells become factories for more virus, instead of factories to help the body make antibodies.

You can see special electron microscope photographs of hundreds of these viruses appearing as little bulges as they poke out from the cell. Eventually they emerge as little round balls, and the cell dies. Millions of virus particles are released into the bloodstream, each one floating in the blood until it touches another

CD4 white cell, bursts, injects its message, reprograms the cell, and the process continues.

The trouble is that despite all our modern technology it is hard to detect an infected cell. They look identical from the outside until they are dying. Nor are we able to find the virus easily when it is floating in the bloodstream.

Antibodies don't protect you

The extraordinary thing about the virus is that its outer bag is formed from your own cell membrane. When it came out from the white cell, it was clothed in cell membrane, so its outer feel is in many ways just like a human cell. It is true that there are some distinguishing marks on the outside of the virus and the body does produce antibodies. However, when the antibody latches on to one of these lumps on the virus coating, the lump can break off, leaving the virus intact, just as a lizard sheds its tail.

The problem with HIV is not that the body cannot produce antibodies against the virus. On the contrary, almost every person produces antibodies. That is how we test for infection: not by looking for the virus, but by testing for antibodies. The sinister thing is that the virus appears to be immune to antibodies. No antibodies have yet been found in a human being that are effective in the long term against HIV. That is why a vaccine will be so difficult to find. It is easy to produce antibodies against the virus, but we don't know how to produce one that will prevent infection, because we have no natural model from which to work.

New strains of HIV appearing

The other worrying thing about this virus is its ability to alter its shape. Earlier we saw that antibody-producing cells are specific. An antibody against one organism is only rarely effective against another. If an organism changes its outer coating at all, it is back to the drawing board to make a new antibody. HIV can change shape in subtle ways in the same person over the course of a few months, and a person can be infected with several differently shaped viruses at once, possibly with varying abilities to cause disease. Even worse, HIV occasionally changes its shape radically. We are currently seeing new HIV-like viruses emerging every year or two somewhere in the world. There are at least six HIV strains already. Each of these major variants may have a slightly different ability to infect different groups.

Some strains seem to have lower virulence, as seen in a group in Australia infected by blood transfusions from someone with HIV. Most of them are still well after years, and the virus cultured seems relatively mild. An increasing number of people are infected with more than one type of HIV. Every time someone is infected, there is a minute chance that radical new changes will occur. As the number of infected people worldwide continues to increase each year, so does the risk of new strains emerging. And every time someone is treated with anti-viral medication there is a risk that HIV will develop resistance, especially if people forget to take the medicine or supplies keep running out.

The common cold virus is also unstable. That is why we are always getting colds. I probably have antibodies in my blood now to fifty or a hundred different shaped cold viruses. By the time one of those viruses has infected people between here, North America, Japan, Korea, India, Greece and back again, its shape has changed so much that I can catch the same cold all over again. That is why we are light years away from a vaccine against the common cold.

The flu virus is also unstable, but less so. We can usually reckon on two or three different viruses causing most flu for a year or so before changing. We spot the new ones, make a vaccine, and give it to people each year. This annual vaccine has never been popular. Why? Because it often gives people a mild dose of the very flu they were hoping not to catch in the first place, and also because protection only lasts until the virus mutates.

AIDS vaccine could give you AIDS

Even if – and it's a big if – we could create a new vaccine radically different from any other we have ever made, one that somehow could make the body produce antibodies that latch on to any kind of HIV, whatever its shape, there is the worry at the back of people's minds that it could have some serious side effects.

Vaccination of animals against viruses similar to HIV made some of the animals ill. A shortage of chimpanzees and lack of a true animal model for HIV infection mean that animal testing does not tell us much. Vaccines have to be tested at an early stage on humans. Even if vaccines do not give people AIDS, there is the possibility that they might get ill more quickly if infected later. One reason for this is the suggestion that antibodies against HIV may help destroy infected white cells that were otherwise circulating quite harmlessly in the bloodstream. The immune defences of the body against HIV may actually be part of the reason for illness developing.

Imagine giving 10,000 New York school children the new vaccine. How many years do you think it would take before we could be 100% sure that none of them would ever go on to develop problems with the vaccine? The answer is at least ten to fifteen years because that is the time scientists now think it can take to develop AIDS. Testing of vaccines requires human guinea pigs. On whom are we going to try it? The answer is that trials are being planned to take place in countries like Uganda. This raises big ethical questions, especially as those vaccinated may think they are now protected. First generation vaccines do not work, although they do give us useful information.

There is the possibility that we could make millions of virus particles without the damaging genes inside. This should be safe but may not be effective. Damaged virus particles tend to produce a very poor immune response and are usually very poor vaccines. Almost all the effective vaccines we possess depend on a milder form of the virus actually infecting the body. Polio vaccine is an example. But there is no milder form of AIDS that we dare risk giving people.

Attempts have been made to take a mild virus used in another vaccine (called 'vaccinia') and change it so the outside looks like HIV but is relatively harmless. However, as we have seen, the virus may still turn out to be immune to the antibodies produced. Any vaccine, whether effective or not, will cause all those vaccinated to give 'positive' test results, making detection of infection more difficult in those vaccinated.

So then, in summary, we are a long way from a widely available, effective vaccine. In the meantime, you will continue to read countless spectacular claims. Even if a vaccine existed today that was 100% safe and reasonably effective, it would probably take five years to become widely available at reasonably low cost. When it does come, it will almost certainly be useless at treating those millions already infected. However, work is also continuing on different kinds of vaccines which might help an infected person fight infection.

Hope of drug cure?

Our only other hope lies in a drug that could destroy viruses in the body. We have none that is effective. For forty years we have searched in vain for a single drug that would work well against a virus without killing the person who takes it. When such a drug appears it will almost certainly cure polio, chickenpox, flu, and a host of other diseases from which our only protection at the moment is vaccination. We will undoubtedly find such a drug one day but it is a long, long way off. How do you kill something that does not breathe, does not need food, does not live and never dies?

There are four target areas where HIV might be open to attack in the body:

1. Before it touches a cell and its genetic code is injected through the cell wall.
2. When the genetic code has been unravelled inside the cell and the message is being transferred to the cell brain (nucleus) using a special enzyme called 'reverse transcriptase'.
3. When the cell starts to make new viruses.
4. When the viruses start budding out of the cell wall.

All the newspaper reports of so-called 'AIDS wonder drugs' over the next few years will fall into one of these groups.

Attempts have even been made to flood the bloodstream with small pieces of cell wall (CD4) so the viruses are unable to touch living CD4 white cells. Another method being tried is to inject antibodies ('neutralising') from HIV-positive people to give extra protection to people with AIDS.

Others are now looking closely at the virus to try to find any important piece of 'machinery' which is unique to virus production and cannot be found in a normal human cell. Machines in cells are called enzymes.

Enzymes are what are found in biological washing powders. We understand what they do very well. Like antibodies they are very specific indeed and each enzyme is capable of only one thing. Enzymes either split large molecules into two smaller ones, which is how they loosen dirt in clothing, or they take two smaller ones and join them together. There is a particular enzyme that reads the genetic code of HIV to form the message that reprograms the cell. It is called 'reverse transcriptase'. The body does not usually make it, and only viruses use it. If we could find a way of jamming it effectively without bad side effects, we could prevent viruses from reprogramming cells.

We are able to jam various other enzymes in the body. For example, aspirin and arthritis drugs jam an enzyme which makes the most painful substance known to man: prostaglandin. This is produced whenever cells are injured in the body. Nerves are irritated by it and fire thousands of electrical impulses which your brain understands as pain. By jamming this enzyme, prostaglandins are reduced and pain is lessened.

Poison for life?

There would be one terrible problem with all such potential drugs. If they can be found, they will have to be taken for life. If some cells in the body are already infected, then a drug preventing entry of new viruses into unaffected cells will need to be taken until every reprogrammed cell and its descendants are dead – which could take fifteen years or longer. If we stopped the drug after ten years and a single reprogrammed white cell were to be activated to make more virus particles, the disease could start progressing all over again. This applies also to drugs preventing reprogramming, virus manufacture, or budding from the cell.

Almost all drugs have side effects and this particular range of drugs has more than its fair share. Zidovudine (AZT), for example, which works by jamming the enzyme reverse transcriptase, is also a poison to the bone marrow of the body, which produces all your blood cells. You can die from taking too much Zidovudine for too long, and Zidovudine-resistant strains have developed rapidly. Likewise, there is an entire family of other drugs called HIV-protease inhibitors. But they also are toxic, and dangerous to use without blood tests every two to three weeks. Every year new substances are developed and tried in ever-changing combinations and dosages. And survival of people with HIV on these drugs is improving all the time. The effects can be dramatic. Many AIDS wards in wealthy nations have closed as people with HIV are now living longer and healthier lives. But it is not an easy road, and even with new discounts for poorer nations, and some factories making medicines unofficially, the prices are still far too high for most people. And even if they are free, as we hope will be the case for millions of people in Africa and other areas, the drugs themselves could easily kill people unless their use is properly supervised. (See Appendix G.)

Every drug currently being tested has been found either to be poisonous to some degree or other, or to have little or no anti-viral effect. In fact, some are so obviously dangerous that the only way a licence can be obtained to give them to human beings at all is on the strictest understanding that all the 'human guinea pigs' are going to die soon anyway from AIDS, so a death from the drugs is less serious, even if the hope of cure is remote.

The United States federal government is usually extremely strict on new drugs. Drugs have to be tried on vast numbers of animals for years before they can be tried on humans. But recently they have approved very many half-developed products very quickly, propelled by a ghastly sense of urgency for the million or more United States citizens already infected. The same is likely to happen in many other nations.

So the drugs currently being tried are usually suitable only for those already affected by AIDS, and while some may be suitable only for those who have become infected, they are completely unsuitable for giving to the whole nation.

However, as doctors are now seeing such a large proportion of those infected go on to develop AIDS, the pressure is growing to try using these drugs on more and more people at an earlier stage, or in pregnancy to protect the unborn.

Vaccines – a high risk business

Drug companies are pouring billions of dollars into research to find better treatments, but much less into vaccines. With a lot less work they can rush through testing and licensing, and can bring a new drug on to the market. Advertising is unnecessary. Media hype does most of it, and pressure becomes irresistible from patients who are desperate for any hope of cure. Doctors and governments are forced into using drugs which are very expensive – possibly $10,000 per patient – but may hardly work at all and may actually make the patient worse.

Of course we need research trials, but they need to be carefully regulated. You can spend millions on a treatment for 500 to 1,000 patients, or maybe for the same money get 500 full-time health educators on the road and into schools, clubs, colleges, factories and offices, preventing maybe 20,000 or more extra AIDS deaths a year. New treatments available in many industrialised nations have increased the cost of caring for someone with AIDS from diagnosis to death.

Vaccines are a different matter altogether: they are very complex to make and many doubt we will ever be able to make one for AIDS that works and is safe. A long period of investment is required over five to ten years before the drug company that develops a vaccine is likely to earn any money. Even if a company creates an effective vaccine, there is a risk of financial ruin if the vaccine turns out to have serious side effects. In the United States, public liability laws and the vast size of lawsuit claims make drug companies vulnerable to bankruptcy if they market something which turns out to be unsafe. As a result, a new Bill has been introduced to US Congress designed to protect researchers and manufacturers from liability in testing AIDS vaccines.

AIDS is big business and many other organisations stand to gain or lose millions of dollars over what happens. A furious argument over who first discovered the AIDS virus took place between French and American scientists. At stake were world rights to royalties from every blood test for AIDS. The row took years to resolve.

Some companies also fear that they would have to make their new product available 'at cost' if it turned out to be a wonder cure or an effective vaccine. As we have seen, public reaction can be enormous if profits are seen to be made out of tragedy.

Governments need to look at this urgently. No one expects drug companies who operate on behalf of shareholders to go bankrupt in the public interest. They need to be reasonably sure of a return, or if the risks of heavy losses are too large, they need some kind of financial inducement, such as low taxation on profits from AIDS vaccines. Failure to address this fundamental issue could set back progress by another couple of decades.

Unfortunately, in the absence of large numbers of volunteers for vaccines in places like the UK, trials are taking place in Uganda, Rwanda, Brazil and Thailand. One might question the ethics of this. The vaccines being used today are useless at preventing AIDS. They produce a degree of immune response, but are only a very first step. Yet in a developing country, an injection of 'the latest experimental vaccine' may well create a false sense of security in those taking part in the study. The result could be their deaths.

The vaccines are so unproven, and have such a high risk of potential side effects, that it is highly unlikely that parents of children or teenagers in developed countries would want to volunteer members of their family. So are we so sure it is right to proceed in other nations? It can be argued that no adult takes part without giving consent, but it is easy to underestimate the huge faith many villagers place in a Western doctor with high-tech equipment offering the very latest in medical research. At the moment there is nothing to stop someone in a country like Canada or the UK from going over to Africa and doing research there which would be illegal at home. There are huge ethical issues here tied up with inequality of resources and exploitation of developing nations.

Most vaccines so far have been made using 'recombinant' genetic engineering. Cells are programmed to make millions of harmless virus fragments which are then injected into people. Antibodies to the fragments should then cross-react with intact infectious HIV. The World Health Organisation is worried that a vaccine might emerge which is very expensive and works only against certain strains in specific areas, useless and unafford-able to developing countries. It is now encouraging the development of an infectious non-lethal form of HIV as a vaccine, similar to the vaccine for polio.

There are many examples where people may be making money out of AIDS in various ways. Pacific Dunlop, who manufacture condoms and surgical gloves, saw their profits grow by 31% in six months of a single year due to the AIDS scare.

Viruses as drugs by the year 2010?

There is a fascinating possibility that by 2010 scientists and doctors will be able to program back to normal any cell that has already been reprogrammed by a virus. Suppose a cell has been taken over by a virus and the book of life is now altered. In the laboratory they painstakingly write a new message and put it into genetic code. Then they (somehow) place the new code into an empty virus bag. The test-tube virus is now allowed to touch a white cell. It enters and releases the new message which programs back the book of life so it reads normally.

If you are familiar with computers, it is a bit like recreating a corrupt disk. We are a long way from this, not least because most viruses get cells to produce a special chemical called interferon as soon as they have entered, preventing a second virus from entering the same cell, whether a wild one or a test-tube virus.

A major step forward in human reprogramming was taken in 1990, with children who had adenosine deaminase deficiency. This gene defect is something children are born with and means white cells fail to work properly. The result is an illness like AIDS, with early death.

In a remarkable breakthrough, scientists at the US National Institute of Health located the correct gene, inserted it into viruses built in the laboratory, removed defective white cells from the child, infected the cells to program them back to normal, and then replaced the cells. The child was cured – but only for a short time. Others have carried the work on and in 2002 the result was a permanent cure for a child. To do the same in HIV-infected white cells would mean overcoming the interferon locking system HIV activates once inside a cell, designed to prevent other viruses from entering.

AIDS as biological warfare?

Some have suggested that AIDS is the result of a laboratory accident. HIV was made, they say, in a search for new germs for use in wartime and it escaped, or was tried out on a few human guinea pigs and spread wildly across the world.

Although we now possess the means to make viruses far more deadly than HIV, we know that HIV virus first appeared at least as far back as the early 1970s and probably as early as the 1950s, at a time when such technology did not exist. Similar naturally occurring viruses are common in some animals in some countries and have probably been around in one form or another for centuries.

Twenty-five years ago we hardly understood anything about viruses and could not even locate the human code for insulin, let alone anything else. It is extremely unlikely that this virus was first made in the laboratory, although it is conceivable that it mutated in a laboratory from an animal virus used to infect human cells in a test-tube experiment.

Testing claims for 'wonder drugs'

When you read a newspaper report, take great care. Medical journals are full of papers which contradict others published only a month or two before. This happens because some studies are badly designed or have very few patients in them. If you throw two dice three times and get three sixes, two ones and a three, you could write a little report saying that you conclude that the dice contains lots of sixes, no twos, and no fours or fives. Everyone would laugh at you because they can pick up the dice and look at them. So what went wrong with your research? You threw the dice too few times to comment and you failed to understand how dice work.

Now if, on the other hand, you threw the dice 10,000 times and half the time they came up with sixes, you might correctly conclude that the dice behave as if they are weighted. If you wrote a newspaper article telling people that all dice from a particular shop are weighted people might believe you – particularly when they hear you threw the dice 10,000 times. You and they would be wrong. How can you generalise about all dice when you tested only two?

You may think these illustrations are an insult to your intelligence, but research workers all over the world make classic blunders every day in the same way. You may not think it possible, but it is.

Take the pill, for example. A very effective contraceptive, but is it safe? Every now and then there is a large increase in the number of pregnancies, many of which unfortunately are ended by abortion. These usually follow some report or other from somewhere in the world that the pill may cause some rare cancer or problem with blood or whatever.

Even if the reports are true – and they are often contradicted by others published months before or after – there is a vital fact missing. None of the reports points out that to be pregnant carries a risk to life. A small risk, but a risk nonetheless. Abortion also carries a risk. The risk to most women is far less from continuing to use the pill than from changing to the notoriously unreliable condom with the possibility of a new unwanted pregnancy.

So then, how do we assess the newspaper scoops on new wonder drugs? Ask yourself what the drug does. Where does it act on our scheme of things earlier in the chapter? What are the risks of taking it and how long do you need to take it? How many patients has it been tried on and how many of them have died? Have the results been published in a reputable scientific journal? Many so-called treatments turn out to be elaborate hoaxes or frauds. Recently a woman was jailed for providing a useless preparation for a fee. People feel better after eating chocolate if you tell them it contains a wonder drug. This is called the placebo effect. Did these patients know they were being given a wonder drug? If they did, then no wonder they reported feeling better. Your own doctor will be able to advise you on these things. The vast majority of so-called wonder drugs are nothing of the sort, so do not be too disappointed by the negative reaction of your doctor when you show her a press clipping.

When several research papers say the same thing, when each study contains a large number of people with objective results – for example, numbers of patients still alive after five years – then we can start to feel more confident.

New approaches to therapy

Several new approaches have been developed, all of which are experimental, yet offer hope for the future.

1. Combination therapy

By using anti-HIV drugs in combination, so that the dose of each is kept low, side effects are reduced and the virus is hit hard. This approach helps prevent drug resistance developing in new virus mutations. The WHO free anti-viral programme uses combination therapy. (See Appendix G.)

2. Liposome delivery of drugs

Liposomes are protein bags similar to ones which occur naturally in the body. They fuse with cell walls, so the contents of the liposome (genes or medication) end up inside the cell. This could be helpful in the future, and is becoming a method of delivering new genes to the lungs of people with cystic fibrosis.

3. Gene therapy

This covers a very large number of different approaches, all designed to help the body fight HIV by adding new genes to human cells. These genes can be designed to help cells block infection, or to help prevent virus multiplication.

4. Virus competition

This approach uses another relatively harmless virus to control HIV. For example, scientists have found a human herpes virus (HHV7) that only targets CD4 cells, the same ones that HIV infects. When CD4 cells are occupied by HHV7, there is some evidence that HIV is prevented access. Inactivated HHV7 shows some effect too. There is a possibility then of a live vaccine one day: a mild virus targeting CD4 cells, spreading in the same way as HIV.

5. Preventing auto-immune reactions

There is some evidence that many dying white cells are destroyed not by HIV directly, but by the body's own defences which have been made aggressive by HIV. For example, an attack on infected white cells can easily damage 'innocent' uninfected cells. Indeed, one part of the HIV structure looks and feels very similar to part of a CD4 cell, so a reaction against HIV could also wipe out white cells directly. It might seem a strange approach in someone with an immune deficiency, but there may be a rationale in some cases in the future to dampen down another part of the immune system using drugs, in order to keep someone well. It all depends which bit of the immune system is dampened down. As we have seen, HIV damages just one part. The rest functions normally, or is even overactive.

6. Blocking cytokine production

We know the cancerous Kaposi's sarcoma is caused by HIV operating together with another agent we have yet to identify. It is a serious condition in people with AIDS and a common cause of death. It seems that HIV makes some white cells over-active so they produce a large amount of a chemical stimulant called cytokine. As a result, cells lining small blood vessels begin to divide and the sarcoma develops. By blocking cytokine production it may be possible to help prevent Kaposi's sarcoma.

7. Developing a spermicidal cream

For those seeking to avoid sexual infection with HIV, there is an urgent need to develop a new spermicidal cream which is highly active in destroying HIV. This could be used in addition to a condom.

In summary, then, HIV infection is highly complex, involving new, dangerous genes being added to white cells. As gene technology advances rapidly we may hope to see real progress towards a safe, effective, low-cost vaccine or cure. However, the advances being made at present are painfully slow, despite a vast global research, testing and treatment effort. This must focus our energy all the more urgently on prevention.

Having seen what a virus is, and how HIV enters and destroys a cell, we can now begin to look at what happens to the body when large numbers of these cells start to die.

CHAPTER THREE
WHEN CELLS START TO DIE

The virus causing AIDS enters the blood and quickly pene-
trates certain white cells (called 'CD4' cells or 'T4' cells) in the
body. As we saw in the last chapter, they program the white
cells, after which there is often little or no trace of the virus at
all. This situation usually lasts for six to twelve weeks. During
this time the person is free of symptoms and antibody tests are
negative.

First signs of illness

The first thing that happens after infection is that many people
develop a flu-like illness. This may be severe enough to look like
glandular fever, with swollen glands in the neck and armpits,
tiredness, fever and night sweats. Some of those white cells are
dying, virus is being released, and for the first time the body is
working hard to make correct antibodies. At this stage, the
blood test will usually become positive as it picks up the telltale
antibodies. This process of converting the blood from negative
to positive is called 'sero-conversion'. Most people do not
realise what is happening, although when they later develop
AIDS they look back and remember it clearly. Most people
have produced antibodies in about twelve weeks.

Latent infection

Then everything settles down. The person now has a positive test, and feels completely well. The virus often seems to disappear completely from the blood again. However, during this latent phase, HIV can be found in large quantities in lymph nodes, spleen, adenoid glands and tonsils. We do not know how many people will go on to the next stage. As we saw in an earlier chapter, at first doctors thought it might only be one in ten, then two or three out of ten. Now it looks as though at least nine out of ten will develop further problems.

San Francisco studies show that in developed countries, without use of the latest therapies, 50% with HIV develop AIDS in ten years, 70% in fourteen years. Of those with AIDS, 94% are dead in five years. The rate of progression can be much faster in those with weakened immunity from other causes, for example drug users, or those in developing countries. It can be far slower in those on various treatments.

Most scientists and doctors are convinced that if we follow up infected people for long enough – maybe for twenty years or more – then all or nearly all will die of AIDS, unless they have died of something else in the meantime, such as a heart attack or cancer. How long can someone live before some infection triggers production of more virus and death of more white cells?

The next stage begins when the immune system starts to break down. This is often preceded by subtle mutations in the virus, during which it becomes more aggressive in damaging white cells. Several glands in the neck and armpits may swell and remain swollen for more than three months without any explanation. This is known as persistent generalised lymphadenopathy (PGL).

Early disease progression

As the disease progresses, the person develops other conditions related to AIDS. A simple boil or warts may spread all over the body. The mouth may become infected by thrush (thick white coating), or may develop some other problem. Dentists are often the first to be in a position to make the diagnosis. People may develop severe shingles (painful blisters in a band of red skin), or herpes. They may feel overwhelmingly tired all the time, have high temperatures, drenching night sweats, lose more than 10% of their body weight, and have diarrhoea lasting more than a month. No other cause is found and a blood test will usually be positive. Some used to call this stage ARC, or AIDS related complex.

You can easily panic reading a list of symptoms like this because all of us tend to read about diseases and think instantly we've got them. Chronic diarrhoea does not mean you have AIDS. Nor does weight loss, high temperature, tiredness or swollen glands. These things can be particularly common in many developing countries.

At the moment in many countries there is an epidemic of viral illnesses which cause fevers, tiredness, rashes and other symptoms that last a long time, always go away completely, and have nothing to do with AIDS. See your doctor or go to a clinic for sexually transmitted diseases (STDs) or genito-urinary medicine (GUM) if you are unsure.

Late HIV illness – AIDS

The final stage is AIDS. Most of the immune system is intact and the body can deal with most infections, but one or two more unusual infections become almost impossible for the body to get rid of without medical help, usually in the form of intensive antibiotics.

These infections can be a nightmare for doctors and

patients. The desperate struggle is to find the new germ, identify it, and give the right drug in huge doses to kill it. The germ may be hiding deep in a lung requiring a tube (bronchoscope) to be put down the windpipe into the lung to get a sample. The person is sedated for this. It may be hiding in the fluid covering the brain and spinal cord, requiring a needle to be put into the spine (lumbar puncture). It may be hiding in the brain itself. It may hide in the liver or gall bladder or bowel. It can hide anywhere.

Chest infections are common

The most common infection is a chest infection. A 23-year-old man walks into his doctor's office with a chest infection not responding to antibiotics. He is flushed and has a high temperature. He has been increasingly short of breath with a dry cough for several weeks. He becomes breathless and has an emergency chest X-ray. The X-ray is strange. Could this be AIDS? Samples are taken from the lung. The man is rushed to intensive care and is too ill to ask if he would agree to a blood test. Within two days he is dead. In Western nations a strange germ is commonly found in his lung: pneumocystis carinii. This is incredibly rare except in AIDS.

He may or may not be reported as a statistic to the centre collecting information on AIDS. This is voluntary and doctors are busy. If he had died a day or two earlier, the cause of death would have been thought to be pneumonia. Yet another silent victim, unnoticed and unrecorded. Our statistics may be incomplete, and remember, no test was done for HIV. In African nations, the organism causing chest infections is most likely to be TB – just another case among all the rest, and perhaps not blamed on the real underlying cause, which is immune damage from HIV.

Without anti-retrovirals, average life expectancy if you develop your first pneumocystis pneumonia is just over two years. 78% survive the first episode, only 40% survive the second. You could live for over three years, or you might be dead in three months. Each new chest infection could be your last. Often people seem only an hour or two from death, then pull around, recover completely, and go home for several months until the next crisis.

We know that 85 out of 100 people with these chest infections in Western nations are infected with pneumocystis carinii, but many are infected with several things at once. Worldwide, the commonest HIV-related chest infection is tuberculosis. As HIV spreads, TB is on the increase, with possibly a million extra cases a year at present as a result of HIV. Latent TB infection is common in the general population. HIV damage to CD4 white cells allows reactivation, rapid deterioration and death.

Damage to nervous system

Half of the people with AIDS will develop signs of brain impairment or nerve damage during their illness. For one person in ten it is the first symptom. HIV itself seems to attack, damage and destroy brain cells in the majority of people with AIDS who survive long enough. The virus is probably carried into the brain by special white cells called macrophages, which then produce more virus there. Brain cells have a texture on their surfaces similar to CD4 white cells which enables the virus to latch on and enter.

The damage happens gradually and often is not noticed until a significant part of the brain has been destroyed, when a brain scan will show a shrunken appearance with enlarged cavities. The signs can be threefold: difficulties in thinking, difficulties in co-ordinating balance and moving, and changes in behaviour. Sometimes the problems are caused by other infections spreading throughout the body, or by tumours, all brought on by AIDS.

Brain damage affects children as well. In one study, sixteen out

A diagnosis of AIDS is made whenever a person is HIV-positive and:

He or she has a CD4+ cell count below 200 cells per microliter, OR

His or her CD4+ cells account for fewer than 14 percent of all lymphocytes, OR

The person has been diagnosed with one or more of the following AIDS-defining illnesses:

Candidiasis of bronchi, trachea, or lungs
Candidiasis, esophageal
Cervical cancer, invasive
Coccidioidomycosis, disseminated
Cryptococcosis, extrapulmonary
Cryptosporidiosis, chronic intestinal (>1 month duration)
Cytomegalovirus disease (other than liver, spleen, or lymph nodes)
Cytomegalovirus retinitis (with loss of vision)
Encephalopathy, HIV-related
Herpes simplex: chronic ulcer(s) (>1 month duration) or bronchitis, pneumonitis, or esophagitis
Histoplasmosis, disseminated
Isosporiasis, chronic intestinal (>1 month duration)
Kaposi's sarcoma
Lymphoma, Burkitt's
Lymphoma, immunoblastic
Lymphoma, primary, of brain (primary central nervous system lymphoma)
Mycobacterium avium complex or disease caused by M. Kansasii, disseminated

Mycobacterium tuberculosis, any site (pulmonary or extrapulmonary)
Mycobacterium, other species or unidentified species, disseminated
Pneumocystis carinii pneumonia
Pneumonia, recurrent
Progressive multifocal leukoencephalopathy
Salmonella septicemia, recurrent
Toxoplasmosis of brain (encephalitis)
Wasting syndrome caused by HIV infection

Additional illnesses that are AIDS-defining in children, but not adults:

Multiple, recurrent bacterial infections
Lymphoid interstitial pneumonia/pulmonary lymphoid hyperplasia

(The 1993 AIDS Surveillance Case Definition of the US Centers for Disease Control and Prevention.)

of twenty-one children with AIDS developed progressive brain destruction (encephalopathy). But any part of the nervous system can be damaged in adults or children, not just the brain, and AIDS can mimic just about any other disease of nerves.

Children with HIV

Worldwide, around 3 million children have HIV infection and half a million die every year. Altogether, 83% of children with HIV will show some kind of abnormality in their white cells, or will have symptoms, by the time they are six months old. Problems can include large lymph nodes, enlarged liver and spleen, failure to thrive (small for age), small head, ear infections, chest infections, unexplained fever and encephalopathy (brain deterioration).

Of those showing symptoms within the first year of life, half die before the age of three. However, with improved treatments children are surviving longer. A common pattern is beginning to emerge: a child may become unwell in the first year or two of life with different chronic or acute infections, yet with treatment is able to carry on for many years, possibly even into adolescence with many ups and downs. Pain and other symptoms are often overlooked in these children.

Blood tests are often confused by the presence after birth of the mother's own antibodies. All babies of infected mothers will test positive for around the first year, whether infected or not. Most babies who test positive at birth turn out to be uninfected. The greatest risk to the baby is the birth process itself and breast milk. Dramatic reductions in infection rates can be made if the mother is given anti-viral medication before and immediately after birth. This is one of the most appropriate occasions to use anti-viral drugs in the poorest nations. But it should always be done under strict medical supervision.

There is a very slight risk that children who later test negative may still carry HIV. If first infected in the womb, the child may regard HIV as part of itself and not react to it. We are still in the early stages of learning about HIV in children.

Skin rashes and growths

The majority of people with AIDS develop skin problems which are usually an exaggeration of things common to most people, such as acne and rashes of various kinds. Cold sores and genital herpes may develop, or warts. Athlete's foot in severe forms, ringworm and thrush are common. Rashes due to food allergy are also common – no one knows why. Hair frequently falls out. Drug rashes frequently occur, often due to

life-saving co-trimoxazole used for treatment or prevention of
the pneumocystis carinii pneumonia.

Kaposi's sarcoma develops in up to a quarter of the people
with AIDS (depending on the country and route of infection).
This produces blue or red hard, painless patches on the skin,
often on the face. In the majority of these people it is the first
sign of AIDS. Tumours can spread to lymph nodes, gut lining
and lungs where they can be confused with pneumocystis pneumonia. The growths may be caused by a second virus that is
allowed to grow more easily if you have AIDS. Treatment
consists mainly of radiotherapy and chemotherapy, including
injections of the lesions.

Because it often affects the face, or may be visible elsewhere
on the body and is so distinctive, people who develop Kaposi's
sarcoma often feel especially vulnerable. In fact, people usually
live longer if they first develop this tumour than if they first
develop a pneumonia. Kaposi's sarcoma is less common in
drug users with AIDS, presumably because it is caused by a
second virus also found in gay men, which is then activated by
HIV.

The other common cancer is a tumour (lymphoma) which
develops in the brain or elsewhere in the body.

Problems in gut, eyes and other organs

Almost all people with AIDS have stomach problems from
strange infections and cancers caused by AIDS and HIV
attacking the gut directly. All three cause food to be poorly
digested resulting in diarrhoea and weight loss. Stool samples
can be examined or samples can be taken from within the gut
using special tubing (endoscopy) to see if there is a second
treatable infection in addition to HIV.

AIDS can also seriously affect sight in up to a quarter of
all those with HIV by allowing an infection of the back of the
eye (retinitis). This is usually caused by cytomegalovirus and

is sometimes amenable to treatment. In addition, the virus can cause damage to other organs of the body such as the heart.

Changing disease pattern in adults

In different parts of the world, AIDS tends to have its own characteristics. This may be due to the pattern of other illnesses present in different communities, which explains why TB is the commonest cause of death from AIDS in Africa and Asia. Different patterns may be related to different co-factors (gay men compared to drug injectors, for example), viral differences or possibly genetic differences.

However, patterns are changing. For example, the incidence of Kaposi's sarcoma is falling among gay men with HIV in a number of countries, while it is rising among drug users. Some of these changed patterns are because of altered treatments; others are due to other factors.

As survival times have increased, other problems have emerged which are far more difficult to treat. These include blindness due to cytomegalovirus, progressive multifocal leucoencephalopathy (weakness, muscle wasting, difficulty thinking), cryptosporidiosis (which causes various infections), mycobacterium infections and cryptococcal meningitis.

In addition, as we have seen, advanced Kaposi's sarcoma can bring its own problems, with lung involvement causing shortness of breath and triggering chest infections, gut involvement causing obstruction or sudden bleeding, and with blockage of lymphatic drainage causing swollen limbs or face, skin ulceration and infection.

In a quarter of those dying with AIDS, the exact cause of death may be difficult to establish, with profound weakness, loss of weight and multi-system failure. Many infections can be chronic, low grade and difficult to diagnose, and when diagnosed can be hard to treat. Indeed, post-mortem examinations show that half of all HIV-related diseases found at autopsy had not been diagnosed during life.

In the early days in many countries, those with AIDS often spent a long time in hospital, as doctors battled to get to grips with the complex spectrum of illnesses. Now people with AIDS are usually able to spend more time at home, with many treatments given in clinics or in the home. However, many have multiple problems and need practical help, backed by nursing care and symptom control, to stay at home in comfort and in control of their own lives.

Later on in this book we will look at the practicalities of setting up community care programmes.

Many people who are ill are now opting not to have every symptom investigated, when the price is valuable time spent in hospital, unpleasant tests, and treatments that may have side effects.

AIDS diagnosis in developing nations

In developing countries it can be hard to make an accurate diagnosis of AIDS because of the lack of HIV testing facilities. The World Health Organisation proposed a clinical case definition, combining symptoms and signs common in AIDS. This has been used as the basis for AIDS statistics in many countries, but is inaccurate.

A study of hospital patients in Zaire showed that the case definition missed 31% of AIDS cases (definition not very sensitive), and 10% of those it identified as having AIDS were errors. The case definition misses people dying with severe HIV illnesses which do not fit the definition. For example, deaths from streptococcal pneumonia are far more common in those with HIV, yet such deaths were not included.

The commonest manifestations of AIDS in Africa are gross weight loss, chronic diarrhoea and chronic fever – the picture of the 'slim disease', as AIDS is known in African countries.

However, it is difficult to exclude other causes for the same symptoms and signs.

Deaths from tuberculosis are another problem. TB is probably the most important infection in those with HIV in Africa. High rates of TB infection are found in those with HIV and the risk of death from TB is greatly increased in those with HIV. However, it is questionable whether all those with TB and HIV can be diagnosed as AIDS cases, since many have TB anyway. Many with TB lose weight and have fever as well as a cough. Therefore in the absence of HIV testing, many with advanced TB are likely to be labelled as AIDS cases using the WHO case definition.

In the light of all these problems, a revised case definition has been agreed. You may wonder how it is possible to be sure of the right diagnosis without laboratory facilities, and the answer is that it is very difficult.

Some have pounced on this difficulty to suggest that there is no AIDS in Africa at all. This is nonsense for many reasons. For example, death rates have soared in the sexually active age groups as HIV infection rates have risen. TB and other illnesses have been around and studied in detail for decades. Something new is happening. Secondly, when people diagnosed with AIDS from African nations are cared for either in countries like the UK, or in very well-equipped hospitals nearer home, it is clear that there are gross abnormalities of their immune systems indicative of AIDS, with positive antibodies for HIV and damaged white cells.

AIDS-related illnesses in Africa

The spectrum of illness seen in AIDS in African nations can vary, particularly in places where HIV-2 is more prevalent. The pattern is very different from developed countries:

Candida (thrush) in the mouth	80–100%
Oesophageal candidiasis	30–50%

Tuberculosis	30–50%
Cerebral toxoplasmosis	15–20%
Herpes zoster (shingles)	10%
Cryptosporidiosis (diarrhoea)	50%

Most people have several problems. (For further discussion on the needs of those with AIDS and how to meet them, see Chapters 10, 11 and 14.)

So, now that we have reviewed how the virus attacks cells and causes diseases associated with AIDS, we are in a position to look at some of the ways the virus can enter the human body and how we can prevent it from happening.

CHAPTER FOUR

HOW PEOPLE BECOME INFECTED

Different groups of people tend to become infected with HIV for different reasons. Children, drug addicts, sexually active homosexuals, and heterosexual men and women all develop AIDS in particular ways. Whole family groups are now becoming ill.

How children get infected with HIV

Just under a million children get infected with HIV each year. A preventable tragedy.

Infection before or during birth

HIV can cross the placenta in the womb, and can also infect during labour, when the baby swallows amniotic fluid and blood – up to 30% of infected mothers will give birth to an infected baby for these reasons. If anti-viral medication is given before birth to the mother, and for a short time after birth to the baby, the risk of transmission from these causes can fall to as little as 5%–8% (results vary according to different studies). There is some benefit from anti-viral therapy even if only started during birth, or only used in the newborn baby. Broadly speaking, anti-viral therapy will more than halve transmission rates if properly used.

Some people used to think pregnancy could shorten the life

of a woman with HIV. Doctors now think the risk of rapid deterioration is not very great.

Infection just after birth

Breast milk can carry the virus from mother to child. This may account for up to half of all infections from mother to baby. One critical factor may be when the mother becomes infected, since virus levels are highest shortly after infection. The risk of infection to a baby could be 29% if the mother is infected while breastfeeding, with 10%–14% additional risk if the mother is infected before delivery. As a result, many hospitals in the United Kingdom have discontinued milk banks for sick babies. Questions have been raised over what advice to give mothers in developing countries. Conventional wisdom is that the risk of death from diarrhoea and vomiting due to contaminated bottle feeds is too great to allow mothers to stop breastfeeding (artificial feeding is a major factor in the deaths of 105 million infants a year). The balance of risk may vary according to the individual and the local situation, especially if the mother is known to have HIV.

So if you treat an infected mother before birth, and she does not breastfeed, the combined reduction in risk to the baby is huge: perhaps a fall from as much as 30% down to less than 8%.

Vaccinations/injections

In Eastern Europe and Africa, infection has spread through the use of the same needles between patients. If there are only a few needles left which are not hopelessly blunt, the temptation is great to immunise a whole clinic with a single needle. Blood from one infected child can spread the disease to others in the group. In some parts of Africa and Eastern Europe, many medicines are injected rather than swallowed. Many mothers seem to prefer it.

Transfusions and blood products

Education of health care workers is critically important: they need to use fewer injections, less blood, and take great care. In most countries today the blood supply is now safe. However, there is always a risk because the widely used tests for antibodies to HIV do not pick up recent infection (in many cases six weeks or more). Someone could be highly infectious, with huge numbers of virus particles in the blood they donate, yet test negative.

Incest/sexual abuse/child prostitution/early teenage sex/drugs

A 13-year-old girl shyly came up to me with a friend after a talk I gave to her class. I had to ask her teacher to leave before she could bring herself to speak. She wanted to know if someone could get infected with HIV through being raped. She was thinking of someone in particular. I had to say yes.

One unfortunate trend in high-incidence countries such as Thailand or Uganda has been the targeting of young teenage girls for sex by older men, who hope they will be less likely to be carrying HIV than adult women. This is one reason why the ratio of infected teenage girls to boys can be higher than five to one.

Child prostitution is becoming a global problem. In Taiwan there are an estimated 60–200,000, while around a million children are thought to be traded as sex slaves each year in South East Asia. UNESCO estimates that 800,000 children work as prostitutes in Thailand alone, while child prostitution is also growing in other parts of the world.

How drug addicts get infected with HIV

Drug addiction is a global problem. 8% of the value of all international trade is now illegal drugs, according to UNDP. Drug addicts become infected by sharing syringes and needles. A common habit is to rinse the last dregs of drug out of the syringe using your own blood, drawing blood out of your vein and injecting it again. This means the next person to use the syringe will inject a lot of virus into the bloodstream if the previous person is infected with HIV. It is far more dangerous than if a doctor pricks himself with a bloody needle. In that case the amount of blood involved would be much less. In Edinburgh, the virus spread from one addict to infect between 1,000 and 2,000 other people in eighteen months. In Thailand, 50,000 drug addicts were infected in two years, with other countries likely to become similarly affected.

The drug addict population is hard to estimate. Addicts do not like to stand up and be counted. Those with children are often scared their children will be taken into custody. Others are just shy of any official contact. I have visited drug injectors in their homes in Manipur, North East India, in villages where up to 8,000 out of 40,000 inject heroin daily, and 4,000 have HIV as a result. The stigma is so great that a villager risks being killed if identified as having HIV.

AIDS has the potential to spread quickly in drug injectors, although in some countries there has been a very encouraging drop in needle sharing, and infection rates among drug injectors have stabilised. A growing number are starting to inject drugs other than heroin, such as amphetamines. The risk is still the same.

Some governments are providing free needles, having found that addicts will be less likely to share them, despite the suggestion that issuing needles may actually accelerate the growth of drug abuse. It certainly makes things hard for the police.

Drug abusers (including alcoholics) have an increased risk of becoming infected with HIV in other ways. When they are 'under the influence', judgement is impaired and risks may be taken. Safer sex, discretion and caution can be thrown to the wind. The same with safe injecting practices. Drug addicts are often thought to be hard to educate, not only because they are hard to find and possibly hard to motivate (some addicts can have a kind of death wish), but also because, even if they decide to be careful, they may forget in the rush of the moment. However, education does work, to the surprise of many.

The third extra risk is that by injecting all kinds of foreign substances – including dirt, germs and powdered chalk – the immune system is weakened. Addicts frequently come into clinics with huge septic boils, rashes, or strange fevers (septicaemia). Huge chunks of muscle can rot away, especially in drug users living in poorer nations with less access to medical care. They are in no fit state to fight HIV. Infection is more likely and deterioration probably more rapid. An infected addict should be encouraged to stop. However, it can be even harder to stop if you know you may be dying anyway.

Drug users may also be at risk of becoming infected when they are in prison. Most addicts end up in prison at some time in their lives. Containing the spread of HIV in prisons is difficult. Many people are calling not only for condom issue (which could be illegal in prisons), but also for needle provision. However, a bloody needle and syringe make a formidable weapon in the hands of someone who may be infected. Prison officers fear attack. In the meantime, injectors may be at greater risk of sharing in prison than in the community. In most prisons a wide range of drugs are freely available from illicit sources. In the absence of needles, even greater risks may be taken. An ACET prison worker recently talked to a man who had shared parts of a ballpoint pen as a 'needle' to inject drugs into his neck.

How practising homosexuals get infected with HIV

In America and Europe, HIV has spread rapidly through gay communities. There are two reasons for this. First, it does appear that someone who allows a man to push his penis into his rectum and ejaculate there has a particularly high risk of getting the infection. The lining of the anus is fragile. The lining of the rectum is also likely to bleed during anal intercourse, especially if a pre-sex douche (enema) or a dildo (artificial penis) is used. It is possible that some cells in the rectum have surfaces particularly suited for HIV to latch on to and can become a reservoir for infecting the whole body.

Anal intercourse has always been known to carry a health risk: hepatitis B virus is spread easily by this route and many active homosexuals appear to have chronic low-grade infections of various kinds that may then lower their resistance to HIV. Anal sex is not unusual among heterosexuals in the United States and the United Kingdom. In some surveys, up to one in ten of women questioned reported having had anal as well as vaginal sex. Anal sex alone is not the reason for the spread of HIV. The biggest reason of all has to be found somewhere else, which brings us to perhaps the main reason why the gay community is experiencing an epidemic.

If you are an active homosexual, a major predictor of infection has to do with the number of different men you have had intercourse with over the last few years. It is true that some practices carry a particular risk of trauma and infection, eg 'fisting', where the hand and sometimes the forearm are inserted into the rectum.

The AIDS epidemic has forced social psychologists to ask some basic questions about human behaviour – questions that may be embarrassing and which have been hidden behind closed doors for decades. It is very hard to get honest answers to these questions, but they are important if we are to predict how the disease might spread in order to plan effective education.

One of the big surprises to emerge from a recent large and authoritative sexual survey of 18,000 people in the UK was how few men said they had homosexual partners. While the famous Kinsey study in the USA (1948) had given figures of 37% of men having had a homosexual experience to the point of orgasm, 10% exclusively homosexual for more than three years and 4% lifelong homosexuals, the UK study showed a different pattern. Less than 5% had ever had a homosexual experience, and only 1.7% had had sex in a homosexual relationship in the last five years. When the latter result was separated out, great regional differences were found: 5% in London and only 1% in the rest of the country.

The results caused an uproar, because they challenged the established view that about one in ten of the male population was a sexually active homosexual. However, the figures were not so much of a surprise to those running sex disease clinics, or working in the AIDS field. For some time, people had been quietly saying that the sexually active gay community seemed to be far smaller than originally thought. This was vitally important in making forecasts about HIV spread and numbers of AIDS cases. After all, if a London clinic found that a quarter of all gay men attending were HIV-infected, it was essential to know if that was a quarter of a total of 2,000 men, or a total of 10,000. Within a few weeks, similar surveys were published in France and the USA. Both confirmed the basic findings. Most experts on sexual behaviour have now concluded that the Kinsey study was flawed.

One of the things that shows up is that sexual behaviour is far more chaotic than many people imagine. For example, a United States study has shown that possibly one in four men who have sex with other men will also have sex with women. In the UK, a national sex survey showed that 59% of men having anal sex with men had also had female partners.

Sexual preferences sometimes changes with circumstances. A starving man on a desert island will eat strange foods. The reason why there are serious outbreaks of all sexually transmitted diseases (including HIV and AIDS) in prisons is that many men who behave heterosexually outside prison, practise homosexually in prison. In addition, male rape is a common form of initiation, bringing fear, humiliation and respect for 'the boss'.

Surveys show that some homosexual men later marry and maintain exclusive heterosexual relationships. However, the most startling fact to emerge from many studies has been the enormous number of different partners some homosexual men have in a year. Over half those attending a London clinic said they had had between 6 and 50 partners in a year. Many had between 51 and 100, and a few reported more than 300. Common meeting places are certain well-known public toilets, gay bars and other venues.

The contrast with the heterosexual group is enormous. Very few men will claim to have slept with more than fifteen women in a year. The vast majority claim to have had only one partner in any year. Incidentally, that is still unsafe. Each different partner each year is a new risk, even assuming faithfulness on both sides for twelve months. Serial monogamy is very common and is not the answer to AIDS.

When a prominent churchman was appointed as an Episcopalian bishop recently, he was shocked and outraged by what he found in the gay community. What made people do this? What happened to a sense of belonging or relationship? The answer he discovered was that, in 'coming out', many gay men had felt able to leave behind conventional restraints. By deciding to sample 'the fruits of the earth', with no relationship ties, many found a new freedom. Even people living together in stable homosexual relationships for years were expected to explore regularly outside those relationships. Public disapproval of gay partnerships also tended to make stable relationships difficult to form and maintain.

Gay people have felt totally ostracised and rejected by society. Beaten up in alleyways, labelled as perverts, and victims of relentless low-grade discrimination, they have often felt misfits. Rejected by family and former close friends, many have found tremendous security and self-acceptance among others who have been through an identical experience. The feeling of togetherness is strong. At last they can be themselves without fear of rejection. This fear is often of heterosexual men; women are usually more tolerant.

These feelings of intense rejection, isolation, loneliness and vulnerability are then magnified a thousand-fold by AIDS. The totally false label of the 'gay plague' has stuck, and has reflected on a whole community. That community has responded with an amazing mobilisation of talent, resources and kindness to support and surround people with AIDS with love – victims, as they see it, not of AIDS, but of horrendous prejudices and discrimination.

No wonder the gay community is so sensitive to the hostile attitudes of some parts of the church. Many people in the gay community have seen AIDS as something that has generated openness and an unprecedented care and concern from people who are not gay: 'Things will never be the same again.' However, others have predicted a possible backlash.

How women get infected with HIV

Historically, in many societies, women have been disadvantaged sexually and vulnerable to sexual abuse. It is still true today that it is very difficult for women in many parts of the world to protect themselves against HIV from a dominant male partner.

In African countries, such as Malawi or Kenya, the majority of infected women in some groups have been celibate before marriage and monogamous since, yet have been infected because of the unfaithfulness of their partners, or because partners were infected before marriage. Some experts have expressed concern at the effect of new Western influences, undermining traditional family values in developing countries, and encouraging higher rates of partner exchange.

Long-term relationships can also clearly carry a great risk where no precautions are taken. Often women may have no idea their husbands are infected, but even if they suspect so, they may be unable to do anything about it. One woman I spoke to after an open-air presentation on AIDS in Uganda, told me she was certain her husband was infected because he was continually unfaithful with a large number of partners, but she was unable to make him change to using a condom with her. She was powerless and lived in fear of her life. These are important issues in prevention, but may lead to confronting cultural norms in a way which could be seen as imperialism. Sensitivity is needed (see Chapter 14).

Sensitivity is also needed in tackling dangerous traditional practices in some countries, such as widow cleansing, where the brother of a man who dies is required to have sex with the widow. This is hazardous if the man died of AIDS after infecting his wife with HIV.

Women can be at risk through anal sex, which is far more common among heterosexuals than many people realise. As we have seen, a number of Western nation surveys of young women have suggested that up to one in ten has experienced anal intercourse at least once. This carries possibly twice the risk associated with vaginal intercourse, partly because of the possibility of trauma to the delicate anal and rectal lining, but also because there are cells in the wall of the rectum that have receptors for HIV which can be infected directly.

Women are at high risk as commercial sex workers, particularly as clients may insist that no precautions are taken, or may indulge in violent sex or anal intercourse.

The main risk in low incidence countries is in sleeping with a man who has had sex at some time in the last fifteen years with another man, or who has injected drugs, or who has had sex with women in nations with a higher incidence of HIV. Once may be enough, for him and for her. They will probably never know, because the man will never say. The average interval between marriage and the wife discovering her husband's homosexual preferences is between five and fifteen years. Women can also become infected from a heterosexual man who has been infected by another woman (commonest in developing nations) or who is a drug addict. Very rarely a woman can catch HIV from nursing her child with AIDS.

Lesbians are one group of people, apart from those who are celibate, where HIV infection is almost unknown. I know of only one or two cases where a lesbian woman has infected another. However, there may be many more infected who are as yet unknown. Lesbians are at risk if they inject drugs and have heterosexual relationships as well.

How heterosexual men become infected with HIV

A heterosexual man becomes infected by having sex with a woman who injects drugs, by injecting himself, or by sleeping with a woman who has previously had an infected partner, the latter being the commonest reason worldwide. He will never know unless she tells him. Sex on a single occasion with an infected partner can be enough to infect, although the risk from a single act is very small – probably less than 1 in 200 for non-traumatic vaginal intercourse, unless there is some other factor, like another sex disease (see Chapter 6).

In some developing countries initiation rites such as male circumcision with a communal knife or ritual mutilation can risk HIV spread. Such practices need to be discussed sensitively. Circumcision reduces the risk of HIV transmission, probably because the risk of other sexually transmitted diseases is lower.

AIDS and the church

Some churchgoers contracted HIV before they became Christians. It can surface after they have begun new lives and are happily married, when they may infect their wives and possibly their children as well. Others who regularly attend church lead double lives: a person can pretend to be one thing for an hour or two a week, and probably at work too, while beneath the respectable veneer he has a drug problem or is sleeping around with men or women. The result may be AIDS.

For some today there is no double life. The risky lifestyle is maintained openly, in defiance of traditional church teaching, perhaps in a church led by someone with liberal views. And, tragically, as we will see in Chapter 14, a small but increasing number of church members are becoming infected while serving as doctors and nurses in high incidence countries where they are exposed frequently to medical hazards.

CHAPTER FIVE
QUESTIONS PEOPLE ASK

Every day I am asked questions about AIDS, usually the same ones over and over again. Some are based on reasonable fear – of getting the disease from sleeping around, for example. Others are based on unreasonable fear – maybe a fear of going swimming. Here are some common questions and some answers to enable your fears to be reasonable.

Q. How is AIDS caught?

You cannot 'catch' AIDS. You acquire infection with HIV, the virus which, after several years, can produce the condition we call AIDS. The virus is spread almost entirely through sex and the sharing of needles or syringes. Other routes are extremely rare, except infection through untested blood in some developing countries, broken or faulty equipment, or inadequate supplies of reagents. Spreading the virus through normal social contact is unknown. The risk from kissing is very, very low indeed.

Vaginal, oral, or anal sex can transmit the virus from a man to a woman and a woman to a man. Oral (orogenital) or anal sex also transmits in both directions from man to man, and oral sex from woman to woman. Other sexually transmitted diseases will make infection more likely. Wherever sores (which may be hidden and painless) or pus are, there the virus will be in large amounts. These areas are also entry points.

Tears, saliva and urine can contain the virus, but almost always in tiny amounts. The amount is greatly increased by eye, mouth, or urine infection. White cells in saliva carry the virus in up to nine out of ten people with AIDS. The virus needs to enter the body to cause infection. Swallowed virus particles are kept first in the mouth by gum and cheek linings, and do not enter the blood unless you have mouth sores or cracked lips, then in the continuous pipe we call the gut. They are destroyed by stomach acid. They cannot enter the blood once they enter the stomach. Virus particles inside your gut tubing are no more a part of your body than a plastic bead pushed up your nose. (See question on communion cup below.) Urine will not usually contain much virus unless there is a urine infection.

With the exception of sweat, all other secretions from the body may contain virus, especially that from wounds. The virus cannot enter the body through the skin unless you have a wound, a rash, or some other cracked area on your skin. The most vulnerable place for this is your hands. Gloves are the best protection.

If you are going to 'take a risk', a condom will reduce that risk. Condoms do not give you safe sex but it is safer, and condom use reduces your risk enormously if properly carried out.

Injecting drugs with a shared needle is dangerous. Non-injected drugs, including alcohol, may impair judgement and make risks more likely. Poppers may directly damage the immune system, as may other drugs.

Safe sex means only one thing: for two people who are currently uninfected to enter into an exclusive, faithful relationship for life, with neither of them injecting drugs with shared needles. The trouble is, you may never know. If someone wants to sleep with you really badly he or she may never tell you about previous risks or a drug habit.

Q. Should I take the test?

Remember that it is no good turning up at the STD clinic or your family doctor the day after you have taken a risk. You need to wait at least six weeks, and ideally three months, for your blood to have time to become positive if you are infected. During this time you must not be in any further risky situations.

Why do you want the test? Are you ready for a positive result and all that could mean? Who would you tell? Could you keep it a secret? Remember, it could result in a strong reaction against you from the people who find out. Will you be able to live with that? Are you sure your family doctor will be able to prevent the result from leaking out? It has happened before. Is the receptionist going to know? Are they discreet? A positive result could prevent you from getting a mortgage or life insurance cover. You should think through these issues, with professional help. A positive result carries huge implications for life. However, it is often easier to change behaviour after a test result. Tests save lives and allow treatment. So we should encourage people to get tested.

As more people in the poorest nations gain access to antiviral therapy, the reasons for them to be tested are growing stronger. Until now, very little could be offered, but new WHO initiatives mean that several million people on very low incomes will receive these medicines which can prolong life for many years and save the unborn from becoming infected.

Some church leaders in high incidence nations are insisting that engaged couples get tested before they can be married. This seems to me to go beyond traditional Christian teaching. But the fact is that tests save lives. And anyone who loves his or her partner will want to be tested if they have been at risk. How terrible to kill the one you love through fear of finding out the truth.

Q. How accurate is testing for HIV?

HIV testing is now very accurate, but it is important to realise that HIV tests need repeating and can occasionally be wrong, especially with 'instant' tests in the field, away from laboratories. There are two main ways of testing for HIV: indirect and direct. Because HIV is so small and difficult to find in the body, the cheapest and simplest way to detect infection is to look for antibodies that people make to fight the virus. These are very specific to HIV, like a spanner shaped to fit a nut.

The most widely used test is called ELISA. Results are usually confirmed using a second test called Western Blot, but can be confirmed in some cases by a second slightly different ELISA test. In most cases, the antibodies can be detected after about six to eight weeks from the time of infection. In newborn babies there is an added difficulty because the test is confused by the presence of maternal antibodies until around the first year of life. That's why all babies of mothers with HIV test positive for several months, even though most do not have HIV.

The first ELISA tests were not as accurate as the ones today, with higher false positive results. There is some evidence that malaria antibodies may have produced a significant number of false positives in some African countries in the mid-1980s, and that the tests were also muddled by other infections. However, the tests are now much more specific, although it is true that if someone has HIV infection, the antibodies against HIV can produce a false positive result when testing for malaria.

ELISA is designed to be ultra-sensitive, picking up every person with HIV antibodies, but the more sensitive the test, the more likely it is to react positively to other things. In a population where the level of infection is very low, up to 70% of all those testing positive with the ELISA tests will turn out to be negative when the ELISA is repeated. Proportions vary with the exact tests used.

An initial false positive result can be caused by many things. For example, recent vaccination against influenza will produce a positive ELISA test in around 1% of uninfected people. Hepatitis B vaccine can also confuse the test. In almost every case, these incorrect results are sorted out by a Western Blot, which is highly specific to HIV. In many countries, second or even third tests are carried out on the same sample so that false positives are eliminated immediately. If you wish further technical detail, read on; otherwise skip to the next question.

In the Western Blot test, virus building blocks are made in the laboratory. A number of different fragments of viruses are separated and 'blotted' onto a special surface which is then cut into strips and exposed to the serum sample. Core proteins (p24, p55 and p17) and envelope proteins (gp120, gp160 and gp41) are used. People with HIV tend to produce antibodies to all these bits of HIV. When serum is added to the membrane, together with special markers, you can see a series of colour bands where anti-HIV antibodies have reacted.

A person is only diagnosed as HIV-infected using Western Blot if antibodies are found to at least two of the bands p24, gp41 and gp120/160. Depending on the population group, between 20% and 70% of repeatedly positive ELISA tests are confirmed using Western Blot.

ELISA
99.3% of infected people are identified (very sensitive)
99.7% of uninfected people correctly test negative (specific)

Western Blot
98.9% of infected people are identified (sensitive)
97.8% of uninfected people correctly test negative (very specific)

Combining the results of both tests increases accuracy. However, it can be seen that if 10,000 people are tested with

ELISA, we can expect that 0.3%, or 30 people, will test positive even if none of the 10,000 is infected. The proportion could be higher if the test was carried out only once, and if testing facilities were poor, as is the case in some countries.

Some samples show a slight reaction to one or two bands. These are called 'indeterminate results'. There are three reasons for this. First, some people may be in the very early stages of infection, so antibodies are not yet fully present. A repeat test a few weeks later will sort that out.

Secondly, some may be infected with HIV-2, which is similar enough for antibodies to cross-react against HIV-1 to some extent.

Thirdly, it may be a true false-positive result: the person may be completely healthy and not infected with any kind of HIV strain. This is very rare.

People with very early infection, or infection with HIV-2, usually show a reaction to the viral core protein p24 first. Between 60% and 90% of HIV-2 infection is picked up with an HIV-1 ELISA test.

Although the 'window period' between infection and antibody detection is usually regarded as about six to eight weeks, at least 95% will test positive after twelve weeks (usually a lot more) and 99% by six months. International standards are maintained at a very high level by the World Health Organisation, which regularly sends out test samples to over 100 laboratories.

Some people can be ill or dying with AIDS and still test negative. The reason here is that their immune systems are so severely damaged that they have lost the ability to form antibodies. The diagnosis is usually obvious from symptoms and other laboratory tests looking at their white cells.

It is possible to test for HIV directly, not waiting for antibodies to develop. This method looks for viral genes – the DNA instructions that the virus inserts into white cells to hijack them into virus factories.

A special chemical reaction is used called PCR (polymerase

chain reaction), which can multiply a million copies of viral DNA in three hours, and, combined with other equipment, can detect as little as one piece of viral DNA in ten microlitres of blood. The test has been useful in some situations to detect possible infection far earlier than antibody tests. More than 90% of antibody positive people also test positive by PCR, but not all. The technique is extremely sensitive to cross-contamination from previous samples. It is very easy to get false positive results.

Viral culture is another method of testing, where attempts are made to obtain HIV from white cells. It can detect 50% of HIV-infected children at birth, unlike antibody testing.

In conclusion, then, HIV testing is usually now very accurate indeed, although the initial test result always needs to be confirmed.

Q. Can saliva be used instead of blood to test for HIV?

Saliva testing is convenient and fast, and depends on finding antibodies to HIV in the mouth. A few drops of saliva are absorbed onto a special pad inserted into the mouth for a few minutes. The length of collection time is important. The fluid can then be tested using exactly the same equipment as for testing blood. Saliva collection has been used to screen prisoners, drug injectors, and now applicants for life insurance. However, studies show the results are not yet quite as accurate as for blood testing – for two reasons. First, the collection method may not adequately collect antibodies, particularly if the collection period is too brief. Secondly, food residues and other proteins in the mouth may confuse the test, although this is less of a problem as testing methods improve.

By packaging a simple saliva collection device with one of the latest 'instant' testing kits, the technology now exists to market a do-it-yourself home test for HIV, available from chemists. However, there are grave concerns about this. While there may be a market among people who do not want anyone else to know their result, or those wanting to test new partners or prostitutes in the bedroom, there is a real danger that people will misunderstand the implications of the result, or even take their own lives if the test result is positive and they are not given adequate counselling.

Q. Are all those with HIV going to develop AIDS?

We do not know whether all with HIV will develop AIDS, because we have not been following people with HIV long enough. As we have seen, in Western countries where anti-viral treatments are not used, 50% are ill within ten years and 70% in fourteen years. Progression is often more rapid in the poorest nations. Long-term survivors are an interesting and important group because they may have within their genetic make-up some kind of enhanced ability – complete or not – to contain HIV infection. Unfortunately, when we study the immune systems of long-term survivors who are well, we find the majority show some signs of immune damage. Of course, the longer people survive, the more likely it is that they will die of some other cause in the meantime, before AIDS develops.

Q. Is it possible for people to get rid of HIV once infected?

There have been a few cases where there has been good evidence of HIV infection, but after a year or two, no trace of virus anywhere in the body can be found. Although it is still too early to be sure, some experts believe that these individuals may have succeeded in eliminating HIV.

It also seems possible that a certain group in the population with particular genes may have some kind of constitutional protection against HIV infection. This should not surprise us. Just like bacteria develop resistance to antibiotics because susceptible bacteria die, leaving one or two variants with natural protection, so we would expect to find among millions of different human beings, a few with gene variations which protect.

By focusing on how the genes work, we may be able to find a

way of protecting the rest of the population. By analysing people's genes, we may also be able to predict in the future what treatments will be most appropriate, and at what stage.

Some individuals exposed to HIV show no sign of HIV infection by antibody tests or by PCR viral antigen testing (see question above on test reliability). However, their white cells show signs of sensitisation to HIV, suggesting that their immune systems have encountered HIV but have eliminated it within days of exposure.

As we will see later (see questions on mosquitoes and kissing), it may be that one reason why HIV seems not to be very infectious might be that many people have an ability to destroy a limited number of HIV particles. A small exposure would then fail to infect many people. One US study has suggested that up to 65% of HIV-negative gay men, 45% of negative drug users and 75% of health care workers accidentally exposed, all show evidence of sensitisation, but not infection. The same research workers found strong evidence of HIV sensitisation in around 2% of the US population, which is not surprising if the official figure of 1 million HIV-infected is correct.

Q. Are some types of condom safer than others?

There are hundreds of different brands available, ranging from latex to animal membrane. The ultra-thin/sensitive varieties are most likely to tear, although any condom may tear during anal sex. All latex condoms will rot rapidly if oil-based lubricants are used, and will deteriorate if stored in high temperatures. Animal membrane condoms may permit virus to pass through more easily.

In summary, if you are taking a risk you need to use a thick latex condom. This will reduce your risk enormously if the condom is correctly and carefully used. (See next chapter for further details on condoms.)

Q. Do the results of an HIV antibody test go on my medical record?

In many countries you can go to a clinic and get a completely anonymous test done. However, the results of named tests are very likely to go on your medical records.

Q. I have heard it said that HIV does not cause AIDS and that AIDS in Africa is a myth. What is the evidence?

There have been suggestions that HIV may not be the cause of AIDS, and that the AIDS epidemic in Africa is a myth. This has in part been due to the claims of a US scientist, Professor Duesberg, who has promoted the view that HIV is relatively harmless, and that AIDS is caused by recreational drugs or other sources of immune damage. Connected with this has been the claim that anti-viral drugs are useless, even in those with AIDS, and that they may actually cause AIDS.

Considering how poorly these claims are supported by scientific data, how very few other scientists take them seriously, and how damaging the claims are to the health campaign, it is surprising they have been given such sympathetic reaction by some people. Underlying most of these claims is a conspiracy theory involving alleged multinational fraud by research workers and drug companies, with the collusion of governments and the World Health Organisation. Trying to discuss the issues with some of these people is hard work. They rarely have scientific credentials of any note themselves, and they have an almost messianic fervour in devotion to their cause.

Remember, you can write an apparently well-researched book to make a case for almost any bizarre theory by the selective quoting of scientific papers, just as you can make a bizarre religion out of twisting Bible sayings taken out of context. This is even more true with scientific studies, since such a vast quantity appears each month, so variable in quality and in results. Fifty scientists conducting similar studies over a decade do *not* report the same results. There are a hundred reasons for variations. The truth is gained by studying the consensus, although media headlines are almost always based on single findings which suggest something different from most studies. Much of the scientific literature is complex and easy to misunderstand.

I am asked for clarification almost every week by well-informed people who are deeply puzzled. The confusion is dangerous too. At a recent International AIDS Conference I was handed a leaflet by an AIDS activist titled 'HIV is good for you'.

Here is a brief summary of some of the reasons why almost all scientists working in the AIDS field are totally convinced that HIV is a highly dangerous infectious virus causing AIDS.

1. The appearance of AIDS always follows HIV spread. In every group studied, we have seen the rise in numbers of those ill with AIDS closely linked to the increasing spread of HIV infection some years earlier.

Example: In Edinburgh, the rapid spread of HIV among drug users was followed by a steady rise in those ill or dying. In Glasgow, drug users of similar age, background and lifestyle were much less affected by HIV (HIV hit Glasgow later and behaviour changed in time) and death rates have been much lower. Incidentally, scientific studies have shown that nitrites and other recreational drugs do not cause AIDS.

Example: In many parts of Africa, people have died from illnesses such as tuberculosis in large numbers for decades. However, a large rise in deaths in the sexually active age group has followed spread of HIV into this group, with death rates in two years being sixty times higher in those with HIV.

Some have claimed that HIV has been present at similar levels for decades. This is nonsense. HIV levels in most towns and cities in many nations show that rapid year-on-year rises took place during the 1980s and early 1990s. Indeed, one study in 1986 found HIV levels as low as 1 in 1,000 in some groups, rising since.

Some have claimed that there is no massive AIDS epidemic in Africa and that HIV is being blamed for deaths of people who would have been dying anyway. It is true that diagnosis of AIDS in an individual in Africa can be difficult, as we saw in Chapter 3, but the fact is that death rates in the younger age groups are unexpectedly high – and among the babies of those infected, too. Babies testing positive a year after birth become ill later with AIDS. Those testing negative do not.

Many Africans arriving in countries like the UK with HIV, who become ill and die, clearly have an identical illness to those with AIDS infected in industrialised nations.

Some say there is a cross-reaction between malaria antibodies and HIV tests. As we saw in the earlier question on test accuracy, this was a problem in the mid-1980s, but not today. It is obvious anyway that malaria confusion is not taking place on a wide scale. The numbers in the population with malaria antibodies have remained relatively constant, while the numbers testing positive for HIV have soared. And HIV is found in many areas where there is no malaria.

Great weight has sometimes been placed on comments by some African specialists and politicians that the AIDS problem has been exaggerated by the West and that the actual size of the epidemic is far less significant than has been made out. Unfortunately, almost all doctors and nurses from European and other nations working in government and mission hospitals give a different story, based on first-hand experience of the unfolding catastrophe. Many African experts are not free to talk about AIDS, for reasons we saw in Chapter 1. Indeed, many Western doctors in these nations may also find it difficult to talk until they go home on leave.

Example: Those with haemophilia have received blood extracts for many years without problems. However, once HIV contaminated their supplies, those testing positive for HIV began to grow ill and die – as did their wives and children in some cases. Some have claimed that these haemophiliacs are only ill because the blood extracts of Factor VIII are rejected as foreign to the body and damage their immune systems. Evidence quoted in favour of this is from unpublished early reports that haemophiliacs with HIV are progressing more slowly to AIDS when converted to pure genetically engineered Factor VIII. However, if Factor VIII is the sole explanation, why are uninfected people who have been receiving impure blood extracts for years not developing AIDS? We would also expect those receiving HIV in a blood transfusion to remain perfectly well, when the fact is that they become ill and die too.

Anyone can see the links: a woman receives a pint of infected blood and becomes infected. Six years later she is unwell. Her baby is infected and develops AIDS and so does her husband. But no one else in her family dies. Why? Because a lethal infectious agent which we call HIV has been transmitted from blood to woman, to partner and to baby. These facts are so obvious and so simple to understand that it is extraordinary to me that anyone of even moderate intelligence should insist that there are other explanations.

Example: As we have seen, mothers can transmit HIV to their babies through the womb, during birth and in breast milk. These babies get ill and die of AIDS. Those who do not become infected remain well throughout life. Remember of course that we are not talking here about babies falsely testing positive to HIV because the result is confused by maternal antibodies.

2. The pattern of HIV spread fits AIDS patterns. If HIV is the cause of AIDS, we should expect to find that HIV shows evidence of spread through sexual activity and through the blood, since we know people with AIDS are linked by such contact. And this is indeed what we find, with overwhelming evidence of person-to-person spread of HIV by these routes.

3. HIV targets the cells which are damaged in AIDS. Some have tried to make a case that HIV is just an innocent passenger, not causing illness but just travelling with whatever does do the damage. However, the more we study HIV the more we understand how dangerous it is.

We know that HIV gets inside the same white cells whose death results in AIDS. We know that after an initial brief illness, HIV goes on multiplying in lymph nodes, where large numbers of infected cells can be found throughout the symptom-free period. We know that as virus levels rise, the person becomes more ill. We know that HIV attacks some cells in the brain and in the gut directly, explaining why people with AIDS can have damage to both organs. Although early studies have suggested that only one target white cell in 10,000 becomes infected, more sensitive tests have now detected HIV infection in one in ten cells.

4. Anti-HIV treatments benefit those with AIDS. If HIV is the cause of AIDS, then we would expect drugs used to fight HIV to produce an improvement in those who are ill. As we have seen in Chapter 2, there are a great number of independent studies which show that the anti-viral drugs improve the condition and survival of those with AIDS when used appropriately. It is true that they have side effects, and it is also true that resistance to the drugs can make treatment less effective after a while. As this happens, CD4 cell levels fall, virus levels rise and the person often begins to deteriorate. This is all evidence of linkage.

The simple fact is that babies of mothers with HIV are far less likely to die of immune deficiency if their mothers have been given anti-virals during late pregnancy. Why? Because anti-virals lower the levels of HIV in the mother's blood and this helps save the baby's life. The HIV-does-not-cause-AIDS groups say that anti-virals actually *cause* AIDS, and do not prevent it. This is a ridiculous conclusion to draw from our experience of caring for babies. It is also equally absurd when it comes to adults. And it completely fails to recognise that all over the world there are people dying with AIDS who have never had the luxury of anti-viral treatment, and even in wealthy nations there are people who have been diagnosed late and so not treated before becoming very ill, or who for one reason or another were unwilling at any stage to be treated. They still get ill and die.

Great play has been made by a minority on the discovery of a very small number of people who seem to have an AIDS-like illness with no evidence of HIV infection. I am not referring here to those who for various reasons lose or never develop an antibody response, but those in whom HIV is never found, even with many different detection methods.

There are two explanations for this, neither of which destroys the HIV basis for AIDS. First, we sometimes fail to look hard enough. Even in an illness like TB, it is not always possible to find the organisms. In other cases it appears we are looking at a very rare form of immune problem that has probably been around for centuries, and is nothing to do with AIDS. Such cases account for only a few in a million of those who get diagnosed with AIDS. As we have seen in earlier chapters, there are undoubtedly other factors which can cause acceleration or slowing of disease. These might include other infections such as mycoplasma and the genetic makeup of the individual.

In summary, there is overwhelming evidence that HIV causes AIDS, although, as with the link between smoking and lung cancer, much of it is circumstantial, based on large-scale studies of disease patterns. Just as you cannot prove that smoking causes lung cancer, or that a cancer in a particular person was caused by smoking, you cannot prove that HIV causes damage to the immune system, or that a particular person dying with TB is dying because HIV has weakened their defences. The nature of medical research is to look for patterns that fit everything else we understand about illnesses. If we accept (as most people now do) that smoking is dangerous, then exactly the same logical process forces us to conclude that HIV causes AIDS. The evidence is before the jury, and the result is conviction. The evidence is beyond all reasonable doubt.

Q. Is it safe to share pierced earrings?

No. Inserting an earring can cause a tiny amount of bleeding and the earring can accumulate dried debris. Earrings should not be shared. They should be regarded in the same way as needles. Clip-on earrings are safe.

Q. Is it safe for athletes to share a communal bucket and sponge to wash bloody injuries?

The sponge could transmit the virus by allowing blood from one player into another player's wound. Clean the bucket and sponge with antiseptic between players. The virus can survive in water for several days.

Q. Are contact sports safe?

You are far more likely to die from a broken neck or be paralysed for life during rough contact sports than to catch HIV. For this to happen, blood from an infected player's body would have to be rubbed into a wound on your body. This is extremely unlikely.

Q. Are swimming pools, rivers and lakes safe?

Swimming pools, rivers and lakes are safe (at least as far as catching HIV is concerned).

The only way you could possibly catch HIV at a swimming pool would be if someone carrying the virus cut themselves – say on glass at the side of a pool – and left a puddle of blood which you stepped in, cutting yourself on the same piece of glass. In the pool itself the dilutions are so enormous that I am sure that even if you poured ten fresh pints of blood full of virus into the pool scientists would be hard pushed to find a single blood cell, let alone a virus particle. My wife and I go swimming regularly with our children and we have no intention of stopping. There are many health risks from swimming in lakes or rivers but HIV is not one of them.

Q. What about going to the barber?

This is safe as long as disposable razor blades are used, and preferably disposable razors as well. Shaving tends to draw tiny amounts of blood, maybe too small to see. The old cut-throat razor blade could transmit virus from one client to another unless carefully cleaned after each use with fresh bleach solution. For the same reason, razors should never be shared in a household.

Q. Can the virus survive outside the human body?

People used to think that all the HIV particles became severely damaged after only twenty minutes outside the body. If this were the case, surgeons would only need to hang up their instruments in the sun for an hour before safely carrying on with the next operation. Infection control guidelines are several centimetres thick in many countries. Sterilisation is vital. An important paper shows that although most virus particles do become damaged after a few hours, a few may survive after three to seven days in dry dust, and over two weeks in water, although only under unusual conditions. In freeze-dried Factor VIII, HIV survives undamaged for months, hence the problems for those with haemophilia before heat treatment began in 1985.

Q. Does the virus survive in someone who has died?

As HIV survives reasonably well outside the body, it is not surprising to find that it also survives in those who have died. A recent survey of post-mortem blood examinations showed that HIV could be found in half of those who died, depending on the length of time between death and the examination.

Normal infection control measures used while the person was alive should therefore be continued – for example, the wearing of gloves to prevent contact with body secretions.

Q. How should we disinfect things?

The most important thing is to make sure that instruments and equipment are washed clean of blood and other body fluids before disinfection, as blood residue is a powerful neutraliser of almost all disinfectants. People used to think that a temperature of 56°C for half an hour or so would destroy the virus. This has now been questioned. One study shows that some virus may remain infectious for up to three hours at this temperature.

A solution of one part bleach to nine parts of water (10%) will destroy all virus in sixty seconds unless there are thick deposits of blood or dirt. These may inactivate the bleach, or require longer for the bleach to work.

For some medical purposes, 70% isopropyl alcohol destroys virus very quickly, as does a 2% solution of glutaraldehyde or betadine (povidone-iodine 7.5%). The virus is not destroyed by gamma irradiation or ultraviolet light, both of which are used to sterilise.

Although it is alarming to think that HIV may sometimes remain active outside the body, cases where this has resulted in infection are almost unknown and are confined entirely to puncturing of the skin with blood-covered medical instruments, and other accidents.

The general rule still holds true that outside of sex and shared needles, HIV does not spread.

Q. If I scratch myself with a needle, after it has been used to take blood from someone who is infected with HIV, what are my chances of becoming infected?

Probably much less than 1 in 200 from one accidental needle stick injury exposure. We know this from following up the results of a large number of such accidents. You are far more likely to get hepatitis B (up to a one in five chance) for which you may need a protective injection within a few hours, unless you have been vaccinated previously. This risk can be reduced further by giving anti-viral drugs soon after the event to anyone who has been accidentally injured.

Q. Is it safe to go to the dentist?

Yes, assuming your dentist sterilises or disinfects equipment after each consultation. The risk is not to you, the risk is to the dentist. Every time dentists give an injection or draw teeth there is a slight risk that they will puncture their own skin. If the patient is carrying the virus there is a slight possibility the dentist could become infected. This has already happened. For this reason dentists are now using gloves, masks and glasses when treating people known to be infected. Some dentists are using gloves and masks when treating all their patients. There has been one well-publicised case where a dentist with HIV infected several patients. Despite intensive investigations, we are still no nearer understanding how this occurred.

Some pieces of delicate dental equipment contain fibreoptic cables as light sources and are difficult to sterilise. They should be cleaned carefully, then disinfected, following normal infection control guidelines, eg 70% alcohol or 2% glutaraldehyde for four minutes (although glutaraldehyde can cause tissue reactions and the fumes can be unpleasant).

There is some evidence that the internal air chambers of high-speed dental drills can become contaminated, with material slowly dislodged by air during subsequent procedures. Like many of the other risk areas we consider, such as kissing, the risk must be very small indeed since a case has never been described of infection by this route (that is, patient to patient transfer at a dentist using such a device). Equipment needs to be well maintained and thoroughly cleaned before disinfection or sterilisation between patients.

Q. What about the risk to doctors and nurses?

Doctors are particularly at risk when they take blood. I have accidentally jabbed myself with a needle many times when trying to fill a blood bottle. Needles should never have their sleeves replaced before being disposed of. A third of accidents occur this way. Casualty doctors are in the frontline when sewing up wounds. Again, I have scratched myself with needles several times while stitching injuries, and gloves give only partial protection. At risk most of all are surgeons, whose hands may be deep inside a patient with a lot of bleeding, sharp needles, and poor visibility. A friend of mine, who is an experienced surgeon at a leading London teaching hospital, tells me that he frequently tears his gloves during operations. Blood can also spurt from a small artery into the eye. A growing number of occupational infections have already been reported, but the real impact must be much greater, and not yet detected.

Ideally surgeons would like to know before starting an operation whether the patient is a virus carrier or not so that they can be especially careful during the operation and in cleaning up afterwards. At present, doctors are often denied this information for ethical reasons. As a result, a number of surgeons may die over the next decade.

So far there are very few cases recorded of nurses contracting the infection from dirty needles or blood-contaminated 'sharps'. One case has occurred where the virus is thought to have entered through cracks in a nurse's hands caused by severe eczema. She was attending a patient with AIDS, without using gloves, and her hands were regularly covered in the patient's secretions.

There are several reports of people who have become infected from blood or secretions coming into contact with their skin, usually on the hands, face and mouth. It is certain that many more such incidents have resulted in infections which have not yet been detected. Some of these reports were of people who had no reason to suspect a risk from their patients and were unaware of any accident until they went to give blood and were found by routine testing to be infected. This is quite different from the situation where a doctor pricks his finger with a needle used on a patient in an AIDS ward. In this situation a report is made out and the doctor is tested. Few such incidents are missed.

In the normal course of nursing or doctoring, the risk of HIV infection is minimal. Care should be taken with needles, and good quality gloves should be worn if there are cuts or abrasions on the hands. It is true that a growing number of medical staff have been infected through caring for patients, but this is a tiny proportion of the vast numbers involved in looking after these individuals. (See Chapter 7 for further discussions of ethics and risks.)

Q. Can artificial insemination transmit HIV?

Yes. Artificial insemination carries a risk. To help reduce this, donated semen is usually frozen and stored for several weeks, and is not used until the donor has returned for a blood test to make sure he was not infected at the time of donation. As we have seen, normal HIV antibody tests only detect infection after a 'window period' of a few weeks. There are special techniques for reducing the risk of infection during artificial semination or IVF.

Q. Can I get HIV infection from a human bite?

Bites can probably pass on the infection, but the risk is almost certainly very low. I have before me a report where a boy infected his brother. It is thought that he bit him and that was the method of transmission. There is a small but variable amount of the virus in saliva which, it has been suggested, entered through the teethmarks of the bite.

Q. Where did HIV come from?

Scientists cannot agree on the origin of HIV, and any discussion of the subject generates great heat in those who fear a backlash against certain groups or nations, particularly those in Africa, if it is suggested that HIV originated there. This is unfortunate. The question of origins is a purely scientific one of the greatest importance in preventing the emergence of further plagues like AIDS.

We know HIV has been in existence since at least the 1950s because we find antibodies to HIV in serum samples going back this far. We know HIV is very similar to SIV in monkeys. These animal viruses have probably been around for centuries, particularly in Africa. In the light of this, many scientists have suggested that HIV mutated at some stage from an animal form. However, the animal viruses are equally different from HIV-1 and HIV-2, indicating that if HIV strains are derived from monkey SIV, then the mutations must have happened many decades ago. If the mutation were recent, we would expect HIV-1 and HIV-2 to be much more similar to each other than to SIV.

A form of SIV would need to have entered a human being at the same moment as mutating – not inconceivable if humans were regularly exposed to these animal viruses. Exposure could have taken place in a variety of ways: fertility rites or rituals involving monkey blood, bestiality, laboratory accidents or germ warfare research (one KGB theory used to try and discredit the USA), contamination of vaccine preparations using animal or human cells, transplantation of monkey tissues, insect transmission, or wound contamination.

Each of these possibilities has been thoroughly explored. While we have the technology to make viruses like HIV today, we did not in the 1950s. A special investigation has failed to find a firm link with vaccine programmes, and insect transmission seems extremely unlikely. Rites using animal blood, or accidental contamination of a laboratory worker both remain possibilities.

Q. Can you get HIV from mosquitoes?

This suggestion is worrying people all over the world, especially in Africa, where the number infected with HIV is large and people are used to catching another disease – malaria – from the anopheles mosquito. This is one of the most common questions I have been asked at education meetings in places like Uganda, Burundi and India from 1988 to 2003.

It is almost certain that no one will ever get HIV from a mosquito. The needle-like mouth of the insect is so fine that white cells carrying the virus cannot be carried in it, or on it, from one person to another. Scientists have studied outbreaks of AIDS and malaria. Malaria is no respecter of age or sex: if you are bitten, you can get malaria. However, there are particular age groups that rarely get infected with HIV – older men and women and older children. These people are not immune to HIV – they simply have never been exposed to the virus. They have often been bitten by mosquitoes, however, and may have developed malaria. Tests on a variety of insects show that HIV cannot multiply inside them.

It is likely that several virus particles need to be transmitted simultaneously for there to be any significant risk of infection, and this is something unlikely to happen from a bite.

In summary, infection from mosquitoes does not seem to be happening, and given the very low risk of transmission – even from a medical needle stick injury – we can see why.

Q. What is the risk from a single episode of unprotected sex?

We are unsure. Various attempts have been made to quantify the risk. It may be as low as 1 in 200 for non-traumatic heterosexual vaginal intercourse without a condom (see next chapter). Risk is higher for male to female anal intercourse and first vaginal intercourse in a woman (bleeding), higher during menstruation (for a man), and higher if other sex diseases are present.

A calculation can be made that in a relatively low-incidence area, where 1 in 30 heterosexuals are infected, the chance of infection from a single encounter could be as low as 200 multiplied by 30, or 1 in 600 against. 'Not a lot to worry about,' many heterosexuals might say. In practice, the risk may be higher, because someone willing to have sex in a one-off encounter may have had sex with many others before in similar situations.

These estimates might seem very low, but the lifetime risk becomes very significant when you add up the total number of risk exposures. (See next chapter for condom risk calculations.)

We also need to remember population size. Ten million people taking a risk on average twenty times a year gives 200 million potential risk episodes – and HIV spreads.

The overall message is that HIV is relatively uninfectious compared to many other disease-causing organisms. This helps us put the even lower non-sexual, non-injecting risks into context. The biggest danger can come, not perhaps from a chance one-off encounter through sex or needle sharing, but through regular day-in, day-out exposure from someone who is not known to be HIV-infected. Hence the situation in Malawi, where it is reported that a third of infected women in some groups were virgins before marriage and have been faithful since (see Chapter 14).

Q. If the risk to heterosexuals is so low in low-incidence countries, what is the point of general health campaigns?

Clearly it makes sense to target those most at risk – sexually active gay men and drug injectors, for example – while also targeting those likely to be the risk-takers of the future: those still in school. Teenagers today are the AIDS generation. In their sexually active lives they may well see 1 in 50 of the global adult population HIV-infected, with very high infection rates in many parts of the world.

Since it may take a generation to change cultural expectations and behaviour, we have to start now. Surveys show it is harder to change established behaviour than to prevent it in the first place. So it could be argued that, say, campaigns targeted at middle-aged heterosexuals in the UK are currently likely to be a waste of money, unless they are directed at business travellers, drug injectors and sexual tourists (see Chapter 12).

Q. What about tattoos or ear piercing?

Both of these procedures can be hazardous unless properly sterilised equipment is used. The hepatitis virus has been spread by these methods in the past. Always go to a reputable establishment.

Q. What about hot wax treatments and electrolysis?

The wax should be properly heated between treatments to destroy any virus. The electrolysis needles must be sterilised or discarded. Again, use a reputable establishment. If in doubt, ask what they do to sterilise equipment.

Q. Can you get HIV from acupuncture?

Not if the needles are sterilised or discarded each time.

Q. Is it safe to kiss someone on the lips?

Yes. The risk of infection from a dry kiss is almost zero. A 'French kiss' where tongue and saliva enter another person's mouth carries a higher risk, especially if one person has sores in the mouth, cracked lips, or bleeding gums. However, we have never yet seen a single case of 'mouth to mouth' spread. Even if one or two cases are found, it would not alter the fact that the risk is infinitesimally small. Having said that, I am not sure I would be happy to give someone with HIV long intimate mouth-to-mouth kisses.

Q. Is the communion cup safe?

Yes! However, new revised Anglican guidelines now permit the wafer to be dipped in the wine as a response to the fear. When I visited Uganda, I found many churches had abandoned the common cup. After some teaching, we shared communion together – a very moving experience, as it was the first time in over a year for many.

Fear, fear, fear – threatening to split congregations. But what are the facts?

Fact: the virus can survive in water for up to two weeks under exceptional circumstances.

Fact: the alcohol content in communion wine is not enough to damage the virus.

Fact: the virus can sometimes be found in the saliva of an infected patient.

Fact: the virus particles from one person could be swallowed by another member of the congregation.

On the other hand, however, the number of virus particles in a sip of wine is likely to be extremely small and you are extremely unlikely to get an HIV infection, even if a number of virus particles do enter your mouth. This is because saliva itself inhibits HIV to some extent, and because of an amazing protection your body possesses. It is called epithelium or gut lining.

Viruses or bacteria in your mouth are kept out of your blood by a continuous lining of internal skin which lines your tongue, gums, cheeks, back of your mouth and throat. Swallowed virus enters a continuous pipeline between your mouth and your anus. There is no break in the lining of the pipe. Nothing can enter your bloodstream from inside the pipe (gut, stomach, etc) without being digested first. The digestion process breaks up what you eat into tiny fragments, and then into molecules of protein, fat and sugar. The first part of the pipe is stretched out into a bag full of deadly acid (the stomach) which kills the virus anyway in a few seconds. Even if the virus was made of steel it could not enter your blood – it would just pass out the other end.

So the communion cup is safe and I will continue to drink from it. We are not going to see a great epidemic of AIDS among church congregations because of the communion cup. It just will not and cannot happen. We would first need to see a serious outbreak of HIV through kissing before we began to worry about the communion cup.

Q. Can my children catch HIV from another child at school?

Playground knocks and scratches are extremely unlikely to spread HIV. For this to happen, blood from one child would have to be rubbed into the wound of another. (See earlier question on contact sports.) A 'blood pact' between two children could spread HIV, and secondary school children could spread HIV if they are injecting drugs and sharing needles. This is much more common than many parents or teachers realise. My wife and I would be happy for our children to share a class with an infected child. We are not going to see an outbreak of AIDS spread by school children, except through teenagers injecting drugs or sleeping around.

Q. Can I get HIV from a discarded condom?

The first time many young people ever see a condom is in the street. There it is, lying in the gutter, chucked out of a car window the previous night. There is a small but growing risk that the semen it contains is full of virus. However, it is not going to infect you unless its contents come into contact with your broken skin, which is hardly likely.

Q. Are female condoms safer than male ones?

Female condoms are made of tough vinyl, held inside the woman by an inner and outer ring, so they might be expected to be safer. However, surveys have shown failure rates are almost as high as with male condoms. The reason for failure may be that the condom is hard to keep in place. In a study of 106 women, only 29% completed six months' use. The devices slipped out, were accidentally pushed inside, were uncomfortable, rustled, were noisy and felt cold and sometimes the penis entered outside the condom. A World Health Organisation spokesperson said at a recent AIDS conference: 'It lurks, slurps, glucks and slicks.' However, half the study group said they enjoyed sex more when using them!

Q. Is it true that nonoxynol-9 spermicide cream protects against HIV when used with a condom?

Experts disagree about the use of spermicidal creams such as nonoxynol-9 in the fight against AIDS. While some preparations show anti-viral activity in the laboratory, this is difficult to test in practice. On the one hand, they give added protection against pregnancy and sexually transmitted diseases such as chlamydia or gonorrhoea. On the other, there are many reports of vaginal or cervical irritation, which could provide entry points for the virus.

The World Health Organisation has announced a major research effort to develop an anti-HIV spermicidal cream which could be an effective weapon against infection. However, it will have to be non-irritant to be safe.

Q. Can I get HIV from being raped?

Yes, it is possible. The risk can be higher because the violence used can make abrasions and bleeding more likely, creating entry points for the virus.

Q. Is it safe to have blood transfusions?

The risk is now very low in most countries, due to excellent testing facilities.

However, the test does not pick up, for example, the man who gives blood five weeks after sleeping with an infected prostitute while on a business trip abroad. The test can take three months or more to become positive, during which time a donor could give lots of infected blood to the Red Cross. In rare cases it never becomes positive, even though the person is dying of AIDS. This is because it sometimes happens that people never produce antibodies. At the moment the risk is very low in countries like the UK, because gay men, drug addicts and other people who might have been exposed to HIV have been deliberately asked to stop giving blood, and almost all have ceased to do so. However, as the number of infected people in the general population rises, the number of infected units that pass through undetected also rises.

If I were about to have a major operation, I would ask for as few units of blood to be used as possible. Blood is not so essential as many people sometimes think. We have some excellent blood substitutes now which can replace the first two or three pints of blood lost – unless you started off very anaemic. In the United States there are large numbers of Jehovah's Witnesses who refuse blood transfusions for religious reasons. Few die, however. Major surgery without the use of blood transfusions is now a well-practised art in the United States.

It is sometimes possible to arrange to give your own blood, which can be stored before your planned operation. This makes you slightly anaemic, forcing your body to make a lot more blood cells. By the time your operation takes place, your blood is normal again, and two or three units of blood are ready for you in the blood bank. The shelf life of stored fresh blood is only thirty-five days, which is one reason why not many hospitals yet offer this facility. The other reason is cost.

For a long time, people in some countries who are too embarrassed to go to a sex disease clinic for a test for HIV antibodies, have been going along to give blood because they know that all blood is tested there. This happened a lot until the Blood Transfusion Service woke up to what was happening and tried to stop it. It is terribly dangerous: someone infected last week gives infected blood expecting that it will be detected, but it isn't. The test will not be positive for weeks. The blood slips through and is used in a hospital.

Q. Can I get HIV by giving blood?

Not at all. Some people are afraid of infection and are staying away. But there is no danger at all in giving blood, so long as all the needles used are sterile.

Q. What about babies of infected mothers?

We know that only a small minority of babies born to infected mothers will turn out to be infected themselves, although all will test positive for the first few months (see question on testing and Chapter 4). Breast-feeding significantly adds to the transmission risk, although advice in developing countries is often to continue because of the danger of death from gastroenteritis when bottle-feeding.

Q. What is the risk from oral sex?

The risk from oral sex is unclear. To be sure that orogenital contact is the route, it is necessary to find couples for whom other methods of intercourse have not taken place, and this can be difficult. Among gay men there can be a tendency for some to admit to oral sex but not to anal sex, although both have taken place.

Studies available suggest orogenital contact can transmit HIV, so care should be taken. There is much we do not yet understand. For example, spread from saliva is unknown from kissing, although the virus is present in saliva. The lining of the mouth and gut of an adult seems to give some protection, yet a newborn baby is very much at risk from HIV in breast milk.

Q. Can I get HIV from a toilet seat?

For this to happen there would have to be fresh blood on the toilet seat in contact with breaks on the skin or genitalia of the next user. The more likely scenario might be an infection from one of the organisms which cause diarrhoea in someone with HIV. This can be prevented by normal washing of hands after using the toilet.

Q. Can I get HIV from sharing a toothbrush?

This is theoretically possible, but we have never seen infection by this route, despite careful studies of many families where one person is infected. Brushing causes tiny amounts of bleeding from the gums, so a toothbrush should be used by only one person. Likewise, articles such as towels or razors (even electric razors) should not be shared.

Q. Can I get HIV from the skin of someone with AIDS?

If the patient has weeping boils or other skin problems causing the skin to crack, bleed, or produce secretions, then care should be taken. The secretions may carry virus. Remember, however, that virus on your own hands is not going to infect you unless there are breaks in your own skin. Hands are especially vulnerable, so cover cuts with waterproof bandages and if in doubt, use gloves. Several cases of infection have occurred following heavy contamination of broken skin by blood or secretions. Infected blood on the face of a person with acne or a skin rash has been known to transmit the virus.

Q. Is HIV present in sweat?

Although HIV can be found in many body fluids including blood, tears, saliva, semen, cervical secretions and breast milk, extensive tests have failed to detect HIV in sweat. However, all other body secretions should be regarded as potentially infectious.

Q. Am I more likely to get HIV from an infected person if my hands are cut or sore?

People with eczema should be especially careful to wear gloves when likely to come into contact with secretions from someone with AIDS. The thousands of tiny cracks and itchy blisters are entry places for the virus. Cuts should be covered with a waterproof plaster. Gloves should be worn by all people whenever handling anything covered with secretions or when lifting or turning a person in bed. Obviously gloves are not necessary for normal social contact, handling of crockery, or unsoiled clothing.

Q. Can I get HIV from mouth-to-mouth resuscitation?

The same principles apply as for French kissing or communion. I once found a man who had collapsed three minutes previously on the pavement outside Liverpool Street Station in London. I gave him mouth-to-mouth resuscitation for twenty-five minutes until the ambulance arrived. Every time I lifted my mouth after giving a breath he spluttered back at me. By the end I was covered with his saliva. It was over my face, in my eyes, in my mouth and in my lungs. But that man walked out of the hospital despite it taking forty-five minutes from his heart stopping to his arrival in the emergency room.

You can reduce the risk enormously by covering the mouth with a handkerchief and breathing through it. Hospitals and ambulances carry a special tube connecting your mouth to the dying person. It has a valve preventing air and secretions blowing back in your face. They should be standard issue, but since they make resuscitation more difficult it probably would not make sense to use one unless you were already familiar with it.

Mouth-to-mouth resuscitation saves lives, and if you do not do it because you are afraid of getting infected, you may have to live with your conscience for the rest of your life. The Good Samaritan was the one who took the risk of being mugged or injured to stop and help a dying man lying in the road.

For an ordinary person, in a low-incidence country, the risk of the other person carrying the virus is low. The risk of catching the virus would be more for someone who knew that the person who had collapsed was positive, had AIDS, was a drug addict, or was a sexually active homosexual.

Q. Can you pick up any other infections from looking after someone with AIDS?

Yes. There are three possibilities: TB, which can develop rapidly in someone with AIDS; cytomegalovirus; and other infections causing diarrhoea.

People with AIDS are 100 times more likely to have TB than the average person, although the kind of TB they have is often less infectious to others. If someone walks into a hospital and has widespread TB, one of the first questions doctors ask now is: 'Does this person have AIDS?' In healthy people, tuberculosis is usually easily treated.

As we have seen, tuberculosis is the commonest reason worldwide for someone with HIV to die. The natural immunity that most people have to the microbe is destroyed, so people die quickly of TB. Therefore it comes as no surprise to find that worldwide TB cases are on the increase, even in industrialised nations such as the USA or the UK.

One worrying problem has been the recent emergence of new strains which have resistance to most drugs used against TB. Someone with HIV needs to take antibiotics for long periods. It is difficult to eradicate the infection without some natural immunity to help. If medication is taken intermittently, there is a risk that resistance will develop. If health care workers become infected with these strains, treatment can be difficult, although fortunately many have protective immunity due to exposure to TB as a child, or from vaccination.

To reduce the risk to care workers, it has been recommended that people with HIV who have unidentified chest infections should be regarded as potentially infectious for TB. It is also suggested that in areas where multiple drug resistance is a problem, staff should be tested for TB every three months.

The other hazard, the cytomegalovirus (CMV) infection, is very common and usually quite harmless, but can be crippling to someone with AIDS.

Some ask if pregnant women are at risk from cytomegalovirus infection picked up from someone with AIDS. CMV infection is very common in the general population. Some 50% of women of childbearing age may be actively infected at any time, without any signs – unless the immune system is damaged. About 1% of uninfected women become infected with CMV during pregnancy. CMV can cross the placenta and infect the unborn child, almost always after new infection. In 1,000 births, around three to four babies are CMV-infected. Of these, 10–15% have a CMV-induced abnormality such as brain damage and/or deafness.

A few hospitals offer screening for CMV antibodies to nurses working in high CMV incidence areas such as AIDS wards. If antibodies are absent, women are advised to work elsewhere. However, there seems to be little hard data to support this advice, and the additional risk to the unborn child appears to be extremely small. Official advice is that no special precautions are necessary for the care of HIV-infected people excreting CMV, but that good personal hygiene should be followed, especially hand washing, after contact with respiratory secretions or urine. Good personal hygiene will prevent other bowel infections being transmitted. Apart from TB, the risks are entirely the other way round: the simple cough or cold a well person has could make someone with AIDS seriously ill.

Q. I have heard that cats can give toxoplasma infections to those with HIV. Is this true?

It used to be thought that toxoplasmosis in those with AIDS might be linked to cat ownership. One person with AIDS I used to visit at home even called his cat Toxo! Fortunately, a study has shown that where toxoplasmosis develops it is almost always the result of activation of a previous infection. No cases were found of recently acquired infection.

Q. What is the importance of a 'doubling time'?

The doubling time is the time it takes for the number of those with AIDS or early infection to double. It used to be six months in many countries first experiencing the disease, but is now averaging three years or more in many countries.

A story is told of a famous chieftain who was agreeing the price of a piece of land. He had a chessboard in front of him with sixty-four squares. He said his price was a grain of wheat on the first square, two on the second, four on the third, eight on the fourth, and so on. The deal was agreed. What the other man did not realise was that by the time he got to square sixty-four, all the grains of wheat in the entire world would not be enough! In around ten doublings you reach a thousand, but by twenty doublings you reach nearly a million. By thirty doublings the number is impossible even to imagine.

A doubling time of six months to a year means it only takes a generation to multiply current numbers by billions. But current numbers infected worldwide are already reckoned as millions.

Another way of looking at it is that all doubling times have to slow down.

Q. Could we all be wiped out by AIDS?

No. The spread is likely to slow down as many of the people with multiple partners and drug addicts become infected. The length of time for the number of new cases to double is getting longer in most countries. At the start of an epidemic in a small community the doubling time is often six months. After a few years it usually lengthens to more than a year or two. This is still very serious, but at least it shows some sign of hope. In Africa, South East Asia, and parts of Latin America, other factors such as other sex diseases are encouraging the spread in ways we do not fully understand. Outside these areas the spread throughout the general population will continue, but almost certainly more slowly. Eventually, we hope there will be a cure (although conceivably not for ten to twenty years).

The only way the whole of mankind might die would be if this highly adaptable, unstable virus were to change its method of transmission. Other similar viruses can be spread through droplets – coughing and sneezing. We really do not understand fully why this does not happen with HIV. We are all hoping this will never happen in the future, but it could, and the more people who are infected each year, the greater the chance of such a mutation. If it happened, many millions could die rapidly unless we found a cure in time. We saw in the 2003 outbreak of SARS the threat of new mutant viruses, bringing back memories of the 1918–19 Spanish flu epidemic, which infected 400 million people, of which 30–40 million died.

Q. Why not test everyone and separate infected from uninfected people?

I am horrified when people ask me this question. This is a recipe for concentration camps. Also, it would not work: many infected people would be missed due to the test not becoming positive for up to nine months after infection. Many who think they are positive would disappear and go underground. The days when any country could close its borders are over – particularly EU countries where border controls have been abolished. Millions of people travel to other countries each year, many illegally. People would have to enter quarantine after being abroad even for twelve hours, because that is long enough to share a needle or have sex. And quarantine would have to be for up to nine months. During this time the person would have to be kept in solitary confinement in a prison cell so there could be no possibility of sexual intercourse or sharing needles. What would happen to business trips or to tourism if no one could travel without being in a 'sex-free' prison for up to nine months first? What are you suggesting? An iron curtain, even more effective and destructive than was the one in the East? Husbands and wives separated? Children never able to see an aunt or an uncle except in a room with a television camera?

Even if the epidemic is controlled in one country, if all neighbouring countries have rapidly increasing problems then HIV will find its way in. That is why, even if I agreed with the concentration camp idea – and I find it utterly repulsive – I would think it stupid to try it. The answer has to be a worldwide answer. The only alternative is to close all borders, airports and sea ports, and blow up any ship, pleasure boat, or plane that approaches the coast.

Q. What is the cause of same-sex orientation? Is there a gay gene?

I am regularly asked after AIDS talks why people turn out to be heterosexual, homosexual or bisexual, and I often wonder what is behind the question. Is it a reaction against gay sex as perverted or abnormal? Is it a desire to promote gay sex as natural and acceptable? Or is it just curiosity?

I am going to attempt to answer the question because misconceptions continue to inhibit a compassionate response to gay men with AIDS. One hears statements like, 'He chose to be gay', linked to an 'it's his own fault' attitude.

Although, as we have already seen, most HIV infection worldwide is heterosexual, people's views of gay sexuality can be profoundly important in the response to AIDS in countries like the UK, where gay men comprise the majority of those who are ill or dying.

At the risk of being rather simplistic, it could be said that in the past many of those approving of homosexual relationships may have tended to the view that people are 'born gay'. And those disapproving of such relationships may have tended to the opposite view: that people become homosexuals either as a result of upbringing, or as a result of individual choice.

What are the facts? There is certainly evidence that our sexual orientation can be profoundly affected by what happens to us as we grow up, but there is also growing evidence that our genes may have a degree of influence too.

Classical psychoanalytic theory has pointed to the family dynamic, and a common pattern of a weak or absent father and a powerful or dominating mother being more likely to result in a homosexual son. Another model has suggested that sex abuse can drive the person either towards same-sex relationships or away from them, depending on the circumstances. The model breaks down, as do all the simple models, because there are many with a same-sex orientation whose childhood and adolescence were quite different.

In the 1950s and 1960s two studies were done of identical twins reared apart. These kinds of studies are very interesting, because they help us settle the nature/nurture argument, as each pair of twins has identical genes. Any differences must therefore be due to factors operating after birth. If sexual orientation were purely pre-programmed, then such twins would always have the same sexual feelings. The studies found there was a link, but not a complete one. Many sets of twins were found to have the same orientation, but not all.

The nature/nurture debate can get very heated. Some may say that a genetic influence on sexual orientation justifies homosexual relationships as normal. Others may say that if there really is a gene, it must be just as abnormal as the one causing cystic fibrosis and should be eliminated from the population. My own view as a Christian is neither of these two extremes. My understanding is that God loves us whatever our genetic makeup. Genes in themselves are morally neutral, yet a part of our fallen world. The real question seems to be how we choose to live with them.

Some Christians get very agitated over the issue, because they feel that an environmental explanation based on 'unfortunate experiences' is easier to cope with than the thought that our Creator might have 'designed us like that'. However, to be consistent, if we take the line that all genes in all people are as God designed and originally intended, then we are forced to the odd conclusion that God intended people to have haemophilia, cystic fibrosis, or a host of other conditions programmed by genes.

The traditional Christian view on illness and suffering has been that God created the world perfect, but gave us free will. When man fell, sickness and decay entered the universe. This makes sense of the observation that we probably all contain rogue genes, useless genes, harmless genes, beneficial genes, dangerous genes and genes which are just part of the varied normal human condition. It then becomes a matter of heated theological and biological debate to decide which category so-called 'gay genes' might fall into.

This is something which needs sorting out. A tough secular world has a knack of quickly destroying embryos which do not fit the fashion of normality. Christians have been remarkably united in condemning such a utilitarian approach to life, and there is a strong consensus between Evangelicals, traditional Catholics and the Gay Christian Movement. All are utterly opposed to the possibility of destroying embryos on the basis of a possible gay gene, although perhaps for different reasons.

There are those who are troubled over the question of choice. Some make the suggestion that if sexual orientation is environmental, people can choose. Since people do not choose their parents, the circumstances of their upbringing, or to be sexually abused, I cannot see it makes any difference if sexuality is more or less genetic or environmental.

I cannot find any evidence that people choose to have homosexual feelings. On the contrary, many are troubled by them and wish they were heterosexually inclined. People can, however, choose how feelings are expressed in terms of behaviour. This is a deeply sensitive, complex and controversial area, and one which has caused confusion in the church to the detriment of those ill with AIDS. Confusion and uncertainty mean people are unsure how to respond.

As we will see in a later chapter, personal views have to be laid aside in order to care unconditionally. The day your views or mine, whether they be on politics, lifestyle, religion, race, sexuality or any other factor, begin to affect the care we give, is the day we should stop trying to care for people. Doctors, for example, should be struck off the medical register for refusing to look after someone on the basis of race, lifestyle or because they have an unacceptable illness. If we cannot accept, love and care for people as people, then our care is almost worthless.

You do not have to agree in order to care. You might have a completely different outlook on life, but that does not take away the possibility (or indeed the obligation) of giving loving, sensitive help to another human being in great need. Some people fear that expressing care condones behaviour they may consider immoral. If that is the case, then nursing someone with alcoholic liver cirrhosis would also be unacceptable, or helping someone who fell under a car when drunk. Or is it just a special judgement to be imposed on those who are practising homosexuals? (For further discussion see Chapter 8.)

Q. What should I do if I'm worried about infection?

If you are concerned about HIV infection, the first thing you could do is change your lifestyle: have one partner (currently uninfected) for life and do not inject drugs. You may feel you have good reasons to be worried. You need expert advice from a physician with experience in this area as a result of which you may want to be tested. You need to think this through carefully. The decision to be tested is not straightforward and you need good preparation if you decide to go ahead. If the test comes back positive, things can happen very fast. In the upset you can end up sharing the result with someone who then lets you down by telling other people. The result can be a lost job – or worse – so you need to have thought through what you will do if the result is positive. However, a positive test could prolong your life by allowing you to enrol for free or low-cost treatment.

You may have been required to have a test because you are about to get married. Many people are choosing to get married somewhere else to avoid a test. But this is one area where testing is especially important: here are two people committing themselves to each other for life and probably intending to have a family. I know people who have decided to be tested because of their past lives, out of courtesy and respect for a future spouse or partner.

A positive test result needs checking a second time to be absolutely sure. The result can occasionally be wrong. A confirmed positive result means your body has been exposed to the virus. Some of your soldier cells will have been reprogrammed. We have to make sure that those soldier cells stay asleep for as long as possible before being stimulated by other infections into producing more virus particles.

Anything that would improve the health of an uninfected person is also likely to give the very best chance of health to someone who is infected. Boosting your immune system will also help your body keep well if some of your soldier cells are starting to die.

Eat a balanced diet, avoid physical exhaustion, and pace yourself in what you do. Exercise regularly and be careful about situations you know are likely to leave you completely drained emotionally. It seems that some people can live for many years – even decades – with this virus. The longer you live, the more likely it is that we will find more effective treatments or even a cure.

A lot of people may try to exploit your fears by selling you all kinds of treatments or remedies. Before you spend your savings on these things, just remember that every drug company in the world would love to find a natural substance that could work well for people with AIDS. Every folk remedy you hear about has already been examined and rejected by scientists or is as yet unproven. Most of these things gain their reputation because people who take them often seem to improve. However, as we have seen, what makes people with AIDS ill is usually the other infections that invade when the soldier cells are damaged. The natural course of the illness can be a series of dramatic ups and downs. People then credit a folk remedy for an improvement that was bound to happen anyway.

I do not want to stop you from trying these things, but many people have wasted a lot of money on 'cures' that are totally worthless.

You may panic because, having read this book, you think you are suffering from the early stages of AIDS. This illness is a great mimic of other less serious conditions. For example, a fever together with swollen glands for a while is quite likely to be caused by glandular fever. All kinds of things can produce rashes or diarrhoea. If you are worried, you should see a physician.

However, you may know that you are a carrier of the virus, and your physician has confirmed that the virus is now making you ill. Exactly the same things apply as for those infected but feeling well: basically, take care of your body to give it the best environment to protect you.

If you are infected with AIDS, you have probably already become an expert on the disease. Some days you may feel able to handle it and other days you may feel you are not coping at all. Sometimes you may find yourself caught between facing the practicalities of dying and wanting to build plans for the next two decades. However you became infected, and whatever your background, not far from where you live there are other people in the same situation who may be able to help you. AIDS is too big a burden for anyone to have to carry alone.

Often it is more harrowing to watch someone else suffering than to be in the situation yourself. You can feel helpless and frustrated. On top of all that can be the exhaustion that comes from giving care twenty-four hours a day, seven days a week. There can also be a lurking unease that your partner may have infected you or that you infected your partner. All these things can produce high levels of anxiety and stress.

Again, I urge you to link up with various agencies, where they exist, for practical and emotional support. You may be encouraged to know that many partners have not infected each other, even after long periods of unprotected sex. You will need to think through that whole area now in the light of the next chapter in this book about condoms and the advice to partners of infected people.

Q. Is there an answer to AIDS?

A simple answer to AIDS is, in the words of a doctor from Northern Ireland, an 'epidemic of faithfulness'. An epidemic of faithfulness would have a major impact on the epidemic of AIDS, along with testing blood donations, taking care over sterilisation and disinfection, and discouraging the sharing of needles and syringes by drug addicts.

In the words of the World Health Organisation: 'The most effective way to prevent sexual transmission of HIV is to abstain, or for two people who are not infected to be faithful to one another. Alternatively, the correct use of a condom will reduce the risk significantly.'

All these questions are important. However, the biggest question in my mind is this: Are condoms really as safe as everyone seems to think they are? Is the emphasis on condoms for safer sex simply because we can't think of anything better to say, or is it really grounded in fact? If it is safer, how much safer is it?

CHAPTER SIX
CONDOMS – THE TRUTH

Whenever I talk to young people in Africa, India or Europe about AIDS I find the same thing: they think that using a condom will prevent them from getting HIV. The truth is that it may greatly reduce the risk, but some risk still remains (even assuming everyone who wants to use them is guaranteed they will always be available and affordable. This is a massive challenge in two-thirds of the world). Condoms are expensive for poorer nations when provided on a national scale in sufficient quantities to rubberise all sexual encounters. Even 140 million condoms would not last Africa more than one night – and then what do you do? International donors have been promoting messages that they have often failed to back with adequate financial commitment and infrastructure. The result has often been an approach which is not only culturally insensitive, but also unsustainable. (See more on this important issue of condom distribution campaigns in Chapter 14 – Special issues in poorer nations.)

But in any case, as every doctor knows, condoms can be unreliable. If a hundred couples use condoms for contraception, up to fifteen of them could be in clinics each year asking for abortions. If you are about to take a risk, you should use one – it could save your life – but don't kid yourself it's totally safe. For a start, they vary in quality. A survey of 50,000 condoms from 110 brands on sale in Europe, Brazil, Indonesia and Thailand showed only 3% to be 'very good' (strength, aging, no holes); 48% were 'poor' or 'very poor'. No condoms on sale in Italy, Portugal or Spain were 'very good'.

In one UK survey, holes were found in up to 32 out of 100 condoms of the least reliable makes. These holes were gross defects, not the microscopic holes seen in some latex (5 micron, HIV is 0.1 micron), which are far less significant. The British Standards Institute permits up to 3 out of 100 to have holes in them when they leave the factory. In the USA, government standards allow only 4 condoms out of every 1,000 to have leaks. But users still experience a failure rate of between 3% and 15%, which is the percentage of women who have an unwanted pregnancy using this method of birth control over a year.

A spokesman from the London Rubber Company (Durex) admitted that if incorrectly used, the failure rate of condoms could be anything from 25% up to 100%, and there are real problems with teaching people how to use them – not least because of illiteracy.

The condom is the least reliable contraceptive in wide use. It's as bad as the diaphragm or cap with spermicide. Many violently disagree. They say it is a superb contraceptive; it is people who are unreliable. They put it on too late, or inside out, or tear it, or forget it, or let it fall off. They say people are unreliable but the condom is reliable, if properly used. But it is easy to have an accident with a condom. Condoms are unreliable compared to, for example, the pill. That is why the pill is so popular in Western countries, not just because it is a more convenient method.

Things are worse than they appear from the pregnancy rates. Out of 100 couples, 10 will have great difficulty in conceiving anyway. Five will probably never be able to conceive for various reasons, including previous infections with sexually transmitted diseases.

After four months of trying to conceive, only about half of an average group of women will succeed in becoming pregnant. If they used a perfectly safe method two out of three times that they had intercourse, it would take a year for half to become pregnant. If they used the method for ten out of twelve months of the year, then 25 out of 100 could be expected to get pregnant in a year. If they had unprotected sex for one month a year and used the method for eleven months, then it could be expected that over 12 of them would become pregnant in a year.

What this means is that if condoms produce a failure rate of around 12 in 100 per year, then they must be leaking often. It is about the same thing as having intercourse for a whole month without any protection at all but taking the pill the rest of the year. Somehow or other secretions from a man and a woman are very frequently meeting each other.

This conclusion is confirmed by a study of 2,000 acts of intercourse by 80 heterosexual and 7 homosexual couples, with 14 types of condoms. The overall failure rate from slippage or rupture was 11.3%, even higher than the 1 in 12 (8.3%) theoretical rate predicted above.

Think about it: a woman can only become pregnant on three days a month – while ovulating and shortly afterwards. After a single accident with a condom there is only a 1 in 10 or so chance of it being a fertile day anyway. Even if it were, pregnancy may not follow. However, it is possible to catch HIV infection every day of the month. The overall risk of pregnancy after one episode of unprotected sex is 2–4%; the risk of HIV from an infected partner after unprotected vaginal sex is probably 0.5%, or 1 in 200 in the absence of other sexually transmitted diseases. An increasing number of people have become pregnant because they switched from a more reliable contraceptive to the condom because of AIDS.

If up to 15 out of 100 couples each year are actually managing to conceive despite condom use, there must be frequent accidents, probably 1 in 12, from the figures above. If you are having sex regularly with an infected person, it is like throwing dice. Every time you throw a double six is how often the condom has let you down. Would you trust your life to a condom? Remember that one episode of unprotected sex can be enough to infect you. Over the next few years there will be a growing number of angry men and women who have become infected, despite using a condom. They thought they were safe.

Various reports have been published on couples using condoms where only one partner has tested positive. In one study, up to a quarter of the healthy partners became infected with HIV in only one to three years, despite use of the condom. Others may say these people were careless. All I am saying is that if correctly used, the condom can be a reliable contraceptive and will almost certainly reduce enormously your risk of getting AIDS, but the reports show that it is hard to use safely.

Another study of partners using condoms suggests that the risk of catching HIV is reduced by 85%. That sounds excellent, but it is not. If you persist in sleeping regularly with someone who is positive, or with numbers of unknown people who are possibly positive, then eventually, condom or no condom, you may get AIDS. Vaginal or anal sex using a condom is not a no-risk activity.

> 'The most effective way to prevent sexual transmission of HIV is to abstain, or for two people who are not infected to be faithful to one another. Alternatively, the correct use of a condom will reduce the risk significantly.'
>
> World Health Organisation
> World AIDS Day 1991 and 1992

Consider the following calculation. Let us assume the estimate many use is correct, and that the risk of transmission is roughly 1 in 200 per episode of unprotected sex with an infected partner. Let us assume 95% protection from the condom for the sake of argument, or a twenty-fold risk reduction. This would give a total risk of 1 in 4,000 per episode of protected sex. Let us assume a couple has sex just under three times a week, or 150 times a year. The risk of the partner becoming infected in one year, despite using a condom, then becomes 3.7% or almost 20% in five years. If we only rate the condom protection as 90% instead of 95%, then the five-year infection rate could rise to 40% or 7.4% per year.

How do these theoretical estimates fit with experience? An Italian study of almost 400 women with infected partners found the following:

- 1.2% always using condoms were infected per year overall
- 7.3% not using condoms were infected per year overall
- 12.3% not using condoms regularly, and with highly infectious partners, were infected per year
- 2.6% not using condoms regularly, and with partners of low infectiousness, were infected per year

Partners were considered highly infectious if their white cell (CD4) counts were low or if they were becoming unwell. Inconsistent condom use increased risk around six times. Anal sex doubled the risk. AIDS in the partner trebled the risk.

In another study, almost 200 women with HIV-infected haemophiliac partners were studied. Between 1985 and 1992, one in ten became infected. The risk of infection increased with time as the men deteriorated. It is very difficult to obtain meaningful figures for these risks because there are a number of variables: stage of infection, sexual practice, the presence of other sex diseases, frequency of intercourse, frequency of condom use. For this reason different studies can give varying results.

A combined European study of 563 heterosexuals with infected partners in stable relationships from nine countries was carried out between 1987 and 1991. People were enrolled in the study month by month, so some were part of it for only a short time. Altogether, 12% of the men and 20% of the women became infected. For men, the risk increased with the stage of the illness, and intercourse during menstruation. For women, the risk increased with her age, the stage of the man's infection and anal intercourse. None of twenty-four couples who always used a condom became infected.

We do not know what the risk is from a single sexual contact with someone who is positive. It certainly depends on many other factors, such as whether either partner also has gonorrhoea or syphilis. Any sores will be full of white cells and virus. Circumcision reduces risk. It seems people are most infectious for the first twelve to fifteen weeks after infection with HIV, and then years later when beginning to feel unwell again. Genetically, some individuals may be more susceptible than others. In conclusion, it seems the risk from a single accident with a condom, or a single unprotected contact, is small, but some have become infected this way.

Condom manufacturers' literature states that condoms are designed for vaginal sex only and are not suitable for protection from HIV transmission by the anal route. Particularly hazardous is the use of oil-based lubricants, as these rot the rubber in minutes. Recently, some new 'extra strong' condoms have been marketed, with lower failure rates for anal intercourse.

What is safe sex?

So what is the correct health message? It is that condoms do not make sex 100% safe, they simply make it far safer. Safe sex is sex between two partners who are not infected. This means a partnership between two people who are uninfected – perhaps they were virgins – and who now remain faithful to each other for life and do not inject drugs. If you are going to have sex in an unsafe situation you are foolish indeed not to use a condom, and you must use it very carefully every single time. But don't kid yourself that you will never get AIDS. (See previous chapter for further background on risks.)

Because condom use also provides a measure of protection against other sexually transmitted diseases, and because the genital ulceration caused by STDs makes the body so vulnerable to HIV, it may be that a key part of condom protection is reducing the incidence of ulceration. This is particularly so in developing countries.

How to use a condom more safely

A condom is tightly rolled up. Make sure it is the right way around. It will only unroll one way. If you have sex in the dark you may need to turn the light on. The teat at the end is there to collect all semen and fluids from the man. This needs to be squeezed empty of air or the condom may leak. With one hand holding the teat, the other is used to roll the condom gently over the entire length of the erect penis. This needs to happen soon after the man is aroused for two reasons: first, a small amount of fluid emerges from the end of the penis during arousal as part of the body's natural lubrication before the man enters the woman. This can be full of virus. Secondly, during arousal a woman produces a lot of secretions for lubrication. These may also contain virus if a woman is infected. The early use of the condom is to keep any genital contact separate from the start.

Wear and tear

A woman usually takes longer than a man to become fully aroused and will usually find things more satisfying if there is continuing caressing before her partner enters her. During this period a condom may unroll partly or fall off altogether. It may also suffer general wear and tear. It can snag on a woman's jewellery or on her fingernails. This can happen if, as advocates of condoms suggest, the woman helps the man put on the condom as part of lovemaking. Damage caused at this stage is usually obvious straight away. The real danger time can be when a woman helps her partner come inside her. Fingernails and jewellery can cause a minute tear in the condom which enlarges during intercourse. The result is discovered on withdrawal.

Rapid exit

Withdrawal must be prompt for two reasons: first there is a small risk of semen leakage along the shaft of the penis, especially if the teat was full of air. Secondly, as soon as a man has reached climax, the penis starts to soften and what was a tight fit becomes a very loose fit. Condoms can easily leak or slip off inside a woman. The condom end must be held gently as the man withdraws.

Most people dislike using condoms

A huge international campaign has been carried out to try and make the condom more acceptable. When used carefully in the way described above, many couples find it disruptive and they dislike it: it is a real turn-off. It is the same whether you are in the USA or Africa. What's so romantic about a condom? After all, that is one reason why people stopped using condoms when the pill came along. The other reason was their unreliability and the constant fear of pregnancy. It was the pill, not the condom, that brought about the so-called sexual revolution of the 1960s.

So the reasons why couples dislike the condom are:

1. To put it on carefully takes precious seconds out of a continuing experience. Some men find that by the time they have got it on, and they are happy it is comfortable (and this may need a couple of tries), their erection has disappeared. The woman is left hanging around and rapidly loses her momentum. Trying to find where you put one, opening the packet, and getting it on correctly can be a joke, but it is disruptive.

2. Making sure it does not roll off can cause tension in the pre-intercourse stage of lovemaking.

3. Checking it is still intact immediately before entry causes further delay.

4. Many men say that the layer of rubber reduces what they can feel (although some who tend to ejaculate too early may find that an advantage). Some women dislike the thought of a piece of rubber in such a personal area.

5. For many couples a central part of their celebration of oneness is to be lying together, with the man inside, immediately after both are satisfied. Many people enjoy being able to 'cool off' in each other's arms like this. Correct condom use requires the man to withdraw immediately. Some see it as a rather abrupt and savage end to a marvellous experience.

6. Some find disposing of the used condom rather revolting. The best method is to tie it up carefully, wrap it up in toilet paper, and flush it away.

In addition there is another vital factor: the very fact that a condom is being used, other than merely to provide some protection against pregnancy, implies some slight anxiety about whether a partner is infected. This can cause tension.

Are people using condoms more?

It is extremely difficult for a woman, with no current boyfriend, to buy a packet of condoms and keep one in her bag. In doing so she is having to admit to herself, and any prospective partner, that she plans to have sex soon – perhaps with someone she hardly knows. When she goes out for the evening, it can be hard for her to take a condom. In doing so she is admitting that she might have sex with someone tonight. Many women feel that carrying a condom makes them look promiscuous, when they feel they are not. A further major problem is when to produce it. A romantic evening is turning rapidly into something more. Are you going to show you don't trust the other person by reaching for a condom? Will the other person take offence at the implication he or she has been sleeping around? Insisting on a condom may take a lot of self-confidence and courage on the part of the woman. Female condoms may be easier, although pregnancy failure rates can be as high as 12%.

Because there are so many natural social barriers to condom use, a major part of some prevention campaigns has been the message: 'Be confident in presenting your partner with a condom.'

How to minimise the disruption

Be prepared. Talk it through with your partner. Practise! But there is another way: change your lifestyle. So many pamphlets tell us how wonderful 'safe sex' is. They say how fulfilling it is just to rub bodies together and have a cuddle. They describe a vast number of other things people can do to have sex safely together. That is not what most people call sex.

The choice is so obvious and clear. Find someone you love and trust, someone who is not infected at the moment and will remain faithful to you for life and to whom you will remain faithful. Then you can enjoy unlimited, anxiety-free sex.

Free love

Your philosophy may be that if people want to, they can sleep together without any great relationship, and with no strings attached. 'We live in a free world and people should be free to do what they like.' Maybe you feel that ultimately you want to be married but you want to have fun now. Friends of mine are afraid that their relationships will become tame and boring if they get married. Or they say, 'A piece of paper won't make me love her any more.'

I am constantly seeing the casualties of this attitude. Life is unfair. Somehow it is usually the woman who comes off worse: she is the one who may become pregnant, and her risk of catching HIV is twice as great as the man's risk from her. She may suffer the chronic pain of pelvic inflammatory disease or cervical cancer. And the woman is often the one who is most devastated when a relationship breaks up.

Free love is fine until your lover leaves you at 43 years of age, and you still have had no children because he would have walked out. A whole generation of people is growing older. The pensioners of tomorrow will have no wives, no husbands, no children, no family. All they will have is a few casual relationships and old memories. No wonder many are deciding that enough is enough. They decide that the right person has not come along, so they are staying single and celibate, yet forming long-lasting, warm, caring friendships.

Someone was saying in a newspaper article once how exciting it was to commit adultery. She was saying there was nothing wrong in it. There were some angry letters in response. One woman said that adultery was wrong for lots of reasons: for her it had meant an elaborate web of cheating, deceit, small lies and big lies. It meant the total betrayal of the trust of another. No wonder it causes such terrible bitterness and hurt. Adultery wrecks marriages and damages children. Surely this is not the best plan for human relationships.

Women leading the way

There are huge differences between the attitudes of boys and of girls in many countries. Some boys want to 'score' with as many girls as possible. Their reputation and image may depend on sleeping with every girl they go out with. Many girls are disgusted by this attitude. They want commitment, friendship, companionship, security – and then they will give themselves in other ways. Romantic ideals live on, even though there has been a trend in some Western nations for girls to take the lead a lot more in relationships, and in sexual conquests.

In most countries, marriage remains very popular, with girls leading the way. I find similar differences expressed almost every time I go into a school to take an AIDS lesson. Girls are often more worried about the consequences of sex than boys. Many boys could not care less. It is the girls who seem to worry most about getting pregnant or being let down. Part of the next education phase needs to be among teenage girls and young women, many of whom need little convincing about the desirability of being in a warm, loving, caring, exclusive relationship. This strategy should be designed to give them moral support when under pressure to 'sell themselves cheap'.

It is strange that many men want easy women to have fun with, but deep down prefer by far the thought of marrying a virgin. We need to cultivate a new age where romance is in, self-respect is in, faithfulness is in, marriage is in.

I don't think it's clever to sleep around or get divorced. The people I admire are those who work at relationships, who are good at relationships, who have good, happy marriages, who can handle things. What's so smart about walking out on every problem? I respect and admire, too, those people who have made a positive decision – for whatever reason – to remain single and celibate.

Advice to someone married to a 'positive' spouse

You may be afraid that you or your spouse is already positive. For many women with partners infected through medical treatments it has been a terrible shock to discover that their partner may have been HIV-infected several years before, without either of them realising.

This is an agonising situation, in addition to many others where one or other partner is known to be infected through other routes.

Such knowledge can place a severe strain on even the strongest relationship. One big question is over the future of the
sexual relationship. Will it continue? What adjustments need to
be made? To what degree does the uninfected person wish to
'take a chance'? There are no right or wrong answers, and each
couple will need to find their own way forward, with the help of
those experienced in HIV counselling.

The important thing is to realise that many people are still
uninfected after several months, or even years. As we have seen,
it seems that the risk of infection rises when the person becomes
ill. Before then the risk may be much lower. You may want to
be tested yourself. If you are positive, neither of you need take
as many precautions. If you are negative, then the following
guidelines are sensible:

1. Use a thick, strong condom carefully (see earlier in this
chapter).

2. You may want to reduce the frequency of your lovemaking
where the end result is penetrative sex. But be sensible: stopping altogether may cause terrible tensions and actually result
in a rushed mistake. Arousal may be much stronger after abstinence and then it is not so easy to be careful. Do not make love
while a woman is menstruating. If she is positive, the blood will
probably contain virus. If she is negative but her partner is positive, she may be more vulnerable. Explore lots of other ways
to express love and affection – through sensuous, arousing,
intimate touch.

3. Deep kissing, where saliva may pass from one mouth to
another, is probably not a good idea. Dry kissing carries a
much, much lower risk. Oral sex is not sensible.

4. An infected woman may wish to seriously consider avoiding
pregnancy as there is a significant chance that any child born

may also be infected or be orphaned at a young age. So use a second method of contraception, such as the pill, as well, or consider sterilisation. This is a very difficult and traumatic area.

Another huge problem is that many women know or suspect that their husband is at risk of carrying HIV, but can do nothing to protect themselves for cultural reasons. They find it hard to discuss their fears with their husband and feel helpless. New testing and treatment programmes may help by encouraging such men to come forward, identifying those who are infectious and offering them treatment, as well as counselling on prevention.

In this chapter we have looked only at the effectiveness of condoms and risk reduction using them. There are, however, major questions over their promotion in many developing countries. In African nations or in South East Asia, for example, condoms may be unaffordable, unacceptable and difficult to obtain. There are also many ethical questions linked to the promotion of condoms, especially in the minds of church leaders. We look in more detail at these issues in Chapter 14.

We have now looked at the whole issue of the spread of AIDS and some ways to reduce the risks of getting infected. But the fact is that we have never been faced with a disease which confronts us with so many conflicting moral choices to do with rights and freedom. Some of these issues threaten to tear society apart. We consider the most important of these in the next chapter.

CHAPTER SEVEN

MORAL DILEMMAS

The reason why AIDS is such a sensitive issue is because it touches on so many different aspects of conscience and morality. Different moral dilemmas present themselves in different cultures and nations.

AIDS is a development issue

AIDS is a disease which thrives on poverty, and spreads fastest in the poorest nations with the least health or education infrastructure. That means scarce medical resources available to treat huge numbers of people, or to prevent further spread. And it also means we *must* take a holistic view of AIDS, and see it as a development issue, not just a health issue. For example, what's the point of educating a young girl about HIV if she is an orphan of civil war and can only stay alive by selling her body to soldiers for sexual favours? If you want to save the lives of girls like her you need to think about setting up projects that will generate income, as well as provide education programmes.

Or you could do something as simple as providing microloans to help people set up their own businesses. For example, five women could club together to borrow enough for a sewing machine that will keep them all busy.

The fact is that the better educated people are in general, and the more economic choices they have, the more likely they are to be able to follow health advice. It's also a fact that the spread of AIDS is one of the fastest ways to wreck an economy, and to put back a country's development by twenty years.

So HIV and AIDS education should be an integral part of every development programme, whether it be a clean water project or a new school. It costs nothing extra to build it in to everything that's done. The best programmes often cost the least, and use local people, who bring HIV awareness into whatever they are involved in, as a part of everyday life.

Difficult decisions

Nations with the most HIV infections have very few resources, and in these situations there are huge pressures on doctors and nurses to use every dose of every medicine wisely, to treat larger numbers with less expensive methods, rather than treat very few and turn everyone else away.

Every day very difficult decisions need to be made about what is appropriate and what is not. For example, if a hospital has a supply of anti-viral drugs, who gets them and for how long? For the same money as treating and monitoring ten people with anti-viral drugs for a year, you could save the lives of hundreds of children with malaria or dysentery. You could also provide painkillers, anti-diarrhoea medicines and chest infection antibiotics for many with AIDS, prolonging many more lives much more effectively. Is it morally right to use anti-virals at all in countries with less than $5 a year per person to cover all health care?

Even with recent price reductions, anti-virals remain some of the most expensive (and poisonous) medicines in these nations and are still far beyond the reach of ordinary men and women if they were to buy the medicines themselves. Should the hospital or clinic use government health budget or donations from wealthy nations to buy these drugs? And it's highly dangerous for people to just go into a pharmacy to buy the medicines and treat themselves without proper hospital or clinic supervision.

In poor countries, how can you spend a huge proportion of the total hospital or clinic budget for drugs on a very expensive treatment for a few people who will remain uncured and at best will gain only a few months of life? This may seem a cruel attitude if it is your own life that could benefit from the anti-virals, or the life of someone you dearly love, but it is also cruel for one person to have his or her life extended by a few months at the expense of a hundred others who could be permanently cured of other conditions.

Rationing has always been with us, and it happens in every government or private hospital in every country of the world. Doctors do the rationing in government hospitals, and insurance companies in private hospitals, by placing a limit on what they will pay for.

So does that mean that anti-virals should not be used at all in poorer nations? Not at all! For a start, some may wish to spend their own money to prolong life by a few months, and that is their choice. Secondly, there is overwhelming evidence that a short course of anti-viral medication can save the life of an unborn baby if given to the mother in late pregnancy and during the birth period. A short course can also save the life of a doctor or a nurse who has been accidentally exposed to HIV.

It seems to me that in such situations anti-viral drugs are most appropriately used when the aim is to prevent transmission, by giving for a short period, rather than trying to prolong the life of someone already infected. So then, use of anti-virals for pregnant women should be part of every prevention programme. And that's expensive.

The 3 by 5 WHO programme aims to provide 3 million people with anti-retroviral medicines by the year 2005, so the cost of anti-viral therapy could fall to zero for many hospitals and clinics. But it still raises a question for international donors about right use of scarce resources by donor countries. For example, it is total madness to provide expensive anti-viral medicine for free to a hospital that doesn't even have enough rubber gloves for midwives to deliver babies, nor enough antibiotics and anti-malarials to treat children dying with far commoner diseases. And what happens if free supplies run out or are interrupted by inefficiency, corruption or conflict?

This is an agonising area. But prevention *must* take priority over care if we are to stop AIDS deaths. You only have today to save someone from becoming infected with HIV. You have the next decade to plan their care if you fail. One infection cleared up today is a life saved, and a family protected. One infection prevented today may be a hundred lives saved over the next decade, because of the way that HIV tends to spread.

Of course prevention and care go hand in hand. Those who care have powerful stories to tell which can persuade people to change how they live. And it is also true that one of the most effective ways to prevent spread is to help identify who is carrying HIV, so they can protect those around them. The promise of anti-retroviral treatment can be a great incentive to encourage people to get tested.

The importance of prevention

It is a question of balance and urgency: people always tend to be pulled towards the immediate needs of the person they are caring for. And often the result is a catastrophe.

I see this especially in church and Christian programmes, which are driven by compassion for the sick and the vulnerable. Christians feel the urgent need to show the unconditional love of God to all affected by HIV – and we are right to feel this way. But we must not neglect preventing more tragedies.

What's the point of having a wonderful hospital if every person who comes in is already fatally ill from a disease that could easily have been prevented? Do you go on blindly caring for people one by one with infinite compassion until the whole city is dead, or do you go to the root cause and stamp out the problem?

The trouble is that care is popular, and prevention is not. People will give millions to build a hospital, but only a few thousand to fund community educators. Churches will devote buildings and people to create a clinic, but spend almost nothing educating youth in their area. In a world affected by AIDS this is total madness.

Imagine a flyover being built over a busy road in Mumbai. It is not complete. One stormy night the diversion signs are blown down and a stream of cars and lorries drives up over the flyover and in the dark monsoon rains they plunge off the unfinished bridge and crash down ten metres below. As a doctor, I rush to help, and no sooner am I pulling one seriously injured man out of his vehicle than another car lands near me with a desperately injured family inside. I rush from car to car, shouting for help and for ambulances.

But such an emotional and well-meaning response would be misguided, foolish nonsense. Every ten seconds another vehicle is shooting across the bridge and crashing to the ground.

I *must* tear myself away from the sick and the dying, ignore their cries and pain, and run as fast as my legs can carry me to the place where the signs have fallen down and raise them again, seizing other men and women to wave down the traffic, block the road, start a fire, and do whatever we possibly can to stop another thousand tragedies.

But when it comes to AIDS I see churches, organisations and individuals rush to care, without putting even a tenth of the same effort into preventing further deaths. Every single one of the people with HIV who come to you for care is someone you cannot cure. And every single one of those infections was preventable. That is why we *must* focus on prevention.

Prevention, prevention, prevention

A friend of mine called Phil Wall has launched one of the biggest AIDS orphan programmes ever created. It's called Hope HIV and is a wonderful scheme. I am proud to be associated with it. But he realises that we have to look at prevention, too, for the sake of the next generation of children, who want to grow up with their mothers and fathers still alive.

Here is the challenge for any church or relief and development organisation. Look at your budget for HIV-related work. For every dollar, shilling, pound or bhat that you spend on helping those with HIV or their families, are you spending an equal amount saving lives through prevention? This is a challenge, because it is always easier to raise money for care. But to fund care programmes only is incredibly shortsighted. No wonder we are losing the global battle against AIDS. No wonder the number of new people infected every day is now twice what it was a few years ago.

Let this be your watchword – prevention works!

Euthanasia – a word to those who care for others

I remember going to see a man dying at home. He asked me to kill him as an act of mercy. Euthanasia literally means 'mercy death'. In some countries it is legal. Why did he ask? He was in no pain because of the proper use of painkillers, nor was he feeling sick. He had a very slight cough but was eating quite well. His mind was superbly clear but he was confined to bed and unable to walk. He knew he was dying and talked about it freely and without fear. He had a faith and felt he knew where he was going.

But his life had lost its meaning. He felt he would rather be dead than continue like this. Some doctors in some countries would have killed him. He would have been in a coffin by the following morning. But let's look at the situation more closely, because many different emotions are tied up together and need separating. This man felt a terrible burden was being placed on his wife. They had a happy marriage and his illness was destroying it. He had always taken the lead in their relationship, and now he felt helpless.

It is rare for someone to ask for euthanasia without the sense of being 'a burden on other people' being a major factor. If we give way and agree, we are then killing people because they feel they are too much trouble to family or friends. This is a hazardous course. We are killing people because, say, a friend, partner, or child is getting fed up and resentful. When do you agree that the patient is too much of a burden on others, or disagree and say that others are coping fine?

Sometimes I have been asked to 'put someone away' – to admit them into a hospital or hospice. Tensions are rising at home, or maybe there is no love lost and the relationship has been non-existent for years. The carer takes me to one side and says, 'I want him put away somewhere.' My first priority is to ensure that if someone wants to die at home, he or she should be able to do so. Therefore it is vital to provide care and support for relatives and friends to enable that to happen.

On the other hand, there are times when we have to admit someone to a hospital for 'social reasons', which usually means the collapse of support at home. You cannot force people to care, nor are they always physically able to do so. Their home may not be a suitable environment. Or they may have no home at all. However, whatever the situation, one tries to ensure that the sick person's wishes are observed. An atmosphere of resentment, hostility or tension produces unimaginable, unbearable pressures for someone who is dying. They often feel compelled to agree to going back to a hospital or even to ask for euthanasia.

The second major reason why people make this request is because of depression. I am not talking about natural sadness. To feel overwhelmed by sadness because of leaving loved ones, losing strength, and because of dashed hopes for the future is normal. It would be abnormal to be spectacularly cheerful in such circumstances. Natural sadness is not depression. Depression is where feelings of sadness are out of all proportion to the situation.

This exaggeration of natural emotion can be caused by all kinds of things, including hormonal changes or chemical imbalance in the body, and it needs treatment. Occasionally it is because lots of minor or major sad events have been brushed under the carpet for years without tears or low spirits. Behind the mask of ecstatic happiness there has been a growing mountain of grief for losses of various kinds. Eventually something happens and the mask cracks. The person cannot hold back the flood any longer. An exam is failed or someone breaks into the house and the person has a major breakdown. People think they are 'off balance', crying all the time for no obvious reason, because they fail to look deeper to the root of major hurts and losses over a longer period of time. Some have breakdowns in adult life because of childhood sexual abuse by a parent, for example – a deadly secret that has never been shared.

When someone is depressed, he or she always loses a sense of self-worth. Everything is useless and hopeless. Everything is an effort. They develop self-centredness or a feeling of being a burden.

Suicide is becoming increasingly common in many countries. Indeed, the wealthiest nations have the highest suicide rates. Money cannot buy inner contentment and peace, nor purpose, nor a sense of meaning, nor love. These things you will find in great abundance in the very poorest communities of the world. I have seen a brightness of spirit in the slums of Calcutta, and among the very poorest in Uganda, that you will rarely find in Europe or America.

If a person is very ill, they will be unable to commit suicide without help. Would you sit and watch a friend who was depressed, but not physically ill, swallow a hundred tablets without trying to stop him or her? No. Nor would you give the person a bottle of pills if he were unable to walk. You see, depression is quite common when you are unwell. When the body is physically low it can affect the brain so that you feel an exaggerated sadness.

Someone who approves of euthanasia must be absolutely sure that the person is only naturally sad, and not depressed. Even psychiatrists find it hard to distinguish between the two. Depression always lifts, given time, with or without treatment, although treatment may shorten its course. Are you really going to kill someone who is emotionally ill, who may feel differently in a few weeks? Are you going to kill someone who is feeling a burden, when he may be under pressures from others that you do not understand? You may say that you would, because you feel his quality of life is awful. But who are you to judge?

Many people find it emotionally traumatic and disturbing to be with someone who is ill or disabled. Many panic phone calls are made by people – even professional carers – who cannot cope with their own anxieties. You may be in danger of agreeing to kill someone because you have a problem coping and this colours your reaction to the person's request. With your own reaction, the patient's mood, and subtle pressures from others, you are on dangerous ground to do an irreversible, eternal act.

If you are still unconvinced, consider the following, especially if you are a doctor or a nurse and are regularly caring for people who are dying. A nurse visiting dying patients may get a reputation as an 'angel of death'. People know death is never far away when she visits someone in the next bed, or a neighbour on the street.

Doctors and nurses are in a vulnerable position. If ever there were the faintest suspicion, grounded in fact, that foul play had been committed, we would lose all trust from patients and other colleagues. I cannot warn you strongly enough. If you practise euthanasia as part of care of the dying you will bring into disrepute not only yourself, but also the whole area of terminal care, an area which scares many people anyway.

From my own perspective, to harm a patient is to break part of the ancient Hippocratic oath. As a doctor, I understand how we are made, and that there is more to life than life. There is a mystery here. No one can create life, and life is to be respected. Issues like abortion and euthanasia have cheapened human life, but I believe human life needs to be treated with the highest regard. I will never commit euthanasia and I believe the man I mentioned at the beginning of the chapter was actually relieved when I told him so. I took away an unbearable pressure. It was not an option. If I had said that I was willing to do it, he would then have been faced with a ghastly sense of obligation. This man was unusual in any case. Most people who ask for euthanasia do so because of unbearable pain and other symptoms. With proper control of symptoms, and accurate information, the terrible fears about what will happen as they get worse usually melt away.

Fortunately, those attempting euthanasia often fail – even doctors. I remember coming onto a ward one day to see a patient. When I looked at the drug chart I was amazed to see that three vast overdoses of a particular drug had been given only hours apart to this person without her consent or knowledge. There had been no suggestion of asking for euthanasia. As it was, she survived and died peacefully in her own time a week or two later. In that case, the staff had been unable to cope with their own distress. Let's stop playing God in secret, behind closed doors. Let us give people control over their own lives. Let us offer dignity and self-respect. And above all, let us have respect for human life.

Withholding treatment

We need to make a careful distinction between withholding treatment and euthanasia. We may make a carefully planned decision not to start a particular treatment. Or we may decide to stop treatment that is artificially prolonging life or directly causing distress in someone who is near death and for whom the possibility of recovery is extremely remote. This is not euthanasia. Relatives, friends, staff and patient can all be involved in the decision, although responsibility for it must always rest firmly with the treating doctor.

Someone who is very ill with an incurable disease may decide it is not possible to cope with another long struggle with lots of tests and special treatments, and may decide to stay at home to die. Radical, mutilating surgery may be declined by a cancer patient. Most people with cancer or AIDS die of chest infections. Pneumonia used to be called 'the old man's friend', because it allowed a stricken body finally to die peacefully. At that stage, it may not always be appropriate to leap in with aggressive treatments, even assuming they are available.

The people who have problems with such decisions are usually scared of death, or see death as failure. They may be too emotionally attached to the patient to let him or her go. Failure to use common sense in this area, failure to see death as a natural conclusion to the process of living, drives many doctors, and especially surgeons, to absurd lengths, ridiculous operations, and ever more exotic procedures, designed to fight to the end whatever the costs. Doctors often do this because they feel guilty. They may have raised hopes too high in the first place, but the person gets worse and is justifiably puzzled, upset and angry. And so the doctor feels under pressure to do something, anything, to stave off the inevitable.

We must learn to allow the body to die. Every year new medical methods make death more elusive. In some countries doctors can now keep a person's body warm and healthy for many years without any brain function. This is not medicine. This is inhuman science gone mad.

Living wills

As a reaction to what some people in wealthy nations see as bad medical care, they are now writing down in advance what they want to happen towards the end of their lives, and they want it to be legally binding. Communication is always a good thing and anything that helps a doctor to understand a patient's wishes is to be encouraged. Many treatment decisions are difficult and a strongly expressed view can be very helpful, even if written in advance.

It can be difficult to ensure that you are allowed to die. And here I am not talking about euthanasia, which is a deliberate act designed to kill. If I was dying of very advanced illness with many complications, I would make it absolutely clear to my doctor that my next pneumonia should be my last. There is no need to 'strive officiously to keep alive' when the end is in sight, so why pump me full of antibiotics?

However, once a written directive is backed by law, then doctors risk prosecution if the exact wording is not followed regardless of circumstances. Medicine practised by lawyers? How could you agree if you thought the person might have been depressed, under pressure or feeling a burden? How could you be sure that every medical option had been fully explained and understood? And what if the diagnosis or prognosis had been wrong? These issues also affect the euthanasia debate, of course, and many legal experts say an Act of Parliament for 'living wills' or 'advance directives' could be a back-door route for legalised euthanasia.

Involving the police, magistrates, judges and juries is no way to care for the dying; much better to encourage good communication, compassionate common sense and expert appropriate treatment, taking into account the expressed wishes of the individual.

Suicide

Suicide is a common terminal event in people with AIDS, usually early in the illness. But tragically it is also common in people who have had a positive test result, especially if any counselling afterwards was poor. A small but growing number are also committing suicide because they fear they have AIDS.

When someone has lost his job, been thrown out of his home, been rejected by family and deserted by friends, it is not surprising he feels suicidal. Glances in the street and people muttering in the shops are easily imagined but may indeed be quite real. News of AIDS spreads only too fast. We need to show that we really care and go out of our way to make infected people feel accepted, loved and welcome. If someone is depressed it may be wise to ask if they have ever thought of harming themselves. Don't be afraid of putting the idea into the person's head. You won't, but the answer is vitally important.

If the person says no, then suicide is much less likely. If the person says yes, then ask if they have thought out how they would do it. Most people have not. Someone who can describe to you with clinical detachment and in great detail exactly how he would kill himself is probably at great risk.

The doctor should be told, and the individual should be persuaded to seek medical help. Any hoarded tablets, or other parts of the plan, should be destroyed. Often someone who is suicidal has secret supplies.

Threats of suicide can be a most powerful means of blackmail, however. 'If you leave me I shall throw myself under a train.' 'If you go on holiday for two weeks I shall probably drown myself. I won't be here when you get back.' But like euthanasia, suicide is harder than people think, and the after-effects of an attempt can be horrible.

Suicide is often attempted as a cry for help. Particularly tragic is the person who takes twenty paracetamol tablets expecting to go off to sleep. After most of a day has passed, the person walks into casualty looking sheepish. The psychiatrist is asked to help. It was a cry, not a serious attempt, but the liver is now permanently damaged. Within a few days the person begins to die an awful death and is dead in a week. Many over-the-counter preparations contain paracetemol.

HIV testing without consent, or mandatory testing

In some countries a doctor who tests someone's blood without prior agreement could be struck off the medical register or prosecuted. However, most doctors feel the need to do so under special circumstances – usually where they believe the patient's life may be at risk through not knowing that he or she has HIV or AIDS.

The reason for the rules is to protect people who are infected. Although they may be free of any signs of illness for years, it is a hard secret to keep, and the knowledge that you are positive can be totally devastating. People lose jobs, houses, friends and partners as a result. They cannot get a mortgage, a car loan, or life insurance.

The other reason for the regulations is, strangely, the ultimate protection of society. Control of sexually transmitted diseases has always been hard. People are reluctant to seek help, and so the disease is untreated and more people are infected. The whole ethos of an STD clinic is to provide a non-judgemental, tolerant, relaxed, attractive atmosphere, with easy access and long opening hours. Clinics pride themselves in being busy, with people coming from long distances because of the pleasant atmosphere. Judgemental, condescending behaviour will put people off and they will stay away and continue to infect other people. It will drive the problem underground, endangering the health of the whole community.

If people believed that while attending a hospital clinic for an unrelated condition, or while in a hospital being prepared for an operation, a sample of blood would routinely be tested for HIV, this would result in many being too scared to seek medical help at all. People would die at home of appendicitis or even from treatable chest infections as a result of developing AIDS. The entire problem would go underground.

But take the plight of a surgeon: would it not be better for him to know when it was appropriate to take extra special care not to cut or scratch himself? It would be wrong to refuse to operate on someone who was ill and needed surgery, but what about someone wanting cosmetic surgery? Is it right for someone who may know he is HIV positive to ask a surgeon to take that risk when the patient's own life is not at stake?

Most emergency rooms now use paper strips to close minor wounds instead of stitches. With small wounds the results are almost always just as good, if not better, than with stitches because stitches can get infected and cause a body reaction. Metal surgical clips can be used to close wounds after surgery. It has been suggested that they should be used with all patients.

The fact is, a large number of doctors and nurses worldwide are going to die of AIDS over the next decade or two unless there is a cure or a vaccine. Accidents with needles and during operations happen in every hospital every day, and most are too minor to report – but still capable of transmitting infection. It is worth considering the total lifetime risk to a medical student, beginning to train as a doctor in a country like Malawi, where up to half the patients on hospital wards are infected.

The argument in favour of selective testing without consent is that the alternative is to assume that everyone is positive and take incredibly elaborate precautions. Time may be wasted and lives lost. Some countries are now preparing to force certain groups of people to be tested. Military recruits in the United States army have all been tested routinely for some time. Iraq is testing all long-term visitors to the country. I think some people are going to disappear rather than be tested.

However, unless a cure is found quickly, HIV testing will become part of the routine work-up before any operation in a number of countries. It will be justified by surgeons as in the patient's interests, on the grounds that fevers and chest infections after the operation may be mistaken for normal consequences of anaesthetic and surgery, the correct treatment will not be given and the patient could suffer.

The public climate is shifting rapidly in many countries. For example, in the USA a jury decided that a woman had committed fraud by not disclosing her AIDS illness to a surgical team before having a breast reduction operation. One of the team accidentally cut herself with a scalpel and became infected. She was awarded compensation of over $100,000.

HIV testing will be done on many patients in hospital wards with unusual symptoms of almost any kind. AIDS is such a complex disease because it opens the body up to so many other kinds of illnesses. It must therefore be on a physician's list of possibilities for an enormous number of people who are ill these days. In wealthy nations, with wide access to anti-viral treatment, testing without consent will become widespread and justified on the grounds that prompt treatment with anti-virals could prolong life – although the real motive may be different.

It may seem shocking to test people for a disease without their knowledge, but we have been doing it for years: blood testing for syphilis is common for similar reasons. It mimics such an enormous number of diseases. People are not always confronted with their result. In fact the vast majority of blood tests are done with what is called 'implied consent'. By agreeing to come into a hospital the person is accepting treatment, including allowing a blood sample to be taken 'for various things, such as to see if you are anaemic'.

However, the great problem is keeping the result strictly confidential. Medical teams must improve at this, especially family doctors and occupational physicians in work places.

Counselling following a positive test is vitally important. As we have seen, it is not uncommon for someone to commit suicide following the discovery of a positive result.

Revenge sex and other situations

What do you do if someone you know is positive and has decided to get revenge on society by having sex with as many other people as possible? A man visiting New York woke up after a date to find 'Welcome to the AIDS club' written on his mirror. He is now infected. A man was recently murdered after announcing to the man he had just had sex with that he was positive. He had made the mistake of laughing.

This opens up the broader issues of confidentiality. A man is positive and has no intention of telling his wife, who is wanting to have a baby. If she is positive, pregnancy could mean death for her and her child. Do you just sit back and wait for the inevitable? Human rights are always complex. You cannot have rights without responsibilities. If someone is raped, should that person have the right to insist that the rapist is tested?

Many doctors recognise that a small minority of people may be using their right to confidentiality as a passport to injure and destroy others. Practice varies among 'contact tracers' in sex disease clinics. Some will contact partners without the person's consent as a last resort if the person will not co-operate despite many hours of counselling.

It is incredibly worrying that a number of people who know they are positive return to clinics only a few weeks later with a new infection of gonorrhoea. Some will have contracted this from promiscuous behaviour without a condom. They have been wilfully putting others at risk.

For the sake of the community, some think that prostitutes and commercial sex workers should not be allowed to practise if they are positive. But that is far easier to say than achieve, unless prostitution is legalised and brothels licensed by the government. How many men do you think each sex worker services each year? In some countries the answer can be up to 10,000.

Another problem is that control measures can backfire and make the situation worse. For example, a crack-down on the Thai sex industry by police resulted in people being reluctant to come forward if they thought they might have HIV. As a result, doctors had great difficulty monitoring spread.

Infected doctors, nurses and dentists

While health care workers may be anxious at times about the risk of being infected by their patients, there is also enormous public concern in low-incidence countries about the far smaller risks of being infected by an HIV-carrying doctor, nurse or dentist. We know the risk is small because, despite the growing number of infected care workers, very few cases of care-worker transmission to patient have been seen.

In high-incidence nations it is hardly practical to insist that only HIV-negative health care professionals carry out operations, even if it were ethical to insist on testing health care workers. You would land up decimating hospital teams and the results could be far worse for general standards of patient care. The surgeon may have HIV but he or she may be the only surgeon within a fifty-mile area of rough jungle roads. What would you prefer – an infected surgeon or no surgeon at all? It's yet another example of the way in which well-meaning officials in a distant land can write policy guidelines which are worse than useless in a poor nation.

In the wealthiest nations, where there is near hysteria at times over these issues, contact tracing is the standard response of a hospital when they find out a surgeon has HIV. There have been several cases recently where infection of a surgeon only came to light after the person had treated a very large number of people. Hospital authorities have often been unsure what to do. How do you trace such a large number of people, many of whom may have moved more than once over the last ten years? Even if you have a complete list of addresses and phone numbers, how long would it take to contact them all?

It is not surprising that information has sometimes leaked out in an uncontrolled manner before helplines were ready, or before a proper public announcement. Often the individual has been quickly identified in media coverage, making his or her life a misery, affecting family, violating privacy and confidentiality, and making it less likely that others will come forward promptly if they think they too could be infected.

The risk of someone being infected by a health worker is very low. For example, a surgeon would need to be cut badly without realising; so badly, in fact, that he or she cuts right through the glove into the pulp of a finger, and then carry on with the procedure so that blood contaminates a patient's wound. This is hardly likely. Nevertheless, we have to face the fact that in a tragic series of events a number of different people became infected by the same dentist, and we have seen the more infectious hepatitis B virus transmitted from a surgeon to patients.

Care workers in wealthy nations who think they may be infected, and are or have been involved in invasive procedures, have a well-recognised duty to arrange to have an HIV test, and to inform their employers promptly if the result is positive. In the case of the surgeon, the issue is not just transmission of infection, but also the possible loss of manual dexterity, given that late HIV infection can sometimes affect the ability to perform complex tasks.

The British Medical Association, the Royal College of Surgeons and the UK government agreed together that those involved in invasive procedures (operations, injections and other procedures where wound contamination could occur) should cease if they are carrying HIV. They should receive practical help and support in switching to non-invasive medical jobs. In practice, this can often be quite difficult, and a terrible blow to an experienced surgeon, for example. The General Medical Council has gone further and said that doctors failing to disclose they have HIV to a senior colleague could be struck off the medical register.

Hospitals in turn clearly have a duty to do all they can to protect the confidentiality of the individual, and to provide appropriate help. This is also in the public interest. It is surely against the public interest to broadcast the name of an infected surgeon on TV news if it means another ten infected surgeons vow to take their secret to the grave.

Hospitals in wealthy nations also clearly have a duty to recall patients where there has been a risk of infection, for example during an operation. It is essential to retain public trust, and if people feel there has been a cover-up, the result can be a backlash against the very people we are trying to protect. People do not need to be told the identity of the member of the health care team who is infected. It is true that many will guess, but it is better for a few hundred to guess than for it to become national knowledge. Ideally, patients need to be contacted by letter or telephone before they hear in the press. They need to be offered access to telephone advice, or a personal interview, and a test if they wish.

There should be an agreement with national media to abide by a code of practice so that if, say, an infected individual is named in the local press, that name is not then regarded as national information in the public domain. The hounding of individuals in some countries has been truly disgraceful. Where do you go? Where do you live? What about your children? Once photographs are printed, the end of normal private life has arrived. This is a bitter reward for someone who has had the courage to be honest and open.

Unless doctors and other care workers can be assured they will be well treated, they will delay coming forward, if necessary until days before death. If this continues to happen, pressure may become irresistible to test all surgeons on an annual basis, which would be cheaper and less traumatic than the recalling of up to 30,000 patients a year.

Compulsory testing would be a great step backwards. Once you start with surgeons, where do you stop? Airline pilots are already routinely tested by some airlines, because of worries about mental performance. Before we know where we are, a great number of different groups could end up being tested on a regular basis, with resultant loss of freedom, breaches of confidentiality, oppression and fear. Nevertheless, the introduction of routine testing for some health care workers is inevitable, unless surgeons agree to testing on a voluntary basis.

Sex education in schools

While HIV infection raises many issues, so does prevention, most of all among young people in schools. What is an appropriate message to give them? What is the right age to give that message? Should people be allowed to opt out of hearing the message? Many have feared that some groups will use AIDS as a platform, either aggressively promoting certain lifestyles as normal to young teenagers, or pursuing a right-wing moral crusade. But young people clearly need to know the facts about HIV, and they also need room to think through for themselves how they are going to respond.

Christian-based AIDS organisations have been very successful in developing schools programmes, and presenting the facts in a context which encourages people to see sex in terms of health, relationships, choices and their long-term future. Most schools reject a simplistic message based on using condoms, and they also reject a moralistic approach. However, they do want values to be communicated in a way which gives a positive view of waiting for the right person and of being faithful. See Chapter 12 for fuller discussion.

Age of consent

One traditional way to discourage sexual activity in the young is through a legal minimum 'age of consent' below which sexual activity becomes a crime.

The age of consent varies widely from one country to another, even in Europe, and from one kind of sexual activity to another. In many countries, there are campaigns to lower the age of consent, particularly where it is much higher for homosexual acts. The law is a blunt instrument with which to regulate private behaviour between consenting individuals. Prosecutions are rarely brought, except where there is evidence of exploitation. Pressures are likely to grow for a unified age for both heterosexual and homosexual sex.

Some argue, on the basis of their own views on morality, that all homosexual acts should be illegal, and therefore an age of consent of 16, 18 or 21 is too low. However, there is inconsistency in the argument, since the same people may regard adultery or heterosexual sex before marriage as morally wrong, but would not make these things illegal.

The basic question is this: Do you want to see people put in prison and receive a criminal record for violating the age of consent as it stands? If the answer is no, then the age of consent needs review, or it could make a mockery of the law.

Telling the truth

I will never forget the day I went to visit a particular person who was dying at home. I was accosted by an anxious relative who was convinced that the only reason I was there was to tell the patient his diagnosis and that he was dying. Nothing I could say would convince her otherwise. She was terrified. In fact, we found as a team that working with this family became impossible. The sticking point was when I said that although I would never mention his probable death to the patient unless he himself asked, I was not prepared to lie to him. I might give an indirect answer such as, 'Why do you ask?' or, 'You don't seem to be getting any better, do you?' but I was not prepared to say, 'Of course you're not dying. Don't be stupid!'

The reason is very simple: trust. One day he would have realised I was lying. Actually, as far as I could tell from what he said, he knew he was dying anyway – most people do. Most people with cancer or AIDS have guessed what is happening long before they are told, although there can sometimes be

denial, associated with fear or guilt. Having established myself
as a liar whenever it suits me, to save embarrassment or to calm
fear, what happens when the person asks if they will die in terrible pain? This time I answer truthfully, but will I be believed?
Often when people are first referred, they are convinced they
are going to 'suffocate to death'. They may have terrible nightmares and be consumed with fears. Every time they get a cough
we get a telephone call, and the reason is overwhelming fear of
what may be around the corner.

The truth is that no one suffocates to death these days.
Hospices have advanced our care of those with lung disease
enormously over the last twenty years. That is the truth – but
will the public believe it? Fear of death can be worse than the
dying itself.

Trust is the most powerful tool a doctor has. It is the reason
why support teams and hospices are so successful. They inspire
trust because they do not engage in the same frauds, cover-ups
and webs of petty deceit that are practised daily on the wards
of every hospital. If only doctors realised that people see
through it all!

The reason for dishonesty by doctors, families and friends is
simply this: we like to pretend that death does not exist. AIDS
then hits us like a thunderbolt straight between the eyes,
because it brings us face to face with death and all our deepest
fears.

But before we take a look at the whole life-and-death issue, I
want to turn to just one more moral dilemma which I get faced
with every day as a church leader. The question people ask is
this: Do you agree with those who say that AIDS is the wrath
or judgement of God?

CHAPTER EIGHT

JUDGEMENT OF GOD?

Is AIDS an expression of the judgement of God? I have often been asked this question by church leaders, although far less often today than when we started AIDS work in the late 1980s. It is one of those areas where you know that any phrase or sentence you say or write could be turned into a banner headline. I am also aware that you may be one of the thousands of readers who will judge this book by whether you agree with what I say. You will either be pleased you bought it or want to burn it, saying I am judgemental or a heretic or a liberal. What follows is a personal view from someone who takes seriously what the Bible says.

It is also a view consistent, as far as I can see, with the historic teachings of the church on sexual behaviour over 2,000 years, whether Orthodox, Catholic, Anglican, Episcopalian, Baptist, Methodist, Lutheran, Presbyterian, Independent Evangelical, Indigenous, Pentecostal, New Church charismatic, or whatever. In fact, Christian teaching on sexual behaviour and morality has been remarkably consistent and united, as it is today outside certain groups within particular denominations in wealthy nations. The big issue is how a traditional Christian view on morality can be equated with God's call to perfect love.

In the early days of the AIDS epidemic, medical advice was that AIDS was spread only by anal sex. The public impression was that unless you were gay you could not get AIDS. A number of clergymen and church leaders then grabbed their Bibles and began a series of private and public pronouncements denouncing homosexuality, listing plagues described in the Old and New Testaments, and declaring that this was obviously God's plague on homosexuals – obviously as it only appeared (at that time) to affect them.

This attitude was not confined to Western nations. In Uganda, it was reported on state radio that a goat, speaking in a loud voice, had prophesied that the AIDS epidemic was a divine punishment for mankind's wickedness in not obeying the Ten Commandments, and predicted a terrible famine. It terrified local villagers and died shortly afterwards.

Such reactions were fuelled by a distorted perception of sexual sin which is part of our culture and not part of Jesus' own sayings. Incidentally, I find it is usually men who are so vehement in condemning the homosexual man. Women are far more tolerant. Yet the same men are more tolerant of two lesbians. Why? Does God find sex between two men more offensive than between two women or in an adulterous relationship? AIDS is almost unknown in lesbians.

Church leaders who declared AIDS was God's judgement on homosexuals must now be acutely embarrassed. By the early 1990s it was already obvious that there were many more women and babies infected than there ever were homosexual men. As we have seen, 98% of new HIV infections worldwide are now among heterosexuals. The 'judgement' theology was then adjusted by some church leaders to include all who are promiscuous – which again is acutely mistaken. What do you say to a million children dying in Africa or elsewhere as a result of medical treatments, such as injections or infected blood or infection in the womb?

When coupled with the public image of the church as 'anti-condom', the comments about AIDS being the judgement of God have been doubly negative. The Catholic Church in particular has been extremely uncomfortable with AIDS campaigns promoting condom use, while strongly advocating compassionate care and understanding. Protestant churches tend to be more relaxed, as long as condom use is placed alongside the options of celibacy and faithfulness.

It is hard to generalise, and responses vary with country and area, but the Pope restated the official Catholic position on AIDS by encouraging compassionate, unconditional care, along with self-control, chastity and faithfulness. Many were dismayed at Vatican suggestions that even married couples where one is infected should not be allowed to use condoms. With 92 million members in Africa alone, the Catholic Church has great influence.

Nothing new

'Judgement of God' theories are not new. Several centuries ago, a plague for which there was no cure swept the known world. Signs of infection were absent, sometimes for many years, and controversies raged over which country it had all started in. It was spread by sexual intercourse. I am referring to syphilis, which, as we have seen, only became curable with the advent of penicillin in 1944.

Many saw syphilis as a disease that God inflicted on the sexually immoral. This had two effects: the search for a cure was inhibited or actively discouraged; after all, you were interfering with the natural course of judgement. Also, those with syphilis were treated in a less sympathetic way: 'It is their own fault and they put society at risk.'

A friend of mine spent some months in a certain developing country a few years ago. Many men came into the hospital clinic where he was working because they had difficulty passing water. Gonorrhoea infection had caused scarring and narrowing of the delicate tube (urethra) inside the penis. Sometimes these people would have full bladders and be in great discomfort. The way to treat this is by pushing a series of rods into the penis, each one larger than the one before, to dilate the stricture. This causes excruciating, unbearable pain unless you use local anaesthetic cream. It is so painful that most surgeons in the United Kingdom do the procedure under a general anaesthetic. Yet in this clinic anaesthetic cream was stacked on the shelves while men were screaming out in agony.

Greatly shocked by this, my friend asked why the pain-killing cream or a full anaesthetic was not being used. The answer was that this was an immoral disease and the person must be punished. I wish it were not so, but these people had been influenced by the atmosphere and culture imported by church missionaries. What has that appalling attitude got in common with the way of Jesus?

You may recoil from this, but you must realise that, in many other countries, parts of the church are still fostering similar attitudes to the very same kind of epidemic. The words are not the same, but the same atmosphere of rejection of the person is there. If you want proof, ask yourself why it is so easy to raise money for AIDS orphans but so hard to raise money to save the lives of young adults who have many partners. Fortunately, things are changing

Be consistent

If AIDS is an expression of God's judgement, then syphilis was too. I cannot see any real difference between AIDS and any other disease, from the medical point of view. The causes and mechanisms of illnesses are different, but people still need care. In the Old and New Testaments, the agent of the wrath of God is often recorded as being an angel. It is portrayed as a supernatural intervention that is selective. Contrast this with AIDS, caused by a virus that has probably existed in some shape or form for thousands of years. It has existed in animals for a long time, and maybe also in humans. The explosive spread, as with syphilis, has been along the lines of international travel and sexual relationships. It behaves according to the rules of every other infection, with its own particular preferences and effects.

As I asked at the beginning of the book: What is so special about AIDS? In one sense, nothing at all. You have been misinformed. The reaction of extreme fear associated with AIDS is unusual. But fear, lack of visible symptoms and a high death rate from a viral disease are not the same thing as God's judgement. For me, the key to the whole thing is the attitude of Jesus.

Caught in the act

In chapter 8 of John's Gospel there is an important story. At the crack of dawn, Jesus was at the temple teaching a huge crowd. Sitting and standing, or leaning against the walls, they listened quietly as Jesus sat and taught. It was still cold under the thin sunlight, and the vast stones were damp with dew. Jesus' voice quietly rose and fell. There was silence apart from an occasional cough or the bleat of an animal outside.

Suddenly, all heads turned at the sound of a great commotion. Twenty or thirty people burst in, shouting and screaming. Jesus stopped. He was used to such interruptions. They happened almost every day. Perhaps it was friends bringing someone wanting to be healed, or the authorities, hoping to provoke a confrontation and arrest him.

A woman was thrown down at his feet. She and Jesus stood up together. She had been discovered in bed half an hour ago with another woman's husband. Caught in the act. The men who had brought her were furious, seething with anger. They demanded a response from Jesus. 'The law says we must drag her away, pick up rocks and boulders, and stone her to death. What do you say?'

It was yet another trap and Jesus knew it. If he agreed with the law they would drag him away and stone him for being judgemental and severe. If he did not agree they would arrest him for being too liberal.

Who's perfect?

Jesus did nothing at all. He said nothing at all. The mob were pressing in, repeating their question over and over again, pushing and shoving aggressively. All the while, the people in the court were watching and waiting. Tension was rising. Someone was going to get hurt. Either Jesus or the woman was likely to be lynched, and the very forces which could have prevented it were standing right there in the temple.

Jesus crouched down on the ground under the harsh glare and threats of the men. He wrote on the ground with his finger. The shouting and abuse got louder.

Finally, Jesus stood up and looked at them. Instantly there was quiet. Jesus looked into the eyes of each man standing there. 'You who are so perfect; you who have never cheated anyone, lied, or been selfish; you who are always so perfectly loving and kind; you who never lose your temper; you who are so generous; you who have never had a lustful thought. Yes, you come forward now, come and take a stone, come and throw it at this woman. Be the first to throw.'[1]

Jesus looked at each man in turn, but they shrank away, uncomfortable under his gaze. He crouched down again and stared at the ground as he wrote with his finger in the dust. The older men began to peel off from the crowd and disappear down the temple steps. One at a time they left in silence. Gone were the shouts, the threats, and the abuse. Eventually no one was left – only those who had come to hear Jesus teach.

---

[1] 'If any of you is without sin, let him be the first to throw a stone at her' (John 8:7).

No condemnation

Jesus stood up. The woman was still standing there, her head hung in shame, humiliation and embarrassment. She stood afraid, unable to move, afraid of the men waiting outside, afraid of what Jesus was thinking.

Jesus looked at her. Spies in the crowd were ready to slip out and report that Jesus had been trapped: he had given himself away as a liberal by letting an adulterer go free.

'Where are they?' said Jesus to the woman. 'Has no one condemned you?'

'No one, sir,' she replied. Jesus then said two vitally important things. 'Then neither do I condemn you.' And then he added, 'Do not sin again.'[2]

The authorities had caught a man and a woman making love. One of them was married to someone else. They let off the man and judged the woman. Double standards: their own they excused, the other they condemned. As far as they were concerned, they were just expressing the natural wrath and displeasure of God, but Jesus rejected their whole attitude. Jesus was concerned, not just with actions, but also with attitude. As far as he was concerned, to have an adulterous fantasy could be as bad as committing adultery. One person may be no worse than the other; it was just that one had the opportunity and the guts to actually do it, and the other had no opportunity, or was too afraid.

The man who is angry with his brother can be as bad as someone who kills. Read what Jesus said for yourself. Actions are not everything. What goes on in the secret places of your heart and imagination is also vitally important.[3]

---

[2]   John 8:11.
[3]   Matthew 5:21–22, 27–28.

Never do it again

Jesus did not distinguish between the subtleties of wrong. We are all wrong. We have all done wrong or thought wrong. None of us is perfect.[4] As the only perfect man, he was the only person who had the perfect right to condemn the woman, but he did not. Why not?

Because he loved her and he understood what it was like to be tempted.

Did he excuse her? Not at all. Did he encourage her? Not at all. Did he allow her to get off free? Not at all. He rebuked her. He told her she had been wrong. He told her never to do it again. He told her never to do anything else wrong again. 'Go and learn from your lesson' was his message.

They were all wrong: the men were hypocrites. When Jesus said that, every single one realised it was true. Every single one of them had had lustful thoughts and fantasies about other people's wives at some time or other. Every single one of them, if they were really honest, knew that deep down inside they were not as nice as they tried to appear on the outside. Only they and their families knew what they were really like at home with the door closed. Only they knew how selfish and mean they could be sometimes. Their own consciences convicted them, and they backed away. In some ways they were no better and no worse than the woman. If she deserved stoning, so did they.

The trouble is that in every town, every village, every church, every country – and maybe in your home, maybe in yourself – there are attitudes just as revolting to Jesus as the attitudes of that crowd: judgemental, harsh, intolerant, vicious, cruel and bitter. 'No!' you may say. 'I'm not like that, nor is anyone I know.' But let me ask you some questions.

---

4 Romans 3:23.

Banner headlines

What is your attitude to a clergyman who is prosecuted for sexually abusing children? Banner headlines continue to hit us over church leaders who have been charged with sexually assaulting children.

What is your attitude to a married priest who is discovered in bed with another man's wife, or in a public toilet with his trousers and pants down, having anal intercourse with another man?

In most circles, inside and outside the church, the reaction to these things is shock and outrage. You say it is despicable because of his position. That person has undoubtedly lost his ability to lead a congregation. He has been living a charade, a facade behind which lies a guilt-ridden twilight world, or else he has rewritten the rule book to make his conduct compatible with his faith. But in your sweeping anger you have condemned him. Your outrage is identical to that angry crowd confronting the woman.

Double standards

Clergy do not have some super gift of God that keeps them perfect. In fact, the Bible does not distinguish between clergy and laity at this point. We are all a royal priesthood. All who claim to be Christians are called to live up to our calling. None of us is exempt. There are no double standards. As you would expect, we read in Paul's letters that there are minimum standards for life and conduct laid down for those appointed to positions of leadership in the church, and certainly such responsibility brings special accountability. However, these minimum standards, such as managing the household well, being sober and self-controlled, are no more or less than those expected of all of us. It is interesting that the lists of qualifications are all to do with character, not gift or experience.[5]

---

[5] 2 Timothy 3:1–13; 1 Peter 2:9; Ephesians 4:1.

Individuals who behave in the ways described above need to be accepted as people, while we may not necessarily accept everything they do or say. But we find this almost impossible. We either accept the person and what he or she does, or we reject both the behaviour and the person. It is not what you say but the way you say it that can be most important. Some people say they care about drug addicts but give out an atmosphere of coldness. Some people say that as Jesus loved all people, they too accept all people, but they still display deep-rooted prejudices at every turn. You who are perfect – you cast the first stone.

God calls us to accept all people and to extend his love to them, regardless of whether or not we agree with what they do. 'Impossible!' you say. 'How can this be reconciled with God's absolute standards?' But Jesus came for all men. He came, not for the perfect, but to invite 'sinners to repentance'. Did Jesus come to bring forgiveness and peace to the repentant murderer? Of course he did. God's love and mercy are so unbelievably great that if even Hitler had genuinely repented and given his life to God in that bunker in 1945, the Bible tells us he would be in heaven now. Some Christians find this hard to accept. They cannot understand the true reality of God's mercy and forgiveness. Deathbed conversion is real. The thief crucified next to Jesus was told that within a few hours he would be with Jesus 'in paradise'.[6]

Judgement without tears is obscene

You may reject all this; you may go through the Bible, quoting texts about God's wrath and anger. It is possible to be correct, but horribly wrong. It is possible to be right about God's displeasure, but to lack love. A well-known Christian leader once said that 'to speak of judgement without tears is obscene'. Where are your tears? Go and find your tears of grief for those

---

[6] Matthew 9:13; Luke 23:42–43.

who are suffering, dying and, so you say, in line for judgement. When you have found your tears, then talk to me of judgement – but start with yourself.

Reaping natural consequences?

It is a fact of life that everything has consequences. If you drink and drive you may injure or kill yourself and others. If you sniff cocaine you may get a hole inside your nose – the nose was not designed for cocaine. If you line your lungs with tobacco tar you can get a chronic irritation which may result in coughs and cancer. If you eat badly cooked chicken you can get food poisoning. If you sleep with someone who is not a virgin, you could catch a number of illnesses which he or she may have caught from a previous partner.

These things are so obvious. The issue of cause and effect is also a central theme in the teaching of Jesus. The Bible teaches that we are creatures of choice. We are not automatons. We are free to choose God's way or our way. If that were not so there would be no point in telling us how to live because we would be unable to respond in any other way at all. But with freedom comes responsibility. The Bible teaches that each of us will have to give account one day for everything we have said, thought, done or should have done and did not do.[7]

The Christian position is that within the Bible our loving Father has recorded guidelines for healthy, stress-free, fulfilled living: how to be healthy and whole. So what is the Christian view of sex? Here is a personal view.

Unlimited sex

Sex was invented by God to be enjoyed. It is one of the most amazing and intensely enjoyable experiences God has given

---

[7] Matthew 12:36.

mankind. In God's plan, he intended a man and a woman to marry and in the context of commitment, care, love and understanding, to explore together the kaleidoscope pleasures of physical love. God intended husband and wife to have unlimited sex: as often as they both would like and enjoy. Out of that beautiful, loving relationship were to come children who would grow up feeling loved and secure, with a mum and a dad, grandparents, aunts, uncles and cousins. God loves families. He created human beings to belong to each other, and those whose families had died or were far away to be cared for, if they wished, by other families or communities.

Our bodies were not designed for sexual encounters with multiple partners. Such a lifestyle has consequences. It is physically unhealthy. Before AIDS, promiscuity was already becoming more and more unhealthy. It was fairly risky until the advent of antibiotics dealt with gonorrhoea and syphilis. Then some penicillin-resistant strains of gonorrhoea emerged, along with various other infections such as herpes and chlamydia (Pelvic Inflammatory Disease). Now we know that early sex and multiple partners can also cause cervical cancer. This was all before AIDS. Promiscuity has always been unhealthy. Now it can be fatal.

Sleeping around has always been emotionally hazardous as well. The result is usually destabilisation of any semi-permanent or permanent relationship. Although polygamy was practised in the Old Testament, its track record of success and happiness is disastrous. Read the story of Abraham. Adultery usually has catastrophic consequences for one person at least. I have yet to come across a case where it did not. Divorce, too, is nearly always a traumatic disaster, leaving lifelong scars. Sleeping around fractures relationships and will always be emotionally risky, unless there are no relationships. If there are no relationships then nothing is at risk. A prostitute or commercial sex worker has no emotional investment in her client, nor her client with her, so there is no loss or trauma. However, there may develop a more sinister and deeper damage to the ability to form lasting, loyal commitments. The risk is a lonely bankruptcy of friendship and support after middle life has sapped physical drives and taken its toll on attractiveness and vitality.

Sleeping with multiple partners can have permanent spiritual effects, too. The Bible teaches clearly that sex is a wonderful experience and one of the deepest mysteries known to human beings. When a man and a woman sleep together, the Bible says they become 'one flesh'. We see the physical expression of this spiritual event when a 'half cell' (sperm) from a man fuses with a 'half cell' (egg) from a woman and the two become literally 'one flesh'. In that moment of history a new being is formed; life is created.

When two people have sexual intercourse, the Bible teaches that, irrespective of whether conception occurs, something has taken place which can never be undone.[8]

Sex was designed as the ultimate expression of exclusive covenant love between a man and a woman. Devoid of relationship, it is robbed of its quality and enjoyment and becomes a mere mechanical sensation. No wonder many unmarried people reject sleeping around and choose celibacy. They see through the glamorous veneer to the emptiness beneath. Those who are promiscuous are often driven into further and further searches for the ultimate in sexual satisfaction. Once you have divorced the physical act from the whole-person experience you have no hope at all of true fulfilment. Women usually realise this sooner than men. None of these things will satisfy your heart. You have been cruelly deceived and there may be consequences.

The Christian position is that when we break any of God's designs for living we create tension in our relationship with him. God is perfect and cannot tolerate sin. Nor can he reward

---

[8] Genesis 2:24; Matthew 19:4–5; 1 Corinthians 6:15–20.

us with the warmth of his love and approval when we have turned our backs on his best for us. Sin affects your nearness to God if you are a Christian, and prevents you finding God if you are not. There is nothing especially wrong in sexual sin, although its effects can be very destructive of relationships and communities. As we have seen, there is one sense in which it is no more displeasing to God than any other sins against others.

I feel I must say again that often we fall into absurd double standards. People reject adultery or homosexual acts as more wrong in some way than lying or cheating or stealing or being cruel or hating someone. There is no such distinction in the Bible when it comes to separation from God. Sin is sin; the other differences are merely cultural values and must be rejected. The Bible teaches that we are all imperfect. We all think wrong, feel wrong and do wrong. We all fall far short of God's standards. None of us deserves any reward or favours from God, and there is nothing we can do to earn his pleasure. That is why I believe no one has the right to turn and point the finger at someone with AIDS.[9]

Impossible barrier

You can never be good enough. Human imperfections always remain an impossible barrier between us and God. Without Jesus Christ, you can no more put human beings and God together than oil and water: they always separate.

That is why Jesus said, 'I am the way and the truth and the life. No one comes to the Father except through me.' There are, we are told, hundreds of ways to God. Maybe, but they don't lead you to a personal relationship with a God who is almighty, omnipotent, unknowable, unreachable and untouchable. Other religions may promise some kind of ethereal consciousness, but

[9] Ephesians 2:1–10.

that is no substitute for a personal relationship. The reason is obvious. Other religions say that closely following a certain formula for holiness will deal with your imperfection. If only it could. The best formulas in the world, and the most ardent efforts, might possibly get you a mile or two nearer God. The trouble is that our imperfections distance us from God by several light years! Even after a lifetime of devoted holiness, you would have a chasm of several million miles to cross.

No wonder Jesus himself said he was the only way to oneness with God the Father. Christians believe the good news that God himself provided a rescue plan for mankind because significant movement by us in his direction was impossible. So God himself moved towards us and entered our time-space world. He came in human form as Jesus.[10]

When Jesus died, that whole issue of separation was dealt with for all time. Every single thing that separated us – all the consequences of our wrong doing and wrong attitudes – was lumped on Jesus' shoulders. As a sacrifice for all time he, the perfect God-man, allowed himself to die for us so that we might be forgiven and released from the consequences of what we have done. The result is now a doorway – a narrow one – to union with God our Father. You enter the door, not by justifying to God what a wonderful person you are, but by believing and accepting all Jesus came to do, and by making a decision to give your life to him in obedience.[11]

Unless you really understand the way the Bible portrays this separation and how Jesus overcame it, you will never fully grasp what Jesus said to the woman and the accusing crowd that morning. In fact they were all finished. None of them had the remotest hope of peace with God. The men and women in the crowd, the adulteress herself – they were hopelessly blocked from a relationship with their Father. That is, outside of follow-

---

[10] John 14:6.
[11] Romans 8:1–4.

ing, believing and trusting in Jesus, the only way, the truth about God and the means of finding the life of God.[12]

Changed lives

To all those who accept Jesus as Lord and turn away from everything wrong (repent means to turn around), he has given a brand new life. That is why Jesus told a would-be follower that he had to be 'born again'.[13]

When I became a Christian, in one sense I died. Baptism is a symbol of my burial. When I rose out of the water it was a symbol of my new birth. The Bible says I am now a new creation: 'The life I now have is not my life, but the life which Christ lives in me.' This is another mystery.[14]

When someone becomes a Christian, the results are often dramatic. Parents or children become easier to live with. Marriages enjoy a new start. Friendships are transformed. A friend of mine who became a Christian invited all his friends to his baptism (we use a local swimming pool). They all turned up with their heavy metal leather jackets and boots. Two were so amazed at what had happened to their friend that, when they saw it wasn't just a passing fad, they became Christians as well. When you've seen the real thing, who wants a substitute? Ordinary people, changed by something outside themselves.

A friend from the United States told me that he became a Christian partly through his mother's conversion. She was dying of severe kidney disease. The poisons were steadily accumulating in her body. She was not a believer but went to a healing meeting. She was prayed for, and felt she had been instantly healed. She went back to the clinic as usual. The doctors were amazed. All the results of medical tests on her kidneys had

---

[12] Romans 6:6–14.
[13] John 3:3.
[14] Galatians 2:20.

returned to normal. Life was never the same for her. She became a Christian, and so did her son some time later.

I met someone recently after an AIDS talk. He told me he had been a heroin addict until three or four years before, when he had become a Christian. He had broken the habit immediately and is now a leader in his church. This is not unusual. Jesus gives people power by the Holy Spirit when they become Christians.

You can be free to choose God's way even though chained to all kinds of things – addiction, childhood memories, or parts of your own human nature. Jesus came to set you free. You choose to follow him and he does the rest. You exercise your will and he will give you all the resources you need.

Father's love

After a meeting at a medical school, I overheard a conversation between a medical student and a member of the hospital Christian Union. She was basically asking why she couldn't believe in God. 'I admire you people. I wish I could believe. You have it all together. You know where you are going. It's all right for you.'

I joined in. I asked her if she really wanted an answer to that question, because I believed God wanted to answer it for her. I told her that God loved her whether she believed it or not. I told her the story of Jesus and the woman at the well. Jesus broke the taboos by asking her for a drink. He then told her to go and fetch her husband. She replied that she didn't have one. Jesus agreed with her: 'You have been married five times and the man you are now living with is not your husband.' She was shocked.[15] How did he know? She rushed to the village to tell them about this man who knew everything about her.

Such insights can be a part of Christian life today. I prayed

---

[15] John 4:4–19.

silently for a moment and then said to the young woman that I felt that part of the reason she could not believe was because of her family. She had never known what it was to feel loved, especially by her father, and so could not accept that God could care about her, or love her as his child.

She sat down and started to cry. Tears poured down her face as she talked about her childhood, not a particularly unhappy one, but one devoid of open affection. She was hurting, bruised and wounded. I asked if she wanted me to pray for her emotions and her past. She agreed. Even before I prayed, her eyes seemed to open and she found she did believe deep down. But it is hard to trust a heavenly Father's love if you have never experienced an earthly father's love. After we had prayed she made it clear she wanted to give her whole life to God. She realised she had been living life her way and now wanted to live God's way. She wanted to turn her back on the past and begin again. She gave her life to God in a very moving prayer. There were tears in my eyes and in her friend's when we had finished.

About a year later I found myself sitting next to her at a conference. Friends had told me previously how much she had changed, how much happier and fulfilled she was, and how her student friends had all been along to various things with her to try and puzzle it out.

Father's discipline

People who have never known love find it hard to accept love – whether from a friend, a spouse, or from God. In the same way, people who have never known the balanced firmness and discipline of a loving father and mother can find it hard to understand the discipline, firmness and standards of God.

Jesus loves all people, but not necessarily what people do. He got angry and violent with traders using the temple area to make money out of pilgrims. He walked through the stalls, tipping up the trestle tables and throwing their goods on the ground. There was chaos: their best wares and coins were flying everywhere. Then Jesus came at them again, this time with a whip of cords to drive them right out of the temple. 'Gentle Jesus, meek and mild' is not the whole Jesus of the Bible. And yet he loved them.

Many of Jesus' words to religious leaders were aggressive and cutting, with biting sarcasm and savage wit. Wherever he went he slaughtered hypocrisy, double standards, false religion and disregard for God's holiness. Today we shrink from preaching on many of the things Jesus said because they are so strong.

The thing on which Jesus was strongest of all was love. 'Love your neighbour' is hard enough, particularly when the story of the Good Samaritan shows us that our neighbour is whoever we come into contact with, regardless of nationality, background, circumstances, or personal risk.

Loving your neighbour is not enough

Jesus then made one of the most devastating commands that has ever been made. Loving our neighbour is totally inadequate. We are also called to love our enemies, to express God's perfect love to those who hate us, despise us, want to hurt us and beat us up. Jesus calls us to love those who rape us and cheat us, and those who twist and distort the things we say. He commands us to pray for people who persecute us or spitefully use us.[16]

This is not a command to mere forgiveness – though that itself is painfully costly and hard at times. This is a command to actively, positively seek to express warmth, compassion, kindness and understanding to those we humanly would hate and regard as our worst enemies. We are told to pray for their happiness. This was not idle talk: Jesus lived out his message all the way to his crucifixion.

This may seem objectionable, impossible and bizarre – but it

---

[16] Matthew 5:44–48.

is what Jesus said. After all, even the most horrible people tend to be nice to their friends. What is so special about being nice to your friends? What is so remarkable about loving those who love you? Nothing at all. We are called to be a visual aid, an active demonstration, a living temple of God's supreme love. Even more amazing is that God's love for us is incalculably greater than our love for others – because God is infinite and perfect.

Just as we are commanded to love, regardless of response, in a way which is totally without conditions or strings attached, so God our Father loves all people regardless of their response to him.

Now, can you see that God does not hate or reject people because he does not like what they do? He weeps over our slowness, our obstinacy, our self-centredness, our stupidity.

When it all goes wrong

When God made creation, he designed man and woman to be physically united in a marriage covenant, to be perfectly loving and perfectly faithful. What happens when it all goes wrong? When people make each other's lives hell in a desperately unhappy marriage? When people cheat each other in adultery? When people sleep around without the covenant commitment of marriage? When people express their sexuality by torturing their partners for pleasure? When children are sexually seduced by adults? When it all goes wrong, what is the response of our Maker?

Sadness and dismay is his response. Where people choose to ignore a relationship with him, the result is no relationship with him. A living death, a living hell. An eternal disaster of constant separation. It is not that God's will is for any to be separated from him, but rather that God is holy. If we choose to live outside Christ there can be no reconciliation.

So does God condemn the adulterer? Not at all. He is sad at the resulting separation from the one he loves. Does God condemn the practising homosexual? Not at all. He is sad at the distance the sin creates. Does God condemn the hypocrite, the liar, or the person who is mean with money? No, he is sad that the person has missed the way. Does God condemn the person whose rages spill over into violence? No, he is sad that the person is driven by these things.

However, the Bible teaches us that God's sadness and God's anger are closely linked. God is angry at some of the things we do. His anger is the result of his perfect holiness and justice expressed through creation. God, although our loving heavenly Father, can never compromise. Anger and judgement are the discipline sides of love, to those who refuse to turn away from what is wrong, and refuse to follow him.

The tension between God's love and God's anger is difficult to understand. God is himself a mystery to the human brain, limited in time and space to a four-dimensional world.

You reap what you sow. If you sow a certain way of life, you will reap the consequences of it. That is not God's wrath or judgement. That is a normal part of living. God is a loving Father whose wish it is to see the whole of creation united with him again as was the original plan.[17]

It is not his desire to see anyone perish, but for all to come into their full inheritance – a life outside the limitations of space and time, a wonderful life for ever free from anguish, pain and suffering.[18]

However, we are created in freedom, and with that come guidelines and responsibilities. With choices come consequences – some of which are, we are told, unpleasant. We are warned that we cannot always undo what we have done. The biggest consequence of all will be having to face our Maker after death with our track record. That may not be such a pleasant experience. It may be a terrible shock to those who thought

---

[17] Galatians 6:7.
[18] John 3:16–17.

God didn't even exist. But at that time there will be no further opportunity to undo what has been done. The result will be separation from God, with all the time-space world stripped away. We will experience either the continuation of a relationship – or the lack of it. There are people right now who are separated from God and know it. They need to be reconciled to him and experience the warmth of his love.

People think finding God as a Father is very complicated. But becoming a Christian is as simple as apologising to God in your own words for living life your way and agreeing to live life his way, turning your back on the past, acknowledging Jesus as Lord to be worshipped and obeyed, and trusting him for everything. That is the way to experience the love of God as your Father. That is the way to find forgiveness and cleansing for all you have ever done wrong, and that is the way to receive the help, comfort and power of the Holy Spirit.

There are others who are separated from God and have no idea at all. So consumed are they with earning money, building a business, or making a nice home that they pay no attention to the empty spaces inside. Many of these people finally start being real about themselves when confronted by their own imminent death.

'If only I had known what I know now'

People who become Christians in later life often say, 'If I had known what I know now, I would never have got divorced. I would still know my kids. I wasted so much of my life. Why didn't anyone tell me before?' They probably did. It's just that it takes a sudden jolt to shake us out of our complacency. Maybe that jolt is the death of a friend, adultery by a wife or husband, the death of a child – or diagnosis of AIDS. With AIDS there is an added dimension. Maybe if the person had become a believer a decade ago, he would not be infected. He could still have been alive in twenty years' time.

Sometimes, of course, people really never have heard before. In the church we can tend to think everyone knows what Christianity is, but in fact very few do in many nations. Saying a prayer or two when in trouble and going to church do not make you a Christian. Being a follower of Jesus is what makes you a Christian. Jesus said that even the devil believes. It is the desire above all else to do God's will that makes the difference. 'Whoever cares for his own safety is lost; but if a man will let himself be lost for my sake, that man is safe.' In businesses we often talk of the cost/benefit analysis. Is a project likely to be worthwhile? In the church we major on benefits, but when did you last hear a sermon about the cost? Jesus majored on the cost, just as he majored on choice, responsibility, accountability and consequences.[19]

Strong stuff

It was Jesus himself who said that if my right eye causes me to go wrong then I should pluck it out (figuratively speaking) and throw it away, rather than 'be thrown into hell where the devouring worm never dies and the fire is not quenched'. Strong words from the strongest man the world has ever seen. You may not like them and I may not like talking about this whole area, but it is part of the truth. To say otherwise is to make God out to be some amoral, ethereal substance, able neither to feel nor to think, an indescribable, unknowable something-or-other as vague as energy or cosmos. My God is more than that: Author, Originator, Prime Mover, who created a conscious, moral, decision-making, spiritually aware creature capable of relationships. Man was made in God's own image, a creature to have a relationship with his Maker, who is revealed to him in terms of an ultimate relationship: that of Father to child.[20]

---

[19] Luke 9:23–25.
[20] Mark 9:43–48.

How do we respond?

Even those who passionately defend their promiscuity or adultery or homosexual sex on moral grounds concede that if I found a friend of mine, a leader of a church, was having an affair with another man's wife, I should tell him to stop. In fact, I usually find that people outside the church are even fiercer in speaking out against such behaviour than many within the church. Those in the church are expected to behave! If I ask why, they say that a clergyman must act in a moral fashion. I agree.

The Bible is quite clear that those who call themselves Christians are called to be loving, kind, generous, honest and either faithful to their spouses or celibate. To remain single, following the example of Jesus, is shown to be a positive, releasing decision, because it frees the person enormously to be mobile, able to go wherever God wants. The Bible is exceptionally clear in outlawing sex between unmarried people and sex with other people's spouses. Sex between two men or two women is considered in just the same way as sex between unmarried people. For those in the church, it is forbidden. Sex between a son and his mother or a father and his daughter or with animals is also outlawed. In fact any form of sexual intercourse outside of marriage is utterly forbidden.

Sex is not unique in this regard. To bear a grudge is also forbidden. To be moody and feel sorry for myself all the time is forbidden. To get drunk is forbidden. The way of Jesus is the way of perfect love.

This feels very negative, but then boundaries always feel negative. I used to tell my son when he was four years old that he could cycle around the park but he must keep within sight of me. I am sure he thought I was being negative. Boundaries are essential. Any child psychologist will tell you what happens when children don't know their boundaries. They are always testing to find the limits of what is acceptable, to say nothing of being constantly at risk through lack of supervision. When

174 THE TRUTH ABOUT AIDS

there are no limits – or worse, when the limits always vary – a child will become insecure and can grow up immature.

Boundaries for healthy living

Out-of-bounds areas are marked for protection and safety. Modern wars have left hundreds of square miles of deserted land surrounded by barbed-wire. The reason is that hundreds of thousands of tiny plastic explosive charges lie inches beneath the soil. Treading on one can cost you a leg or a foot. These land-mines cannot be detected, because they contain no metal, and they cannot be destroyed.

It would be strange if there were no fences, no barbed-wire, no warning signs. You can climb over if you like. No one will stop you, although they may shout at you not to be so stupid. You have been warned by people who care and by people who knew that your instinct would be to run over the beautiful inviting fields and meadows.

The out-of-bounds areas laid down for us are not some great negative moralistic statement, but warning signs: 'Enter here at your peril. It could cost you.' It will cost you. It will cost you emotionally, physically, psychologically, and will certainly cost you spiritually. When we flout God's guidelines for life, whether by being selfish, dishonest, gossiping, being unkind, or by being unfaithful or uncontrolled in our sexual lives, there are spiritual consequences. It creates tension in our walk or communion with him. It creates a barrier that can only be removed by confessing to God that we have been wrong and have disobeyed. This is the only route to forgiveness, cleansing, wholeness and inner healing.

In conclusion

My own view, based on a thorough reading of the Bible, together with the historic teachings of the church, is that AIDS is not an expression of the wrath or judgement of God, but is a part of the world of cause and effect in which we live. When it comes to the practicalities of healthy living, the Bible confirms what common sense tells us: that we are not designed for multiple sexual partners and there is another way to live. However, all those with AIDS need our unconditional care. Such basic Christian principles are timeless and cultureless, transcending all people groups.

A Christian response to AIDS

We need a vision to meet the challenge to demonstrate the love of God and teach people how to live healthy lives. Part of this will be seeking to challenge and fight oppression, stigmatisation and prejudice wherever we find them, and also to challenge our society to reconsider its values. The church in every age is called to be salt and light, transforming the whole of society by its witness and work, not just the lives of believers.

We need to recognise that the church has also contributed to the AIDS situation today by failing in previous decades to give a clear lead, to challenge behaviour, to model an alternative life-style and to proclaim the gospel. Many of those finding faith today are finding faith when the HIV damage has already been done.

So, having considered some of the questions about sexuality and moral codes, we need to look at one other big issue before we look in detail at how we can respond practically: the issue of death. It's an issue I have often faced as a hospice-trained doctor.

Death and dying are no strangers to me in cancer work, yet walking onto an AIDS ward for the first time was quite a shock. This was an acute hospital ward of mainly young men, many of whom would be going home. What kind of care people ill with AIDS receive will depend to a large extent on whether the rest of us have sorted out our own death and

176 THE TRUTH ABOUT AIDS

mortality, or whether we are going to pretend death doesn't exist. The medical world is not known for its honesty – least of all over life and death issues – and the church is also struggling. Why?

CHAPTER NINE

SOME LIFE AND DEATH ISSUES

I will never forget the first person I met with AIDS. He was a young student, desperately ill, lying in a side-room of a busy hospital ward. He was anxious, sweaty and panting for breath. His hands gripped the sides of the bed with fear. His thin face was covered with an oxygen mask, his chest was covered in wires and tubing. He was alone and about to die.

From that moment on I found I was involved. Here was a human being, made in God's image and in great need. How could I respond other than to care and help, laying aside any personal feelings I might have had about his lifestyle, and the means by which he had become infected?

Dying without family, friends or dignity

I asked about his family and his medication. I was told his parents lived some distance away, knew nothing and thought he was fit and well at university. He did not want them to be contacted because he feared a terrible reaction when they found out what was wrong. He had hidden his illness from them completely.

I was told the simple medication I suggested could not be given because there was a chance he might pull through. In my view, the team would be phoning his mum or dad just a few hours from then, to inform them of the death and of the diagnosis. By the time his parents arrived his body would be in the mortuary, sealed in an opaque body bag following an agonising death. What kind of care was that?

I came off the ward feeling angry, upset and frustrated at the lack of response to suggested medication changes, and realising that life would never be quite the same again. I later found out that almost three-quarters of those with AIDS in the UK lived within ten miles of my home and place of work. I quickly discovered that many others were dying badly, in pain, alone, afraid, separated from those they loved, and often trapped in a hospital ward because no one could care for them at home. At the time, many services available for other illnesses would not get involved. There was a massive gap.

In the prime of their lives

The most shocking thing of all was that, unlike a cancer ward where people tended to be retirement age or older, here was an entire ward of young people in the prime of their lives, every one of whom was going to die from a totally preventable, rapidly spreading infection. As a care-of-the-dying specialist I could not turn away, whatever the reasons for the illness, or the lifestyles of those who were ill.

I had had mixed feelings about even visiting the ward. Some of my colleagues had refused to get involved and I had felt less than keen. After all, so they told me, AIDS was basically a sex disease of gay men. Was this really an illness I wanted to become heavily involved in?

Correct but horribly wrong

My Christian background told me that most of those infected were ill because they had rejected God's ways. It was easy to feel detached or even critical. It was also easy to react with embarrassment when confronted by a whole ward of young gay men, many of whom were openly expressing physical affection and intimacy.

So often as Christians we do nothing, or find ourselves rushing to open our Bibles and to declare to ourselves and to others that something is wrong. Yet in that first response we can lose sight of God's mercy, love and forgiveness.

Just one more statistic

I went back to the ward a few days later to find the young man had died the day before. They had taken my advice. They found, as I predicted, that medication to relax and help remove fear and feelings of breathlessness had improved his condition. The level of oxygen in his blood had gone up, not down. Far from killing him, the medication had allowed the inevitable to take place with comfort, dignity and peace. He saw his family before he died.

As a result of this experience I began, with others, to set up hospice-style home care teams for people with AIDS. Many with AIDS told me that the emphasis should be on 'living with AIDS', not on dying. My reply was that such an approach was fine so long as you were well, but many were dying badly. Doctors also reacted, telling me there was no 'terminal phase', that AIDS was totally unlike cancer, and that the emphasis should be on active treatment. A part of these two reactions was undoubtedly fear of death or death denial, but those who were dying so obviously needed help, and there is often a stage of chronic illness and gradual deterioration when palliative care is needed.

Death denial

Since 1945, those in industrial nations have been living in an escapist, death-denying society. What is so peculiar about dying? It is just as much a part of the cycle of life as birth. The reason is that we are afraid of death. Death is the terrible unknown, which robs and destroys. This fear can spill over into panic, and lead to fear of illness, operations, flying, or many other things. As we will see later in this chapter, this has a profound effect on doctors and what they do.

The church in the West is full of the same death-denying mentality. This can lead to a watered-down gospel, which promises good things now (peace, security, happiness, prosperity) because all the future rewards (heaven, eternal joy and peace with God) have lost their meaning. People who are always talking about heaven can be regarded as needing a psychiatrist – and yet that is the hope that drove the earliest Christians towards their goal. The prize St Paul was absolutely determined to win was God's call to the life above in Christ Jesus. He was perfectly content to continue this life as long as God wanted because to 'live is Christ', but 'to die is gain'. So what has gone wrong? If even Christians are afraid, what hope is there of dealing with the fears in the rest of our society?[1]

Christians in wealthy nations have so much to learn from the churches in poorer nations. Here death stalks even the youngest and the healthiest as a daily reality, and life on earth is uncertain. Eternal life is more real. The result is often an attitude to daily living which is far closer to the attitude of Jesus himself, who taught us not to worry about tomorrow for tomorrow has troubles enough of its own. Jesus mocked the rich man who laid up wealth in his barns and then suddenly died. Jesus taught us to lay up treasure in heaven, to focus our attention, not on what is seen, but on what is unseen; not on things, but on our relationship with our heavenly Father.[2]

---

[1] Philippians 1:21; 3:7–14.
[2] Matthew 6:19–21.

The church's reaction to death

Consider the attitude of many churches (particularly in developed countries) to someone in their congregation who has just been told he will be dead by Christmas. The younger the congregation, the more extreme the reaction, which is why many of the rapidly growing churches are in difficulties over this whole area.

Horror

The person, his family and the church recoil with horror at the prospect of death. Having carefully put aside all thoughts about getting old and the body wearing out, and having ignored the absolute inevitability of death, the news comes as an inexplicable, unexpected disaster. The deaths of friends, colleagues and relatives at similar ages and stages have always been faced with the philosophy of 'it will never happen to me'. The shock now produces devastation.

Frantic search for cure

Every avenue is pursued and every door pushed. Second opinions are sought. Ever more mutilating procedures are discussed. The treating doctors often drive this madness along themselves, as a part of their own feelings of inadequacy and failure. 'Cure at all costs.'

Desperate prayers

Fear of death is perhaps what lies behind some of the tremendous drive towards supernatural healing in the church. Books on healing are bestsellers. Healing conferences are packed. Healing meetings have standing room only unless you arrive very early.

Within a congregation there is a drive to desperate prayers – and maybe fasting. These are not the balanced prayers of faith, however, but the desperate prayers of fear – the gripping, overwhelming, paralysing fear of a terrible disaster. The person being prayed for may be totally at peace about 'going home', but others, because of their own fears and emotional problems, are utterly opposed to allowing events to take their natural course.

Please do not misunderstand this. I believe God does heal supernaturally. Major healings of conditions that doctors are unable to cure may happen every day – and I say this as a doctor. I regularly pray for people to be healed and sometimes things happen. This recent growing experience of God's healing power has gone hand in hand with a renewed emphasis on the work of the Holy Spirit, who had become a mere nebulous, ethereal 'thing' in the life and teaching of the church. The Holy Spirit is described by Jesus as the agent of his power, and I am sure we are going to see far more evidence of that power over the next few years in countries like the UK, where our rationalistic mindset seems to make supernatural intervention more unusual, compared to many developing countries. God has given gifts and resources to the church and he expects them to be used.

Miraculous healing

People often ask me if I know of any cases of miraculous healing of those with AIDS. The answer is that a number of reports are circulating, many from developing countries, but none yet that I know of relating to people in the UK, or of cases I have been able to verify personally.

However, if we believe that God made the universe in an outpouring of almighty, cosmic power, then it follows that the same God must have power and authority over every aspect of what he has made. He can boil a kettle of water at his command, turn water into wine, turn your home into rubble, move a huge tree twenty feet, quieten a storm, create a second moon to go round the earth, or remove a virus from someone's body.

God's kingdom – now, yet still to come

Scripture teaches us that God, in his infinite wisdom and mercy, has chosen to constrain much of his own power at this stage in the earth's history until the second coming of Jesus. In the meantime we have been given a foretaste of the coming kingdom.

There is a sense in which the kingdom of God is already here. We are encouraged to pray. When we pray according to God's will, we are told that God hears us and desires to act in response.

The truth is that in all things God is sovereign. Who is healed, and why, remains a mystery. Far fewer people are healed at the moment than think they have been healed. But unless we get our fears of death sorted out we will never have a true perspective on healing.

Confusion

Let's be honest. Usually people are not healed. Even those with special gifts of healing have low success rates with serious illnesses like cancer or AIDS. This often leads to confusion – especially if people have been convinced that healing will take place or has already occurred.

There is a lot of unreality in the church over this issue, and much of it is the result of the fear of death, and the teaching by some that God wants to heal everyone who is sick. Unless there is honesty, openness and integrity, any healing ministry will be brought into disrepute. If you think you have been healed, then, just as Jesus told the lepers to get their cure certified by the priests (the medical experts of the time), get yourself checked out. Are you afraid of an X-ray? If God is God and he has healed you, the X-ray of your arthritis-ridden hips will be normal. If you have been healed of high blood pressure, your reading will be normal, and will remain so when (under medical supervision) the drugs are stopped.[3]

---

[3] Luke 17:14.

Some conditions flare up and die down, so it is hard for a doctor to certify a cure until some time has gone by without any further episodes. Examples of such conditions are asthma, ear infections, sinusitis, epilepsy, arthritis and AIDS. Because of the so-called placebo effect, many symptoms, such as pain, may disappear for minutes, hours or weeks, simply as a result of suggestion; yet the disease may remain.

Questioning

The person or family may be angry. 'Why hasn't God healed me when he healed someone else in our church? Why not me?' This can try the faith of the ill person, their family and their friends.

Isolation

All too often, separation occurs between those who have faith that healing has already occurred or is about to be completed, and those who are being faced with the daily reality of subtle changes in health, growing weakness, steady loss of weight, depressing blood tests, increasing pain or shortness of breath. One group can be praying and fasting while the other is also praying but is tied up with the important process of preparing for death. This is a tragedy, especially if the latter group is tiny or non-existent apart from the ill person. If both groups are substantial, the result can be a split congregation.

Dying people tend to be marginalised anyway. We kid ourselves that we are caring, but we are in fact rejecting. This has always been so for cancer patients, which is part of the reason for the establishing of hospices, and it is especially so for AIDS patients. Apart from all the terrible fears and fantasies about touching a person who is dying with cancer (many deep down fear they can catch cancer, even though they know this is irrational), there are all the intense fears of catching a plague related to AIDS.

When you don't know what to say, the result may be either ludicrous conversation or oppressive, awkward silence. Because both are uncomfortable, many people shy away from visiting someone who is near death or has been bereaved. If they do visit, the conversation is stilted and often meaningless to the ill person, who finds entertaining visitors exhausting. Visiting times can become nightmares: the time of day when the patient is most vulnerable, when literally anyone can burst onto the ward into their bedside chair and be immovable for an hour – unless someone else arrives. For further discussion of grief and loss, see Chapter 10.

So what is the answer to it all? The answer I believe lies in understanding the mystery of life and of death. Because nearly all my medical work has been concerned with those who are dying, dead or bereaved, I have often been confronted by this issue.

'He had just left his body behind'

The first dead person I ever saw as a medical student was a huge, bloated, blue-faced man who had been pounded and punctured during a cardiac arrest. Doctors had jumped on his chest and jabbed him with needles. He came around, groaned, vomited and died. They shocked him again, pounded him some more, sucked out the vomit and eventually gave up. I waited and watched. Everyone drifted away. The curtains were abruptly closed off. Who was he? Who were his family? What about his wife?

I remember holding his hand and praying for him silently as he lay there, his brain gradually dying. A junior doctor came in armed with huge needles and began practising entering a vein in the neck. I asked him to stop, but he refused. He carried on until he got bored and wandered out. That doctor was in charge of the patient, but couldn't be bothered to find out if his wife was waiting outside. His whole attitude was cynical, as though the man was merely an object, a piece of meat.

I was angry and upset. How could people who had been

trained to care react like this? I vowed no one I was with would ever die in such indignity.

As a Christian, I believe I understood something the doctor had completely missed: a profound mystery had just taken place and I had been privileged to be present when it happened. Here was a man, a person, an individual with personality and energy, who in a moment had left this world, which is bounded by space and time. While I watched, he had just left his body behind.

Going into the dissecting room for the first time as a medical student is a strange experience. Here are people laid out on slabs; people of all shapes and sizes, distorted by long immersion in formalin. Hard skin and fixed muscles. Empty shells: no one there, all long since departed. This is a mystery, the key to understanding life itself and our Creator.

That is why I count it such a privilege to look after people who are nearing the end of their lives. It is a spiritual event. Some would say that the nearest an atheist gets to a religious experience is his own death, and approaching death heightens spiritual awareness in every way.

This is why deathbed conversion is so common. As we saw in an earlier chapter, Jesus welcomed the dying thief into his kingdom. It seems strange that a patient who becomes a Christian in the last week of life should be loved by God in the same way as a faithful believer who has served God for decades. But Jesus said that the first shall be last and the last shall be first. Those who care need to look out for clues to what is going on: a newly opened Bible on the bedside locker, a crucifix which appears one day above the bed, a rosary in the patient's hand. These are all ways in which people tell us that things are changing inside. Sometimes conversion takes place without a word being said. A man I admitted to St Joseph's Hospice announced he was an atheist. Two weeks later he asked to see a priest. The man had undergone a radical turn-around as he approached the end.

Without faith, death is the ultimate enemy; death is the robber and the destroyer. With faith in Christ, death is merely a doorway to eternity. Faith confronts us with an issue: will I enjoy eternity when I get there? Will eternity with God be heaven – or will I find eternity an unpleasant hell?

Because I have found forgiveness, inner peace and reconciliation with God through turning to Jesus, I am looking forward to dying. While I am alive I am delighted to be allowed time here to spend with my family, building up the church, serving the community, worshipping and praising God – which is one of the most enjoyable things in my life – and telling people the good news, extending God's kingdom. However, I am just a visitor passing through. There is nothing here which compares to what is to come. The next life is the true reality – because it is unchangeable. The earth we live on, the solar system we inhabit, the other galaxies, the whole cosmos as we know it today, has a very limited existence. You and I can outlive it all.

When we begin to find God's perspective on this time-space world, then death truly loses its sting. Even AIDS loses its power. As doctors, the death of a patient is no longer failure, but the natural transition from one existence to another. Death is not taboo any longer. We can talk about it and face up to our own mortality.

When we are with a patient who asks us if he is going to die, he can sense that we are at peace and not afraid. We can stay with him and not run away. We don't avoid spending time with him, but are able to share experiences. We will not abandon him because hope of a cure has abandoned us.

As a student, I spent a four-week residential elective at St Christopher's Hospice. It wasn't necessary to have a faith in order to work there, but those who had no faith didn't tend to last very long.

If you are a Christian, I believe you have the answer. For you the mystery is understood. You know the meaning of life and the meaning of death. You understand what is happening when someone is dying. You can give meaning and hope to a person who is reaching out to God. Because Christ himself lives within you, you bring Christ to each person you meet. Every time you speak, smile, or take someone's hand, that person comes into touch with some aspect of Christ himself.

We have seen how AIDS is sweeping across the globe, leaving a terrible trail of human destruction. The only solution for the foreseeable future is a radical change of values and human behaviour. Failure to deal with fundamental issues like death and dying now compounds the problem of providing good care. AIDS makes us think through again our views on sexuality and life itself. It confronts us at the very root of our being and, at the end of the day, leaves us with choices about how we respond – not just to AIDS and those who are dying from it, but also to the ultimate issue: What is the meaning of life? What is the meaning of *my* life? Am I really just a collection of molecules, or is there another dimension?

There is another question: What is the church going to do about AIDS? What Christian response can be made and how do we make a start?

CHAPTER TEN

WHEN CHURCH MEMBERS NEED HELP

How are you going to care for people with HIV in your church, especially when people in churches may still be worried about things like the communion cup? How are you going to look after church members dying at home?

Exploding myths

Priority number one must be to get educated. Church leaders need to be up to date and well informed. Books, conferences and visiting speakers are all ways to achieve this. Even a ten-minute presentation as part of a Sunday service can be long enough to bring home the impact of AIDS, if done by someone with personal experience of the illness, possibly from an organisation working in the field as a Christian agency.

Church congregations need clear information about risks, the communion cup and about social contact. They also need clear teaching on some of the ethical issues involved. Teaching needs to be given about God's accepting love, as well as his standards, emphasising the need to care unconditionally, and prejudice and judgementalism need to be challenged (see Chapter 8).

Caring for church members

We tend to think of AIDS as something 'out there' rather than a problem within, yet AIDS is also marching into the church. Any growing church that is seeing people come into faith, having their lifestyles changed and their lives transformed, is likely to find imported HIV sooner or later.

Infection usually survives conversion

It is sobering to think how many of your congregation have come into faith in the last ten years. If many have done so, then HIV may be nearer than you think. Conversion or a rediscovery of faith can happen gradually or suddenly, but infection always remains, barring God's intervention in a miracle of healing.

AIDS time bomb in the church

As we have seen, someone who joined a church in 2003 may have been unknowingly infected in the mid-1990s. The person may be perfectly fit and well today, and in a few years' time may be a recognised leader with many responsibilities. One day that person may come to you looking obviously unwell after having been afflicted with various medical problems for some time. Now they have tested positive for HIV.

This scenario has already become a common one in many African nations. The pastoral implications are huge when you have a congregation which has mushroomed from maybe 500 to 5,000 in five years and you realise that up to a fifth of your adult members could be carrying the virus.

AIDS and pastoral issues

It is a huge step for someone to tell you they have HIV or AIDS. In many cases it means revealing intensely personal things about the past – things which have been prayed over, confessed and forgotten years ago. This is in addition to the shock of coming to terms with a future death from AIDS. It often seems particularly tragic when someone who has made a fresh start has to pay such a very personal and public price for what happened so long ago.

Such tragedies can tear churches apart, with people asking over and over again why God has not chosen to heal the person after the greater miracle of life-changing conversion.

Can you keep a secret?

Once someone in your church has told you they have HIV or AIDS, a journey has started which will probably have a profound effect on you and the church over many years. Confidentiality is important. As we have seen already, we live in harsh times when it comes to AIDS. Violence, discrimination, verbal abuse and hostility are common reactions in many nations from an intolerant minority; common enough to create an atmosphere of tension and fear if the diagnosis becomes known.

A diagnosis of AIDS or HIV infection is sensitive information which may need to be kept strictly confidential for a long time. You may be able to create a supportive environment in the church. However, churches are by their nature public groups meeting in public places. Anyone can turn up to meetings and new people join. You cannot be certain how one or two on the edge of things might react, especially those who perhaps have not been Christians very long or who have deep personal problems of their own.

People with AIDS may leave your church

I remember talking recently to a mother with a young child. She told me that she had moved 100 miles away from her church after the news that she had HIV gradually spread. She said the church had been caring. She had felt accepted and cared for by the leaders and supported by her home group, which met in someone's house during the week.

Unfortunately, once her situation became widely known in the church, she began to notice a change. She felt people were avoiding her. No one wanted to have her child to play any more. No one wanted to share the communion cup with her. She felt isolated, insecure, rejected and afraid. After a few weeks she left. I am pleased to say she is now happily settled elsewhere.

Her story made me think. The same could so easily have happened in my own church, or in any church for that matter. Much of the supposed rejection could have been her own hypersensitivity and insecurity, but it is quite likely that one or two may have made inappropriate comments, or behaved in a hurtful and unkind way.

For these reasons we need to address the issue of who is told before the event, rather than working out a policy an hour after realising someone has HIV. Do all the leaders need to know at this stage? What about their spouses? If one person in the church knows, will others be told – 'just for prayer, of course'?

Big leaks can start slowly

News may leak gradually before an explosion occurs. Take the situation of four senior leaders who know, each confiding in one other person over the next six months. Each of the new four also confide in one other, while the four leaders also tell two or three others. The result is that in just twelve months at least fourteen to sixteen people already know. After the second year the number knowing has grown to twenty, and by the third year to twenty-five.

One day a conversation is overheard by someone else who very likely tells another ten in as many days. By the end of the month people at work have found out and are saying they will refuse to co-operate unless the person is laid off. The result could be loss of job, loss of income, public humiliation and a big question mark: Does every other person in the church know?

Now is the time to prepare

Churches for whom all these things are quite new and unfamiliar need to prepare now, before someone turns out to have HIV. Perhaps someone in your church is already infected, but he or she – or you – has yet to find out. Sometimes I am asked to speak to a church because the leaders are now aware of someone with HIV who is becoming unwell. They realise people are going to guess soon and they want help now, so when people find out there will not be any panic. It would have been better to have organised the visit the year before.

It can be hard to know when to widen the network of those who are aware of the situation. The timing and occasion are best determined by the person with HIV. The process becomes easier if one or two new people are told at a time, before involving larger groups. Often the person with HIV feels anxious about possible reactions. As each person is found to be accepting, warm and encouraging, it helps to overcome the big lie which says that people will reject once they know.

This fear of being known is a curse, because it robs and destroys friendship. Whenever someone lives under the shadow of discovery, there will always be deep insecurity. It is only as we find people still love us despite our failings that we begin to see and feel what the love of God is like.

Openness can bring release

The more open we can be, the more AIDS becomes normalised as a part of our suffering world, and in turn the easier it is for others to be open in the future. More importantly, the more open we are, the easier it is to organise help. So in general it makes sense to be as open as possible, given all the constraints of the local situation and culture, and all the cautions above.

If you are unsure how to proceed, one rule of thumb is to operate on a need-to-know basis. And as illness develops, the need to know becomes gradually greater for a larger circle of people.

Practical care at home

The needs of those with AIDS living in the community are in many ways exactly the same as the needs of those with other kinds of illness. There is always the need for friendship, but often the greatest needs are practical. It is easy for barriers to form and people feel unable to ask for help because they feel they are a burden. On the other hand, wanting to help can make us feel awkward and embarrassed, not knowing what to say or do.

Here is a brief outline of ten practical steps that any church can take to support a church member. Most of these also apply to caring for others in the community. This is not a definitive guide. Many of the basic principles of care are valid in different cultural and economic situations, but other aspects require adaptation.

The greatest help is often the simplest – things that anyone can do, whether they live in a Manhattan apartment or in a house of corrugated iron and plastic on a rubbish tip in Brazil. It doesn't cost money to be kind.

1. Show you still care

Someone with HIV is likely to feel especially vulnerable after telling you the news, or knowing that someone else has told you. What will your next meeting be like? Will there be a smile, a hug or an awkward turning away? People may think it won't make any difference, but is that really true, or are they just pretending? They can think they are a liability, an embarrassment, a burden on the church. Go out of your way to express appreciation, acceptance, love, care and support in those first critical days.

Learn about the illness so you are well informed and can help others later on who may be struggling with ignorance.

2. Maintain friendship

Try to maintain as much normal life as possible. The person who has HIV will probably want to carry on as usual rather than be dragged down by thinking about the illness all day long. Be sensitive to changing physical needs, moods and feelings about the future. It is perfectly normal for people to swing from optimism to pessimism, from grand plans to the depths of despair, from acceptance of the situation to denial.

This is just part of the process of adjustment to grief and loss. Often we think of grief as an emotion triggered by the death of someone we love. However, grief is a process of adjustment triggered by losses of any kind. As we have seen in earlier chapters, the losses for someone dying with AIDS are numerous and often devastating. Loss of health, memory, sight, physical comfort, sleep, control over one's body; loss of future plans, ambitions, hopes and dreams; loss of friends, family, job, physical attractiveness, energy; loss of independence and freedom; loss of life on earth. It is no surprise, then, to find people oscillating between denial, anger, sadness and acceptance, or with mixtures of all four. AIDS can be a heavy burden to carry.

3. Listen to the questions

The Psalms are full of heart cries towards God. 'Why is this happening to me?' 'What is God doing?' 'This seems so unfair.' Questions and statements like these are cries of pain and anguish which need a listening ear rather than a trite reply. The person may just want you to sit and listen while they express their feelings. There are no simple answers to human suffering, as Job's friends discovered.

Anger can often be directed at others such as members of the family, neighbours, friends, doctors, nurses, volunteers and members of the church. Anger and sadness are closely linked. They can both be a part of the process of grieving for a life that has been unexpectedly shortened. The anger may be directed at you, too. It is important not to take such rejection too personally, and to continue to offer friendship.

Sometimes anger can become a test of friendship. You may be on trial yourself. Is your love great enough to keep coming back? In the meantime, while offering continued support, there may be another who is better placed to maintain the closest links.

4. Open your home

Be ready to offer a meal, or a place to stay or sit quietly during the day. Often a change of environment can help, not only the person who is unwell, but also the other carers. Many with AIDS have no real homes or families. Many have been effectively orphaned by their condition, or by previous circumstances. Many are living on their own, or with friends, in situations where dying at home may be difficult, or impossible. As we open up a network of homes and relationships, we are offering new choices to people who may feel they have none.

5. Draw others in

In our desire to preserve confidentiality, to care and to protect, it is easy for intense relationships to develop, and to reach a situation where 'lock up' occurs. It is easy as a carer to convince yourself that no one understands the person better than you, and that you alone have an 'inside track' on the situation. You want to be involved in all decisions and to be present at every discussion. It is easy to have mixed feelings about others becoming involved. Yet that very intensity can become more than the relationship can bear when illness develops.

As the situation unfolds, it is wise to draw others in. As a church leader myself, I feel it is vitally important that at least one member of the church leadership is closely involved, providing pastoral support to the person and to the carers, spotting signs of pressure or difficulty and helping to find ways through.

At every stage you will need the backing of the person concerned to involve others in this. If this is constantly blocked at every turn, you may have some hard talking to do. I have seen many situations break down at home, with people landing up in hospital simply because no one was willing to think seriously about the future.

6. Seek expert help

At some stage or other you are going to need expert help. It is all very well providing emotional support as a friend, but as events unfold you may need extra professional advice and support either from a clinic or from a community service. It may be that there is no local service available, in which case even telephone advice can be helpful.

Community care varies from country to country, but the trend in many places is towards caring for people in the community. Neither the richest nor the poorest nations can afford to keep people with AIDS in hospital when they do not need acute medical care.

As we have seen in Chapter 1, anxiety can produce many of the symptoms of early HIV illness, and as in other areas of medicine it is possible for people to convince themselves and others that they have HIV when there is no evidence of this. Because medical confidentiality is so strict in many nations, it is only possible for health care professionals to obtain confirmation of diagnosis after written permission from the person concerned, and even then it can be difficult. However, such confirmation is important. It is not unknown for fraud and deception to be practised, in order to get extra attention or material help.

7. Be ready for the long haul

Both those with HIV and those who care for them can be bewildered by rapid changes in the illness. One week there may be such a marked deterioration that they assume the end must be near, while the next week things may be back to their usual state. AIDS is a disease of ups and downs. People can be close to death, yet recover with prompt treatment, and be home again. In many countries people with AIDS are living longer with improved treatment, as we have already seen. Therefore it is wise to plan for a level of support that may need to be sustained for a long time.

People often ask me when the end will come. The answer is that no one knows, although we can often be certain about one thing: death is not here yet. With onset of new symptoms it is natural for everyone to become anxious. I often say to people that although it is true they are going to die of this illness, barring a miracle or a sudden new discovery, it is also true that they are not dying at this moment. We can often look back and see that maybe over the last few days things have actually improved a little.

One of my greatest joys has been seeing people begin to make realistic plans again: a last holiday, a project to complete, friends to see, a place to visit. Our aim is to redeem time; to give back dignity, freedom and choice. That is why expert care is so important. When it comes to practical care, nothing is more rewarding to me than something as simple and important as being able to give someone their first good night's sleep in months, so that the following day can be enjoyed.

8. Fear of death can be worse than death itself

Remember that the process of dying can be far more worrying to people than death itself, particularly if the person is sustained by the hope of eternal life. Common worries can include losing control over bowels or bladder, becoming mentally feeble with loss of memory, becoming disabled and confined to a wheelchair, losing hair as a result of chemotherapy for cancers, having to be washed and dressed by another.

Other worries can include the fear of uncontrolled symptoms of pain, breathlessness or other kinds. Finally, there is also the fear of losing control, of others marching in as strength fades, and of the wrong decisions being made.

The way to deal with these fears is to address them, and to try to discover what lies behind them. I remember someone asking me one day whether he would suffocate to death. There was real fear in his eyes as he gripped my arm, waiting for the reply. Before answering, it occurred to me to ask why he was asking the question and, even more importantly, why he asked that day, when I had been visiting so regularly.

The answer tumbled out that he had woken in a terrible fright the previous night in the middle of a nightmare. He had seen himself lowered into the ground in a coffin while still alive. Despite his shouts and his hammering on the sides of the box, they had covered him with earth. He had suffocated to death.

We were then able to talk about the dream, and I was also able to promise him, first that he would not suffer from feelings of suffocation if he developed a pneumonia, and secondly, that death when it did come would be certain. No one would suddenly whisk him away. He could remain in the house for some time. As a result of the conversation he felt at peace and the fear never returned. It is an important principle to find out what lies behind a question before wading in with an insensitive and immediate response.

9. Support the carers too

Sometimes all the attention can naturally fall on the one who is ill, ignoring those giving most of the support. But partners, children, other family and friends can unexpectedly run out of steam. Things can become too much as they juggle jobs, other responsibilities and the needs of someone with AIDS. An effective early warning system is vitally important. Sometimes it's the case that very young children are having to do most of the day-to-day caring.

Those doing all the work need to know they too have someone who is special to them, watching out for their own needs, stepping in with practical help, sharing the load, providing a shoulder to cry on, and being a friend in times of trouble. The greatest help is often practical. You could spend an hour a day counselling a carer who is near breaking point, when the time might have been better spent sitting in the home for a morning or an afternoon so the carer can go out. Perhaps you can take the person who is unwell out for the day, or have them to stay for a night or two, possibly longer.

Don't wait for people to shout for help, as they will often tell you much too late. Keep in touch regularly, even when things seem to be going very well. Time can fly by. Write a note to yourself in the diary to telephone or drop round again.

Be honest about your own needs, to yourself and to others. You are a special person too in God's eyes. He loves you too. Allow yourself to be vulnerable. Let the right people see when you too are feeling the strain and are hurting inside. Obviously you need to be careful not to share too widely, nor to dump your own emotional needs on someone who is ill, or on the main carer, but maybe sharing that you are human too will encourage someone else. Be ready to say no, to draw the line, to have recovery time of your own. That is why it is a good idea to involve a few others. You never know just when you will need their support.

10. Be ready to help around the clock at the end

You will need to be well-organised if the person wishes to die at home. It is likely that the last day or two, or even longer, will be quite harrowing. There may be a need for a continuous presence in the home, in addition to professionals coming in and out. You may need to identify a few sensible friends who would be willing to help on a rota basis, and who are acceptable to the person who is ill. The main need is likely to be for the sort of help that a caring relative would provide, to help in various practical ways.

On the whole, the care approach is the same as would be taken locally for any illness, whether you are living in Kampala or Bangkok or San Francisco. The only thing you need to take extra care about is exposure of skin to body secretions. Spillages of blood or other secretions should be wiped up wearing a pair of gloves. The easiest thing to do is mop up using disposable paper towels, and then to soak the area for two or three minutes with a freshly made solution of one part bleach to nine parts water. The area can then be cleaned in the normal way (see Chapter 5).

Gloves are not needed at other times. As we have seen, intact skin is an excellent barrier to HIV. Even if there is some skin contact with secretions, infection is most unlikely to occur unless the skin is damaged. It is wise to cover cuts with a water-proof plaster before going into the home.

Although this may all seem rather daunting, hopefully you will not be managing on your own. In many countries you will find health care workers are also providing support and advice. In other places, churches have found themselves having to develop their own community services because there is nothing available in their area.

When the moment of death comes, those in the home can feel uncertain as to what to do. There is no need for great activity when someone dies. The normal cultural rituals can be observed, remembering that secretions from the body will still be infectious. There may be one or two who need to be con-tacted, and would like to be able to say goodbye before the person is taken out of the home.

I want to look now at extending our care from our own church to the wider community.

CHAPTER ELEVEN

OTHERS NEED HELP TOO

Caring for church members is one thing, but what about those with AIDS who are part of the wider community? They may be dying in the most terrible conditions. Are we able to sit back and ignore their plight? Incidentally, their needs are largely the same and the ten-point guide in the previous chapter gives a good foundation for action.

In some churches, as soon as you talk about getting involved you can sense a problem. Some say it is far more important to deal with the root of the problem by preaching the gospel and seeing lives changed. However, the teaching of Jesus makes it clear that the two need to go together. Evangelical churches emphasise the need to preach the gospel. However, it could be said that evangelism without love is an obscenity to God, because a gospel message without love is a gross denial of what God is like. Love will always go further than words to meet practical needs. As Christians, we are called to love people as an expression of God's love, not as a means of manipulating them into joining the church. We love because people are worth it, made in the image of God.

Over the centuries, the church has pioneered many aspects of medical care that we take for granted today. Almost all of the first hospitals and associated caring agencies in many countries were started by Christians. Medical care was spread all over the world by a small army of dedicated men and women who often died, far from home, of the very illnesses they went out to fight. Their living conditions were dire and primitive in Africa, Asia, South America or China.

A missionary tradition

Those men and women were driven by an overwhelming compassion for those in other nations, many of whom were often without care and without hope. For them, bringing treatment for leprosy, malaria, tuberculosis or smallpox was bringing the practical love of God. As a result of that work, churches in South America, Africa and Asia are the fastest growing in the world, often at a rate enormously faster than the birth rate. These countries are now sending missionaries to mainland Europe, the United Kingdom and the United States.

I cannot find a closer parallel to AIDS today than the situation with leprosy a century ago. Now is the time for the church in the West to climb off the fence, to stop taking pot-shots at the tip of the iceberg – the bit they see (erroneously) as consisting entirely of promiscuous homosexual men and drug addicts – and to start considering the whole picture. There are millions of men and women dying worldwide, as well as those dying on our doorstep. God calls us to accept all people and extend his love to them, regardless of whether or not we agree with what they do.

Public involvement

Church leaders and congregations need to be visibly involved in the wider community, and not just seen to be caring for their own. They need to be quoted in the local press, on local radio, and down on record in the national media as declaring a commitment to get involved. The message is that we care about what is happening and we want to make a difference.

Leaders especially need to come forward and to be examples.

They need to be filmed talking to people with AIDS, holding their hands, receiving communion with them, or giving them a hug. At the end of the day, actions like these are the things that really encourage others. Fears are not dispelled by words alone, but by seeing that other people are not afraid. If church leaders cannot do this, then efforts to mobilise the congregation will be useless. It costs nothing to lead the way like this.

Community support

Is it practical to set up a small community support group to help those outside the 'family' of the church? How could we go about it? What about those who cannot be cared for at home? Could we use a church building to provide some sort of residential care or hospice for those who cannot manage at home?

Experience has shown that these things are possible in a wide variety of community settings, whether in a country like the UK or one like Uganda. The approach may vary greatly according to the local situation, but the overriding principles of compassionate care remain the same.

Everyone cares for their friends

Jesus said that caring for our friends, or members of our own social network, is something that everybody does: it is not a great sign of his kingdom. He said that true love is to care for those who are not members of our own family; people we would not normally associate with; people we do not like and might not be naturally drawn to. In fact, Jesus went even further and told us that we were to love our enemies, those who want to stab us in the back, those who run us down, those who hate us, those who undermine us, those who attack us, those who are against us.[1]

If this is the test of true love, then we can never be content to care just for our own. The test of true love will be our willingness to care for others in our community and for the children

---

[1] Luke 5:43–48.

left behind, without any hidden agenda or additional motive other than that which drove the Good Samaritan.[2]

Jesus wants us to care as the natural response to the need of those around us. He wants us to care because he cares and we are channels of his care. As people come into contact with us, and feel our touch, our love, our compassion, they are coming into contact with something of Jesus himself.

As we have seen in a previous chapter, this is a mystery. As we enter a room, we carry his presence into the place. I remember how, as a junior doctor, working in a busy hospital, I came into contact with a great number of staff. Once or twice I came home and talked to Sheila, my wife, about a particular nurse on one of the wards who seemed to radiate something I had come to recognise in the past.

She had never said anything, neither did she wear some kind of badge or symbol. I remember after some months, with slight embarrassment, I asked her if by any chance she was a Christian. Of course the answer was that she loved the Lord very much. It showed. She carried the aroma of Christ with her. You can smell believers as they walk into the room![3]

So our calling is not to shut up the love of God in some kind of Christian ghetto, just caring for each other, but to allow that love to be expressed through caring for others.

Isn't care the responsibility of the government?

Some say that it is the responsibility of the government to care, not the church. I believe it is the responsibility of both. One of the primary responsibilities of government is to spread wealth and resources by collecting taxes and providing services and benefits, whether in education, health care or road building.

The balance between individual, group and government

---

[2] Luke 10:25–37.
[3] 2 Corinthians 2:15–16.

responsibility is a political question, but one thing is clear: as Christians, we are called to be our nation's conscience, responding to need ourselves, and also encouraging a compassionate government response.

Where possible, I believe it is entirely right and proper that the government contributes to or provides some or all of the running costs of church-based care and prevention programmes, so long as the running of those programmes remains within the church and there is no loss of control. We need to be careful that Christian initiatives do not become mere extensions of government or international agencies, particularly now that (finally) a huge increase is being seen in financial resources given by wealthy nations and multinationals to fight AIDS in the poorest nations. That is why we need such a clear vision about what God is calling us to do. Without that we will be rapidly swept off course by someone else's vision, politics or priorities.

The issue is care for people, closely linked to social justice and basic human rights. If I am healthy, well fed and have a high standard of living, then the teaching of Jesus is that my 'neighbour' too should not starve or be deprived of the basic necessities of life. The church is one vehicle for provision; voluntary agencies and government departments are others. All can work together to get the job done.

Partnership between church and funding agencies can impose useful disciplines. It can help us think through what we are doing, as well as encourage us to measure our effectiveness and to plan strategically. (See Chapter 15.)

In many developing countries, the government depends on international aid, often channelled through Christian agencies, with projects overseen jointly by the donor and national government. These arrangements are often very successful, because governments are able to tap into an established network of Christian medical missions that have been providing first-class care and prevention programmes in the country for decades. This is increasingly being recognised by international donors, even though in practice it can be hard to connect donors and faith-based networks together.

The test of unconditional love

The test of unconditional love is twofold when it comes to AIDS. First, does it matter to you how someone came to be infected, or why someone's parents have died? Will that knowledge alter the way you see that person or the way that person is treated? Many people feel it is easier to care for an orphan or a dying baby than for an adult who is ill. That is certainly the situation in Romania. Everyone wants to help AIDS babies, and the care of adults or the need for prevention can almost be ignored. But is that the way of Jesus? Our love is unconditional because it is the same expressed to all, regardless of how they have come to be ill.

Is our love always the same?

The second practical test of unconditional love is perhaps even more important. Two people are dying with AIDS, and one has indicated he or she would like to become a Christian. Does this person get better care than the other? If so, then our care has become conditional. This is a real challenge to us and should cause us to consider how we think and respond to a variety of situations in the church.

Some may say that there is a sense in which God's love is full of conditions – this is the basis of God's judgement. Perhaps Chapter 8 needs reading again to see the whole thing in balance.

Community care or caring for our own?

If, in subtle ways, our care has become conditional on whether the person shows signs of wanting to join our church, then the programme needs redefining. It is not really community care at all, but just an extension of church life. That may be fine to you, but other agencies may be extremely reluctant to ask you to help, unless it is to care for those who already have a strong Christian faith.

Building on what we have

The advantage of home care is that you do not need a building, or even a formal office, in order to begin. You can start by resourcing the work from within the existing structures and facilities of the church. Indeed, it is possible to provide very effective AIDS care through general care programmes, so long as people are adequately trained, and those with AIDS locally are willing to receive help from a non-specialist agency. As we have seen, in most countries of the world the church has a huge established caring network, and a long track record of delivering high-quality care. There may be other care programmes running already which can be extended or adapted to help those with AIDS. There are no blueprints for success. You will need to adapt lessons others have learned to your own situation.

Care at home is fine as far as it goes, but what do you do when care at home is impossible? What about hospices or other kinds of specialist care centres?

Caring in a residential unit/hospital

Even if we set up a community programme, there may be people we are caring for who cannot manage at home. For a variety of reasons they may need to be cared for in a hospital or a hospice. For example, they may need stabilising and monitoring on anti-retroviral therapy as a part of WHO initiatives such as 3 by 5. They may need expert treatment of complex symptoms. Many churches have access to buildings, or may consider buying one. How can we tell if this is a sensible way forward, and how can we make sure the project will be successful?

Why hospices have grown in wealthy nations

Over the years, I have talked to a number of people who were set on starting some kind of in-patient unit for those with AIDS, whether in a country like Uganda or in the UK. Some of these are for end-stage care. What exactly is a hospice? The hospice movement has grown enormously over the last twenty-five years, having had its origins in the UK earlier this century.

It is aimed at providing a place where those with terminal illnesses can find peace and security in a specialist environment with a particular expertise in symptom control. Hospices are usually separate from hospitals, are often independently funded, and seek to provide emotional and spiritual support, as well as practical care.

The hospice philosophy spread fast from the 1970s onwards, in the UK at first and then elsewhere, because traditional medicine seemed obsessed with cure and had little time for the incurable. At the same time, those with symptoms such as pain were often very badly treated. Hi-tech medicine has sometimes lost touch with the needs of people. Thus the drive to build these hospices often came from relatives of loved ones who had died badly.

When AIDS became more and more evident, most of those who were ill in many countries were treated at first by specialists in either sexually transmitted diseases or chest problems, neither of whom had much experience of looking after the dying.

The aim is to help people die well by caring for them as whole people, physically, emotionally, socially and spiritually. The unit of care is not just the person who is dying, but also the family, or the group of people around that person. (See Appendix D on holistic care.)

However, we do need to be 100% certain that a dedicated unit for HIV really is the most appropriate solution, keeping in mind facilities available for other conditions in the country. It may be a very poor use of resources to have a well-fitted-out specialist

AIDS unit in a city where general medical and surgical facilities are extremely limited. In that situation a separate AIDS facility may be a luxury that cannot be afforded and is likely to be a magnet for many with a huge variety of other conditions. On the other hand, as we have seen in the wonderful work of the Mildmay in Uganda, centres of excellence can provide a wide range of services supporting other hospitals and clinics as well as training of large numbers of health care workers.

There is a real need for expert advice. For example, you may have access to a property, but after all the costs of conversion you may still not have a building which is practical. It may be better to build something from scratch.

Forming a ten-year vision for your care unit

Whatever the type of in-patient care you plan to provide, whether active treatment or end-stage nursing, you will need a steering group or committee prepared to see the vision through and sustain it. You need long-range plans and vision – for at least ten years. It may take you three of those years to get from agreeing the plan to being able to welcome your first patient. It is all too easy to go bankrupt with a beautiful building. Most people like to see something for their money, so they give to capital projects and are less happy to support staff salaries. Other approaches can be considered. For example, there may be a need for something more like a halfway house between what you would expect in a hospice and what could be provided at home. (See Appendix A on capacity building.)

One common solution has been to adapt an institution that was built for another reason, and is now redundant, for example a centre for leprosy or for those crippled by polio.

AIDS orphans – how have churches responded?

Whenever we care for young people who are dying, we may find children swept up in the process. Churches have responded in many creative ways, depending on the local situation. I remember visiting a Ugandan village where many adults had died. At first there were just a few orphans, but then numbers had grown rapidly. In Africa, a child who has lost even one parent is likely to be in big trouble, because the family may already have been living at a subsistence level. To lose both parents is usually a disaster, especially if the family is large with maybe six or more dependants.

There were 400 orphans in this village. What should be done? Many grandparents were spending their time trying to help bring the children up. The children had no source of income, no one to pay their modest school fees, so they had dropped out of school. Nearby was a village that had been closed by the government. The generation of parents had been wiped out. Only grandparents and children were left, and the village could not survive.

It is easy to march in and build orphanages as residential institutions providing love, education and care, but it is often not the best answer. There may be a simpler approach. Attending to one area of need may release the community to provide the rest.

If school fees can be found, the problem can be greatly eased. It is a tragedy that the local schools, which may offer an excellent education, may be half-empty because AIDS orphans are dropping out. It can be unwise to educate them separately as this may reinforce the isolation and stigma. It can also be a mistake to house them separately, as integration into village community life may be more difficult later on as adults. They may have difficulty finding husbands or wives, as they do not belong. Institutions can never provide the same experience of home as a family.

Sponsorship in families

For these reasons, an effective way to help in a country like Uganda can be to provide school fees or other simple support such as teaching them how to repair their houses and grow food. Often this is all that is needed. The children are then in their own communities, hopefully back in class with their friends. They are supervised and may even be fed in the middle of the day. Sleeping accommodation at home is often far less of a problem and in some countries in Africa the food supply may be adequate and inexpensive. Families usually grow most of their own.

Sponsorship in the home means that hundreds of orphans can be cared for individually in as normal an environment as possible. It is low cost, with few extra staff needed. The staff role becomes that of a community visitor, advising, monitoring, supporting and encouraging. Sponsorship schemes are funded by a number of different relief and development agencies, such as Tearfund, in partnership with local churches and national agencies.

Every country and community is different and we need to be very careful about transporting models that seem to work from one place to another. It may be that with very little outside help, local people are able to set up a school of their own. I have seen very inspiring examples of what can be done with almost nothing by villagers with faith, determination and vision. But as I say, there is more to survival than school. Many children with no parents need to be taught how to grow food, repair their homes and sell their produce.

Orphanages may be needed

Although we have seen that community placements can offer good provision at low cost in some countries, this may not always be possible. If the network of extended families and village resources is totally overwhelmed, then institutional help may be the only alternative. The principles of running such places are the same as for any other orphanage project. It is good not to separate those who are orphans because of AIDS from those orphaned by other events such as war, tuberculosis, accidents or malaria. In practice, it's hard to separate children out on this basis in any case. Orphans are orphans, and in many cases younger children may not even be certain what killed their mother and father.

The scale of the problem defies comprehension. In many areas at the moment, 9- or 10-year-old children are acting as mum and dad to younger brothers and sisters, often after nursing their own parents until they died. The children have to collect firewood and water, cook their own food – and grow it – supervise young ones and repair their homes. They have nothing.

Just a very little help can make all the difference. One project in eastern Uganda has been helping children rebuild their huts, so at least they have somewhere safe and dry to sleep at night. The workers also give out food and other essential items. Another in Zimbabwe is supporting over 2,000 orphans on a budget of less than $2,000 a month. (See Appendix E for more on setting up orphan projects.)

Income-generation projects

There are often situations in developing countries where a small amount of capital and training can equip people to become self-sufficient. Small micro-loans can make all the difference: for example, to buy a bicycle so that charcoal can be carried from the field beside the house up onto the main road and down into the city. It's not only orphans who are growing up and need to provide for themselves. Older women who have been widowed or who are otherwise vulnerable may have no means of survival, shelter or subsistence except through sex. In some countries the women may be seen as commercial sex workers; in others they may be seen as bar girls, or 'kept women'.

In Uganda there are thousands of women without family support or jobs. Many survive through the gifts of a number of men who stay with them regularly when in town. AIDS campaigns are useless to those who will starve without providing sex. A small cottage industry can enable a number of women to find a new life, with new freedom, dignity and control over their own lives – lives free from the constant fear of exposure to HIV. For example, in one area a group of women were given pigs and other livestock to breed and sell, as well as to feed themselves and their families. These issues are also important in countries like Thailand. One project there has set up a needlework industry for former sex workers.

As in every area of this terrible epidemic, it is easy to feel totally overwhelmed. Where do you start? How do you begin to tackle such a vast, global, growing problem? The answer is to start somewhere.

As George Hoffman, founder of Tearfund, once said, you cannot change the whole world, but you can change someone's world somewhere.

If, as a result of your help, an adult with AIDS is able to die at home, free of pain and at peace; if a family of children, recently orphaned, are taken into a home and cared for together until they grow up; if, as a result of an AIDS lesson, five young people are still alive in ten years' time who would otherwise have died of AIDS, then you have indeed made a big difference. Just think what 100, 1,000 or 10,000 people could do together. Just think what could be achieved by the whole church across your country, across the continent, across the world.

Jesus did not heal all the sickness in the world. He came and touched the lives of those around him, giving hope and purpose to a suffering world. As we ask God to show us who our neighbour is, his answer could involve us in the lives of those in another continent, or in the lives of those who live next door.

Some are called to give care in practical ways. Others are neither called nor gifted to set up or be involved in projects, build hospices or start agencies. However, there are many other ways to be supportive, through prayer, financial help and encouragement.

The importance of prevention

Whenever we begin caring for those with AIDS, we are faced with a terrible thought. Here are a growing number of people dying of a very unpleasant and incurable disease, yet every day many more are becoming infected, becoming ill, dying or becoming orphans. If we cannot cure it and the virus is spreading so fast, then we must urgently do all we can to prevent further tragedy and destruction.

Our greatest moral challenge is to spend as much time, energy and finance on saving lives as on caring for those affected by HIV. You can give all the care in the world and not beat AIDS – you will just get busier every year. You can spend all your efforts on prevention and maybe, just maybe, all the care programmes will have to close down because there is nothing left for them to do. There is a middle way: we fight the disease, and we care for those affected. Both should go hand in hand. But what is actually happening in almost every church-related programme across the world is neglect of prevention in favour of care. This is a route to future disaster. Churches talk about both, but their actual spend on prevention is usually tiny compared to care, orphan support, income generation and so on.

But prevention is difficult. It's easier in some ways to set up a care programme. What is our message? Can Christians agree? We need to decide what to tell our children, since they are in the frontline and in most danger, and we need to tell them in a way that is most likely to help them see the risks and change their behaviour. School is an ideal place to start, but what do we say and will our message actually change behaviour?

CHAPTER TWELVE
SAVING LIVES

Why prevention is often swamped by care

What do you do if you are walking along the road one day and two cars spin off the road in quick succession as they reach a dangerous bend? Do you run to help the victims? Do you run up the road to yell a warning to traffic? Do you go into a house and phone for an ambulance and the police?

Most of us respond to the immediate, which is why in many countries care for those with AIDS is eating up most of the AIDS budget. Prevention is usually an afterthought in spending terms, which is madness considering that although infection is lethal and incurable, it is almost totally preventable. Infection is also very expensive.

Economics of prevention

Effective prevention campaigns could halve new HIV infections, according to the World Health Organisation. A global programme in all developing countries would cost less than the price of a can of Coke for each person in the world. The saving in direct and indirect costs could be as great as $100 billion.

Prevention saves huge care costs

The economics in favour of prevention are staggering, yet little action is taken. Each life saved through education saves not only the costs of care but also the losses to the economy from that person's untimely death. How much does it cost to save a life? The figure is harder to come by, but let us argue from common-sense principles. Let us suppose that a schools worker with experience of working in home care spends a whole year taking classes in schools and talking to young people. He or she may see up to 8,000 pupils in the year, as well as talking to a large number of staff, parents and others. Let us suppose that only one individual changes behaviour so that infection is avoided. That educator would still probably have saved the government more than their annual salary in care and treatment costs and losses to the economy.

Health education is free

How many lives do you think a good educator could save? Ten? Twenty? Thirty? Fifty? High impact AIDS prevention is quite simply one of the most cost-effective things a government can possibly spend money on. The reason for this extraordinary fact is that, in industrialised nations, AIDS is such a difficult and expensive illness to treat. The drugs used are some of the most complex and costly ever produced. Until recently, anti-viral medicines were so expensive that a doctor in Uganda would have had to save every penny he earned for ten years to pay for one year's treatment of just one person.

In poorer nations the costs to the wider economy are also very significant, especially when AIDS strikes a significant number of senior executives, civil servants and community leaders in the country. Then there are the indirect costs caused by loss of business confidence, and companies pulling out to invest in other nations.

The cost of AIDS

The cost of treating one person with AIDS in the UK is the same as the Ugandan government spends on the entire health budget for almost 15,000 people for a year. But education is cost effective in Uganda too. I am excluding here, of course, any other measure of cost apart from economic. How can you place a cost on human life?

I have sometimes been asked by people in developing countries to help provide supplies of 'wonder' drugs. The trouble is that, as we have seen, these drugs just delay death and they are toxic, so complex laboratory monitoring is needed. Other cheaper medicines can have a far greater impact for the same price.

For example, many people with AIDS will be helped by receiving antibiotics to treat chest infections, anti-fungals to treat thrush in the mouth, anti-diarrhoeal drugs and painkillers. But none of these may be available on a regular basis to those in rural areas. A year's supply of anti-viral medication for one person could be exchanged for medicines to prolong life and control symptoms in up to 200 people with AIDS. These are very difficult and controversial issues.

When deaths damage the economy

The indirect cost of AIDS is the biggest problem in many developing countries. When a young person dies who is well educated, highly skilled and a key person in some part of your country's economy, a part of that economy dies. For example, if a factory in Malawi loses four out of six of its directors from AIDS in a year, you can be sure that production will fall, and so will the export orders, further damaging the economy.

If key designers, sales and marketing executives, engineers or people with mechanical skills die, then there is a cost to the government. The economy shrinks. Although this is hard to measure, and you may not think it matters when unemployment is high, in the longer term the loss is significant.

But this talk of finances is to reduce humans to items for sale or purchase. People are worth more than a few thousand pounds. Whether they are famous or unknown, people are people and have value for who they are as individuals. Yet, as we have seen, many governments spend practically nothing on prevention in comparison to care.

Ten years before health savings

Unfortunately, as with anti-smoking campaigns, prevention costs money up front, while government spending will have to continue for at least another decade because HIV, like tobacco, has a very slow effect. With HIV prevention, health services will probably see no real reduction in illness from today's prevention campaigns until well into the next decade.

Does health prevention work anyway? How do we know if any of the millions spent so far have had any effect at all? All health promotion tries to demonstrate cause and effect, persuading people that the effects are so terrible that it is worth paying a big personal price to stop doing something they like doing very much.

Behaviour can change

Studies have shown that behaviour does change, and can do so quite quickly. However, the most significant shifts in behaviour take some years to achieve. Infection rates among teenage girls in Uganda have fallen dramatically over a decade, from 23% to 5% by 2002, with smaller but significant falls also in Zambia. Similar successes have been seen in Thai men. Infection rates per year have fallen from 143,000 to 29,000 people a year in Thailand over the last decade. We have also seen huge changes in the sexual behaviour of gay men and drug injectors in America and Europe.

However, most success stories have happened after the community concerned began to see significant numbers of AIDS deaths. It is far harder to persuade people to change behaviour at an earlier stage of the epidemic. We have seen huge changes among drug injectors in several countries, many of whom have ceased sharing equipment or injecting as a result of education. We have also seen condom sales increase in many areas following AIDS campaigns targeted at the general population. All these changes have been seen in a very short space of time compared to the slow response to anti-smoking campaigns. This gives us some hope for the future.

But relapse is common, and risk-taking is on the rise again in Europe and parts of Africa. Every year is a fresh challenge with a rising generation of new youngsters taking risks for the very first time, and an ageing population of others who decide to take a chance that would have worried them a lot five years ago.

Young people take the greatest risks

Half of all new HIV infections globally are in those who are younger than 25 years old, so prevention must start young. However, surveys show that those changing behaviour the most as a result of campaigns are those who would be likely anyway to be settling down and changing partners less frequently. For example, in the UK and some other countries, gay men aged 35 to 45 have reduced their number of partners, while younger men unfortunately seem to be taking bigger risks again. We see this in the rising number of young gay men going to sex disease clinics with new cases of gonorrhoea – a sure sign that they are having unprotected sex.

Those in the firing line are young people. Every year, in many countries, the age of puberty falls a little more. The reason is unclear, although it is related to increasing body weight in girls. At the same time, the age of settling down is being effectively pushed in the other direction, with longer training and apprenticeships and changing social pressures.

Male sex drive is strongest in those who are youngest and it hits boys at a time when they are least able to handle it all emotionally. A 12-year-old boy and girl may be experiencing strong urges to explore sex at a time when they are incapable of working out a stable adult relationship. These pressures continue to fuel the debate for and against lowering the age of consent (see Chapter 7).

Sex education needs to start at a younger age

In many countries, the average age for the first sexual encounter has been falling for many years. In Uganda, a survey of teenage mothers found that 70% had their first sexual encounter before their fourteenth birthday. We know that in many towns and cities in the UK, over half of all 16-year-olds are sexually active, possibly with an even higher figure in some other nations. Research in the USA has shown that the number of partners people have in their lives can be directly related to the age they first have sex.

Young girls are particularly vulnerable to HIV and other sex diseases because of the immaturity of the female genital tract, particularly in those who are 13 years old and younger. This may be part of the reason why one Ugandan study found that there were five times as many 15- to 19-year-old women with AIDS than men of the same age. It's the same in older women. In Kisumu, Kenya, for example, in 1998, the prevalence of HIV infection among women aged 15–29 was 23%, while in young men it was 3.5%.

The other reason may be that young girls in many countries are targeted by older men as being less likely to be infected. It is also true that for physiological reasons a woman is twice as likely to get HIV from an infected man than a man is from an infected woman.

As we have seen, it is far easier to prevent risky habits than to change them once established. Parental attitudes and religious faith have also been found to be important influences on teenage sexual activity.

Incidentally, we also know there is a big link with smoking in some nations, alcohol in others. One study in the UK has shown that those who smoke under the age of 16 are six times as likely to be sexually active as those who do not, possibly because both activities are to do with wanting to take risks, to experiment and to rebel.

For all these reasons it is obvious that we need to start young, and that a big part of any national campaign needs to be directed towards schools, or where young people tend to meet, since in some countries less than half of all teenagers attend full-time education. Those becoming teenagers today are entering a different world. Unless we find a vaccine or cure for HIV, they are going to see some difficult things. With 1 in 200 of the whole global adult population already infected, they are likely to find this has risen to 1 in 100 by the time they have children of their own.

The AIDS generation is growing up

With the epidemic out of control in most of the world, our young people urgently need to be prepared to live in an AIDS world without dying. But what do we say and how do we put it across? Clearly the way we present a message will need to change with the audience and the context to be most effective. An approach for committed Christian teenagers may need to be different from that used in a secular school.

At the most basic level there is no point in preaching a sermon about immorality based on Bible verses, when your audience does not even believe in God. They are unlikely to be impressed by your arguments. A more pragmatic approach is needed. Yet for those wanting to base their lives on the teachings of Jesus, a talk explaining what the Bible teaches about sex will be very helpful.

AIDS in the church youth group

Because of the time delays between infection and illness, it is far more likely that you will find the church youth leader asking for help than one of the teenagers. Teenagers developing illness are more likely to have been infected at a much younger age – from infection at birth or from medical treatments, for example.

Teenagers in church get pregnant

Surveys show that not only is teenage pregnancy a real possibility in most churches, but also sexually transmitted diseases, including AIDS. Most churches find these things hard to face. It can be a terrible shock to find that the daughter of the church leader is three months pregnant, or that 'nice young lads' have been buying and selling drugs on church premises.

Unless we think that somehow our church is entirely separate from and irrelevant to the community in which we live, we mustn't be surprised to find that the things which go on in almost every street in the land also go on from time to time in the lives of those connected in some way with our churches.

Starting sex education earlier in churches

We need to take sex education and AIDS prevention seriously with the young people in our churches, before they become sexually active. The survey mentioned above shows us that this means starting before they are 16, and probably at around the time of puberty, or even earlier.

Some may feel that insensitive approaches to these subjects at such a young age are only bound to encourage experimentation. I agree. All sex education should be carried out sensitively in a balanced way, emphasising the positive aspects of marriage, family life and waiting for the right person.

Unfortunately, in a video and satellite age the fact is that, whether you are aware of it or not, many 13- or 14-year-olds are regularly watching 18-rated pornography, either in their own homes with borrowed videos, or in their friends' homes while parents are out or busy.

As most parents know, many 9- or 10-year-olds are now regularly watching 15-rated films in the same way. Older people also need to realise that, because ratings have become more relaxed, this means that 10-year-olds are now seeing things which would have been X-rated some years ago.

Educating parents is vitally important, as is encouraging them to take the primary responsibility in these areas which is rightfully theirs.

Sex in the playground

Children are bombarded with images and stories of sex. Playground talk of sex has increased to such an extent that parents are now finding their 5- to 8-year-olds asking for explanations of the things they are being told by other boys and girls at school.

In such a sex-obsessed world, the almost complete silence of the church is nothing short of bizarre, especially as the Bible itself is full of stories about sex, sexual imagery and sexual standards.

We need to face what is going on and break the sex taboo, bringing our discussions about it into the frame of normal Christian conversation and experience. We can no longer live in this two-worlds unreality. We are letting our young people down.

'Sex is dirty . . . so save it for someone you love'

We need to be careful about the mixed messages we give in church. For example, 'Sex is dirty . . . so save it for someone you love' can be the mixed message left in the mind of an impressionable child brought up in the church. Another conflicting impression can be: 'Sex is wonderful . . . but don't tell the children about it.'

We need to communicate that sex is a wonderful gift from God, an amazing experience, as we saw in Chapter 8. We need to teach that God very much approves of sex – it's the waste of sex outside marriage that causes him grief. Sex was invented by God as a gift to humankind.

We need to include teaching about sex as part of the overall programme of the church. After your Sunday service, a number of your congregation may be going home from church to enjoy it with their spouses; their children are obsessed with it; the television and videos from the corner shop are full of it; and the Bible is very explicit about it. So why are we still avoiding it?

Role models do matter

We need to make sure youth workers in the church are capable of handling the subject, and, more importantly, are able to set a good example in their own lives. Young people need to see role models worth following – models that are exciting and that work. They need to see in the marriages of the leaders of the church an attractive alternative to the often temporary relationships they see around them. We live in a generation which has almost lost the memory and experience of happy, lifelong commitment, yet is searching for it.

The answer is to include sex, sexuality and AIDS as topics in what the church is already doing.

Schools programmes

Teaching in church youth groups will only reach a few. What about schools? There can be few lessons which are more controversial. As soon as we think about education on sex or AIDS in schools, we find ourselves caught up in polarised debate. We find strong opinions expressed about the general approach, the content, methods, context, teacher support, parental opinion and the age it should happen. Millions of words have been written and tens of thousands of hours have been spent in training or in discussions, yet very little is actually happening in many countries.

ACET England (now part of Oasis and called Esteem) has developed an education programme with a simple, practical, low-risk approach which has become immensely popular with teachers, with a take-up rate of our materials in up to 60% of secondary schools. While it can hardly be regarded as a blueprint for success, there are general lessons to be learned, a number of which can be adapted to the situation in different countries. Similar programmes are run by members of the ACET International Alliance in countries such as Scotland, Ireland, Russia, Czech Republic, Slovakia and Uganda.

Instead of getting caught up in discussions of educational theory, it is possible to start from the other end – from the point of view of a teacher facing a sceptical class for an AIDS lesson. Teachers face real difficulties. Educational committees and self-appointed experts can generate a wide variety of materials that may be 'politically correct' and fit with the latest fashions in education, but which turn out to be completely unusable.

AIDS education is literally a matter of life and death. We are in a race against time. Our aim is not only to inform but somehow to persuade people to change – to change hearts and minds. Information is useless without action, without commitment. Life's too short to pack children's brains with more data about HIV unless their lives are changed as a result. And, of course, persuasion is an art: it is about helping people to make up their own minds, to take their own decisions, to take hold of their own futures.

Here is a summary of twenty findings based on the situation in the UK and some other countries. A similar process in other nations will produce some differences, but fewer than you might think.

1. HIV/AIDS education in schools is sensitive

Schools work is a sensitive issue because people cannot agree on what should be taught. Staff, parents, governors and national regulations all need to be respected. Be careful to use appropriate language. AIDS prevention is difficult because on the one hand we want to hold attention, to be relevant and to have impact, while on the other we must not upset or offend. AIDS prevention is most effective as an integral part of sex education or education about the risks of addiction. However, in educating about sex or drug abuse, we always have to ensure that we are not just feeding the imagination and encouraging experimentation.

2. Facts alone are of limited value

If you go into a classroom and try to give an AIDS talk, you will see that facts alone can be a waste of time. Teenagers in low-incidence countries like the UK are bored rigid with AIDS, and those in high-incidence countries may think they already know everything. The whole subject has been done to death by the media. People need to see AIDS is real before they are going to listen to you talk about it, or seriously consider changing their behaviour. They also need to see it all in the broader context of sexual health, teenage pregnancy, drug addiction and other issues such as self-esteem and self-confidence.

3. Family deaths change behaviour

As we have seen, behaviour often changes dramatically when someone experiences the death of a family member or close friend. The trouble is, by the time many young people in schools today begin to see deaths among their friends, we will have a much higher infection rate. In a schools lesson in Uganda I asked for a show of hands from all those who had been to the AIDS funeral of a family member. Most of the hands shot up. They needed no persuading that AIDS was for real and they were keen to listen.

4. We need to make AIDS real to pupils

One way to help make the illness real to pupils is to ask people with AIDS to visit schools. Unfortunately, this can be very difficult to organise and is unlikely to be possible in low-incidence countries, except on a small scale, for several reasons – the commonest given being the risk of anti-heroes. Many schools do not wish to bring in someone with AIDS who might become something of a role model regarding previous lifestyle. Teachers in the UK had a shock over their campaign to prevent drug abuse. The government produced striking posters with the slogan 'Heroin screws you up'. The picture showed a young man with boils on his face, looking quite ill and sorry for himself. A number of schools requested these, but found the posters kept disappearing without trace. It seemed that teenage girls were pinning them up on their bedroom walls. The boy had become an anti-hero, the latest pin-up idol. Others may be sensitive about someone coming into school who might want to promote gay lifestyles. That leaves only those infected through heterosexual sex or blood products, many of whom are not enthusiastic about being in the public eye in this way. It takes great courage to walk into a school where you are unsure of people's reactions.

Another effective way is to use educators who have been involved in the care of those dying at home with AIDS locally. This has been ACET's approach.

A comprehensive review of prevention programmes by the World Health Organisation has shown that person-to-person prevention is especially effective, particularly when 'peer led'. In other words, where the target audience can identify with the educator by reason of similar age, background or experience. In other areas of prevention this has been very successful – using infected commercial sex workers to reach sex workers, or truck drivers to reach truck drivers.

5. We need to use professional educators working within a moral framework

AIDS education is often relatively easy for a church organisation to provide, compared with a secular agency, because many schools want sex education within a traditional but compassionate, caring moral framework.

ACET International projects provide educators in various countries to take individual lessons, teams to teach larger groups, and materials and training for school staff. Teaching methods vary, with interactive questionnaires, class discussions, role play, dramatic presentations, conferences for large groups and formal teaching, assisted by overheads, charts, colour slides or video. Every country and situation is unique. Care credentials are helpful: educators who have helped care for people dying with AIDS are able to talk from experience and have instant credibility. There is no longer a 'boredom factor' when you are talking about real people dying of a real disease.

Formal educational qualifications are unnecessary so long as individuals are carefully selected for their communication skills with young people, and are properly trained. Paper qualifications do not mean someone will be able to persuasively alter the behaviour of teenagers in school. The personal values and lifestyle example of the educator are a very important part of the message. Extra security is provided by the presence of the class teacher. AIDS is then placed in the whole context of sex education, in the framework of relationships and commitment, empowering people to make their own choices and helping them find their own ways to say no to sex or drug abuse if that is their choice.

6. Success breeds success

The best advert for your training programme is personal recommendation based on past experience. A good reputation is essential, and takes time to build. Everything needs to be of the highest standard. Endorsements are helpful from health authorities and other influential bodies, including religious organisations where culturally appropriate.

You can transfer reputation and success from one country to another or from city to city, riding on the back of success and solid reputation elsewhere. This is why networking and being part of international alliances or recognised federations is important. But, conversely, take care, because your reputation can be damaged by the actions of others some distance away.

7. Compulsory HIV/AIDS education opens new doors

A further impetus has been given to schools work on AIDS in many countries by changes in the national curriculum, as has been happening in eastern and western Europe recently.

8. Help pupils find their own answers

People often ask whether we preach, or why we don't, depending on their position. The answer to both is the same: pupils need to work out their own answers. There is no point at all in trying to back up what you are saying from the Bible if you are talking to people who have never read it, don't believe in it and don't even believe that God exists.

You will merely undermine your message by convincing people that you are giving a biased view of this confusing epidemic. You will be open to the accusation that you are manipulating the facts to get people to accept a Christian lifestyle. We are only in the classroom for an hour or two on a limited number of occasions, yet the message needs to last a lifetime. Experience has shown that a long-term impact is more likely if pupils take part in the presentation, and come to their own conclusions about changing behaviour or avoiding risk.

The relationship of trust and respect built between the educator and pupils is a key element. They need to feel able to talk freely, and to feel that what is being discussed matters and is being covered in a balanced way.

9. No need to preach

While it is true that you cannot preach, our experience is that you do not need to. The facts speak very loudly for themselves.

It is also true that the kind of person the educator is, and the way he or she comes across, can communicate a lot.

When people see someone who is young and single, who enjoys life, has a sense of humour and a normal sex drive, yet is not sleeping around, then a new role model is created. These things can emerge in response to pupils' own questions, which can be quite probing. The lessons should be designed to help them talk frankly and openly.

Young people are very perceptive and can detect double standards, double talk, lack of integrity and hypocrisy. Teaching one thing and doing another totally destroys any impact you might have, and makes it certain that behaviour will remain unchanged at best, or become even riskier at worst. That's a very important reason why Christian educators have proven so popular with parents and teachers in many countries, especially when they know these educators are also linked to care programmes which bring compassion as well as an example that can be safely followed.

The idea of using role models of college age in schools is not new. Many studies have shown that if pupils are presented with an older person who has an overbearing authoritarian manner telling them to 'be good', they are likely to react adversely. Some may even be more likely to take risks in the future as an expression of rebellion against authority.

Teenagers are often far more concerned about their own health than adults realise. A US study found a high level of concern about AIDS, schoolwork, making friends, sex, discrimination and dental problems. Teenage girls were also worried about violence, rape, menstruation, abuse, pregnancy, sadness and being overweight. Boys were concerned additionally about homosexuality, car accidents and low weight.

10. Classes can be large or small

Many theorists say that only small classes are useful. In practice, you are often limited by the timetables and priorities of the school. If teachers already have booklets or other usable materials and are teaching the subject themselves, then they may be very grateful for an outside presentation to a large group to help reinforce the message.

Drama can be an effective way to communicate to larger groups, although it is very labour intensive and expensive in terms of the number of pupils reached per hour. Drama has been particularly helpful in reaching populations in developing countries, including variations such as the use of puppets in performances.

The aim is to make the illness real so teachers can teach about the disease with greater attention from their pupils. The greatest impact then comes in smaller groups where there is time for discussion and feedback, and where the educator has an ongoing presence in the school. The key is continuity. Behaviour change is most likely to occur when a group of people are involved in a 'journey' together, as a result of which their group culture changes. And that all takes time. But surely it's worth time to save a life?

Believe me, when you've had the deeply distressing experience of caring for lots of people with AIDS who got infected as teenagers or young adults, and a teacher invites you in but says you've only got ten minutes with a large group, you grab the opportunity. *Any* chance to raise the issues of AIDS is a chance not to be wasted and, who knows, you may convince the teachers that they need to do more – lots more. Of course one also needs to look at cost/benefit and how practical it is to do short visits if there's a distance to be travelled.

I often begin by saying, 'This is the most important school lesson you will ever have in your entire education, because this is the one that will save your life or the lives of your friends.' Or, 'Unless your own peer group behaves very differently from those who left this school in the last decade, you too could find yourselves going to the funerals of many of your closest friends.' Or, 'I'm here today because I don't want to be looking after you with AIDS in ten years' time.'

11. Teachers need to be closely involved

Most teachers want to be involved, although work pressures are so great that it can often be very tempting to leave the classroom to get on with preparation elsewhere. ACET International Alliance educators in England and some other countries always ask the class teacher to be present during sessions. Although some are surprised, because they expect pupils will be more inhibited, we have found the advantages more than outweigh the disadvantages.

The aim is to equip and give confidence to class teachers, not to de-skill them so they feel the need to leave it all to outside specialists. Watching us at work gives them confidence. Teachers often feel able to take over much of the work in future years, thus increasing the impact of our work.

If an outsider comes in to talk on a subject like AIDS, the danger is that the message will be entirely disconnected from everything else in school. Even worse is the possibility that there may be conflicting messages.

When teachers are present, this guarantees that what is said fits in with what they want. It also guards against complaints from parents – there is a witness to exactly what actually happens in each class. You never know when a pupil might make some kind of accusation about, say, insensitive language, or when a parent might make an unjustified complaint. Finally, it ensures that what the school is teaching about HIV is as accurate as possible.

Because every class is not only a pupil presentation, but also a teacher training session, a small number of educators can have a big impact over a year. Between classes there is also the opportunity to talk with staff informally, or to meet the head teacher and advise on syllabus priorities.

Evaluation is essential. Another big advantage of having teachers remain in class during presentations is good feedback. It is essential to evaluate any programme, particularly in schools. I have always encouraged teachers to complete evaluation sheets at the end of presentations, but they may prefer to wait until after the following week's lesson when they have had feedback from the pupils themselves. From time to time whole classes are asked to complete evaluation forms rating the presentation and booklets.

12. Sexual orientation is a separate issue

Many schools in developed countries are very anxious about how gay relationships will be presented in an AIDS talk, because a high proportion of people with HIV in these nations were infected through gay lifestyles. There is always a risk that an AIDS lesson by a visiting educator could open up all kinds of sensitive areas in the classroom, including lengthy discussions about sexual orientation, detailed descriptions of anal sex, oral sex and ways to masturbate, demonstrations of putting on condoms and the promotion of gay lifestyles in schools. The teacher may have to spend the next few weeks sorting out the chaos!

Whatever our own views are on these areas, we need to listen carefully to what parents, teachers, governors or community leaders think would be most helpful. Schools usually prefer an objective, low-key approach, using non-emotive language in a matter-of-fact way. They do not want an AIDS lesson to be hijacked by other issues.

It is always best to use plain language where you can, so, for example, I prefer to talk of sex between people of the opposite sex, or sex between men and women, or sex between people of the same sex, instead of 'heterosexual', 'homosexual' or 'gay'. The latter two terms are very unhelpful and misleading, because many young people are unclear whether you mean someone who has a particular attraction to someone of the same sex or someone who is sexually active. And there is another reason. As we have seen, six out of ten men who have homosexual relationships also have sex with women. Some may not think of themselves as gay or bisexual.

If you are careful with language, it is unusual to find problems in the classroom or with parents. We are not there to talk about why or how sexual orientation develops, nor is it the job of schools in most countries to comment on the appropriateness or otherwise of gay or straight sexual activity, except as a health issue.

13. Drug use or misuse must be discussed with integrity

A significant proportion of new infection in many countries is caused by injecting drugs, so it is essential that we tackle this important area. Many are likely to have been offered drugs or to have experimented by the time they are 17 or 18. The first thing we have to recognise is that there is something of a double standard in many countries. Many who are against 'drugs' are in fact addicted themselves, either to nicotine or to the most commonly abused drug in many countries – alcohol.

We need to acknowledge these things before we can talk sensibly with young people about the use of cannabis, ecstasy or crack, or the injection of drugs. Cannabis is far less physically addictive than tobacco, and perhaps less dangerous to general health. However, there is certainly a lot of evidence that those using cannabis regularly may be less careful when it comes to thinking about sex. As a relaxant, it removes sexual inhibitions – but then so does alcohol, and alcohol is a very important element in unsafe sex. Using cannabis may introduce the user to a circle of friends or a way of life where it becomes part of the norm to try other things. These are usually given freely at first. The charging comes later. And then some may need to move into selling drugs to cover the costs of their own habit. An injector may well be injecting all kinds of things – not just heroin, or what has been sold as heroin. We need to get across the message that sharing needles or syringes is the quickest way to get HIV.

An important part of the approach is to help pupils see how they can avoid situations where they know they will be under pressure to accept drugs. We also need to help them see how they can say no in such a situation, while preserving their self-esteem.

14. Condoms need to be discussed in context

The most obvious question facing any educator in schools is how to discuss the condom issue. Christians may have all kinds of objections to the way in which condoms seem to have been promoted as the answer to AIDS. These need to be laid aside when we think about going into schools. We need to take an objective look at the facts, and once again listen to teachers before deciding our approach.

Excellent protection, but not 100% safe. We have looked at the failure rates of condoms for pregnancy and HIV in Chapter 6. A survey of 18-year-olds in Glasgow asked for a description of 'safer sex', and 84% mentioned condoms, 68% some aspect of partner selection, but only 2% mentioned abstaining from certain sexual activities as an option. A very one-dimensional message is being given; yet abstinence must increasingly be recognised as a valid – and 100% safe – option, and should increasingly becoming a central part of thinking on prevention.

Testing is a real alternative. It is hard to think of a more absurd approach than just promoting condoms, particularly in view of the pregnancy failure rates we saw in Chapter 6. If you think through what the campaigns are saying, the conclusion is that all sexually active adults should use condoms in all relationships for life if either has ever had sex before.

This is a ridiculous message. What happens with couples who have been faithful to each other for years? Are we really expecting them to go on using condoms in addition to the pill for the rest of their fertile lives? What happens when the woman wants to have a baby? Are we seriously expecting women who have gone through the menopause to continue using condoms with their lifelong partners till they die of old age?

As we have seen, the answer is that HIV testing is an excellent alternative to condom use. It costs less to have a test than it does to buy three months' supply of condoms. If both partners are uninfected, they can enjoy anxiety-free, rubber-free sex for the rest of their lives. They will, however, need to be able to trust each other not to have other relationships or to share needles if injecting drugs.

The testing option has hardly been mentioned by many governments, and has been missing from poster and TV campaigns because it is not politically correct. Various highly influential pressure groups have persuaded governments that testing is still too sensitive and controversial, mainly because of discrimination. However, the situation is changing in developing countries.

No need to roll condoms on bananas. People often ask whether we give out condoms in the classroom. Of course the answer may vary from country to country, but my own view is that it is almost always unnecessary and inappropriate. Most parents of teenagers would be horrified if we were to roll condoms onto bananas in front of their children. We are in the business of giving an all-round message on AIDS, only one part of which is to explain the value and limitations of the condom.

If schools wish to demonstrate the use of condoms, we would expect that to be a part of their overall policy on sex education, after having carefully consulted with parents and governors. In my experience, few schools feel a demonstration is necessary, desirable or appropriate.

Teaching people to sin safely? While some outside of schools want all educators to demonstrate condom use and to teach teenagers that it is good to have fun with sex when you are young, others are horrified, saying that even to mention condoms in class is to invite people to 'sin safely'. Surely, they say, there is a danger that in even talking about sex and condoms we may be encouraging promiscuity.

In the context of a school class we are called to give the facts, recognising these are sensitive issues and that some church groups feel very uncomfortable talking about condoms. Christian agencies working in the AIDS field are certainly not wanting to encourage sex outside of marriage, but it would be absurd to avoid any mention of condoms at all. Even if you say condoms should only be used by people who are married, there may be many situations in the future where a couple have got married knowing that one partner is infected from the past. Are their lives also to be placed at risk through a ban on all information about condoms? Young people live in the real world – as do you and I – and we need to demonstrate that in a realistic down-to-earth approach. (See later for Catholic approach and other church issues in relation to condom discussions.)

Condom summary. In summary, then, we need to make pupils aware that there are several ways to reduce the risk of HIV or avoid it altogether. As the World Health Organisation says, the most effective way to prevent sexual transmission of HIV is to abstain, or for two people who are uninfected to remain faithful to each other. Alternatively, the correct use of condoms will reduce the risk significantly. We need to get across that having sex without using a condom could be suicidal with a partner who may be infected. However, condoms may let you down.

15. Ethnic minorities often welcome a Christian approach

Over the years, ACET has gained a lot of experience teaching in different kinds of schools in different cultural areas. The same approach to AIDS has found great favour across the spectrum, including schools which are 95% Asian with Muslim, Hindu and Sikh children and parents.

Parents appreciate educators who have a moral framework for their own lives which is similar to their own. Many from other religious groupings or different ethnic backgrounds are deeply devout or traditional, and find Western or secular sexual standards shocking, upsetting and worrying as they consider the future of their children.

16. Catholic schools also welcome sensitive AIDS education

The sensitivities in Catholic schools tend to be greater, although this varies very much from school to school and from country to country. The big issue for Catholics is whether condoms will be mentioned.

Some Catholic schools take the view that it is permissible to talk about how HIV spreads, how it causes illness, and how to help with HIV, but not to mention condoms unless pupils ask directly. Others are more relaxed, so long as the lesson is placed firmly in the context of the Christian ideal of sex as part of marriage for life. The range of what is permitted varies from area to area and country to country.

As in every other school context, the best approach is to treat each school and each class individually, discussing with teachers the approach they want, and any particular sensitivities of the school or of the particular class. This is the only reliable way to avoid misunderstandings, to ensure we serve schools well and to make certain we are operating as part of their team.

In Northern Ireland, the same educator, programme and materials have found warm acceptance in both Catholic and Protestant schools. The problems are therefore often more imagined than real. The key is a strong relationship of trust and respect built with individual educators.

17. Lesson content needs to vary with age

Some schools will want to educate pupils who have not yet reached their teenage years. This is perfectly possible without offence or difficulty, but the content will need to be adapted under the guidance of teachers. It is not necessary, for example, to explain about sex in order to teach that babies can be born with HIV. Some aspects of AIDS can be taught in the context of geography, science, hygiene and other school topics.

Countries vary greatly. In Uganda, for example, elements of sex education and AIDS are often taught to children as young as six. The reason is that in towns or villages where up to a third of the population is HIV-infected, most children will have seen members of their own families die from AIDS. The illness dominates local life, and some explanation has been found to be necessary. In comparison, such topics are very difficult to discuss with young children in a country like Thailand.

18. AIDS education needed before some leave school

With many pupils leaving school at the age of 16 in countries like the UK, and far younger in some other countries, AIDS education must start earlier. A recent survey in Scotland showed that those leaving school early are often much less likely to take notice of public health messages later, and this group may take greater risks than those who carry on with general education. School education is therefore particularly important for this group.

19. Establishing traditional behaviour patterns as most common can be very effective

Behaviour is often influenced by peer pressure, or by what people think everybody else is doing. Media and peer group conversation tends to exaggerate reality, however. 'Almost all my friends sleep around.' 'Most of my friends use drugs.' 'Hardly anyone these days is still a virgin by their eighteenth birthday.' A lot of talk, but little or no performance.

Can these impressions be changed? A US study compared two approaches to the prevention of smoking, alcohol abuse and use of marijuana by schoolchildren. The first method taught skills to pupils to help them refuse unwanted offers. The second corrected false impressions of how many other pupils were actually experimenting, and what most others in the school thought of this behaviour.

The second 'normative' approach worked well in altering

reported behaviour one year after the programme. Although the first had fewer measurable effects these two approaches are particularly effective when used together: giving people the self-confidence to say no, while also helping them see that they are following the majority when they do so. It is essential also to reinforce the positive behaviour of the large number of teenagers who do not abuse alcohol or other drugs, or take sexual risks. They are without doubt the majority in most parts of the world.

This is really important. Those who say no to drugs or sexual activity as teenagers need to understand that they are in good company. Despite all the noise, most others in the classroom have made exactly the same decisions and share the same values. Far too often, teenagers have drifted into risky behaviour after becoming convinced that abstinence is eccentric and that they needed to take risks just to be seen to be normal. This is particularly tragic, since the pressures on them are based on cruel deception, totally false impressions which will ultimately kill some of them.

Normalisation of abstinent behaviour could be the most powerful weapon we have in using peer group pressure.

Take the use of drugs. Even in a country where most teenagers have tried something by the time they leave school, the situation is far less bad than it appears. The majority of those trying drugs will have done so only once or twice, and other regular users give up after a brief phase. Why? Because they didn't like it or because it is 'un-cool'. Surveys show that 'lifetime' use of drugs is far higher than figures for how many teenagers have used drugs in the last six months. *It's time to talk about the truth. Saying no is normal. It's what most young people do!*

20. Social skills and peer resistance training work

Many studies have shown that classes designed to help pupils develop the ability to say no are effective in behaviour change.

Facts are essential to understand the problem, and personal presentation is vital to make the problem real, but pupils may still take risks against their wishes if they feel insecure about themselves, have a poor self-image, or are afraid of being looked down on or laughed at.

Surveys show that the problems and issues faced are remarkably similar from country to country. This is also true in the experience of international groups like ACET. While cultural sensitivities vary and may require adjustment of content and approach, many basic issues such as motivation, communication and long-term behaviour change remain the same. People are people after all.

The impact of all schools programmes is likely to be greatest when mass media campaigns are also part of the overall national picture, as studies on teenage smoking have shown.

Dealing with criticism

In such a sensitive area, whatever one does will be criticised. The test of whether you have the balance about right in schools is probably when you are criticised from several different sides equally, but none too severely.

Constructive criticism must always be taken seriously, especially if it relates to conduct or lesson content. That is why evaluation forms are essential. You want to pick up a slight problem with an educator's approach long before there is a complaint.

We need to understand the background to the criticism. For example, there are hundreds of self-appointed experts in the UK when it comes to AIDS prevention. Hardly any of them have any real experience of teaching about AIDS in schools, or if they do it may be in just one or two schools which are unrepresentative of the country as a whole.

Coping with the 'thought police'

Sometimes comments made from 'non-school' sources can be vitriolic. Valid points may be being made, but I often wonder why they have been allowed into so few schools themselves if they are such experts on getting the message right. Why have their own resources and leaflets found so little favour?

The classroom is a uniquely difficult and sensitive environment and my feeling has always been that it is up to teachers and pupils to tell us what they need.

We must allow teachers to get on with the job. They are the experts; we are the assistants. Failure to recognise this has been the reason why so little government-sourced material has been used in schools in some countries such as the UK. It is nothing short of a scandal that a modest schools programme, intended as no more than a pilot to show what could be done nationally, should turn out to be one of the largest programmes of its kind in England (Oasis Esteem).

Perhaps there is little new under the sun when it comes to HIV prevention – or criticisms of it. Negative reactions to schools programmes run by Christian organisations have tended to be very repetitive along ten main themes.

Objection 1: 'Large classes are a waste of time'

It is obvious that the more time spent with a group of pupils, and the higher the presenter-to-pupil ratio, the greater the impact is likely to be, but we have already seen that larger classes may be the only ones on offer in a school. A school which opts for a single large presentation one year as an experiment, will often open up more of the timetable the following year. Most schools need time to find their way forward.

Objection 2: 'Faithfulness to one partner is a naive suggestion'

Some think it is hopelessly naive even to mention the option of being faithful to one person, let alone staying with one partner for life. It is interesting that in almost every class I have been into, pupils have worked out for themselves the options – and benefits – of abstention and monogamy.

When you ask them what 'safe sex' is, there are usually two reactions. If you ask who has seen the slogan 'Condoms mean safe sex' or 'For safe sex use a condom', you will often find every hand shoots into the air. Almost always they have misread official slogans by dropping the 'r' off the end of 'safer' to remember 'safe'. However, when you ask pupils what they think, those with an ounce of common sense tell you that safe sex is certainly not achieved by using a condom. They know friends or relatives who became pregnant using them.

I would argue that it is hopelessly naive to expect that pupils are going to decide after your lesson to use condoms every time they have sex until the day they die, when the alternative of a test in a long-term relationship is so simple. Also, many people are searching for love that lasts.

Objection 3: 'Suggesting celibacy and monogamy as options is moralistic'

Some say that you should not make any suggestions at all about behaviour, nor propose any role models. 'Pupils should be totally free from any proactive or directive approach.' They say it is moralistic to talk about keeping to one partner or to suggest not having a sexual partner at all.

In reply, three points need to be made. First, medical facts are morally neutral. It is a medical and human fact that it is possible for people to refrain from sexual activity or promiscuity, and that this can be a very healthy way to live – for a start it protects you from sex diseases. Secondly, in countries like the UK there are legal requirements to present sex education 'in such a manner as to encourage those pupils to have regard to moral considerations and the value of family life'. Thirdly, even if such an approach was not required by law, the parents and governors of most schools in the country would insist on it anyway.

Having addressed a number of parent/teacher associations, it is obvious that some of the most conservative parents are those who were themselves teenagers in the 1960s or 1970s and are now deeply concerned about their children living the way they did in a pre-AIDS world. Many still want marriage to work for themselves and most of all for their children.

Objection 4: 'If you don't show people how to use condoms they won't bother or they will make mistakes'

It is true that people should be encouraged to familiarise themselves with a condom before they need to use one. The best place for this to happen is in the privacy of one's own home, where the packet can be opened, the instructions read, and the condom examined and, if necessary, experimented with. Demonstrating condoms to children under 16 years of age could be taken to be encouraging under-age sex in many countries, and even over that age you could land yourself in trouble.

Objection 5: 'Visiting speakers are dangerous because they do not fit into the overall work of the school'

We have already discussed the importance of each educator becoming, in effect, an extension of the head teacher's own staff in the school. Nothing is worse than a hit-and-run approach with no continuity, no follow up and little impact.

We have noticed that many schools see huge advantages in having outside carer/educators. They have impact because they are involved in care. They are respected experts. They are seen as non-threatening and not part of the establishment. They are often easier for pupils to talk to. They bring a fresh perspective to the school.

Objection 6: 'Not enough time is given to gay issues'

AIDS prevention is about preventing HIV transmission through risky sexual practices and drug injecting, not about sexual orientation. This important area is a part of overall sex education, personal life skills and social education. In any case, as the epidemic unfolds, gay issues are increasingly irrelevant in the global AIDS picture.

Objection 7: 'You fail to point out that you are almost 100% safe in low incidence countries unless you inject drugs or have anal sex with a gay man'

Objections 6 and 7 are almost opposites of each other. If we spend time on the relationship between a gay lifestyle and AIDS, we create the impression that AIDS is just a gay problem, when, as we have seen, AIDS is an increasing threat to heterosexuals in industrialised countries, and a huge risk in developing countries. If we spend no time on gay lifestyles we create the false impression that all in our society are equally at risk.

The 'politically correct' thing to say is that there is no such thing as an 'at risk group', but only 'at risk behaviour'. While it is important that we teach people not to hide behind labels and prejudice, we may be in danger of splitting hairs. It is certainly true that the risk of a gay man picking up HIV from a sexual encounter in a gay bar in London is hundreds of times greater than the risk of a heterosexual man picking up HIV from a girl he meets at a party in the north of England. In the classroom, however, we have only a very short time to put across the simple message that AIDS is real, HIV is spreading and these are the ways to protect yourself and those you love. Although the risks are low, it is a fact that some have become HIV-infected after a single episode of unprotected sex (see Chapter 6).

Objection 8: 'Fear of getting AIDS is a very negative way to motivate change'

People object if you talk about the illness as it really is. But we know what we are talking about. AIDS is a very unpleasant illness, with many unpleasant symptoms which are difficult to treat. People do not just live with AIDS, they die too.

I often say to classes in schools that I hope we do not ever have to look after any of them. After all, that is why I am there: to try to save their lives if I can. If they carry on behaving like some of those who left the school over the last few years, then it is likely that doctors or nurses will be caring for some of them too. This is a frightening thought and it greatly disturbs me.

A few years ago people were reluctant to talk about dying with AIDS because it created a negative image. This is ridiculous. If you create the impression that to have AIDS is to be a hero, that living with AIDS can be fun, that you can live for many years and there is a lot of hope for a cure, then don't be surprised when people decide there is nothing to worry about.

Objection 9: 'You are creating a negative view of sex'

Some say that if we talk a lot about the dangers of unrestrained sexual activity, then a new Victorian age of sexually repressed people will emerge. I have met some HIV educators who have openly told me that one of their purposes is to help teenage boys and girls feel happy about their bodies and about their sexuality, so that they feel free to enjoy themselves.

Half the emphasis of their presentations is therefore on sexual enjoyment – for example, teaching young girls about orgasm – and the other half is on how to have fun more safely. They say this is realistic and fits in with what the pupils are doing anyway. As you can imagine, they very rarely get the chance to give such presentations in UK schools.

This approach certainly fits well with our culture. You only have to wander into a video shop to see what I mean. Western culture has produced conditions for the rapid spread of HIV and AIDS by encouraging a casual view of sex, through mass communications with a global influence. But our culture is out of date and needs to change in our post-AIDS world. There is no such thing as free sex without cost. At the same time, Western influence has had a huge effect on liberalising sexual constraint in many traditional tribal cultures. Where premarital sex or adultery was once prohibited and rare, promiscuity is now common.

As we have seen, surveys show that the younger someone is when they first have sex, the more likely they are to have multiple partners. There is also a strong relationship between the age at which a girl first has sex and her risk of cervical cancer. This cancer is often caused by a virus which is sexually transmitted. It appears that the immature cervix of a young teenager is particularly vulnerable to infection. Deaths from cervical cancer are increasing, despite intensive screening programmes.

Other sexually transmitted diseases are emerging for which treatment is difficult or impossible; for example, genital herpes, which produces clusters of highly infectious and painful blisters from time to time throughout life, and genital warts, which require repeated treatments with caustic substances. In the last twelve months alone, 250 million people worldwide became infected with a sexually transmitted disease. The highest incidence is in 20- to 24-year-olds followed by 15- to 19-year-olds.

In these circumstances, I feel as a doctor that we do our young people a gross disservice if we pretend that sex is always wonderful, totally ignoring the pain and devastation felt by many pupils in almost every class because of marriage break up, or the collapse of stable relationships outside of marriage. On many occasions, unfaithfulness is at the root of the problem. It is always the children who suffer, caught up in conflicts with split loyalties, and with possibly two 'mums' or 'dads'.

A national UK survey showed that children of divorced parents often continue to suffer well into adult life, when they are more likely to be unemployed and experience psychological difficulties. There are real costs attached to so-called sexual freedom and these need to be clearly taught and understood.

It is also vitally important to give a very positive message about sex as a wonderful experience; something which gives great pleasure and can be very fulfilling, especially when it is an expression of love, respect, appreciation, care and commitment. Sex is something well worth waiting for. The UK Population Trends survey shows that couples living together before they get married are more likely to be divorced after fifteen years of marriage than those who do not.

At this point we start hearing objection number 3 again, with suggestions that teaching is highly moralistic, right wing, Christian propaganda. No wonder schools are voting with their feet.

Objection 10: 'You should teach people other ways to have sex'

The AIDS industry continues to churn out large numbers of guides to safer sex which give long lists of 'low risk' or 'no risk' activities. Examples of 'safe sex' include rubbing each other's thighs, mutual masturbation and 'talking dirty' on the phone to each other while masturbating.

Some seriously suggest we should be discussing some of these options in schools. They have obviously never tried such an approach with pupils. Laughter is the only response you are likely to get from a class if you seriously suggest that rubbing each other's thighs is the same thing as having sex. That certainly is naive. The suggestion may be valid for gay men who know there is a one-in-three chance that their next partner could be infected, but it does not go down too well with teenagers in low-incidence countries.

Why should they bother with such a feeble substitute for the real thing when they know they can enjoy rubber-free, anxiety-free, penetrative sex for life, with the help of an HIV test if they or their partner have been at risk in the past? As we have seen earlier, deciding whether to have a test is a delicate business and all those wanting a test should be carefully counselled first.

Over-promotion can be a problem

Having looked at ten of the commonest criticisms ACET has faced, we need now to look at the opposite problem: over-promotion of a church programme by well-meaning Christians who want to help. A lot of damage can be done. For example, if someone known to be a moral campaigner goes to the head teacher and begins a campaign to get you in, it would be better if that person had never started.

As we have seen above, you need to take very great care indeed before rushing in as an AIDS educator. The reason is that an amateurish and clumsy approach to this sensitive area could jeopardise the work of many other agencies.

If you are already established as a youth or schools worker, supported by churches in the area, then you may be able with care to include some aspects of AIDS in what you are doing. However, you will need to make absolutely sure you get your facts and general approach right. You will have greatest impact, as we have seen, if you have been involved in caring for those with AIDS.

CHAPTER THIRTEEN

NEEDLE AND CONDOM DISTRIBUTION?

While a church organisation can find doors open easily into schools, and the general approach required fits well with Christian values, when we look at other areas of community prevention things can become much more difficult.

It is far easier to bring HIV or AIDS into other aspects of existing work than to set up new programmes. Examples of this might be detached youth work or work in pubs and clubs, among the homeless or among commercial sex workers.

Walking the streets

Detached work can be very successful in reaching all kinds of marginalised groups. Two or more people go out onto the streets, heading for areas where people are known to hang out, especially in the evenings. It might be outside a takeaway food shop on a big estate, or at the bottom of a particular tower block.

Friendships are formed and in that context other things can happen. For example, people can be invited back to someone's house, or literature given out about HIV on the streets. The aim is to create a situation where individuals or groups become interested, and ask questions about how they can protect their own health.

In Dublin, detached workers from ACET Ireland have made

contact with a drug-using community who are, to a large extent, outside contact with health services. A number are ill or dying, and many are infected with HIV. Others have become friends. While other agencies or care workers are sometimes unwilling to go into certain areas, with great fears for personal safety, ACET workers have found this community accepting and protective in attitude.

Giving out clean needles?

In Dundee, Scotland, I have been out with teams where drug users gather round as soon as you drive onto various estates with an (unmarked) van. Often they talk about friends who are unwell and need help. When in their homes, there is also a chance to talk to others about safe injecting and how to save their own lives or the lives of their partners and friends.

This brings us straight into another area of difficulty. Some are injecting with shared equipment because they have no needles of their own. They do not want to give up. Should we issue them with clean needles on an exchange basis – in other words, take a blunt one and give them a fresh one? Are we back onto the argument of just teaching people to 'sin safely'?

Needle exchange programmes have been very successful, dramatically lowering the incidence of needle sharing. However, one problem is that the needles do not always come back – sometimes only half do. This raises fears that, while HIV infection rates may fall, the numbers injecting may rise. The whole issue is very controversial in many countries.

Encouraging a habit or saving lives?

Christians find it is easy perhaps to decide what is right or wrong behaviour, but when confronted by different situations, it can be less easy to know what to do. Let us imagine that you are a worker visiting people ill and dying with AIDS on a big housing estate in Scotland.

Over a period of months, you gradually get to know a group of drug injectors who have no contact with any other source of help. Several need care, and several want to break the habit. You organise help for these people. However, despite your conversations about the dangers of injecting with shared equipment, three of them tell you they will do so again tonight because they only have one needle and syringe between them.

There are several options open to you. You could inform the police and get them all arrested following a raid on the flat. If you do that, you will violate the trust of the group, you and your organisation will never be asked to help again, and those dying on the estate will die without any help at all. Drugs are also freely available in most prisons, so you will have done nothing to solve the basic problem.

You could just turn your back on the situation and walk out, leaving them to infect each other with a warning about the danger, knowing that one or two of them may receive a death sentence that very night from HIV infection.

There is another option: you could decide to help them on their own terms. Despite all your efforts, they are going to continue to take big risks. They are addicted to the habit and are happy to remain so. You could explain that rinsing the needle and syringe with a freshly made solution of bleach in water (one part in ten) before passing the equipment on will reduce the risk of death from AIDS enormously. This is not just a matter of morals; this is quite literally a matter of life and death.

If you decide not to tell them this and walk away, and a few years later you are cradling one of them in your arms as he dies, because he became infected that night you walked away, will you not feel an element of responsibility for his death? Perhaps you can distance yourself from this situation, but what if it was all much closer to home?

What if the drug user was your own teenage son or daughter? Would you not do all you could to encourage your own child to use bleach if he or she was determined to continue injecting with shared needles or syringes? If your own child was about to go to the house next door to borrow a bloody needle from someone you knew had AIDS and you happened to have a clean needle in the house, would you not feel perhaps a need to offer a clean needle? If your son were infected on that occasion, would you not feel you could or should have prevented the tragedy? These are not hypothetical situations. Similar agony and conflict is an ever-present reality for many Christians caring in the community, and unfortunately for some Christian parents.

We need to find the way of Jesus. What would he do? Jesus was always honest, open and hard hitting in what he said, yet compassionate and loving in what he did. I cannot believe that Jesus would sit watching the person injecting death without a warning to stop, and, if disregarded, then giving advice on at least how to clean the needle properly, taking care of hygiene. If he knew there was a box of new needles in the corner, I can imagine him mentioning it – not to promote the practice, but to save life until a time when the person may be looking for help out of addiction, and for reconciliation with God.

I have met a Christian who told me that he would rather sit and watch his son die than tell him how to inject safely. What kind of a dad is that? Some parents are so severe with their children it is no wonder so many teenagers of Christian families reject their parents' faith. Often teenagers are saying, 'If this is Christianity, then you can keep it. It's horrible.' Life in the home is vitally important, because it is there that people see the reality of who we are. What kind of gospel are we living? We need to recognise that even where parents have been wonderful examples, children can rebel, rejecting not only parental authority, but also parental values and faith. We also need to see that doubt is a big issue for many people.

Another churchgoer told me that if her son ever showed any signs of growing up with a same-sex orientation she would throw him out of the home, disinherit him and never see him again, even if he was celibate. What has such harshness got to do with a loving heavenly Father? I shudder to think what would happen if God judged these parents with the ferocity with which they are judging their children.

Jesus said, 'Do not judge, or you too will be judged. For in the same way as you judge others, you will be judged, and with the measure you use, it will be measured to you.' So take care. You had better be near perfect or you may be rightly accused of hypocrisy. Of course, as we have seen in Chapter 8, there are clear standards and we are called to challenge, rebuke and confront behaviour where necessary.

We need to understand that Jesus often behaved in a way that people thought was encouraging others to do wrong. As far as the spiritual leaders of the day were concerned, he showed a profound lack of judgement and gross indiscretion in the relationships he formed. Jesus was heavily criticised for encouraging either financial corruption or sexual immorality by publicly associating, eating, drinking and making friends with 'tax collectors and sinners'.

They felt Jesus was giving out a very dangerous signal that wrong behaviour was acceptable, and that, despite what he said about God's standards, he was actually encouraging these lifestyles. It is the same today. There are some in the church with rigid, black-and-white views on what is absolutely wrong and what is absolutely right in absolutely every situation. They would have had exactly the same problems accepting Jesus as the Son of God as the passionately committed Pharisees did 2,000 years ago.

After much careful consideration and prayer among our team, we felt that we should issue a limited number of replacement needles on an individual basis to some we knew who were injecting, whose needles were blunt, who were unwilling to stop and who would be using other people's needles unless replacements were found. This was not an easy decision and some will criticise us for it. Perhaps the reasons will become clearer as you read on.

It is interesting that Christian doctors, nurses, social workers and missionaries living in the real world usually understand our decision, with many coming to the same conclusions. It is usually those whose lives are most sheltered from those at the margins of society who have the greatest difficulty. Yet that was exactly where Jesus was always found – with the marginalised, the poor, the outcasts, the oppressed, those who had dropped out or rejected the common view of what was right or wrong.

The issue of needle exchange is an entirely different issue from giving out condoms to children in schools. We would not give out needles in school corridors either. The equivalent of needle exchange regarding condom distribution might be a church running a Christian pregnancy advisory service.

We do need to help people find ways to say no if they are feeling under pressure to have sex, and to help them understand the risks they may be taking. However, most Christian doctors in general practice I have spoken to do recognise that there can be circumstances under which they feel it might be appropriate to provide people with condoms. The issue of contraceptives for those under 16 is far more controversial, especially if this is done without parental involvement. If we refuse, the next request could be for an abortion.

Incidentally, I would always prefer advice to be given, if possible, in the context of the family doctor's surgery, but young people are not always willing to go there because they are afraid that Mum or Dad will find out.

Contraceptives for unmarried people?

Ethical dilemmas are faced by Christian doctors and nurses every day. I am not saying it is possible to be certain about all the answers, but it is important that we face the questions. It is too easy to hide behind a sermon or to withdraw into the Christian ghetto of church social life and hope these things will go away. We need to preach practical faith that helps people to live in the real world, not platitudes that just comfort us when we return to our homes at night.

We face conflicting ethical issues when someone who is unmarried asks for contraceptives. In the past, family planning clinics in the UK would only help married women. I am not sure many Christians would want to insist on such a rigid approach today, any more than they would want a law passed making sex outside of marriage illegal, as is the case in some Islamic states. However, it could be argued that giving free contraceptives to people who are living together is directly encouraging immorality. Exactly the same thoughts can apply to helping those with a drug habit. We need to be consistent. What is the answer?

It seems to me that first we need to provide the best possible rehabilitation facilities for any who would like to come off drugs. Secondly, we also need to offer the best health advice for those who want to continue injecting.

If we follow the same line as with unmarried men and women who want protection against pregnancy, then we will be willing to supply not only clean needles, but also bleach for sterilising.

Some say that we are then being inconsistent about condoms in schools. I think there is a huge difference between agreeing to make condoms available to adults wishing to reduce the risk of pregnancy or HIV, and promoting such methods to children or young teenagers.

We agree that adults, by definition, are of an age and maturity to form their own judgements and to make their own choices. In contrast, we accept that young teenagers have a developing maturity which is particularly susceptible to influence and pressure. For good reason, there is widespread concern that giving out free condoms in schools will send a powerful message that pupils are expected to have sex at a young age. There are enough pressures on young people to say yes to sex. Why add to them?

We are all involved in 'grey' areas

Christians are divided on these issues. All I am saying is that we need to be consistent and compassionate. All would agree that needle exchange is not ideal.

The fact is that in many situations, we are faced with limited choices, each one of which will mean thinking through some important principle. The choice to do nothing is no way out because it breaks another principle, which is our duty to respond to human need.

We are being dishonest with ourselves if we think we can avoid these dilemmas, these shades of grey, and live in a world of black and white decisions. Jesus faced dilemmas in his own day: for example, over the issue of whether it was right to heal people on the Sabbath, or whether it was right to condemn a woman who had committed adultery.

All the options may feel wrong

In reality, from time to time we all have to choose options we do not like very much, when something is disturbingly wrong with every option. The reason for this is that we live in a fallen world. Take the example of a child we think may be at slight risk of sexual abuse. We are caught between the desire to protect the child and the need of that child for parents, knowing how difficult short-term fostering can be and the dangers present in many children's homes.

Another example is the response of the United Nations in the past to Bosnia and Iraq or more recently in the War Against Terror. In each case, the autonomy of the sovereign state, and the call to live at peace with one another, is balanced against the need to protect lives, to fight aggression, or to prevent mass genocide. In every situation we need to pray for wisdom and humility, recognising that whatever we decide is the best, there will be others who might take a different line.

Prostitution makes us think

We face the same complex issues when talking with commercial sex workers. As we have seen, there is a strong link between commercial sex and drug abuse. In some cities over half of all sex workers are injecting drugs. Many sell their bodies for sex because it is the only way they can generate enough money to feed a drug habit. Their pimps may be paying them in kind with drugs, food and accommodation.

We can offer those on the street a way out through drug rehabilitation programmes and helping them find new housing and jobs, but many will choose to remain. If they do, then I believe we have the same obligations to teach them to protect their own health and the health of others as we have to educate any other members of our community.

Missionaries make difficult choices

Once we become deeply involved in the community we find very difficult situations to which there are no right answers: every choice open to us presents further difficulties. Missionaries overseas have always encountered these situations and still do so today.

For example, I was talking to someone recently who had been working as a missionary in Thailand. Young girls cross the border from neighbouring countries to work in the cities as prostitutes. Sending a daughter to the big city to work in the bars and sell her body can be as much a natural way of life in some countries as sending children to university is in the UK. Many young girls are expected to work this way and to support their families back home, returning after a few years to settle down and marry. In addition, in some places large numbers of children as young as eight are being sold as sex slaves to brothel owners in neighbouring countries.

The problem now is that many of these sex workers have

become infected with HIV. Those from neighbouring countries cannot return home because they have heard reports that those returning are tested for HIV at the border and any found to be infected have been led away in the past to be shot or injected with cyanide. The girls are effectively owned by brothel keepers in the city and cannot run away. If picked up they would be deported anyway, as they are often there illegally.

Life-and-death choices

A number of churches have programmes reaching out to such girls, many of whom are becoming ill. Some of the girls have formed close friendships with people in the church – the only friends they have – and have become believers. However, it is hard for them to stop being prostitutes for fear of violence or death at the hands of their masters.

The church is faced with a choice: do we encourage them to stop because their work is against God's law? If they do stop, the church cannot risk sending them back across the border. Does it then hide a growing number of illegal immigrants? Where do you hide them anyway, as they are bound to be discovered by the intricate communication network between brothel dealers in the city? If they are taken deep into the country, it is still likely that they will be found eventually. The church will have broken the law and will be in big trouble.

I have been told that at least one church has come to the conclusion that the girls will have to stay where they are for their own safety. They are effectively slaves owned by the brothels since they cannot escape. Therefore, most if not all of the moral responsibility for what they are doing lies with those who are threatening to kill them or to beat them if they do not obey. These are very difficult areas, but they are just the sorts of issues that face us once we move out of our comfortable Christian ghettoes and get involved in what life is like for the rest of the world.

Befriending or confronting?

So then, we need to define our goals: are we wanting to befriend and help people to continue more safely or do we want to confront and offer a way out? There can be a middle way, which is to provide both approaches in the same team or person, but the way you go about it is critically important. You cannot drive into a residential area week after week and meet drug users with disapproving comments, and then expect to build friendships and become a source of advice.

In any case, HIV spread among drug users means we need to have a big rethink about drug rehabilitation. People like Jackie Pullinger in Hong Kong have caught the imagination of millions of Christians with wonderful accounts of how God has delivered drug users from addiction – usually from heroin use. The only treatment used is prayer and friendship. They have found no need for medically supervised withdrawal, and they see a very high success rate.

Similar programmes have grown rapidly all over the world. They work in part by using those who have been through the programme themselves to reach, help and support others.

Unfortunately, while in the past such miracles of new life could sustain a growing work, now many of those who have been through such programmes are found to be HIV-infected. Indeed, many may be ill or dying before their first contact with members of the church.

Drug rehabilitation goals changed by AIDS

We need to redefine our aims. If a drug user is going to die in the next six months with AIDS, is there the same point in weaning him or her off drugs? It is true, however, that if a person continues injecting with shared equipment, then he may be adding further damage to the immune system, and may die more quickly.

Is the aim to enable the person to have a good quality of life and to die well, or is the aim to provide a long-term stable and secure future?

In summary, then, community prevention is a vitally important area for the church to be involved in, but it often raises far greater ethical questions than AIDS education in the classroom does. The basic principle of unconditional love leads us to offer help in a broader way than we might initially feel comfortable with. We need to have a clear moral framework ourselves for our own lives, understanding God's standards and his design for living, but we may need to be prepared to offer a modified approach to prevention when helping those who do not share our values.

We want people to be fully aware of health risks so they can make their own choices. We want to encourage people to avoid HIV risks completely as far as possible, with latex rubber, clean needles or bleach as partial protection, rather than just carry on as before. Part of teaching people the truth about AIDS is teaching them how to reduce risks. While Christians may then be accused of simply teaching people to 'sin safely', we also have to recognise the need to save lives. The key is how advice is given, placing risk reduction in the context of relationships, commitment and empowering people to make their own choices about saying no, taking a long-term view and thinking through what is important to them.

CHAPTER FOURTEEN

SPECIAL ISSUES IN POORER NATIONS

In developing countries, like Uganda, Burundi, Rwanda, Nigeria, Sudan, Tanzania and India, there are many complex issues and questions to face. It is not just a question of setting up community care programmes or reaching young people in schools.

For example, testing becomes vitally important in towns or villages where large numbers of adults may carry HIV. When people realise how many of their friends are infected, they may have one of two reactions. Some may become fatalistic, reckoning they may already be infected so not bothering to take precautions. Others may become very worried, wanting urgently to get hold of a test for themselves and their partners.

Pre-marriage testing – a social time bomb

Any church leader involved in pre-marriage counselling in such a situation will find couples wanting to be tested. In many countries, access to testing is still difficult, with long travel to a testing centre, long delays, lost results and sometimes even doubt as to whether the result you have been given is really yours, or whether the result is accurate.

A church mission could order some of the newer testing kits which produce a result in a few minutes from a sample of blood or saliva, without using costly laboratory equipment. Prices are falling and it is likely that soon instant saliva testing kits will be available costing less than £5 each. The church may also be able to link with the WHO 3 by 5 programme, which is making free testing and anti-viral treatment far more widely available. Testing should only be carried out after careful counselling, for reasons which will become apparent below. It is also important to know the limits of accuracy of these tests. Positive results may need confirmation to rule out a false positive result (see Chapter 5).

Some church leaders in high-incidence countries are now insisting on pre-marriage testing before they will conduct a ceremony. This seems to me too drastic and to go beyond what Scripture demands. It is one thing to discuss carefully the risks of entering a union without testing where one or other may have been at risk, and even to strongly encourage testing, but quite another matter to insist on tests for all. Having said that, one does hope that all those about to embark on a lifetime of commitment to someone they dearly love will want to protect their future husband or wife and not unwittingly kill them. Testing is a very important part of pre-marriage preparation where there have been risks in the past.

Married couples want tests too

Once testing becomes available, huge problems can emerge. Married couples also want to be tested. A wife may be worried about the safety of having sex with her husband, since she is aware he has been unfaithful to her or that he had many partners before they married.

She may be even more worried when she hears that, in one African country at least, one in three of the women who are now dying with AIDS were virgins before they got married and have always been faithful, yet were infected by their husbands.

When testing of married couples begins, it is sometimes found that both are already infected. At least in this situation there is no risk of endangering the other person's life, although children born to the couple may turn out to be infected. The risk of babies being born with HIV can be reduced very significantly by a short course of anti-viral medication given at the right stage of pregnancy (30% to around 8%).

For many couples, it will be found that both partners are free of infection, but other couples will emerge where only one partner is infected. How are such situations going to be handled? Before you know where you are, a small testing programme involving fifty couples could have completely destroyed the marriages of ten of them, with partners walking out or being rejected or insisting on divorce.

So you can see that many churches and Christian groups in developing countries are sitting on a social time bomb which could be triggered by indiscriminate testing. Yet access to testing is vital to help contain spread, and also to identify those who can then hopefully receive treatment.

Counselling before and after testing

Part of the answer is to provide careful counselling to people before offering a test, and afterwards, irrespective of the result. Where one partner is infected, the advice will be to use condoms carefully every single time, recognising that there will be a small risk of an accident (see Chapter 6). Condom quality can vary in different countries and few people realise that latex rubber, as a naturally occurring substance, tends to weaken with time, so the expiry date on the packet is very important. In a country with a hot climate, condoms can deteriorate quite rapidly in storage.

There is some debate about appropriate advice to people where both partners are infected. It has been suggested that since the virus mutates rapidly inside each person, and since each time two people have sex there is a chance of a fresh inoculation, it is possible that those continuing to have unprotected sex may die more quickly. However, there is no real evidence to support this suggestion at present. It is certainly true that if other sex diseases are passed on, then the combined effect of these on someone whose immune system is already weakened could be great.

Engaged couples, or those at the start of a relationship, may be faced with very difficult and traumatic questions about their future if one tests negative and the other is infected.

Condom promotion in Africa

Africa has been targeted, as has much of the rest of the world, with the condom message, which varies in expression and emphasis from country to country. I have already challenged assumptions about condoms and safe sex in Chapter 6.

However, even if you believe condoms to be 100% reliable, there are some serious problems to be considered in developing countries: cost, distribution and culture. It is sobering to realise that, as we have seen, many African nations only have less than five to ten dollars to spend on total health care for each person per year. This has to cover hospital care, clinic treatment, vaccination programmes, provision of glasses and dentistry.

The cost of supplying condoms could wipe out the health service

The entire health budget for a person would be used up in less than three months – just in the cost of providing condoms. A couple of years ago, an international exporter faxed ACET's London offices, offering us 140 million condoms at a few pence each, delivered free to any African port. The trouble was that even if we had had £10 million, the entire consignment would have lasted the continent just one night, or at most two or three – and then what would we do?

The cost of rubberising all sex in Africa would be at least $250 million a year – more than the World Health programme spent on AIDS for the whole world in the mid-1990s.

It is true that budgets have greatly increased, as wealthy nations have finally begun to recognise the AIDS catastrophe in poorer nations as a global issue. But it is still the case that the international community has failed to grasp the magnitude of the problem of a condom-based prevention programme. Bukino Faso, for example, has an illiteracy rate of up to 60% with extremely poor and vulnerable rural communities. Are we really expecting high-tech condoms to be used correctly and carefully every time all adults have sex until the day they die? The naivety, cultural ignorance and arrogance of many health planners in wealthy nations is truly astonishing.

Distribution can be difficult

The distribution difficulties are vast. Let us assume for a moment that the funds are available. We still have a problem. If you give out supplies free, experience has shown with other kinds of programmes that those supplies can quickly disappear – often bought up quickly by traders. Supplies are hard to get hold of, and as the price rises, a limited supply becomes available again in the markets.

To get over this problem, another approach has been used, called 'social marketing'. This has been tried in Congo. With this approach, condoms are not given away, but are made available to wholesalers and retail outlets at low cost for them to sell at reasonable profit.

Condoms are then always in the shops and markets, but at a low price. This approach can work well in towns and cities, but it is harder to make it work so well in rural areas.

A further hurdle to overcome is perhaps the most important of all. Even if condoms are available throughout a country at low cost, people may still choose not to use them. We are assuming that this is despite a comprehensive health campaign operating at every level.

Condoms are a Western 'hi-tech' solution

Many African people live very simply. If you visit homes up country, you may find that the only factory-made items in the hut are a plastic petrol container being used as a water carrier, and a plastic washing-up bowl. There might be in addition one or two pots and pans and a few utensils. There may be a small battery-operated radio, but possibly not.

In comparison, a condom is real hi-tech: here is a very sophisticated item, which is made to precision standard, yet is thrown away after each use. It requires great care in how it is put on and how it is removed, and requires overcoming possible cultural embarrassments or religious objections in order to talk about its use, or even to produce it. They need to be supplied regularly to places where nothing else is supplied, and where there may be a twenty-five-mile walk to the nearest clinic.

So then, condoms can provide excellent protection if used carefully every time, but can only be part of the answer to the explosive African AIDS epidemic. We have to look at other solutions as well (see later), of which the most important are 'faithfulness and abstinence', to use the words of the World Health Organisation.

'Condom dumping' by the West can be resented

The perceived obsession of the West with condoms has caused much ill feeling in Africa. When I have travelled there, or taken part in radio phone-in programmes across Africa organised by the BBC World Service, it is clear that a number of people are very sensitive. First, they may feel they are being blamed for AIDS, since people say it came from Africa and it is their fault.

They are also often very sensitive to 'Western imperialistic' suggestions that there are 'far too many people in Africa', and that over-population is the reason for famine.

Population politics and AIDS

They are especially sensitive to people who seem to have population control as a hidden agenda in AIDS-control programmes. Many are deeply suspicious and angry when they find that Western nations are willing to pump millions into condom distribution, while their own governments are struggling to provide clean water or adequate food.

I am not saying that population control programmes are necessarily inappropriate or a waste of time. On the contrary, anyone who has seen a graph of the world population will realise that current rates of growth are likely to create major problems in some developing countries. Population growth is an important issue.

It is also true that the more people there are in the world, the more conditions are set for new epidemics and plagues to evolve. As we have seen, each person represents a new chance for a dangerous new mutation to emerge. The next few decades will undoubtedly see further new epidemics: we can only hope that they will turn out to be as uninfectious as HIV, and less harmful. If another lethal virus were to emerge, spread, say, through sneezing, and was rapidly lethal, it would pose the greatest threat ever seen to the future of humankind.

In the original 1987 edition of this book I warned of the threat of these kinds of new mutant viruses. The SARS outbreak in China in 2003 was no surprise. Expect more to come.

It is ironic that at a time when a killer plague such as AIDS is out of control, the world population should also be spiralling upwards. Perhaps that is why I have heard people dare to say that they think AIDS is a good thing – to keep the population down.

When the two effects combine together, as in much of Central and Southern Africa, the end result is that population growth is slowed, while the age distribution becomes grossly distorted. You find that the middle-age group has been decimated. The 20- to 40-year-olds, on whom the future of the whole nation depends, are in short supply.

People often use Uganda as an example because it is the most open in discussing AIDS. However, many other countries in Africa have been at least as badly affected. Recent reports suggest similar infection rates as far south as Zimbabwe.

There is a strong link between population control politics

and AIDS prevention programmes. You must remember that African nations are largely dependent on massive foreign government handouts for AIDS programmes. In Uganda, such funding formed a major part of the economy in the mid-1990s, before a period of peaceful rapid economic growth, together with other development programmes. Any visitor to Uganda ten years ago used to notice that many of the vehicles driving round Kampala were owned and run by relief agencies.

Rich pipers call the tune

Attending a meeting of the World Health Organisation in Geneva, I had rather a shock. As an international AIDS agency, ACET International had official observer status and could take part in debates. Round the massive circle of desks and microphones a large number of countries were represented, each with four or five delegates. The scene was just like one of the United Nations meetings you see on the news. There was one big difference. Almost every delegate was white.

Most developed nations were there, but only two African nations were represented, and two from Asia. To be there, and to have a vote, your country needed to be a donor to the World Health Organisation AIDS budget. This meant, of course, that the only countries deciding world policy were the industrialised nations. Because Africa and the Far East would not otherwise have been represented at all, WHO had agreed that each continent could appoint two representatives for free.

The results were striking. After a long discussion by nations like Germany, the UK and the USA, there was a plea for realism by an African delegate. He was listened to respectfully, but the points he made were lost among the many others present. No wonder international aid for AIDS is so often seen as imperialistic.

Many Western donor nations have been reluctant to give via WHO or UNAIDS or UNDP or UNICEF or the Global Fund (malaria, TB, AIDS), preferring to give handouts direct to individual countries. In many cases this means even more nation-to-nation control, which suits the donor well. We have already seen how many countries have been reduced almost to economic servitude by the crippling burden of foreign debt.

Why condom programmes look good

One big advantage of condom programmes is that Western executives thousands of miles away, with no understanding of African tribal life, can then be dazzled by graphs showing millions of condoms distributed or bought each month. They can see data showing how sales are boosted by advertising campaigns and radio broadcasts. This helps keep donor nations happy, knowing that their 'prevention campaigns' have reached millions of people.

So condoms are not necessarily the easy answer you might think when it comes to Africa, although their use may be measurable and attractive to fund.

Despite all I have said, however, we must recognise the importance of condoms in HIV prevention directly, and also indirectly, by reducing other sex diseases which help transmission. Finally, at a time of great unsustainable population growth, condoms also enable families and nations to control fertility.

Testing is a vital part of the answer too, while encouraging people to be celibate or faithful. The treatment of other sexually transmitted diseases is also important. Testing and encouraging no-risk lifestyles do not pose any difficulties for church missions, but treating sexually transmitted diseases can raise a few Christian eyebrows.

We must treat other sex diseases

As we have seen, one reason why heterosexual HIV has spread so fast in some countries may be because facilities for treatment of other sexually transmitted diseases are poor, increasing the risk of transmission.

One of the most effective ways to reduce HIV spread in developing nations is to set up a large number of clinics to treat these other infections. For many churches this is less attractive than, say, suggesting people reduce their number of partners or abstain. Yet this is something we also need to think about.

Mission hospitals have always treated sex diseases as a normal part of overall community health care, but here we are talking about rapidly expanding the number of services as a deliberate anti-HIV strategy. Are Christian supporters in countries like the UK or the USA or Australia going to be willing to fund such work? Will they see it as simply encouraging promiscuity – yet another example of helping people 'sin safely'?

Sex disease clinics in Christian missions

Setting up a successful service to treat sexually transmitted diseases means providing a walk-in, friendly environment where people feel very comfortable to explain what they have been up to and with whom.

If there is the faintest whiff of moralising, then experience shows that people may stay away, defeating the purpose of encouraging them to come forward for treatment. This atmosphere may be difficult for many Christian agencies to provide.

Different messages for different countries?

In all our community prevention we need to take great care to find the right message for each section of our society, each tribe, each ethnic group or each country because even within each country there can be unique problems. For example, in one African nation, ACET has worked with a particular tribe which had an elaborate circumcision rite using a communal knife and likely to spread HIV. Radio campaigns and leaflets in tribal languages were useless in changing the practice.

The answer was to build a relationship of trust and respect with the village chief. When the delicate discussions were over, the chief called the village together and announced that the ritual would now be modified so that it was safe. The process took some time, but the practice has stopped in that village at least. The person who carried out the negotiations was a national of that country.

In another area there has been concern about a tradition that the brother of a dead man should have sex with or marry his widow. If the man died of AIDS, it is likely that the wife will pass on HIV to the dead man's brother.

In some parts of Thailand, it is common for teenage boys to be sent into brothels as part of an initiation ceremony into manhood. It is also socially accepted – or even expected – that adult men will have sex regularly with commercial sex workers. Even with extensive government campaigns and the efforts of many other agencies, these deeply rooted social practices may require a generation to change completely.

In each locality the way of life needs to be respected, understood and incorporated into every aspect of prevention.

In Eastern and Central Europe, AIDS campaigns are swimming against a powerful tide of Western permissive culture, which is flooding into former Eastern bloc countries at an alarming rate. Ever since the collapse of communism in many countries, there has been an insatiable demand for pornography and sexual freedom. While many Western nations are just beginning to question the benefits of liberated sex in the light of marital breakdown, increasing juvenile delinquency and AIDS, many East and Central European countries are enjoying the first tastes of previously forbidden fruit. Russia is also affected by multiple social challenges, with high addiction to drugs and alcohol and major collapse of marriage and family life.

In addition, opened frontiers and mass migrations due to economic chaos and civil unrest have accelerated the spread of sex diseases such as HIV. These countries have also become major corridors for illegal drugs passing from East to West. Most early AIDS cases in countries like Romania were caused through infected blood or contaminated medical treatments, but we are now seeing rapid spread among adults. Changing medical practice as a result of intensive training of health care workers has been far easier than changing the sexual behaviour of a whole country.

Faith – the ultimate weapon against HIV?

Whether we try to prevent HIV with condom distribution, or by encouraging testing, celibacy and monogamy, we are faced with a problem: we know that education encouraging these things will have a limited effect. The reason is that most people do not want to change. Therefore the only secular motivation we can possibly provide is fear.

I have often heard AIDS educators say that we must not give a negative message based on fear, because it will be counterproductive. (Incidentally, that statement is itself a similar negative.) However, the fact is that all successful health promotion works by creating anxiety about what could happen if you ignore the message.

The faith motivation is totally different and ultimately much more powerful, as social psychologists are beginning to recognise. Faith creates hope and new expectations about behaviour and gives people purpose, self-worth and meaning. Christians also believe that faith in Jesus Christ releases God's power in our lives, enabling us to change.

I will never forget meeting the Minister of Health of an African nation ravaged by AIDS, who told us that, although he himself was an atheist, he particularly welcomed the involvement of the church in fighting AIDS. He told us the reason was that we could give people hope so they could bear to hear a painful message, and we could also give people the power to change. Of course it is not us, but we can be the route by which people discover the power of God in their own lives.

Before the communist regime fell in Hungary, secret approaches were made by the communist leaders to a friend of mine, who was heading up an evangelical organisation based in the UK. His work was to smuggle Bibles and other items for persecuted Christians behind the iron curtain.

The authorities asked to meet him because they needed help in dealing with a rapidly worsening drugs problem. They knew that those finding faith often came off drugs rapidly and permanently. A wonderful, low-cost, 'infectious' weapon against drugs was too good to turn down. Instead of threatening him with arrest as before, they unofficially invited him to bring others in. The gospel was proclaimed and programmes were set up. They too had seen the power of faith. Likewise today, in former Eastern bloc countries such as the Czech Republic and Slovakia, there is a great openness to educators who are motivated by Christian values.

As Christians, we can have confidence in who we are and what we stand for. We have an answer which we feel is *the* answer. We can offer sensitive, practical approaches to prevention, based on medical facts. We can also seek to influence behaviour through the rapid spread of faith in the world today. An important part of the answer to AIDS is for the church, as the most powerful organisation in the world, to combine efforts with governments and communities to help save people from themselves.

We now need to turn to an urgent question which faces every health care worker in developing countries, especially where there is a high incidence of HIV. This issue is seen vividly in the letters missionaries send home to their supporters. How can we help prevent AIDS deaths among doctors and nurses?

Missionaries die of AIDS too

I am often asked for advice by those about to be sent overseas by missionary societies. What is the risk of occupational infection?

There has been increasing concern for the health of those giving health care to others; not just from such hazards as multi-drug-resistant malaria, but also from HIV. The main areas of concern are blood transfusions and contaminated equipment if the person is needing care, or medical accidents if the person is caring for others.

So what are the risks, and how can we avoid or reduce them? Fortunately, the risk of infection from a single accident such as a needle jab is known to be very small – even if the person is carrying the virus. Numerous studies from different countries, following up people who have jabbed themselves with needles, or otherwise injured themselves while giving care, have shown that there is around a 1 in 200 chance of transmission from a single accident. This is much lower than for hepatitis B, which carries up to a 1 in 3 chance of transmission.

However, for someone working day in and day out as a surgeon or midwife, for example, in areas of highest incidence, the cumulative risk soon begins to mount.

Exposure to HIV is common

Even assuming your hospital has enough pairs of gloves for you to operate with a good quality pair each time, the chances are that you may tear gloves during long operations several times a week. You hope you do not cut your finger at the same time, but it happens.

In many places, doctors testing patients on their wards using reliable testing methods have found that around half of their patients are HIV-infected. The percentage may be lower for surgical than for medical cases. Let us assume that a busy general surgeon tears one or two gloves each week and that once every month he cuts himself, or spray from a cut artery spurts into his eyes, or there is some other blood contamination of a wound. Let us assume that only one in four of his surgical patients are HIV-infected (it could be higher). A quarter of the time, on average, the blood could be from an infected patient.

Surgeons are working under tremendous pressures. Every time they begin an operation they know that one careless move or unexpected problem could mean HIV infection, with terrible consequences, not only for them, but also for the health of their husbands or wives, for the future of their marriages and for their families.

How big is the risk for surgeons?

The surgeon in our example will be exposed potentially to HIV around three times a year. Each time is like a pull on a fruit machine with 200 possible combinations. How long before you hit the fatal result? The average surgeon working in such an environment will be infected in sixty-six years, but it could happen in the first three months.

To put it another way: if a medical organisation or missionary society is supporting fifty surgeons in high-incidence countries, then it is possible that every two or three years perhaps one or two more of the team might become infected. This has colossal implications for those concerned, their families, for churches supporting them, and for the organisations.

We may debate about exact percentages, but the risk must be acknowledged. So much depends on local infection levels, the quality of gloves, operating lights and other equipment, the skill of the surgeon and the nature of his work. Some operations are far more likely to expose a surgeon to injury than others. Some surgeons in Rwanda did their own calculations based on their own practice. They estimated that one in four of them would become infected after thirty years' operating in their town, which had a seroprevalence of more than 20%.

Unless those sent out are tested regularly, we could have a

situation arising where a significant number have become infected before anyone realises, because of the delay between the time of any accident and the development of symptoms.

A medical organisation may miss an increasing number of future tragedies by just hoping for the best. However, people might argue that once you have taken reasonable precautions, all you can do is trust God for protection and there is therefore little point in regular monitoring of infection. Even if that is so, we need to think now about our responsibility to care for those with occupational infection who may be unable to carry on working as surgeons in low-incidence wealthy countries, where the risks of cross-infection are considered unacceptable. These are big issues.

Reducing the risks to surgeons

There are a number of simple steps that can be taken to reduce risks in surgery. For example, always sew away from your other hand rather than towards it; use blunt needles for sewing fascia or skin; consider eye goggles in operations where your experience is that you often get sprayed (risk of infection can range from 1 in 10,000 to as high as 1 in 200); double check gloves before reusing them; and be extra careful about being jabbed by splinters of bone or other sharp objects. Cover minor skin abrasions on the hands or arms with a waterproof plaster for further protection. Following all the above may reduce exposure by three or four times.

Perhaps, if careful measures are taken, our group of fifty surgeons will only see one colleague infected every three to five years on average. These are all guesses and will depend on local factors, including the stage of illness of the patients, the nature of the operations and the skill of the surgeon. As we have seen, infectiousness increases as AIDS develops.

Risks to health workers can be significantly reduced further by giving them anti-retroviral therapy for a short period following accidental exposure. First reports suggest that this may reduce infection rates by up to 80%. Risk depends on the level of virus in the patient (higher as the illness becomes more severe). A normal course is four weeks, with two or three different drugs. Whether anti-viral therapy is available or not, the wound should be encouraged to bleed immediately after the incident.

Testing all patients before surgery may not be helpful, since the test will miss those infected less than twelve weeks before (which will be a lot of people in countries where HIV is spreading fast). If funds are scarce, many surgeons may prefer the luxury of a new pair of gloves for each operation.

Midwives are in the frontline too

Nurses are also very much at risk in certain situations, particularly midwifery. Some time ago, I visited a hospital in one African country where a number of midwives had died from AIDS. The death toll seemed to be far higher than in nurses from other parts of the hospital, suggesting that many had been infected through delivering babies. We will never be certain, since there were no testing facilities.

The difficulty for midwives is that their exposure to blood can be even greater than in the operating theatre. If labour is difficult, or if a piece of the placenta is left inside the womb, the midwife may need to have not only her hand and wrist inside the mother, but also much of her forearm. No glove covers that much, although waterproof arm coverings, sleeves and gloves have been described. Midwives can finish a delivery with arms completely soaked in blood. Unfortunately, in many hospitals across Africa and Asia there are still not enough gloves for midwives, so many deliveries are being assisted without glove protection. Although HIV cannot pass through intact skin, there may be slight cuts or abrasions on the hands, or less commonly on the arms, which can be an entry point for the virus.

Therefore, if you have friends working as doctors or nurses in high-incidence countries, pray for their protection. There have always been risks to the health of those serving in the neediest situations. Countless Christian doctors and nurses have willingly laid down their lives to bring the gospel to places where Jesus has never been known. Many have died in service, often of the very diseases they spent most of their lives treating.

Ten ways to reduce risks in medical and nursing practice with limited resources:

1. Sterilise cleaned equipment after each treatment. Use autoclaves, boiling, 70% alcohol or a freshly prepared one-in-ten bleach solution in water.
2. Use undamaged latex gloves for operating or midwifery.
3. Use eye shields if spray is likely in theatre.
4. Use blood transfusions sparingly.
5. Get hold of instant HIV testing kits if you have no laboratory equipment – and use sparingly when needed to help save lives.
6. Cover cuts on hands and forearms with waterproof plasters.
7. Sew away from, not towards, your other hand, using blunt needles where practicable.
8. *Never* resheath needles, and dispose of used needles carefully – or keep in secure safe container until washed and sterilised.
9. Use gloves for any procedure where extensive contact of skin with secretions is likely, including handling laboratory specimens. The threshold for using gloves will depend on availability.
10. Ensure good standards of general hygiene, with spillages carefully cleaned up.

. . . and pray.

CHAPTER FIFTEEN

GOOD PRACTICE IN HIV/AIDS PROJECTS

by Mark Forshaw
(Africa Inland Mission)

The church is playing a leading role in many nations, saving lives, caring for those affected, fighting discrimination, prejudice and injustice, fufilling Jesus' command to be salt and light, for the glory of God and for the extension of his kingdom. Here are some stories to encourage you, and some lessons from a number of inspiring projects in different countries, which can easily be adapted to your own situation.

Every one of these stories has a small beginning – perhaps just one individual, touched by the love of God, and deeply affected by what AIDS is doing to the world. These are people who felt they *had* to do something, and who began, usually, with almost nothing. Step by step they have followed God's calling, in fellowship with others, and have learned from those around them as they went. In many cases the road was long and hard, because there were few models for such programmes at the time. But now the programmes they began are an inspiration and practical encouragement to us, and can help speed us on our own journeys. Building capacity is vital.

Start with what you have. It costs nothing to be kind, to care, to go and visit the sick, to look out for orphaned children, to speak to young people you know about AIDS. Make HIV issues a natural part of all your church or organisation does. If every community did that, we would see a global people movement and we would be well on our way to defeating AIDS altogether.

But we must also think on a much larger scale. In many hard-hit nations there is an acute shortage of community AIDS projects which are well run, can prove that they deliver quality services, have a strong track record, are good at telling their stories, are well networked, and are of sufficient size to be visible on the radar screens of major international donors, whose country-based representatives are often greatly frustrated and puzzled as to how they can spend their funds wisely and quickly, avoiding corruption, inefficiency, incompetence and scandal.

This is a major challenge to thousands of Christian agencies who have struggled for many years, depending on God for every penny, unable often to think about the bigger picture, and with little hope that things could be different, yet making a real difference and seeing many answered prayers. When it comes to community projects, 'small is beautiful'. Growth can of course bring its own pressures. Missions built on faith and absolute reliance on God's daily provision, run mainly by volunteers, can sometimes find their values attacked, their Christian basis questioned and their priorities subverted. The key is clarity about mission, purpose and calling – backed by outstanding quality in all we do.

We need to hear God very clearly, be obedient to what he is saying and be faithful in everything. As Hudson Taylor, the great missionary to China, once said: 'God's work done in God's way will never lack God's supply.' But now is a season of great opportunity and open doors. Don't struggle on alone. Link up with those around you doing similar things. Together we can be a great force for change.

Here are sixteen different case studies from recent years. Life is too short to reinvent wheels. Lessons over two decades can help us all to move ahead rapidly and confidently now. You will also find vitally important practical help in the Appendices at the end of this book.

Case study 1: Providing care in Zimbabwe

Dr Geoff Foster, a paediatric doctor in Zimbabwe, founded FACT (Family AIDS Caring Trust) in Mutare, Zimbabwe. In 1988 he saw the pressing need to mobilise the local community to provide care, and churches were asked to suggest individuals willing to be trained to provide care to families and neighbours in their communities. FACT home care programmes are co-ordinated by experienced health workers who are responsible for local teams. Each team is headed by a volunteer, managing other local church volunteers, who provide the actual care to those in need in their areas.

The training of volunteers consists of basic counselling and care skills; bathing and personal hygiene, washing clothes and bed linen, house cleaning, provision of appropriate food and the treatment and dressing of minor wounds. While the main aim is to help those infected with HIV, they are trained to care for all who are chronically ill or dying, maybe from TB, diabetes or simply from old age. When health care of any kind is hard to find, specialist teams inevitably become involved in wider problems.

Volunteers recognise that needs are not purely physical, but also emotional and spiritual, and the formation of serving relationships is the basis for good practical care and supportive counselling.

The majority of those visited are living with members of their families and the role of the volunteers is also to support the family. They offer advice on ways to deal with different infections common to HIV and how to access services available. They also offer emotional and spiritual support to the family carers.

Through these relatively low-skill and low-cost teams a larger number of people are able to receive help within the traditional family and community. Volunteers also contribute to data collection and help with decision-making and planning. Their help is invaluable, because they are involved with the people who are closest to those who need help.

Lessons on providing care

- Community based care reaches more people
- People with AIDS often prefer to be cared for in their own homes
- Be prepared to care for those with other illnesses, not only those living with HIV/AIDS
- Families, friends, communities and volunteers are a resource for care
- Communities must own the work and so must be consulted from the beginning and throughout the life of the programme
- Care in the community gives opportunities to offer support and counselling which can help people to learn and make responsible decisions
- Care programmes should be fully integrated with prevention and counselling work
- Community-based care is more often cheaper than hospital-based care
- Care should be holistic: physical, emotional, social and spiritual
- Effective care in the community is best linked to other services and works in partnership with them (eg local hospitals)
- Effective communication between non-government organisations, community-based care and medical institutions can reduce duplication of services and maximise care of patients
- Communities have many resources within them that can be drawn upon

Lessons on using volunteers

- Selection criteria must be established at the start
- Relevant training is important, both at the start and throughout the programme

- Monitoring and support of volunteers must be present throughout the life of the programme
- Involve volunteers in decision-making and planning
- Make clear to volunteers what is expected of them and when they should refer to paid staff

Case study 2: Prevention programme by ACET Uganda

ACET Uganda, under the present leadership of David Kabiswa, has developed effective resources now used across Africa and even further afield, in India. Like his fellow Ugandan team members, David could not stand by and watch the vulnerable, such as school children, women and street children, become increasingly at risk of infection. Starting in 1990, the ACET Uganda team has developed a three-pronged approach to communication to assist effective and sustainable behaviour change.

First, there is the provision of information, designed to meet individual and local needs. The aim is to lay a foundation for understanding the medical, social, economic, cultural and spiritual issues related to HIV/AIDS. But facts alone will rarely change behaviour.

So secondly, the team attempt to identify high-risk behaviour and to help people make important lifestyle choices based on understanding the options and consequences of particular behavioural practices.

Finally, having been shown the choices, the individual is then encouraged to think through the options. The idea is to reduce their vulnerability to infection, to enable long-term fulfilling relationships, to help them take personal responsibility for their behaviour, to have confidence to make and live by their own decisions, and to respect the worth of others.

As ACET Uganda developed its prevention work, it soon became apparent that HIV/AIDS could not be dealt with in isolation. It was also necessary to deal with general sex education and to encourage the development of relationships through individuals' sense of self-worth and respect for others.

With increased urbanisation, people are facing new economic and social pressures, while traditional social structures are breaking down. Development of life skills, in particular by those most vulnerable, such as young people and women, can equip people to respond more positively to the challenges that they face in life.

ACET Uganda uses a number of interactive teaching methods to provoke people to think and discuss issues that affect them, assisting them to analyse situations they will face and what their response will be. The role of the education team is to develop peer-group thinking that will help reinforce and sustain positive and healthy behaviour.

The methods used include focus group discussions, debates, films and videos, questionnaires and short talks dealing with contemporary issues.

Lessons learned about prevention

- The issue is not primarily raising awareness, but assisting personal and community behaviour change
- There is a need to pay attention to vulnerable groups, in particular women and young people, and to research their needs
- Use varied educational techniques, and tailor education and training techniques to meet the needs of different groups
- Respect and listen to the views of others
- Encourage co-operation, not competitive learning
- Recognise the importance of peer education
- Use interactive methods of learning
- Allow time for reflection
- Make sure your message is clear
- Spend time building relationships first
- Be prepared and equipped to offer counselling to groups and individuals
- Train others to assist in the process

Case study 3: Community mobilisation, Chikankata Hospital, Zambia

The Salvation Army hospital at Chikankata describes its work of community counselling as 'an activity . . . directed towards the genuine transfer of responsibility for AIDS prevention from health personnel and other concerned "helpers" to individuals, families and perhaps most importantly communities'. Such a community-wide interactive approach is essential in communities with high rates of HIV infection. The task of prevention is very great and communities must own the desire to change. Instruction alone is not enough. They need education, information and training from people they respect. The church must mobilise the community.

With the advent of the HIV/AIDS epidemic in southern Zambia, the initial response of Chikankata Hospital was to develop designated AIDS wards and comprehensive community and prevention services. However, it soon became apparent that there were too many people for the in-patient services to handle, and that many of the needs should and could be met by care services based in the community. In 1987 a home-based care programme linked to hospital diagnosis, counselling, education and treatment was established.

The programme allowed people to be cared for in their own homes, and created opportunities to train families in the care of people living with HIV/AIDS. Furthermore, it gives opportunity to discuss HIV/AIDS education and prevention with those in the wider community. The home-based teams are multidisciplinary and include community nurses, nutritionists, and counsellors.

The care programme at Chikankata soon developed into a comprehensive HIV/AIDS programme including in-hospital counselling, AIDS education in schools, child support programmes and technical assistance programmes for other organisations. Chikankata has developed a diverse but integrated approach to supporting the local community, and programmes are tailored to meet the needs of different sections of the community.

These programmes belong to the community that benefits from the services, not to the aspirations of a non-government organisation or health care institution. The word 'community' does not necessarily mean a geographical area, but rather indicates that the local people own the programme. This link between home care, prevention and general community development would not have been so readily achieved through hospital in-patient care. Furthermore, home care has proved to be 50% cheaper than in-patient care. But obtaining such savings requires good planning and management, as community-based care still has many costs attached, including the training and support of volunteers.

Holistic care, whereby the physical, social, spiritual, economic and psychological needs of individuals and the wider community are met, is of paramount importance to the team at Chikankata. The expectations of many in the area had been that the hospital would meet their need for income generation, food production and schools. But the management of the hospital recognised that the use of paid hospital- based community care teams was expensive and that they were increasingly unable to meet the growing workload as HIV prevalence increased. One manager said the community health care structure was being used as a 'Neighbourhood Watch Scheme', and the community would ask for help on a wide range of issues.

The response of the hospital management was to meet with the local leaders and to share their concerns that they simply could not continue to meet all the demands being made of them. The result was the development of Care and Prevention Teams (CPTs), which are run by the community and not the hospital.

The members of the Care and Prevention committees are chosen by the community, not by the hospital, and they address not only health issues but general development matters. Local key stakeholders, such as volunteer health workers, and local business men and women, are invited to join the committee, and hospital-based staff work as team members.

The CPT works with the local community to identify available resources: environmental (water, roads, trees, fertile land), services (hospitals, clinics, donors, banks, schools, NGOs) and human resources (teachers, farmers, politicians, committed individuals). A shortage of money does not necessarily mean a shortage of other resources.

The CPT and the community then agree on a management structure and a plan of action to utilise the resources in order to respond to the community's needs. An influential individual from the local community, or someone particularly committed, is selected by the community to act as the main motivator and link person. The CPT then negotiates with the hospital staff to agree the assistance that can be offered by the hospital to support the community's efforts. This could include regular monitoring and evaluation.

Above all, the CPT strategy encourages the community to take on responsibility for the provision of caring for fellow members of the community who are chronically ill (not only those ill due to HIV/AIDS) as well as those affected by the illness, such as dependants – usually children and elderly parents.

The CPT is also concerned with the prevention of HIV/AIDS, and their focus is on behaviour change. As care of individuals is provided, opportunities arise for addressing the issue of behaviour change in the lives of those individuals.

To quote Dapheton Siame, a member of the Chikankata management team, 'This is not a new way of working, but finding again our old ways of [community] working.'

Case study 4: Church mobilisation, Jinja, Uganda

Under the leadership of Pastor Sam Mugote, members of Deliverance Church, Jinja, formed a group to offer physical and spiritual care to people in their community living with HIV/AIDS. They were motivated by the many needs of their neighbours but also by the call of God's word to care sacrificially for those in need, without prejudice or judgement. The programme grew as other churches saw its positive impact on the lives of individuals, the community and the church itself, and wanted to become part it, or to be allowed to replicate the work.

The Deliverance Church formed The AIDS Intervention Programme (TAIP), the aim of which is to assist churches to develop sustainable support for people living with HIV/AIDS. Churches are facilitated to plan and manage both care and prevention programmes through volunteer-based work in their immediate communities.

The implementers of the work are individual volunteers from churches, the majority of whom are untrained in formal health care, but who have been equipped to provide the basic physical care that people living with HIV/AIDS need in their homes. The volunteers are also trained to provide counselling for the emotional needs of patients and their families. They offer advice on nutritional matters and on the other services available to individuals and families.

Pastor Sam Mugote sees the role of TAIP as assisting churches to develop work that they are already doing. The churches that seek assistance and are selected to receive training share two key qualities. First, they see the need of people in their community affected by HIV and the effect this has on their families and community. Secondly, the church is active in proclaiming the gospel, and telling people the good news of Jesus Christ in word and deed. The role of TAIP is to offer guidance on how each congregation may best direct their vision and skills to offer an effective care and prevention programme.

The TAIP team begin by making an initial visit to a church to meet with the minister, church leadership, and interested members of the congregation. It is important that the leadership not only agrees to the development of a programme but is also actively involved in the work. The church may meet a number of challenges where strong leadership will be needed. Volunteers may face prejudice and will need support and help once they are involved with chronically ill and dying people.

The TAIP team then train and motivate selected members of the church to become a Support Action Group to visit people with HIV/AIDS. The group is encouraged to support one another by meeting together regularly.

The emphasis of the training is to develop relationships with individuals, enabling them to realise that they are loved and have worth. It is from this base of emotional support that the other elements of care can be supplied.

The experience of TAIP has been that the mobilisation of a church can take between six and eighteen months. Volunteers must be selected and trained, and practical experience must be gained between training sessions. Supervision, support and update training are provided by TAIP.

It is the experience of TAIP that volunteer-based projects can be developed more easily in rural areas than in urban areas. The main reason for this is the availability of volunteers with time to care for people outside of their own families. In urban areas there are often reduced family structures and the need to earn a wage can severely restrict the time volunteers have to offer.

TAIP have noticed that often a programme developed by one church will motivate other neighbouring churches to catch the vision.

Lessons learned about church mobilisation

- It must be evident that church members follow a biblical lifestyle
- Leaders must be supportive and involved
- Training must be good and relevant
- Volunteers must be given regular support
- The importance of developing relationships must be emphasised
- Support for families must be included
- It can take up to eighteen months for an effective programme to develop
- There must be clear liaison and communication with the local community
- Such programmes are more difficult to develop in urban areas

Case study 5: Caring for women, Mbale, western Uganda

Throughout the world women are disproportionately affected by HIV/AIDS. Women are becoming infected and dying at younger ages; they may be the victims of sexual exploitation; they may be the main providers of care for the sick and dying. In response to this need, many groups have established programmes designed to target women in particular. One such group is Uganda Women's Concern Ministry, in Mbale, western Uganda.

In 1989, Mrs Edith Wakimire, a local church leader in Mbale, realised that many of her women neighbours were suffering through gender prejudice and disempowerment – culturally, socially and economically. She gathered a group of people together to form the joint committee of the Uganda Women's Concern Ministry (UWCM). Their aim was to improve the social and economic position of local women.

UWCM is predominantly staffed by women and seeks to involve local women in the management of the programmes.

Initially they worked through income generating projects to improve the financial status of women, and to give them personal dignity. These projects have included dress making, agricultural training, community-owned cows and a piggery.

UWCM is located in Uganda's eastern region, mostly in the Mbale district, but with some work in the neighbouring districts of Pallisa, Kumi and Toror. Towns are generally small and the populations are mainly peasant subsistence farmers. By 1990, Edith Wakimire had become increasingly aware that women were developing HIV-related illnesses. She left her teaching career to establish an AIDS programme that would become the central work of UWCM.

The programme's objectives are to provide education and training opportunities for women and children; to offer counselling and support for families affected by AIDS; to mobilise women to engage in income generating activities that will improve their financial status and give them personal dignity; and to provide the basic needs of orphaned children and school fees for their education.

UWCM now provides training in improved agricultural practices, tree planting, raising livestock, dress making and social communication skills for empowering women in their relations with men and officialdom. UWCM team members visit churches, education institutions, community forums and youth camps, conducting seminars on topics such as health promotion, environmental protection, family relationship skills, and the behavioural changes necessary to prevent HIV infection.

Counselling is offered at central meetings and also in individual homes, and UWCM believe this to be their most challenging area of work. A particular concern is with the children of parents with AIDS – finding ways to enable these children to carry on once their parents have died. Short-term emergency assistance is offered to families affected by AIDS, and these grants can enable children to remain at school and supplement a family's nutrition if the ability to earn money or work the fields has been lost.

Sarah is a recipient of UWCM's support. Sarah married in 1982 as a second wife. All was relatively well until 1991, when her 'co-wife' died of AIDS. Sarah was suspected of having bewitched and killed her, and the intense hatred from relatives and neighbours almost crushed her. She desperately wanted to escape from home, but economic insecurity and love for her children forced her to stay.

Her misery was aggravated by the death of her husband the following year. The family had still not realised that AIDS had struck the home and they continued to vent their anger on Sarah for having caused the deaths. She decided it was time to do something.

First, she went to the AIDS information centre at Mbale and had her blood screened. She was HIV-positive. She began to imagine what was in store for her: the coming death, slow but sure, and the plight of her children. But following a meeting with Edith Wakimire, Sarah received regular staff visits to counsel herself, her in-laws and the seven children. She was given advice on income generating activities, some material assistance and sponsorship for the children to remain at school. For Sarah this meant a new peace of mind.

Case study 6: Caring for women and children, SIAM CARE, Thailand

SIAM CARE operates a drop in centre for women, often with their children who are HIV-positive. Because of the social stigmatisation that HIV brings in Bangkok, the need for confidential meeting places for those living with HIV is high. Community rejection of those with HIV is common around the world, but there are some areas, such as Thailand, where it is a particular problem. Those with HIV are rejected by neighbours, employers and even family, so that people who are living with HIV will keep their status a secret. This adds to their emotional stress and ability to access assistance.

The SIAM CARE Drop In Centre provides a safe and confidential place to receive support, advice and training from SIAM CARE staff and volunteers, and encouragement from others in the same situation. The atmosphere that the centre has created is positive, supportive and even fun! A visit to the centre at lunchtime will find children playing, and women cooking their regional dishes for each other to enjoy. In this atmosphere the staff become friends and are able to offer counselling and professional help to the women and their children.

SIAM CARE have also developed a shelter home situated some twenty minutes from their main centre, where up to five homeless women and their children can be accommodated. The women are assisted in returning to the community, primarily through a self-support group that operates from the shelter. Once again, the shelter provides a place of safety, love and respite for women in a culture that can often be hostile towards those who are HIV-positive. The women themselves are involved in the management and running of the shelter for as long as they are there, and there is a culture of encouragement and empowerment – it is not a place where they are expected to rely on service providers.

Case study 7: Working with commercial sex workers, Calcutta

At the Emmanuel Ministries medical centre in Calcutta, there is an excellent relationship between the centre itself, the Samaritans of Calcutta, a secular doctor and government sexual health workers. In their work with commercial sex workers and the rickshaw pullers (another very poor and marginalised group), there is great emphasis on dealing with individuals holistically, addressing their many needs, and not just the issue of HIV/AIDS.

There is a clear commitment to the building of personal relationships in the community and of serving the community in things like the provision of education, and of a shelter for the children of sex workers. Among many activities the children make pottery goods and the women make woollen clothes that are then sold to Christian relief organisations in preparation for disaster relief.

There is integration between care and prevention, and between medical and non-medical care. Former sex workers and their family members are encouraged to provide prevention and care in their own families and communities.

On the medical side, the aim is to include HIV/AIDS as a component of general sexual disease care and prevention. This is important in the light of research that has shown that the successful treatment of sexually transmitted diseases can greatly reduce the risk of HIV transmission. Good health care for these women reduces the risk of stigmatisation they might experience if they are forced to attend STD clinics. This in turn gains the trust and respect of women in the community, and subsequently increases the numbers accessing the services.

The spiritual impact of the work is clear and encouraging. Lives have been changed, and many of those who have undergone detoxification and rehabilitation have become team members. Bible study groups are independently started, and in the Muslim rickshaw pullers group a worship and Bible study meeting has begun.

Case study 8: Working with drug users, Delhi, India

Since 1988, Sharan, in Delhi, has been involved in awareness work and research related to drug abuse. A drug rehabilitation centre has been established, concentrating on reaching people from the slums. Sharan has built up considerable credibility and has developed materials (audio visual, posters, flip charts and drama sketches), conducted workshops and carried out awareness programmes among drug users and slum dwellers. From this base they then went on to conduct weekly general health clinics in seven Delhi brothels, negotiating with the 'madams' to prevent problems for the sex workers. They then began a school and crèche for the children, thus meeting the most heartfelt needs of these marginalised women.

Sharan also seeks to reach out to the customers of the brothels, with the aim of developing behaviour change over a period of time.

In order to increase local sustainability, they offer training to women from the local community, and provide clinics and accessible health care for the sex workers.

Intravenous drug use is a major route for HIV infection in Asia, and there is enormous need among sex workers and in prisons. The work in prisons and in drug rehabilitation centres is in response to prejudice and lack of a tradition of community care. However, the lack of response from the church continues to be disappointing and the need for independent action of Christian non-government organisations will remain for the foreseeable future.

In Sahara, a sister organisation to Sharan, approximately 90% of the team are former intravenous drug users who are now committed to serving individuals resident in the centres.

Of the 104 residents of the Sahara centre, approximately 25% to 40% are believed to be HIV-positive. But all are treated equally. Sahara has very good links with the Sharan detoxification centre, and with their halfway house, where people are prepared to re-enter the community, often in groups of four so as to continue supporting each other.

For both Sahara and Sharan, there is no forcing of the gospel upon people and no obligation to attend devotions, but residents look forward to the times of daily worship. The St Michael's halfway house has good links with the local church, something that has often proven difficult for other AIDS work in Asia. It has taken time, but because the halfway house offers an opportunity for committed individuals, churches are being mobilised as prejudice is broken down.

St Michael's also offers respite care (at any one time, eight out of ten of the residents will have TB), and acts as a day care centre for, primarily, former residents.

Case study 9: Care of drug users with HIV, Manipur, India

In the north-eastern Indian state of Manipur, the El Shaddai resource centre offers community care to drug users and their families.

The El Shaddai counsellors have, on average, ten clients each, and they visit each client two or three times each week. Each counsellor has a locality within which they operate, enabling them to develop relationships within the close-knit communities.

The process of serving the clients begins with befriending the individual. There is no shortage of referrals to the centre, and many of the counsellors are ex-addicts whose friends and neighbours, having seen the changes in their lives, request assistance for themselves.

The common experience of the counsellors is that they will often be met with defensiveness, but befriending helps to break this down. This is followed by a period of 'bringing reality' to the drug user, or to those infected by HIV, helping them to see the situation they are in and their need for help. They are assured that detoxification is a possibility, either at the centre, or through other agencies. During this period the clients are also given awareness education on the transmission of HIV and how their behaviour can lead to increased risk of infection and transmission of the virus.

Most of the drug users are men living with their families, and families often act as the main providers of care. Women, however, can find themselves stigmatised and living on their own. The reason for this is that women who are drug users are generally also involved in commercial sex work in order to fund their habit.

The centre provides support, care, and love to the families of those going through detoxification or learning to live with

AIDS. The family itself is used to help clients stay at home. Families are counselled to forgive and to forget; many of them have suffered greatly as a result of the 'selfish' habit. This has resulted in an unexpected but welcome reconciliation within families.

Parents of addicts are given education on the issues faced by their children and the need for strengthened communication and relationships within the family.

El Shaddai is also providing programmes of care, and prevention of drug use as well as HIV/AIDS in the slums of Imphal. They have developed socially and culturally appropriate policies and practices that have enabled families to provide care, and many individuals have passed successfully through detoxification and received physical, emotional and spiritual care.

The spiritual impact of the work is evident in the establishment of a new church by ex-drug users, Bible study and self-support groups, and the presence on the team of ex-drug users and people living with HIV/AIDS.

Case study 10: Providing an advocacy service, Brazil

The Associacao de Acao Solidaria (ASAS) of Recife, Brazil, provides care and support for people infected and affected by HIV/AIDS. They offer relevant and expert advice on medical and welfare issues, and have established a support group, which cares for the family during the illness, and following the death of a family member.

Families now say that ASAS has been their advocate, a voice for the voiceless, providing important advocacy in political forums, and enabling them to gain access to necessary medicines and health and social services. People entering hospitals and learning of their HIV status have been able to learn from ASAS what their rights are, and have been helped to adjust to their status.

Advocacy is often a new activity for churches, many of whom have previously felt it best to avoid the political arena and to concentrate on care and prevention. However, there are issues of justice here, and often people with AIDS need someone to speak on their behalf. Many churches and Christian organisations are therefore now acting as advocates for those with AIDS, perhaps as they seek improved health care from clinics.

Advocacy requires the developing of relationships with key people and organisations, and facilitating meetings between marginalised groups and people of power. It can happen at many levels – ranging from a local clinic to church leaders working at the national level.

Lessons learned about advocacy

- Develop relationships with key people and organisations
- Do not speak on behalf of people with AIDS or communities unless they agree
- Facilitate meetings between marginalised groups and people of power
- Develop a strategy, define issues and be clear what you want to achieve
- Be aware that prejudices and fears are often strong and will take time to change
- Don't just demand; be prepared to negotiate
- Maintain momentum
- Be prepared for the long haul and allocate time and resources accordingly
- Be prepared for setbacks
- Keep those with HIV/AIDS informed and involved: it is their campaign

Case study 11: Providing a counselling service, Kenya

Counselling has a critical role to play in both care and prevention of HIV/AIDS. People living with HIV/AIDS and terminally ill are very likely to need emotional as well as practical and clinical care. Counselling is an invaluable component of HIV/AIDS prevention programmes for the families of people living with HIV/AIDS and with young people in particular.

Following the development of training programmes in care and prevention across Kenya, the Africa Inland Church Kenya AIDS Team saw the need to address counselling as a separate issue, such was its importance. Under Dr John Chaplin the team have now equipped many 'ordinary' church members to do the extraordinary, with basic training and consistent supervision and support. Individuals provide emotional support to people who feel abandoned and unloved.

Counselling should seek to enable people with HIV/AIDS, and their carers, to cope with the social, economic and emotional problems they face. It should also seek to help an HIV-positive person to decide not to spread the infection further. There are a limited number of qualified counsellors in the developing world, but some aspects of counselling can be carried out by carers with less experience and qualifications. Many organisations call their care staff 'counsellors', understanding that they do more than simply physically care for their clients. They listen and provide emotional support and empathy, but do not provide a psycho-therapeutic counselling service.

Counselling cannot and should not be considered as a completely separate issue. When staff or volunteers provide for the practical needs of people with AIDS, they should also attempt to meet the emotional needs of those for whom they are caring. Organisations do have to be sure, however, that home carers know their limits and have an awareness of when to refer for more qualified counselling.

HIV testing often has far reaching consequences for the person being tested. If positive, it can result in feelings of depression, anger, guilt and fear. In many communities it also leads to an individual facing stigmatisation. It is imperative that where testing takes place there is also pre- and post-test counselling. Pre-test counselling should include explanation of the testing process, implications of the test, risk prevention and coping strategies. If the test is positive, post-test counselling should include emotional support, discussion about sharing the result, onward referral and prevention of the spread of infection. If negative, it is important to utilise the opportunity to talk of future prevention.

Lessons on counselling

- Make counselling a central part of any care and prevention programme
- Ensure adequate training for counsellors
- Provide good supervision for counsellors
- Establish clear boundaries, so that people know when to stop and who to pass issues to
- Establish that counselling should be unconditional and without prejudice
- Emphasise the importance of confidentiality and trust
- Emphasise that listening is more important than teaching
- Counselling should be a comfort – getting alongside people and walking with them during their difficult times
- Ensure that counsellors have correct information about HIV/AIDS and the services available and are able to impart information clearly
- Care for your counsellors – they are dealing with bereavement constantly and they must themselves be counselled

Case study 12: Caring for orphans in the community, Bethany Trust, Zimbabwe

One of the most heartbreaking social consequences of the AIDS epidemic is the number of orphans, together with the increase of households which are headed by a child. The responsibility for income and care, not only for siblings but also for ailing parents and elderly grandparents, is falling increasingly on the shoulders of children.

The principle of empowering the local community to care for their orphans has been central to the work of the Bethany Trust in Zimbabwe, founded by Susie Howe, an HIV nurse specialist of several years' standing. Susie found herself in Zimbabwe and felt compelled to work with local Christians to provide sustainable care for orphans in their communities. Local churches and Christians are encouraged and trained to equip communities to care for the increasing numbers of children in need.

The process begins by discussing with communities and the orphans the needs, concerns and what possible solutions the community can identify for the challenges ahead of them. Volunteers are then trained to provide emotional and practical support for orphans. This could include guidance on planting crops to guidance on growing up. They speak to children, listen to them and then speak up for them when required.

The work is not restricted to child-headed households, but also extends to assisting any family that has suffered the loss of a parent. This ministry is particularly critical for supporting the increasing number of grandparents who now act as sole carers for their grandchildren.

By enabling families and communities to care for orphans and not send them off to orphanages where they may become stigmatised (especially if their parents died of AIDS), the children gain so much. They maintain their sense of belonging to a family and a community, which benefits them emotionally – and also practically, as they are supported in the present and learn relevant skills to survive long term in their home areas.

A similar principle has been adopted in Chikankata (see case study 3). The hospital is now moving away from providing school fees for individual orphans, and towards supporting the economic development of local communities. When grants are made they are for schools, not just individuals. These new initiatives are not AIDS specific, but seek to assist all children in need, not only orphans. It is an integrated approach that mobilises communities and strengthens bonds between children and their community.

In the past, people have often built orphanages as a response to the needs of orphans. But the Bethany Trust has encouraged and trained communities to such an effective extent that in five years it has mobilised the care of over 6,000 orphans in the district of Zvishavane alone. Orphanages can be seen as the last safety net, but before that point is reached there are the existing family and community structures to be drawn upon.

The Matilda Project is another example of a successful project in Zimbabwe which has learned from many of these lessons and now itself supports over 2,000 orphans in other parts of the same country.

Case study 13: Caring for orphans in a centre, Sao Paulo, Brazil

Faced by increasing numbers of children orphaned or in need of care in their area, the Associa cao Evangelica de Apoio e Solidriedade as Pessoas com AIDS e seus Familiares (PRAIDS), with the help of Tearfund UK, established a centre to care for children. PRAIDS is committed not only to individual children but also to their families, seeking to support them practically and emotionally.

Children are encouraged to be involved in the activities of the centre, to develop their ownership of PRAIDS work, and to care for their relatives.

PRAIDS is committed to holistic care of children, and to meeting their spiritual, emotional, physical, and social needs. The children are taught that the centre is their home, not just a place to live, and love is demonstrated through appropriate discipline, and the encouraging of care for themselves and cleaning duties in their rooms.

The schools and medical teams all comment on how the children from PRAIDS are exceptional in their health and dispositions. Children are given opportunities to integrate into the local community by attending local schools and churches, and they play a full role in the life of each institution. PRAIDS maintain contact with whatever family the children have, and support and encourage fostering of the child by the extended family where appropriate.

Local churches are given opportunities to be involved in a number of ways. Some make regular group visits to the centre for worship meetings, play times with the children and to spend time with individuals. The children attend Sunday Bible schools at the churches, and some church families have established links with individual children. This can range from making regular visits, to donations of clothes and toys, or, in some cases, to children being fostered by church families.

Church leaders are delighted that involvement in the work of PRAIDS has positively impacted the life of their respective churches. The senior pastors who direct and manage PRAIDS are held in great respect, not least because they seek to draw upon the human resources of the local community, both church and secular, to support them in their work and to develop awareness in the communities.

Volunteers are supported, with access to team meetings, and directors and co-ordinators make an effort to be available and to enquire as to how volunteers are doing. This is important when someone is chronically or terminally ill, as this can place great emotional strain on individuals. Many of the volunteers are poor and PRAIDS gives them monthly food packages and parcels at Christmas for their families. The gifts in the parcels may be the only gifts their families will receive. Since beginning this limited support for volunteers, the amount of food donations that PRAIDS receives has increased.

Contact between the school and PRAIDS is constant and at different levels, both with management and with other staff, and PRAIDS is seen as dependable and efficient in responding to enquiries from the school. The school feels that they are partners together in the care and education of the children. The school is in a poor area, and PRAIDS often makes donations of clothes for the poorest of children.

When there are parties at PRAIDS the PRAIDS children often invite their school friends, and local children will often go to the centre to play.

PRAIDS demonstrates a level of expertise in managing the care of HIV-positive children that the school wishes they had for other children in the school they suspect of being HIV-positive.

PRAIDS has sought throughout its history not to go it alone but to work with as many of the different groups within the local community as possible. They have a policy of practically supporting other non-government organisations in Sao Paulo, and in other regions of Brazil, by passing on some of the donations of foodstuffs, clothes and other articles they themselves have received. If there is any excess of donated toys or clothes, PRAIDS organise sales to the local community at prices lower than normal second-hand prices in order to serve the local people and to strengthen links.

Contacts have also been developed with businesses. Almost all of the foodstuffs and other essentials for the two centres are donated by local businesses. The experience gained in developing business contacts should aid them as they seek to increase funding from within Brazil.

The services available to PRAIDS beneficiaries are of a very high standard, and this is due in no small part to the positive stance of the Brazilian government towards HIV/AIDS. The government supplies, free of charge, combination therapy drugs that have improved the health of those with AIDS very significantly.

Government HIV/AIDS health teams for adults and children are based at a major Sao Paulo hospital, providing monthly monitoring of health, viral load and C4 count, as well as the impact of drugs combating the virus and medication for opportunistic illnesses. The teams are also available for call out in the case of emergencies, or for house calls.

Lessons on caring for orphans

- Involve orphans and listen to them
- Empower families and communities
- Offer support to all families in need, not only those affected by HIV/AIDS
- Aim to keep children in their communities
- Provide skills that will sustain families, like farming or other income generating activities
- Be prepared to spend time preparing children for the death of a parent – they will be more able to cope with bereavement when it comes. The truth needs to be told, but in a sensitive and supportive way. A number of organisations, such as Servants to Asia's Urban Poor in Cambodia have developed memory boxes or memory scrapbooks. These are collections of photographs and mementoes gathered by the infected parent with the children as a means of holding memories of the parent for the children in the future.

Case study 14: Income-generation activities, Nairobi, Kenya

Pastor Ogutu in the slums of Muthare Valley, Nairobi, Kenya, has established some effective income-generation programmes. He directs a work which provides assistance to families of children in need. Not all of them are infected or affected by HIV/AIDS, but the benefit of such a policy is that stigmatisation is reduced. Pastor Ogutu began by using his own skills as a mechanic to train young men who had been attending the school he had founded in the area. He soon found that the opportunities for them were limited so, after researching the market opportunities for mechanics, he fine-tuned their training. Furthermore, he developed working relationships with garages and they began to trust the quality of his graduates.

(This was an important lesson. In another part of Africa, for example, a local hospital trained men in carpentry to enable them to enjoy sustainable income. Sadly, however, that project found there were more carpenters than the area needed, and this resulted in unemployed carpenters, ill feeling from the existing carpenters, and wasted investment by an organisation in training that had no future use.)

Pastor Ogutu then began to research appropriate training for girls, and has since developed successful training courses in dress making and clothing repair.

It is always important to consider the health status of those infected by AIDS. Individuals may not always be able to work, and it may be necessary to supplement income-generation programmes with welfare grants. Involving the families and supporting communities will assist in the sustainability of projects during periods when people are too ill to play a full part in an activity.

Thai Concern Foundation (TCF) in northern Thailand has created a multi-faceted response to the challenge of HIV/ AIDS. They similarly established groups which give opportunity for self-support, learning and joint advocacy. In parallel with these support groups, low interest loans are offered. These loans assist families when the main income earner is sick and unable to work, or has died. TCF has found that the project has benefited from drawing in others in the community not infected by HIV.

Also in Thailand, Global Inter-Action is assisting people with AIDS by establishing income-generating projects. They also found that the nature of HIV demands the involvement of many family members, and work needs to be home based, because low energy levels can make travelling to and from work too exhausting or even impossible. Integrating people who are not HIV-positive into an activity can also be a way to increase acceptance into the community of HIV/AIDS sufferers.

Lessons learned about income-generation projects

- Previous experience of financial management is essential
- Appoint people with specific skills to avoid wasting money and causing disappointment
- Seek expert help to establish if the project is viable, if there is a market, and if the relevant skills are available
- Be aware that projects for women can actually lead to an increased burden rather than self-reliance, depending on whether the women are actually running their own businesses, or expecting the project to create jobs for them. Check with an external advisor
- People with AIDS should be part of the decision-making and planning process to develop appropriate and sustainable programmes
- Integrate into the local community – projects should be open to other members of the family and community who do not have HIV/AIDS, but without losing original purpose
- Decide what will happen when people are sick and cannot work
- Investigate the provision of grants to cover periods of illness

Case study 15: Working with refugees, ACET Uganda

ACET works with refugees in northern Uganda. They have seen how HIV/AIDS spreads more easily in times of instability when social practices that protect individuals are disrupted or even broken down completely. In early 2002 there were an estimated 15 million refugees in the world – three-quarters of them in Africa – and 80% were women and children. In addition there are an unknown number of displaced people who have been forced from their homes but have not crossed country borders.

HIV can spread at times of social crisis and its impact is greatest in developing countries, the very places least equipped to combat the crisis.

In emergency situations of mass movement, dealing with HIV can often seem less important than providing food, shelter, water, emergency health care and security. But what are the long-term effects of not prioritising the risks of HIV transmission? Relief workers must ask themselves whether displaced people are at risk of HIV infection. This need must also be met, at the same time as short-term issues of security, shelter and nourishment.

ACET recognised the need to integrate HIV/AIDS into initial needs assessment of emergencies and the need to train relief workers in HIV/AIDS. The emergency they are facing now needs to be seen within the context of the emergency which will be produced by HIV in ten years' time.

Lessons learned in working with refugees

- Work with military leadership to provide prevention education for troops
- Provide protection for women and girls
- Support the maintenance of health provision to reduce HIV transmission rates
- Ensure the rapid provision of preventative education
- Consider utilising the host population in provision of services

Case study 16: Working in prisons – examples from South East Asia and Africa

In the face of barriers to working in many SE Asian communities, mostly due to prejudice and lack of a tradition of community care, a Christian NGO has sought to assist Christian drug rehabilitation centres to develop appropriate HIV services, and has also begun work in Malaysian prisons. They set up a community home that offers five men a place for mutual support – a very low cost project that could be replicated elsewhere.

The work in prisons is in recognition of an alternative community. Prisoners have been empowered to recognise resources at hand, in particular their own ability to act as carers for one another while in prison and for continued care following release from prison.

The Prison Fellowship of Zambia have also recognised that provision of care in prisons can be by fellow prisoners if there is a strong sense of community and existing mutual support, and have sought to train inmates in care and education of others. They also act as advocates, enabling those with AIDS to receive support. HIV-positive prisoners offer key insights into the planning and managing of projects and programmes. Failure to meet with a target group can easily result in a failed project: they know their situation better than anyone does.

Time for action

The size of the AIDS epidemic has left many leaders frustrated and impatient with the slow pace at which the church, missions and Christian organisations have responded. Church leadership is key in the mobilising of HIV/AIDS programmes. If church leadership remains unmotivated or, worse, negative about church involvement, time has to be invested to ensure a change in this attitude.

When you have support and encouragement of church leadership, the resources within a church can be more easily mobilised. The word of God and the Holy Spirit motivates people to care. Christians are called to care as Christ did, not just for physical needs of people, but also for their emotional, relational and, ultimately, their spiritual needs. Christians have the opportunity, through HIV/AIDS care and prevention programmes, to express the practical love of Christ for the marginalised, and for all in the community living under the threat of AIDS.

MAP International in Nairobi have for some years produced effective materials and training for churches in responding to HIV/AIDS. They have always sought to be strategic in their work, whether in a local church or group of churches, and they recognised it was vital to train future church leaders at theological and Bible colleges. MAP aim to reach present and future leaders, equipping them with a biblical perspective on the need, outlining a potential response. They prepare leaders to intervene proactively before they are bogged down by numerous funeral services of AIDS victims.

After reading this chapter, maybe you feel that you are not qualified, and there is not much you can do. But the most important thing of all is to do *something*. It costs nothing to care, and you need no organising to go and visit a neighbour in need, to talk to your own relatives about the risks of HIV, to lend someone this book, or to get involved in an existing programme in your area.

The battle against AIDS will not be won by great programmes or by structures, plans and organisation alone. It will be won as millions of ordinary men and women in every nation rise up, determined to take AIDS seriously and to make a real difference. As those who belong to Christ, we have a message of strength and hope, as well as of health and wholeness.

CHAPTER SIXTEEN

A TEN-POINT PLAN FOR THE GOVERNMENT

People often ask what governments of various countries should be doing next. Here are a number of different suggestions, which need to be adapted sensitively and carefully to the country concerned.

1. Determine the extent of the problem

We need to get it right: governments do not have resources to squander on problems that do not exist or are being exaggerated by those with vested interests in increasing their own budgets. Neither do we have time to adjust plans if the AIDS epidemic becomes worse than estimated or changes its character in any way. For example, has education reduced heterosexual spread, but not affected drug addicts? Are new HIV viruses spreading in different ways? After all, as things stand, a person infected tomorrow will probably die. You have possibly five to fifteen years to plan his or her terminal care, but only today to prevent a death.

All discarded blood samples from selected hospital laboratories should have identifying markers removed and be sent to public health laboratories for testing. Only the hospital of origin should be stated. Results will give an indication of spread across the country and will enable local increases to be detected. Hospitals giving cause for concern should then be asked to send regular batches of blood samples with age and sex recorded on each bottle, but no other information.

Monitoring antenatal clinics for infection levels has been a popular approach, but can give misleading results if used as a yardstick for the general population. By definition those who are pregnant are sexually active and therefore likely to have a higher level of infection in general than the whole population.

Whatever approach is taken, consistency is vital from year to year so rate of change can be properly assessed.

2. Target people especially at risk with further new campaigns

Education is most effective when targeted at those most at risk. Young people also need to be targeted before they begin taking risks. It is far easier to prevent risk-taking behaviour before it becomes a life habit than afterwards. Government campaigns are insufficient without continued high-profile publicity for a prolonged period afterwards. Education is easy; changing behaviour is extremely difficult. Smoking kills hundreds of thousands each year, numbers which dwarf the current AIDS problem, yet public health campaigns have taken years to produce change. Sexual drives are stronger than the power of nicotine or the needle.

All educational literature should be clearly marked with date of issue and leaflets should be promptly withdrawn when out of date.

3. Get an army of health educators on the road

The economics of health education are simple in many industrialised nations. Hospital costs for caring for one AIDS patient alone are so high that a health educator only has to prevent one person a year from developing AIDS to save the government or health insurance companies his entire salary. If he succeeds in preventing one person a month from becoming infected, the government or other agencies save a fortune. (See Chapter 12.) In poorer nations, the economic arguments are strongest when targeting those on whom the future of the country most depends, and those likely to be at greatest risk.

The argument for prevention is overwhelming. From travelling around to schools and colleges myself, I am convinced that an effective communicator can save hundreds of lives a year.

One important factor has been left out of most school information packs and is also missing from youth education: the personal factor. Tell your own stories. When I go into a school or college everyone is on the edge of their seats. Why? Because I know people personally who have died of AIDS, people who are dying right now, and I often see people who are dying of it. It is real, so prevention and encouraging positive attitudes are easier.

4. Establish a national training programme for all health care workers

Never has there been a new lethal disease that has spread so quickly to affect so many millions of people. Consider cancer care or malaria: cancer and malaria have been around for centuries. Even so, there are acute training problems. Existing care teams are under strain with conflicting demands from patients and from the need to train more carers.

The explosion of AIDS cases in many countries and the changing appearance of the disease – with new treatments and research likely to make knowledge obsolete – means that a vast, crash-training programme needs to be established. In 1994, long before 9/11, I wrote that if every week terrorists blew up four civilian aircraft on domestic flights killing 1,000 US citizens, a national state of emergency would be declared. Why shouldn't governments treat the AIDS epidemic with the same seriousness as the war against terror? After all, possibly eight times the same number are doomed every day across India, China and many African nations through new HIV infections.

5. Provide a network of specialist advisory teams

Governments should fund specialist teams to advise and support health care workers in the community and various hospitals in high-incidence areas. One aim would be to channel the latest information and techniques on treatment from research centres to those in the field. Such workers can have a remit to cover other illnesses as well, particularly in poorer nations.

6. Recruit extra community nursing staff

People with AIDS are heavy users of nursing resources. Health teams need additional resources for community nursing that can be increased in line with their numbers of people with AIDS.

7. Work in partnership with the church

The church is the largest non-government organisation in many nations and perhaps globally. It represents a massive untapped resource. In many countries, the church has a long history of care provision, particularly in developing nations. Governments should actively seek partnership programmes. The church represents not only an effective resource organisation, but also a powerful influence for behaviour change. The essential government task is to provide overall strategy, leadership and co-ordination. We all need to work together. The problem is too great in many countries for governments or secular agencies to solve on their own. Faith-based organisations have a vital role to play, especially in behaviour change.

8. Increase spending by wealthy nations on prevention in developing countries – and pass on funding to NGOs

In an age when a traveller from the UK can be in Botswana more quickly than the time it takes to drive from the north of the UK to the south, the wealthiest nations must recognise the need to invest in international prevention efforts, even as a matter of self-interest. The AIDS epidemic must not rage ahead unchecked. It is a scandal that the UK government, with its tiny domestic problem, has until recently spent more on AIDS than all the UN agencies for their global programmes on AIDS. No wonder the world epidemic is out of control (except in wealthier nations).

Part of the deal is for developing countries to work hard

ensuring that every dollar of aid goes swiftly and openly to projects delivering practical services to people who need them. Too often red tape and secrecy have created a climate that encourages corruption and other bad practices. In many countries there are unspent aid funds sitting in accounts because of disagreements about where the money should go. Delay costs lives.

Governments should give major priority to funding non-government agencies (NGOs) since they are often much better placed to deliver services quickly in a relevant and efficient way.

Getting spending sorted out will encourage donors, who want to see rapid action and real results.

9. Research into long-term relationships as well as vaccine/cure

Governments and international agencies need to fund further major research into vaccines, cures and better ways to prevent spread. Incentives need to be provided to encourage drug companies to direct their vast research operations towards vaccines.

A comprehensive study of marriage is greatly overdue. What makes a happy marriage? How does one choose the right partner? How can marriage breakdown be prevented? Results can then be fed into schools education.

10. Integration of HIV into government policy

AIDS is too great a challenge to be defeated by budget allocations, programme officers and policy guidelines. Governments in higher-incidence countries need to make sure that HIV issues are a part of every government-funded activity, as appropriate.

The same should be true of all non-government organisations in these parts of the world.

How can I help turn plans into action?

The future is in your hands. You can write, phone, or otherwise make your views known to those in local or national government, to health planners and to church leaders. You can make sure that as many copies as possible of this book (produced without profit and distributed without charge) get to the right people. You may feel that your contribution is small and not worth much, but thousands of others are doing the same. Together we can help turn the tide and build a better place for those who come after us. We are too late to prevent a disaster, but not too late to prevent an even bigger one.

Petitions are useless in comparison to individual letters, so get others to write too. Write to your Member of Parliament or other appropriate government official. Even if not read, your letter will be counted as yet another part of a big vote on the issue. Write to radio or TV producers who have made AIDS programmes. Commend them for good content and criticise the bad. Remember that in many countries, just thirty letters after a programme is enough to influence the producers.

Write to your local legislators, asking them what provision they are making for those with AIDS. If you are dissatisfied with the reply, say so, and send copies of the correspondence to your local newspaper.

Having looked at how the government can respond, we now need to return to our overall Christian vision for responding to AIDS. Is there more needed than just prevention and cure? Is there anything more we need do? Is the church in danger of just becoming an expert provider of AIDS programmes almost identical in many ways to government ones? Are we in danger of losing our way?

CHAPTER SEVENTEEN

A GLOBAL CHRISTIAN CHALLENGE

We have looked at how churches can care, save the lives of young people and develop community programmes for different cultures and situations. However, we need to look again at the call of Jesus and ask ourselves whether all this is enough – or is there something missing? Is this the sum total of a global response to AIDS, or is there another dimension?

Care and prevention are not enough

Many would say the work is complete. We are expressing love to our neighbour and we are also teaching people the medical facts about AIDS, so what more do you want? Surely that is more than enough?

If Jesus had just lived on the earth as a remarkable man, occasionally healing people or using his carpentry business to help people out, he would never have been crucified. If Jesus had merely mobilised great numbers of people to help the poor, to feed the hungry, to care for those who were oppressed, he would have lived till a ripe old age.

The problem people had with Jesus was not what he did, but what he said and who he was. They loved him for what he did and hated him for what he said. Jesus said he was the Light of the World. John's Gospel tells us that the light shines in the darkness and the darkness has never overcome it.[1] Light is always visible, always directional. Its source is obvious, threatening the darkness. In a dark cave you can strike one match and be blinded. The greater the darkness, the brighter the light.

The darker the city, the brighter the light

Jesus said we should let our light shine so that people will see the good works we are doing and give glory to our Father in heaven. Being light, then, is about explaining, about proclaiming, about being prophetic, about going high profile. Jesus said that no one should place a light under a table, but we should hold it up so the light can shine on a wide area. While we are to be filled with humility, we are to take every opportunity to explain and show what God is doing so that people give honour and glory to him.[2]

Letting the light shine

This means being happy to be known as believers, to be identified very publicly as belonging to Christ, to be willing to teach what he says. It means we welcome it when, in a media-dominated world, we find press, radio or TV wanting to report what we are doing, describe who we are, or broadcast what we are saying, perhaps because they recognise that if everyone followed a Christian lifestyle, HIV would disappear as an epidemic in thirty years.

Huge reaction to Christian view of sex

Christian views on sex can provoke a huge reaction. Recently, I was approached by a major publisher and invited to submit a

---

[1] John 1:9; 9:5.
[2] Matthew 5:16.

one-page idea for a book, challenging the supposed benefits of the 'sexual revolution', based on a survey of scientific data on AIDS, other sex diseases, and on the economic, social and psychological consequences of the breakdown of marriage and family life.

The editorial meeting rapidly became a highly charged debate, with passionate, heated arguments over personal life-styles and personal morality. Clearly the idea had touched a raw nerve, a deeply painful area. They realised such a book would cause a massive media storm: 'AIDS expert calls for new moral code'. But they feared the enormous publicity might not result in sales of a book that 'no one will want to read'. One participant was unable to recall such a fierce and stormy debate over any other book. Another publisher took it. It is called *The Rising Price of Love* and it did cause a storm.

Many people are very sensitive to hypocrisy, double standards (for example, church leaders falling into immorality), attempts to put behind closed doors the reality which has only recently come into the open, bigotry, lack of reasonableness, and blind negativism, which they may suspect is based on a fear of sexuality, prudery and a lack of normal, healthy, emotional and sexual development.

Some psychologists might say that the stronger an anti-Christian reaction, the more they might also suspect that deep, dark shadows of latent guilt are being disturbed. In my experience, those who fight the hardest seem to be people who feel insecure and threatened by another world view. Those secure about their own values and lifestyle are generally far more relaxed in open discussion.

Some who have rejected the Christian faith may also be angry for the guilt they still feel, blaming the church for a moral code they are unable to shrug off from their childhood. However, many Christians would argue that God's framework for living is constant and absolute, and that, even without the teaching of the church, there is a 'natural law' of conscience which is an innate part of every person. A sense of right and wrong is a God-given component of our being.[3]

Where is the body of Christ?

So who is the voice of Jesus today? Who are his hands and feet? No single person has the capacity to represent the heart and mind of God. We are told that together as believers we are his body. That is why Jesus prayed so much that those who believed in him would be one. Together we show his love, together we seek to express his voice, together we seek to present his challenge to the world and together we seek to reconcile the world to God.[4]

That is why I am so encouraged to see God's people joining together across the nations, with barriers breaking down, whether as vast numbers of people praying for our world as 14 million people did in many nations in March for Jesus, or whether it is at the sharp end of providing unconditional care to those with AIDS who are dying.

Daring to be different

We are called to fight discrimination, stigma, prejudice, bigotry, intolerance, oppression, injustice and cruelty. We are to encourage love, care, consideration, compassion, understanding, responsibility, commitment, faithfulness, truth and righteousness.

Jesus promised we would be identified, targeted, challenged, mocked, misunderstood and persecuted. The trouble with the church is that so often we have deserved a rap on the knuckles for strident moralism based only on an empty call to be light, without being prepared for the loving sacrifice of being salt. The more fully we represent Jesus, the more we may find that some people love what we do, but hate what we are.

---

[3] Romans 2:14–16.
[4] John 17:20–23.

Called to be wise and innocent

We need to be sensitive and wise. For example, when ACET started home care in London, it became clear from comments made by members of other groups that a number of people were hoping a volunteer would overstep the mark; that we would be 'caught', as it were, insensitively 'Bible-bashing' someone with Christian faith in their home. In UK culture, such an event could have closed down the entire home care programme. We acted with integrity: what we said in public was what we actually did in private. But we took great care to ensure this really was so. These things are very culturally dependent. In some parts of Uganda you are more likely to be criticised for not offering to pray with someone sick at home, than for offering to do so.

The reality is that a holistic model of care recognises that people may have physical, emotional, social and spiritual needs. Conversations about spiritual matters are often started by those who are unwell, and volunteers or team members may often be asked personal questions about their own faith, or people who are sick may ask for prayer, or for a visit from a chaplain or priest. Many people find faith, peace, forgiveness and reconciliation with God at such a time. But faith must never be imposed on those we seek to serve, at such a vulnerable time in their lives.

Criticised for being Christians

At the end of the day, quality of care is critical, as is the quality of training and prevention. If mud starts flying, you want the only accusation that sticks to be that you are followers of Jesus and have perhaps a different world view and a different motivation. The quality of our compassion and care should aim to be the best in our country.

We need to be clear about our purpose: if it is to publicly

challenge the moral climate of our nation, then we had better watch out. If we are going to do more than just occasionally comment about lifestyles or other sensitive issues, in some cultures we may find we have caused so many insecurities in the minds of those we care for that they do not want us to look after them any more. It may be better sometimes to leave such weighty matters to other church leaders.

Once said, comments cannot be unsaid. Off-the-cuff public remarks can be a disaster: you need expert advice from those Christians who are experienced in media matters and used to handling sensitive issues such as AIDS.

An alternative view of AIDS

If our purpose is to present a clear, common sense, no-nonsense, independent view of the epidemic, then that is relatively straightforward. I am often asked for an accurate, informed comment on AIDS by press, radio and television. People seem to want a fresh and different perspective from the rest of the AIDS industry – much of which is beginning to look very tired after years of predictable and increasingly irrelevant responses.

Jesus was always something of a puzzle: people could never quite work him out – or predict how he would respond. If we are to be his light, then we will find we are like that too. We have a God-given responsibility to contribute to public debate, just as Jesus did in his day – for example, over the emotive issues of imperial taxation and allegiance to the Roman occupying forces.

In conclusion, then, a growing number of believers are waking up to the explosive destruction of AIDS. They have clearly heard God's call to care unconditionally for all those who are ill, regardless of how they came to be so, and to do all they can to save lives, challenging societies to think again about what is ultimately important and the future of life on earth.

Time for a confession

In many countries, I believe the church needs to acknowledge its own failure to give a clear moral lead in situations where it would have been possible in the past. We need to confess our corporate neglect of the oppressed, the poor and the marginalised, many of whom have turned to dangerous lifestyles in their isolation and need. We need to confess our apathy and slowness to respond to the AIDS crisis, our blindness to the needs of other nations, and our judgemental attitudes to those outside the church, particularly in view of the frequency of divorce and sex outside marriage in many church networks and denominations.

We need to honour the work of those who have a very different world view to ourselves who got involved years ago, starting AIDS initiatives and setting standards of excellence at a time when the church was wallowing in its own confusion as to how to respond.

Hope and comfort in tragedy

We need to recognise the part we must now play. We can begin to mobilise the vast network of church resources around the world, bringing hope and comfort at a time of terrible tragedy. We can speak of the God of love who never intended the beautiful world he made to end up in such a mess as this. We can continue to do all we can to fight injustice, fear and prejudice. We can speak of God's purpose in creating us, and of friendship and forgiveness.

A global movement

We need to see the church's response to AIDS in the context of rapid church growth. There has never been a time in history when so many have turned to Christ each year, at a much faster rate than the growth of the population. In almost every continent of the world the church is growing rapidly, as idealism and faith in political systems have died, where in many people's lives there has been a spiritual vacuum. It is no coincidence that both

HIV and faith are spreading so fast: in different ways both are temperature gauges of sick societies which have lost their way.

While HIV spread can be an indicator of the loss of traditional values that have held societies together for centuries, spiritual awakening is an indicator of recent rediscovery of purpose, meaning and ultimate destiny.

The pendulum of history is moving

The lesson of history is that fashion and behaviour both change constantly. What one generation counts odd or foolish is often seen as sensible orthodoxy to the next. The great pendulum is never still for a moment. It swings from side to side with unfailing regularity, surprising and shocking each generation, ignorant of all that has gone before. It turns as it swings – tomorrow is unique.

It seems inevitable to me, therefore, that we will see in many parts of the world the emergence of a new sexual culture at some point in the new millennium. Unless a widely available vaccine or cure is found fast, the effects of AIDS will be long lasting on the psyche of many of the worst affected nations, with a ricochet effect in many other countries.

Even if a cure is found in the next ten years, it will not be in time to prevent a scarred generation which has learned through painful experience that having multiple sex partners is a very efficient way to kill yourself and those you love.

Children born in the new millennium are inheriting a new kind of world, with scarce resources, a tendency to epidemics, and with the increasing threat of organised crime, terrorism, civil wars and ecological disaster. They may see worrying pressures grow in some places for a new national, regional or world order almost totalitarian in strength, to give security in a world increasingly torn apart by market and military forces beyond the control of democratically elected governments.

In all this we are called to pray that God's kingdom will come and his will will be done. I believe the church needs to take hold of God's answer to AIDS with confidence; to tell people about the God who invented the wonderful gift of sex and who loves it when we love one another and are faithful to each other, and about his unconditional love and the way to find new life. It is time to proclaim a clear message based on the facts and God's purpose for us all. It is time for us to reach out and care for those who, until now, we hardly realised were there.

Writing words is easy, and reading them is even easier. How are you going to respond? What is your church going to do about AIDS? Are you going to put this book away now on the shelf, or are you going to respond to what you believe God is calling you to do? For perhaps tens of thousands around the world, this is a call to move out of the secure comfort of our churches and into the problems and pain of the city, and a world stricken and dying with AIDS.

You are either part of the problem, or you can be a part of the answer.

APPENDICES

APPENDICES

BUILDING THE CAPACITY OF LOCAL GROUPS
by Isabel Carter

This information is adapted from one of a series of PILLARS guides produced by Tearfund, UK. PILLARS (Partnership in Local Language Resources) guides are designed for ease of translation and printing in other languages.

Introduction to PILLARS guides

These guides are designed for use in small group situations where one or more of the participants are literate and confident enough to lead others in group discussion. They aim to provide material for discussion around a subject, either in isolation, or as part of a regular group meeting – for example of farmers, literacy trainees or Mothers' Union members.

Ideally, just two or three topics should be used each time, allowing plenty of time for discussion of the issues raised and for carrying out some of the practical ideas suggested. No initial training is necessary for the discussion leader.

PILLARS guides aim to increase confidence among group members, so that they can successfully manage change within their own situation, without the need for outside intervention. The idea is to build on existing knowledge and experiences among the members, or within their community, so that different ideas can be tried out, adapted, and used if appropriate, or abandoned if not.

Objectives of this guide

- To help groups become effective in working and acting together
- To encourage record and note keeping
- To encourage communication and openness within a group
- To encourage groups to take positive, autonomous action without outside intervention

Anticipated outcomes

- Local groups will gain confidence in their ability to make changes for the better within their own communities
- Groups will be enabled to keep better records of their activities and to make use of this information in evaluation and future planning
- Groups will experience helpful sharing and networking of information
- Groups will be helped to plan for the future through organising activities and action

Glossary

aim	broad, long-term, important goal
assumption	something taken for granted
co-ordinate	to work together
evaluate	to study or measure the outcome of a course of action
objective	measurable activity which contributes towards achieving the main aim
resource	available money, information or services
risk	the possibility of injury or damage
SWOT	strengths – weaknesses – opportunities – threats

Topic 1: Understanding the purpose of a group

Understanding how a group works can be rather like understanding how an onion is made! All you can see of the onion is the outside layer, unless you cut it open and see the different layers inside. All we usually see of a group are the people and the resources they have.

But if we want to try and understand the group, we have to peel away the layers until we reach the centre, where we discover their vision and values.

Discussion

☐ Discuss the different groups participants are aware of. Try to work out how much you know about them. It will probably be easier to fill in the outer layer or two, but much harder to work out what should be at the centre.

☐ How often do groups start working with the outer layers before they have worked out their central vision? What problems will this bring? What happens if the central vision changes?

Topic 2: Working together

Within a community, there will be many situations where health workers, farmers, teachers, extension workers and others need to work alongside or co-operate with other people. Successful co-operation needs understanding of other people's views, concern for the needs of others and sharing of the same goal.

Take time to listen to what others are doing, how they are doing it and what the results have been. Take time to discuss ways the work could be changed to bring in new skills or people. Always try to build on what others are doing rather than starting again. Always remember that everyone has something to offer.

Discussion

Discuss this quotation by Stephen Corey: 'Seek to understand someone before you seek to be understood.'

☐ What do participants think of this idea?

☐ Discuss any existing co-operation between different organisations in the area. If there is none, discuss what sort of co-operation might be useful.

The following is a good exercise which shows the results of not working together. You will need felt pens, a large sheet of paper for each person, and plenty of table space.

Divide people into groups of four to six. Each group should sit together. Give each person a sheet of paper and ask them to begin drawing a picture of their own choice. It is very important that people do not discuss what they are doing with others in the group.

After a few minutes, ask them to stop drawing and pass their piece of paper on to the next person. Each person should then continue with the incomplete drawing that they have received. Repeat this process until each person has back their own original drawing, and give them time to look at how their own drawing finished up.

Work through the following questions. Include any questions of your own that may have arisen as you watched people take part in this activity.

- When you added to someone else's drawing, did you understand what that person was trying to draw?
- Did you think the additions to your own picture appropriate and relevant? Is your picture better or worse than you had hoped? In what way?
- If the picture you started to draw was changed, how did you feel? Why?
- What did you do if the picture you received was almost complete?
- How did you feel if the picture you received had just been started?
- Was anyone afraid to begin drawing a picture? Why?
- Did anyone find it difficult or easy to add to a picture? Why?

- What conclusions can you reach after completing this exercise?
- How might this exercise affect how you feel about team work in the future?

(Adapted from *Health Care Together*,
published by TALC. Edited by M P Johnston and S B Rilkin.)

Topic 3: Unity is strength

One person working alone may feel unable to do much to change a situation. He or she may have no confidence to make changes, take action or speak out.

A group of people who share the same situation, commitment and values, however, can achieve a great deal. Through working together and supporting each other they can take practical action. This can help build their confidence in themselves as a force for change. Together they may feel able to ask outsiders for advice or help. Together they can be strong.

Discussion

Encourage people to discuss ways in which they could work together. Are there any examples in the community of groups of people who work together? Encourage anyone who is a member of any kind of group to talk about their experiences, both good and bad. Discuss together the potential, the advantages and disadvantages of being in a group.

Ideas might include farmer groups, food processing groups, herbal medicine learning groups, health committees, youth groups and vegetable cooperatives.

Topic 4: The role of leaders

A good leader should provide a stable base for a group, should be able to inspire group members to take action, should be able to keep the group united, should have the confidence to speak out if things go wrong and should always be open to new ideas. However, leaders should also be people who are always ready to listen, especially before making decisions.

People often choose strong individuals with influence and wealth as group leaders. Sometimes this may be the right choice, but sometimes these individuals will lead the group in the way they want, rather than the way most of the members want. A quieter person, who listens well, may prove to be a good leader, especially if they are really committed to the group's well being.

Discussion

☐ Suggest at least five qualities that a good leader should have. Discuss what order of importance participants think these should have. Can you think of people who have one of these qualities? Can these qualities be developed or encouraged?

☐ Discuss the importance of a leader in maintaining and supporting a group. If there is no one person who has all the necessary qualities, are there two or three people who have some of the necessary qualities, who could lead together? What would be the advantages and disadvantages of this?

☐ A useful exercise is to send out small groups to observe together the way in which ducks and chickens care for their young. After a short period, bring groups together and discuss what each group has observed and discussed. How useful is this when considering the role of a leader?

Topic 5: What makes a good leader?

There are three kinds of leader:

1. Leaders who command. They make decisions on behalf of the group and allow little or no discussion with group members. In times of trouble, this may be necessary, but in other situations it is unlikely to encourage the group to grow in confidence and skills.

2. Leaders who consult. These leaders encourage discussion about situations and goals and then make a decision on behalf of the group.

3. Leaders who enable. They set certain limits, but within these limits encourage and enable members to gain confidence in discussing and analysing their situation and in making their own decisions.

Can you identify examples of these three kinds of leadership style. Which style would help your own situation?

Discussion

☐ Can participants think of examples of these three leadership styles? Was each different leadership style appropriate for a particular situation?

☐ Discuss what makes a good leader. If possible encourage thoughtful discussion of local personalities, politicians, characters from well known books or radio programmes or leaders within local organisations. Try to keep the discussion from becoming critical or too personal.

☐ How much does the personal knowledge and experience of a person affect their ability to lead successfully?

Topic 6: How to choose leaders

What is the purpose of the group? What kind of leadership style will be needed? What particular knowledge and skills might be helpful? The likelihood is that there will be no one in the group who will make a perfect leader, but there may be someone who could develop into a good leader.

Take time to consider who should be nominated, based on all that has been discussed.

If a vote is needed to allow members to choose between two leaders, decide how this can be done to allow each person to vote privately without being under any pressure.

Discussion

☐ Discuss what might be needed in a leader for the particular local needs.
☐ What rules should a group have for selecting leaders and for deciding how long people should remain as leaders? Make sure these are agreed before choosing a leader.
☐ Encourage discussion of the practical requirements. Allow people to feel free from pressure both when nominating people for leadership and when voting.
☐ Paper ballots, show of hands, placing stones in piles or in containers are all ways of allowing people to vote. Discuss if these, or other methods, might be useful in your own situation.

Topic 7: The role of Chairperson

A leader may often take the role of Chairperson during meetings, but the two roles are different and can be done by different people. During meetings a Chairperson would do the following:

- Carefully explain issues under discussion and regularly review where the discussion has reached
- Inspire and motivate others during meetings
- Encourage quieter people to share their opinions, views and knowledge
- Keep control of any debate and make sure people stay on the subject
- Allow decisions to be reached by popular agreement
- Make sure that disagreements and arguments do not interfere with the ongoing progress of the group
- Stand back from personal feelings and make good judgements on the group's behalf
- Share out responsibilities and work
- Be approachable and encourage openness

Discussion

☐ Emphasise that this list of qualities may not be complete. Discuss each point one by one and use examples where possible. What other qualities and responsibilities could be added?

☐ Which of these roles do participants think are more important? Why? If most members are literate, these roles and any others suggested could be written out on pieces of paper and then ranked in order of importance.

Topic 8: The role of Secretary

The role of a Secretary is to provide support for the Chairperson, to keep careful notes and to organise the smooth running of the group. A Secretary needs to be:

- Literate – so that a record (minutes) can be made of all the important points discussed and decisions made at each meeting
- Able to write letters and reports on behalf of the group
- Able to arrange the timing and place for meetings and make sure all members have this information, together with details of matters to be discussed (agenda)
- Able to look after and organise any information resources and notes which the group owns

Discussion

☐ This list may not be complete. What other skills might be needed?

☐ What would be the possible consequences for a group unable to keep notes of its meetings and activities?

☐ What are the benefits of good organisation within a small group?

☐ What personal qualities might a Secretary need?

☐ Which of these skills do participants think are more important? These could be ranked in order of importance.

☐ How vital is literacy for the role of a Secretary? Is there any training available for someone who would make a good Secretary, but needs encouragement with literacy training?

Topic 9: The role of Treasurer

First and foremost a Treasurer will need to be trustworthy. They should also be able to do the following:

- Keep careful records of all money paid in as contributions, fees or sale of produce, and of all money paid out as loans, or expenses
- Look after the group's money wisely

- Manage the bank account (if one is opened) and keep cash in the bank for safety
- Report back to members on the group's finances
- Advise the group on the best ways to use their funds

Discussion

☐ What sort of training or experience might be needed for a Treasurer? Where might this be available?

☐ What should group members do to make sure the Treasurer is fully accountable to them?

☐ What help and support might a Treasurer need in carrying out this work?

☐ Are there other qualities which would be useful in a Treasurer? Which of the roles mentioned do participants think are more important? Can you rank them in order of importance?

☐ 'Women make better Treasurers.' Discuss this statement. Do participants agree with it?

Topic 10: The special role of animators

The role of an animator is rarely given a formal title within a group. However, within most successful groups there will be at least one animator. These are people who bring new ideas, enthusiasm and a vision for making change possible. They rarely push themselves forward but they have a real concern for the well being and progress of the group. They don't just talk about new ideas – they make them happen in practical ways.

Animators believe in the potential of people in their communities and they provide the energy that is needed for change.

Discussion

☐ Discuss the concept of an animator. Do participants agree that such people are usually found in each group? How often are they the Chairperson?

☐ Are all development workers in NGOs and church organisations animators?

☐ List the qualities an animator may have. Start by mentioning that they may perhaps be an encourager, an enabler or a trainer.

☐ Can these qualities be learnt and developed in someone?

Topic 11: Group members

Groups are made up of all kinds of people but there are a few types that can be found in nearly all groups:

- Complainers are people who rarely find anything good in other people's views and decisions and are quick to complain.
- Know-it-alls are the people who are always convinced their views are right and often persuade others to follow them, sometimes creating division within the group.
- Quiet members rarely share their opinions and do not want to take any responsibility or make decisions.
- Positive members are the ones who carefully consider ideas before reaching their own view or opinion. They join in discussion and share in decision-making. These people are usually the committed centre of a group.
- Traditionalists are those who dislike change or taking risks with anything new.
- Bridge-builders like others to feel at peace with each other and be happy with decisions made. They take time to sort out disagreements.

Discussion

☐ Is there ever likely to be a 'perfect' group?
☐ Encourage discussion about how members can learn to appreciate the different roles and personalities within the group. Be careful not to allow people to become personal and start making comments about each other.
☐ Which of these different types of people are less common within groups?
☐ Ask participants to suggest practical ways of encouraging different personalities to play supportive roles within a group.

Topic 12: Making the most of meetings

Meetings can be dominated by one or two 'important people' telling everyone what they should be doing. This kind of meeting is not very productive. People are more likely to become involved in taking action if they have been involved in the decision-making process.

Sensitive leaders will encourage group members to take more and more responsibility both during meetings and in practical work. Over time the leader's role may become less important as members become more used to sharing responsibility.

Discussion

☐ To help people reach decisions, especially on sensitive issues, a good Chairperson should have the skills to stop debate, summarise the views expressed and ask for a decision, if necessary by a show of hands. Postponing decisions is usually only necessary if more information is needed. What can group members do when meetings are badly led?
☐ Continue to discuss how to encourage participation at meetings. How

can 'important people' be politely asked to let others have their say? How can women be given confidence to speak and make their views known?

□ How can meetings start on time? How can meetings use time well? How can decisions be reached, instead of postponed for yet another meeting? Should decisions be made early or late during meetings? Why?

□ A good and effective Chairperson is key. They need to prepare for the meeting with a well-planned agenda, which is then followed. Time limits should be set for meetings – and kept.

Topic 13: Setting aims and objectives

A new group must take time to carefully agree on the purpose of the group.

Most groups come together because members all have an interest in a similar idea. This is usually the main 'aim' of the group. However, they should first meet with others in the community to discuss the needs, then agree on exactly how they plan to work together, what their priorities are and how they can work together effectively to reach their aim.

It is usually a mistake to set lots of objectives. Discuss what you hope to see happening in the future. Then try to decide on just a few key objectives.

Discussion

□ First discuss what is meant by 'objectives' and 'aims'. A group will usually have just one or two main aims. These could include supporting their community, improving health, raising income.

□ How can the real needs of the community be understood? How important is it to make sure that activities planned by groups will help meet some of the needs in the community?

□ Groups then need to set objectives – the ways in which they plan to achieve their aim. For example, if the aim of the group is to improve health, their objectives might be to improve the water supply, to build latrines, to have a health worker trained in each village, to support the clinic in their immunisation programme and to teach young people about HIV.

□ What sort of objectives might a group set if their aim was to care for orphans in their community, or to care for those with AIDS who are unwell?

□ What happens if group members have very different ideas on what the group objectives should be? What should happen if they cannot agree? Should groups agree to split at the first major sign of differences? What are the alternatives?

Topic 14: Planning activities with the 'Five Finger' method

Once a group has agreed its objectives it can begin to take action. For successful activities, it is always helpful to first plan them carefully and put them in order of priority.

The Five Finger Questions are a very good way of planning:

- **What** is the action being planned? Why is it needed?
- **How** is the work going to be carried out? What resources are needed?
- **Who** is going to carry out this work? Will they need training?
- **Where** is the work to be done?
- **When** is the work going to be done? How long will it take?

Discussion

☐ Why is it important to ask these questions for every activity which a group plans to carry out? What might happen if they are not asked? Try them out for each activity participants are planning.

☐ If participants do not belong to a group with clear objectives, discuss how they might ask these questions for each of the possible objectives set after the discussion in Topic 13 by the group who wanted to improve health in their community. Alternatively, set some other imaginary objectives and work out what activities would be needed to achieve them.

Topic 15: Planning in a changing situation

When a group plans aims and activities, it is easy to be positive and to assume everything will go well. However, all kinds of things may change how those activities work out. Often things don't turn out as planned.

When planning activities, it is very helpful to consider what may unexpectedly happen to put the activities at risk. For example, key members may become ill or leave the group; there may be a natural disaster; the Treasurer may disappear with the money; another group may start producing the same products.

Once risks are considered, the group will be better prepared to deal with the unexpected and to take steps to reduce risks – for example increasing financial supervision or networking with other organisations.

Discussion

☐ Consider again the group wanting to improve their community's health. First of all, consider what they assume will remain the same. For example, they may assume that the clinic will remain open, and that people will use any improved water sources. Can you think of any others?

☐ Secondly, what possible risks might they have to face? For example, the minimum salary might be increased by the government by 50%, or there might be a major outbreak of cholera or typhoid. Can you think of any others?

□ Think of the assumptions and risks for each one of the objectives you have listed.

□ Repeat this exercise again with some other imaginary objectives.

Topic 16: Measuring progress

Consider what the signs of progress will be for various different activities planned. Ways have to be found to measure whether there has been any progress.

You may *think* that health, agriculture or income may have improved a bit as a result of your planned activities, but this will not tell you very much! If, for example, your activities have included introducing rabbit husbandry, the things you could measure might be:

• The number of farmers deciding to look after rabbits
• The number of rabbits sold for meat
• The number of rabbits eaten by family members
• The number of cases of childhood malnutrition recorded in the local clinic
• The frequency of disease in rabbits
• The income from selling the furs

Over two years, this would provide a good record of the effect of your activities on farmers, nutrition and income, and indicate areas where you could improve future activities. Can you think of similar measures for HIV prevention and care programmes?

Discussion

□ If you start activities and only consider measuring their effectiveness after two years, it may prove very difficult to discover what has been achieved. You need to think before starting work about how you will measure progress. Then you will be able to keep useful records that will show clearly the results of your activities.

□ Consider again the example of the community improving health. What ways could they use for measuring improvements in health? For example, they could see if the number of children receiving vaccinations has gone up, or the cases of childhood diarrhoea been reduced, or whether the number of child deaths in the first two years of life has been reduced, or the number of women going to the hospital for antenatal care who turn out to have HIV has been stable or falling since the project started (although it can be hard to be certain what factors have contributed alongside your own work).

☐ Can you think of other activities and then suggest ways of measuring their effectiveness?

☐ Planning activities like this take a long time, but they will prove very worthwhile. This kind of planning process is especially important if you hope to find funding for your work.

☐ Use all the different stages (aims, objectives, activities, assumptions and risks and ways of measuring progress) when writing funding applications!

Topic 17: New skills and information

A group with clear objectives and plans will usually find it has a need for new skills or more information. Sometimes these can be found within the community or nearby and can be arranged informally. Sometimes group members do not know where to find them.

Try contacting nearby organisations to ask for their advice. People may fear visiting organisations and officials on their own, but acting for the group may give them the confidence to go out and visit with one or two other members.

Training to learn new skills may cost money. If so, ask for advice about obtaining scholarships or grants.

Discussion

☐ Encourage participants to discuss any NGOs, government or church organisations which they are aware of. Be prepared to suggest others. It is also helpful if one member knows somebody who may be able to give advice on several of these organisations. Begin with local knowledge and contacts and build on them.

☐ Discuss where or to whom participants go to ask for advice or information when necessary.

☐ What other possible sources might there be?

☐ Would they have more confidence to visit new organisations or government officials if they went with other members? What would be the benefits of this?

☐ Are there useful workshops or training courses participants are aware of?

☐ Try to find other local groups with similar interests and experience. They may have useful knowledge to share about organisations, government officials and training opportunities.

Topic 18: Local resources

Within the local community there are often many valuable sources of information. Older people in particular are often a huge store of information about the local environment, cultural traditions and customs, and the uses of local plants and animals, particularly for their medicinal qualities.

Discussion

☐ There is a saying that each time an old person dies, a whole library of information dies with them. What do participants think of this saying? How may this problem be avoided? What information is it important to learn?

☐ Discuss what local sources of information participants find useful. Who (or what) do they turn to first?

☐ Are there innovative farmers in the local area who are always trying out new ideas, and as a result are often regarded as slightly odd by others in the community? Can local people visit and learn from them?

☐ Are there herbalists or traditional birth attendants or retired men with experience in local government?

☐ What kind of information is available locally which participants fail to find?

Topic 19: Outside information

New ideas often require new sources of information and resources. All groups need to develop their methods of obtaining such new information. This will often mean building relationships with individuals in organisations, especially where they may be able to help with obtaining useful information about other organisations, suppliers, purchasers of new goods, crafts or products.

What printed information does the group have access to? Many newsletters and some books can be obtained free of charge. Try to build up a small resource centre.

Information may bring the knowledge, power and confidence to make changes.

Discussion

☐ Encourage participants to discuss any useful sources of outside information they have found. Help participants to list all the likely sources of outside information. Which ones have never been used by participants? Why? Examples might include research institutes, universities, British Council libraries and the internet.

☐ What sources of printed information do group members have access to?

How could members share this information? Do any have access to newsletters? Often these will refer to other useful newsletters or resources.

☐ Does the group have any money to buy information in the form of useful books or manuals?

Topic 20: Keeping records

Clear, brief and accurate records should be kept of every meeting. Good records (minutes) mean that any disagreements about decisions made can quickly be checked. They can also be used to look back and check progress.

Good records should also be kept for each activity carried out. Many outside organisations may consider good records an indication of a group's ability to manage resources and funds. They can also provide a record of those present at every meeting. They should always be open to members.

It is a good idea for members who act on behalf of the group to keep a diary or notebook, recording each activity: how many came, what was shared or learnt, what were the results, and so on. This simple idea will provide good records and a lot of information when evaluating the work of the group.

Discussion

☐ Consider the purpose of records kept by any groups or organisations of which participants have experience. Did they fill a useful purpose? How often were they referred back to?

☐ Could they have been more useful? Were members able to see copies of the records? Did they have too much detail or too little?

☐ Consider the present meeting. How would you keep records of the meeting? Is it necessary to record all the discussion or just the decisions reached? Should minutes be as short as possible or as long as possible?

☐ Have any participants kept a diary of their activities? Notes need only be very short, but could still prove a very useful record.

Topic 21: Networking

Contact with groups in similar situations and with similar objectives can be very rewarding. Each group can bring different experiences to share. Networking with several such groups may be even more rewarding. Usually one group or individual needs to be responsible for maintaining regular contact between network members. Networks can keep contact through meetings, letters, newsletters, email links, workshops or informal contacts.

Discussion

☐ Have people ever felt that they are on their own, cut off from help and similar groups? Do they feel they have to struggle alone to find out new skills and information? How encouraged would they be to discover that there are other similar groups?

☐ Networks are ways of linking people together. Usually networks link groups with a similar interest, such as community health, animal traction, sustainable agriculture or literacy.

☐ Members of networks are often linked by newsletters. Sometimes there may be workshops or regional meetings. Sometimes network members are encouraged to visit nearby contacts.

☐ Do participants have any experience of belonging to networks?

☐ Some useful and free newsletters that include HIV focus are:

Footsteps. PO Box 200, Bridgnorth, Shropshire, WV16 4WQ, UK. E-mail: footsteps@tearfund.org

Health Action. Healthlink Worldwide, Cityside, 40 Adler Street, London, E1 1EE, UK. E-mail: info@healthlink.org.uk

Contact. CMAI, 2A3 Local Shopping Centre, Janakpuri, New Delhi 110 058, India.

Child to Child. Institute of Education, 20 Bedford Way, London, WC1 6OA, UK.

Topic 22: Looking back (evaluating)

However much a group has managed to achieve, there will always be many more things that can be done. Sometimes a group will be very successful in some of its actions, whereas other actions may prove of little use. It's always good to set aside time to look back and consider where the group has come from.

Evaluation looks back at what has been achieved, studies the group's records, decides what have been the strengths and weaknesses, looks at how things could have been done more effectively and then makes new plans.

A group who did their planning will find it much easier to evaluate their work.

Take time to be encouraged by progress, however small!

Discussion

☐ Evaluation can take a lot of time, but it can be very valuable, so it is worth setting aside time each year to do this. Would it be helpful for someone from outside to take part in this as they can often see things very clearly? Could you ask another group to help with this?

☐ Often people rely on what they think is happening rather than what is actually happening. This is where surveys can help. For example, people may think that latrines are being well used, until a visit shows that this is not always the case. Decide what would be useful to measure and how the group members could do this.

☐ Carry out a SWOT (Strengths, Weaknesses, Opportunities, Threats) analysis. This can look at the organisation, activities or work of a group. First consider all the strengths, then the weaknesses. Then consider opportunities for new possibilities and finally anything which may become a threat.

Bible studies by Rose Robinson

These Bible studies are designed to use in small groups. They may provide a useful introduction to a meeting where different topics from the Guide are being discussed. Choose a study that will be linked to the topic you plan to study or that is relevant to your situation. During the studies, encourage people to reflect on what they read, to discuss the meaning and the implications and, finally, to pray together about what they have learnt.

Bible study 1 – One in heart and mind

Read Philippians 2:1–4. Is there someone in your life who has treated you in a way that has been a great encouragement, comfort or support to you? Such people help us to realise the value of unity and love.

With any group it is important to agree on a purpose and what we hope to achieve, and to relate positively to one another.

Paul tells the Philippian church to be 'one in spirit and purpose'. Likewise, Acts 4:32 says that 'all the believers were one in heart and mind'.

☐ What happens if a group does not have a vision or purpose, or if the members do not all agree and share the vision?

☐ How should you decide on the central vision of your group so that all the members are fully behind it?

Jesus said, 'Any kingdom divided against itself will be ruined, and a house divided against itself will fall' (Luke 11:17). It is important in any group to consider everyone's opinions, to ensure that each person in the group feels valued and is contributing in a positive way.

☐ Are you listening to others in your group?

☐ Read Philippians 2:5–11. Christ Jesus is, of course, our greatest example. According to this passage, who is Jesus? Yet what was he prepared to do for us? How far will you forego your own position to encourage others?

☐ Read Philippians 2:12–13. Is God achieving his purposes through your group?

Bible study 2 – Leadership (1)

Read 1 Timothy 3:1–10. This passage describes the qualities Paul considered important for leaders in the church. What does Paul say about the person who sets their heart on being an overseer (verse 1)?

☐ Which of the qualities listed for overseers and deacons (verses 2–5 and 7–9) might be important for your group leader(s) and why?

☐ What danger does verse 6 say there is in having a recent convert as a church leader? Could there be the same danger for your group if you had a new member leading?

☐ What does verse 10 say about deacons?

Bible study 3 – Leadership (2)

Read the following verses: Exodus 3:11, Judges 6:15, 1 Samuel 9:21, 1 Kings 3:7 and Jeremiah 1:6.

☐ What sort of people is God choosing for leadership roles here?

☐ What are their attitudes?

☐ What model of leadership does Jesus show us in John 13:3–5? What does God say he looks at when he is selecting a leader? (See 1 Samuel 16:7.)

Having reviewed the qualities and attitudes a leader needs, and the work to be done, many people might feel (as did some of the people in these examples) inadequate and unable to fulfil the leadership role. This can be a healthy attitude if handled correctly, as it means the leader will look for support and not become proud.

Bible study 4 – Leadership (3)

What help might your leader need to fulfil his or her role effectively? The following may give you some ideas:

• God's help (Exodus 3:11–12; Judges 6:15–16)
• Help from others (Exodus 4:10–16; Exodus 17:12; Acts 6:1–7)
• Prayer (Acts 6:6; 13:3; 1 Thessalonians 5:25)
• Resources and workers (Exodus 36:2–3; Nehemiah 4:6)
• Training alongside those with more experience (Joshua – Exodus 24:13; 33:11; Elisha – 1 Kings 19:19–21; Timothy – Philippians 2:22)

Bible study 5 – One body, many parts (1)

Read 1 Corinthians 12:12–26 and Romans 12:3–8.

There is much we can learn from these passages about how a group works together. In any group there are a variety of people but they form one body (1 Corinthians 12:12; Romans 12:4–5) and as such have a commitment to, or belong to, one another (1 Corinthians 12:14–16; 12:26).

☐ What does this mean in practice for your group?

Each member of the group has a gift to use. In these passages several dangers are highlighted when thinking about our own gifts and those of others. What warning does Romans 12:3 give us? 1 Corinthians 12:21–25 teaches of a similar attitude.

☐ What happens when we overvalue our own gifts and undervalue those of others or begin to boast about our own gifts?

Bible study 6 – One body, many parts (2)

The Bible tells us that every person has gifts (1 Corinthians 12:7, 11). Jesus himself also gave us some strong teaching on what happens to those who do not use their gifts (Matthew 25:14–30).

☐ Do you know what your gifts are? And are you using them (Romans 12:6–8)?1 Corinthians 4:7 reminds us that all we have has been given to us, so there is no room for pride. However, what is the opposite danger (1 Corinthians 12:15–20)?

☐ Is your group functioning well, like a healthy body, where each different member is playing their part? How can you encourage one another to do so?

Bible study 7 – Planning

Read 1 Chronicles 22:1–19. David shows us the importance of making good preparations before beginning work. Luke 14:28–30 likewise encourages us to 'estimate the cost' before starting anything, so that people will not laugh at us because we began something and were then unable to finish it.

We can see how the 'Five Finger' planning method applies to this passage (see Topic 14).

- **What** is the action being planned? What did David have it in his heart to do (verse 7)?
- **How** is the work to be carried out? What resources were needed (verses 2–4, 14)?
- **Who** is going to carry out the work? What part did David play and why (verse 5)? Who is given the overall responsibility during the construction phase (verse 6)? What kinds of workers were involved (verses 15–16)? Who else does David encourage to help (verse 17)?
- **Where** is the work to be done? 1 Chronicles 21:18 tells us that David was guided by God as to where to build the temple.
- **When** would the work be done (verses 7–10)?

All the practical details for this project are thoroughly planned: the aim; the site; the materials; the workers; the supervisor; the helpers and the timing.

☐ Who is really in charge of all this planning for the building of the temple? (See, for example, 1 Chronicles 28:18 and 1 Chronicles 29:7–13.) Proverbs 16:3 tells us: 'Commit to the Lord whatever you do and your plans will succeed.'

☐ Are you following this advice?

Bible study 8 – Nothing is impossible with God

Read Judges 7:1–22.

☐ Why does the Lord say he cannot deliver Midian into the hands of Gideon and his men?

☐ What does he not want Israel to end up doing?

☐ Which men turn back first (verses 2–3)?

The Lord uses the way that the men drink from the river to decide who else shall not go with Gideon. The majority of the army kneel down to drink and just 300 men lap with their tongues like a dog, with their hands to their mouths. God tells Gideon that these 300 men are the ones to go into the battle.

☐ How does your group choose who will do a certain task (verses 4–8)?

☐ Do you seek God's advice?

☐ We are told that the Midianite army is huge (verse 12). How does the Lord encourage Gideon not to be afraid and to believe that his small army will win the battle?

Gideon and his men use the resources they have to great effect: they work together (verses 17–18, 20), with each man playing his part (verse 21), 'for the Lord and for Gideon' (verses 18, 20). They know that the victory is the Lord's (verses 15, 22).

☐ How might this passage encourage your group as you face the tasks ahead of you?

If God has called us and we keep our eyes fixed on him, however immense the task seems, and however small our resources are, we will succeed: 'For with God, nothing is impossible' (Luke 1:37).

CREDIT AND LOANS FOR SMALL BUSINESSES
by Isabel Carter

This information is adapted from one of a series of PILLARS guides produced by Tearfund, UK. PILLARS (Partnership in Local Language Resources) guides are designed for ease of translation and printing in other languages.

Micro-credit schemes have been used successfully to help those orphaned or widowed by HIV/AIDS, as well as to provide income for women wishing to find alternatives to commercial sex work, or for those who have HIV and are financially vulnerable.

Introduction to PILLARS guides

These guides are designed for use in small group situations where one or more of the participants are literate and confident enough to lead others in group discussion. They aim to provide material for discussion around a subject, either in isolation, or as part of a regular group meeting – for example of farmers, literacy trainees or Mothers' Union members.

Ideally, just two or three topics should be used each time, allowing plenty of time for discussion of the issues raised and for carrying out some of the practical ideas suggested. No initial training is necessary for the discussion leader.

PILLARS guides aim to increase confidence among group members, so that they can successfully manage change within their own situation, without the need for outside intervention. The idea is to build on existing knowledge and experiences among the members, or within their community, so that different ideas can be tried out, adapted, and used if appropriate, or abandoned if not.

Objectives of this guide

- To demonstrate a variety of ways of obtaining either credit or loans
- To establish good practice in record keeping and planning

- To study the issues involved before establishing either informal savings or credit groups or obtaining loans from outside organisations

Anticipated outcomes

- Understanding and confidence in managing resources and finances effectively
- Appropriate officers to be appointed within groups supported by relevant skills training in record keeping and accounts
- Local groups encouraged to establish systems of micro-credit which are appropriate to their needs and resources, either with or without outside intervention

Glossary

accountable	responsible or answerable to others
advertising	making customers aware of a product
aim	broad, long-term, important goal
credit	money available as a loan
debt	money owed to an individual or bank
evaluate	to study or measure the outcome of a course of action
expenses	money paid out for services and goods
export	transport of goods or products for sale in other countries
inflation	a rise in general prices throughout the whole country
interest	a charge made for borrowing money
loan	temporary use of a sum of money, usually with an interest fee payable
micro-enterprise	a small business, usually run by one person
NGO	non-governmental organisation
objective	measurable activity which contributes towards achieving the main aim
profit	money which remains after all costs have been taken away from income
resource	money, information, human skills or natural products, available to help achieve an objective
revolving credit fund	a sum of money made available as a short-term loan to members of a savings group, who take it in turn to have the loan
savings	money put aside for the future, usually in a bank where it may earn interest

Topic 1: Dreaming

Most people have dreams of what they could do if they had enough money. They may dream of how they might start a small business, such as a bakery, a market stall or as a carpenter.

Discussion

☐ Encourage participants to discuss their dreams and consider what would be required. How would you use a loan of $50 or of $200? In small groups encourage people to talk about their hopes and dreams, and then come together to share them with the whole group.

☐ Do some share the same idea? Suggest they get together to talk things over more.

Topic 2: The problems of credit for the poor

Obtaining a loan from a bank is very difficult if you are poor. Officials will need evidence of your skills in reading, writing and managing money. They will also need evidence of how much property you have in case you cannot pay back a loan. Often a woman can only obtain bank loans in her husband's name.

Discussion

☐ What experiences have members of the group had in dealing with banks?

☐ Encourage participants to share their experiences. Have some people met with problems in trying to obtain a loan? What kinds of problems were these? Have they been able to overcome them?

☐ Have some people been successful in either opening bank accounts or obtaining credit? If so, why? What different kinds of bank accounts have they used or found out about – for example, savings accounts, loan accounts or credit accounts.

Topic 3: Self-help credit

By forming a group, people with no access to outside credit can help each other with credit. A group of about fifteen people, meeting regularly, could agree to bring to each meeting either a small amount of money or an agreed amount of crop or fruit produce for sale. Each group member would take it in turns to take all that week's money or produce.

Discussion

Even this simple system, which needs no bank account or training, still needs certain things to succeed. What might these be? Encourage participants to make suggestions.

Here are some examples of what needs to be considered:

- People will need to trust each other to bring regular payments
- What will be done about those who miss their payments?
- What will happen if group members who fall ill cannot pay but need money urgently?
- How will the group decide the order of who gets the loan?

Topic 4: Revolving credit groups

The advantage of using this system of revolving credit is that no outside help is needed. It is simple to run and can often be added to the ongoing work of a group such as Mothers' Union, a farmers' group, a health committee, and so on.

Discussion

☐ What existing groups are already established locally where revolving credit could be introduced?

☐ Encourage participants with experience in revolving credit to discuss both the good and bad points they have experienced.

☐ How can the work of revolving credit groups be expanded? What might the dangers be?

☐ Such loans will provide only small amounts of credit. How can groups encourage saving in order to provide larger amounts of credit?

Topic 5: Working together to raise income

If no outside income is available, small groups can agree to work together to raise income for a micro-enterprise, or other purposes. A certain time each week or month or season could be set aside – for example, to grow vegetables, to process foods or to produce crafts.

Consider any ways of working together like this which might raise income. Is there an outsider who might bring useful ideas, suggestions, advice or training?

Discussion

☐ Careful record-keeping from the beginning is very important, not just to encourage confidence among group members, but also because it may help to obtain an outside loan in the future. Why might this be?

☐ Money earned from working together can be put into a savings account, after expenses have been paid. Where might the money be put?

☐ How will members know who has saved what amount?

☐ How can members be sure that their money is looked after in a trustworthy way?

Topic 6: Savings clubs

Savings clubs encourage members to save a small amount of money regularly to use for a special purpose. Members may all save for the same event, such as making a visit together or establishing an income-generating project. They may also save individually, for example for a wedding or for Christmas celebrations.

Simple savings clubs depend on an honest and reliable Treasurer.

Discussion

☐ Discuss how establishing a savings club could be added to the regular activities of any group.

☐ What experiences do members have with savings clubs? Have these been positive or difficult experiences?

☐ How should the funds of a savings club be looked after?

Topic 7: The role of Treasurer

First and foremost a Treasurer will need to be trustworthy. He or she should also be able to do the following:

- Keep careful records of all money paid in (from contributions, fees or sale of produce), and all money paid out (as loans, or expenses)
- Look after the group's money wisely
- Manage the bank account (if one is opened) and keep cash in the bank for safety
- Report back to members on the group's finances
- Advise the group on the best ways to use their funds

Discussion

☐ What sort of training or experience might be needed for a Treasurer? Where might this be available?

☐ What should group members do to make sure the Treasurer is fully accountable to them?

☐ What help and support might a Treasurer need in carrying out their work?

☐ Are there other qualities which would be useful in a Treasurer? Which of the roles mentioned do participants think are more important? Can you rank them in order of importance?

□ 'Women make better Treasurers.' Discuss this statement. Do participants agree with it?

Topic 8: Keeping careful records

A group decide to collect a certain sum of money from each member every meeting. They chose a Treasurer who has no experience in keeping records. At the next meeting some members pay in full, others pay half and say they will bring the money later. Others forget. Later the Treasurer cannot remember clearly who has not paid in full and argues with them but soon gives up. When she is asked at the meeting how much has been raised she makes up a sum because she is unsure. People are angry that there is not more. Some accuse her of taking money and ask why she has a new dress.

Discussion

□ What do people think will happen to this group? What action needs to be taken? Emphasise the need to discuss problems before they happen.

□ What can be done if members stop paying regularly but still want a loan? What happens if members are sick or in trouble?

□ How can the group protect themselves against a member who is one of the first to receive the credit and then leaves?

□ How can a group protect themselves from future difficulties such as drought, leading to a poor harvest?

Topic 9: Opening a bank account

Once any group begins to save money, it is important to open a bank account so that the money is kept safe from theft or loss. Two people need to sign each cheque as well as the Treasurer. These people must be able to write their names and must be trustworthy.

A bank needs to be sympathetic to the aims of the group and willing to let them open a joint account. If a group has kept good records, these may help reassure officials of the reliability of the group.

It is useful if the bank is nearby so that deposits can be made regularly. Find out about bank charges before opening an account. If there is a choice, find out about the different rates of interest available and choose an account that gives higher interest, as long as payments and withdrawals can be made regularly.

Discussion

☐ New groups may find it helpful to get advice from someone who already has a bank account, or from an NGO. These people may be needed to give a guarantee to the bank. Can people suggest such individuals?

☐ If inflation is very high, there may be little point in saving money in a bank account as it will just lose its value. In what other ways could groups invest their money? For example, could they purchase building materials or kitchen equipment that could be resold?

Topic 10: Obtaining loans from money lenders

When poor people without savings need money quickly, for events such as illness, family funerals or weddings, they usually turn to a local money lender for a loan.

Money lenders are usually well known, easy to approach and often do not ask for any guarantees before giving a loan. However, the rates of interest they charge are usually very high indeed. Repaying a loan may push a family further into poverty and debt.

Discussion

☐ What are the advantages of using local money lenders? Are there social pressures which make it difficult for people to obtain money from elsewhere?

☐ What are the disadvantages of using them? What alternatives do people have?

☐ Discuss people's experiences with money lenders. Are there examples of people who have become trapped by debt which continues to grow? They may be forced to keep borrowing more to pay back previous loans from money lenders.

Topic 11: Obtaining loans from informal savings groups

Groups with a well established savings system may be able to make loans available to members. When loans are made, it is usual to charge interest. Many groups find that 10–15% interest will cover the costs involved.

The money raised from interest payments should cover the costs of record keeping and banking and the rest should be invested to cover any loans that are not repaid, perhaps because of death or sickness.

At the beginning it is a good idea to make only small loans. Once people have successfully repaid several smaller loans, they can usually be trusted with a larger loan.

Discussion

Imagine the following two examples.

1. Peter wants to establish a tree nursery, and is loaned $50 for a period of two years. The interest is 12%, which means an interest fee of $12 after the two years.
2. Mary wants to produce palm oil. She is loaned $50 for six months at an interest rate of 12%, which means an interest fee of $3 after the six months.

☐ Discuss the reasons behind interest charges. Compare these suggested charges with those of local money lenders.

☐ In the first example, Peter borrowed $50 to buy equipment for a tree nursery. He was allowed a year before starting to repay the loan and then had to finish the repayments within two years. His total repayment was $62 so he paid back $5.20 each month during the second year. He raised this money from the sale of fruit trees.

Mary borrowed $50 to make palm oil. She bought palm nuts from the market, processed and bottled the oil, selling it quickly in the local market. She paid back her loan in full after only six months, paying just $3 in interest charges – making a total of $53.

Encourage members to discuss the implications of making such loans available and look at whether there is any training available locally.

Topic 12: Using money wisely

Money in itself is unlikely to make a difference unless well used. Careful planning is needed, and likely costs, markets and profit need to be considered.

With money in the hand it can be very tempting to spend some on clothes or food. Family members may demand some of the money for other purposes. It may be helpful for other group members to assist with purchasing the planned items as soon as a loan is taken out, to ensure the money is used as intended.

Discussion

☐ Discuss some suggested ideas for raising money, such as rabbit keeping, baking, bicycle repairs, drying fish or making straw mats. What should people consider for each idea suggested? This should include:

• The costs of raw material, tools or animals
• Rent of space

- The time it will take to produce and sell items
- Any local competition
- The likely profit

☐ Discuss any concerns around how to help members spend their loan wisely and safely.

Topic 13: Group security with loans

Taking out loans as a group has a lot to recommend it. Each group member is responsible for making sure other members help to repay the loan. If someone does not pay, other members will want to know why. Groups can usually obtain larger loans, making it possible to buy more expensive equipment or raw materials.

If a member becomes ill, other members may be able to help cover their payments until they recover.

When problems arise, the group members can discuss them and are more likely to find solutions by working things out together. However, things may also go wrong and relationships become difficult.

Discussion

☐ Encourage discussion of the advantages and disadvantages of individual loans and group loans. Do participants know of real examples?

☐ How well should members of such a group know and trust each other?

☐ What would people do if a person wanted to join but others were suspicious of them or didn't like them?

☐ What might happen if members argue or no longer want to work together?

☐ Encourage participants to list the advantages of obtaining a group loan. These could include:

- Ability to buy more expensive equipment
- Working together is usually more enjoyable and more productive than working alone
- If one member cannot make their repayments for good reasons, other members may be able to help
- Successful repayments will give a group self-confidence and encouragement for future plans
- Relationships within the group may develop into real friendship and trust

Topic 14: Obtaining credit from outside organisations

An increasing number of NGOs are able to provide credit for micro-enterprises. If you are fortunate to live near one, then you may be able to benefit from their training, advice and credit schemes.

Groups are more likely to obtain a loan if they can demonstrate that they are capable of keeping clear, accurate records. Evidence of savings will also increase the chance of obtaining a loan.

Many NGOs are likely to prefer making loans to established groups rather than to individuals.

Discussion

☐ Are people aware of any organisations offering loan or credit schemes which operate in the area? What has been people's experience of their activities and conditions?

☐ It is not recommended that churches or pastors take responsibility for credit and loan schemes. Why do you think this is? For example, it would be difficult for the church to provide support for people in difficulty and be responsible for demanding loan repayments. It is better for local Christians to manage a credit scheme and report to local churches.

☐ Encourage people to discuss this and share any experiences.

Topic 15: Setting up in business

Micro-enterprises, which supply goods or services that local people need and that have an easily available market, are more likely to be successful. Ideas should be new rather than setting up in competition with existing enterprises.

Consider what facilities, equipment and labour will be needed. While it is sensible to start small, it is also useful to allow some space to be able to grow and increase production without needing to move immediately.

In addition to obtaining a loan or credit, other legal structures may be required. The enterprise may need to be registered officially. What is the situation regarding tax? If food products are involved, the enterprise may need a hygiene inspection. Is the equipment reliable and safe for workers?

Discussion

☐ How can new ideas be developed? What household products are always needed but could be produced slightly differently? These could include bags, mats, brooms, food products, cooking equipment or lights.

☐ Who else is making such products? How could you vary what is produced? Consider new ideas, variations, colours and different uses, even for everyday things.

☐ It is usually better to start with making products which use locally available materials and tools so that you don't need too much money to start with.

☐ Is there any useful training available? Are there skilled individuals you could learn from? Are there courses available?

Topic 16: Market research

Before supplying products or services, you will first need to find out if enough people will want to buy them. Before you start producing goods, you will need to find out what people really think, what they would like and what price they are prepared to pay. Never make products first, hoping that you will be able to sell them. You will need to ask:

• What products are popular and in demand?
• What is the likely selling price?
• How many are likely to be sold in a day or a week?
• Who else is making the same or similar products?
• Where are they selling their products?

Discussion

☐ What problems may come from relying just on the advice of friends who want to be encouraging? Where should people go to make these enquiries? Should people look just at the local market or is it useful to travel to nearby towns?

☐ What kind of questions should be asked? Who should ask them? How many people should be questioned for their advice? How seriously should such information be taken?

Topic 17: Managing small businesses

The key to success is to understand what customers want and then produce it in ways which allow a good profit to be made.

Costs must be measured accurately and should include every part of the business, including borrowing a friend's vehicle, wastage, replacing equipment, and power charges.

Profit is the sale price, less any costs. Profit can be increased in two ways. First, by increasing the sale price – if the goods are of such high quality or interest that people will pay more. Secondly, profit can be increased by reducing the costs of production – for example, through buying larger quantities of raw materials or through reducing waste.

Discussion

□ What kind of costs could easily be ignored when working out the real cost of producing goods?

□ How can people keep their business money separate from their personal money? For example, money from a recent sale may make people feel rich and be used for personal needs. Money owed to a supplier or needed to buy raw materials may be used to buy food for the family. A simple solution is to use a separate pocket or container for business money.

□ Should all profits be kept for personal use? Should some be invested to build up the business? It may be best to decide what you can afford to take from the business as a salary and take only that.

□ If someone already has a small business, how could a loan help them to improve their profits?

Topic 18: Controlling the quality of goods

Once you begin to produce goods, it is very important to check the quality at all stages. Customers will want value for money and will not continue to buy poor quality goods.

Make sure that all your workers understand what quality of work is expected and make checks without warning.

Buy safe and tested raw materials and use dry and pest-free storage.

Customers notice high quality goods and your reputation will increase.

Discussion

□ Consider a few examples of locally produced products. For example, these could be bags, cooking equipment, processed foods or vegetable oil. For each example, how do customers decide which are good quality?

□ Will it matter if one or two items are included that are not such good quality?

□ What could be done if the work of one reliable worker is always of poor quality because they fail to improve their skills – even though their children will suffer if they lose their job?

Topic 19: Marketing your products

New products will only sell if customers are aware of them. Think of ways of telling customers. Could you get market traders to promote your products in a way which also benefits them? Could you use local radio or newspapers? Could you design posters?

It is usually better to produce goods for a local market. In this way, many costs of production can be kept low. Money will not be needed for transport, fewer goods will be damaged and feedback on sales will be immediate. It is also much easier to build up a reputation for good quality products within the local community.

Discussion

☐ Initially it may be worth spending some money to tell people about your new product. However, a new business may have required a great deal of investment so money is likely to be very short. What are the advantages and disadvantages of spending more money on advertising? How much would be appropriate to spend? Would it be a useful investment?

☐ Some ideas of places where you could consider targeting advertising are schools, health centres, markets, shops or cafes. Think of some examples of products available locally. Consider some appropriate ways of advertising in these or similar places. How could you make it worthwhile for the staff in these places?

Topic 20: Multiplying the benefits

Most small businesses are run by one person with others helping. Sometimes a product may prove really successful and the business begins to grow. However, it is useful to consider whether this is a good idea.

Will the local market be large enough to provide enough customers or will transport be needed to reach other markets? Will demand continue long-term?

Larger production is likely to mean employing more people, training them and managing them. It will mean more detailed account keeping. Is this what you want?

Discussion

☐ There is a well-known saying: 'Small is beautiful'. Is this true in business? Discuss the advantages and disadvantages of either staying small or growing larger to meet demand.

☐ Growth usually means one business taking on more workers and increasing production. However, it could also mean the business agrees to split with several linked businesses working together to meet the demand. Do participants know of any examples of this happening? What would be the advantages? What might be the disadvantages?

Topic 21: Learning from experience

Few small businesses start up and are an immediate success. Success may only come through the experience of many failures. Developing new ideas can be painful and many changes may first be required. Always try out new ideas in a small way, preferably alongside existing goods which already have a market.

Remember that sometimes it may not be necessary to change the product, just to change the way you sell it. Try different ways of displaying products, new labels, new wrapping materials, different sizes, different combinations. If sales of fresh fruit are poor, try drying fruit and packaging it or making it into fruit juice. Try cleaning up bottles of palm oil and designing a bright new label.

Discussion

☐ How many people have tried out a new idea and been discouraged because it failed?

Share the stories. As a group, you may be able to suggest other ways the ideas could have been developed.

☐ Think of everyday products that are used locally. Can you think of better ways of presenting them – for example, different colours, labels, packaging or sizes?

Topic 22: Benefits to the community

One group of people within a community who have learnt to work well together can provide a real encouragement for others.

Their experience and confidence can be shared. People with new skills can train others. They can provide employment. People able to earn extra income will be more likely to buy locally produced foods or services.

Successful small businesses may also encourage others to start, sometimes through example, sometimes through sharing practical help such as buildings or vehicles.

They can encourage young people to see that it is possible to make a living without leaving their communities to find work in large cities.

Discussion

☐ Are people who have made a success of a small business willing to share their experiences? How can this be encouraged?

☐ What are the dangers of trying to copy the same business as someone else?

☐ Do participants have any examples of how one successful business idea encouraged others to begin in the same community?

☐ Just as successful ideas may help others to grow, what happens when businesses fail? Is that likely to have an impact on other businesses? What can be done about this?

☐ What happens within a community if one person or one family is able to make a real success of a small business enterprise? Does this lead to problems and resentment? How can this be avoided?

Topic 23: Producing goods for export

While the local market should be the first priority, sometimes it is worth considering other markets, either in nearby towns, large cities or overseas. High value, lightweight crafts, good quality dried fruits or unusual food products are all examples of goods that may benefit from finding markets elsewhere.

Several producers may find it worthwhile to combine their efforts and work as a cooperative, making either similar or the same products in order to meet the needs of large commercial orders.

Discussion

☐ At what point should producers begin to look for other markets?

☐ Exporting goods usually requires the capacity to produce huge orders on an exact date just once or twice a year. What difficulties could this cause?

☐ Is there anywhere producers can turn to for advice about markets in large towns and cities? What kind of market research might first be needed?

☐ Exporting goods or foods overseas requires the use of all kinds of legal documents such as hygiene inspection certificates, export licences and customs clearance papers. What are the implications of this? Is there anywhere people can go for advice?

Here are some useful contacts for people wishing to sell their goods overseas:

* Centre for the Promotion of Imports from Developing Countries (CBC)
  PO Box 30009, 3001 DA Rotterdam, The Netherlands.
  Fax +31 10 4114081
* Tearcraft
  100 Church Road, Teddington, Middlesex, TW11 8QE, UK.
  Fax +44 208 943 3594
* Traidcraft Exchange
  Kingsway, Tyne and Wear, NE11 0NE, UK
  Fax +44 191 4822690
* Ten Thousand Villages
  Archana Handicrafts, 704 Main St, PO Box 500, Akron PA 17501-0500, USA.

Bible studies by Rose Robinson

These Bible studies are designed to use in small groups. They may provide a useful introduction to a meeting where different topics from the Guide are being discussed. Choose a study that will be linked to the topic you plan to study or that is relevant to your situation. During the studies, encourage people to reflect on what they read, to discuss the meaning and the implications and, finally, to pray together about what they have learnt.

Bible study 1 – Beginnings

Start by reading Revelation 22:13, where Jesus says that he is 'the first and the last, the beginning and the end'. Read also Genesis 1:1, which tells us that, in the beginning, God himself created everything from nothing, by his word.

All of us at times dream dreams. There are things that we long for, but sometimes they seem impossible to achieve. They are so unlikely that thinking about them depresses rather than inspires us. We do not have much hope, and we feel unable to change our circumstances.

Read Romans 5:1–11. In this passage we hear how a hopeless situation is turned upside down by God's love demonstrated to us through the death of his Son.

☐ What words can you find in this passage to describe what we were before Christ died for us? (See verses 6, 8, 10.)

☐ What do we now have through Jesus? (See verses 1, 2, 5, 9–11.)

Even our sufferings produce perseverance, character and an unfailing hope because of the love God has poured into our hearts by his Holy Spirit. (See verses 3–5.) It is hard for a poor person to obtain credit. It is hard for a person who has very little to imagine how they might provide more for their family or improve their situation.

Now read again Romans 5:10. Romans 8:32 also tells us: 'He who did not spare his own Son, but gave him up for us all – how will he not also, along with him, graciously give us all things?'

☐ What do these two verses mean to you?

Bible study 2 – Advice

Read 1 Kings 12:1–17. Solomon has died and Rehoboam, his son, has gone to Shechem to be made king. Jeroboam, who has been promised by God that he will rule ten of the tribes of Israel (1 Kings 11:31), returns from Egypt where he had fled for fear of Solomon.

☐ What do Jeroboam and the people of Israel propose to Rehoboam? (See verses 3–4.)

Rehoboam takes three days to consider this proposal and get advice. Before we make decisions and take action, we should listen to the people we are serving and seek advice from those with experience and wisdom.

☐ What advice does Rehoboam get from the elders who had served Solomon? (See verses 6–7.)

☐ Rehoboam rejects this advice and goes instead to the young men who have grown up with him. What do they advise? (See verses 8–11.)

Israel and Judah have been united and ruled as one kingdom by Saul, David and Solomon in succession. Rehoboam follows the young men's advice: his harsh answer to the people of Israel leads to the split of Israel and Judah.The Bible tells us that good advice is very valuable: see, for example, Proverbs 12:15; 13:10; 15:22. Of course, the very best advisor or counsellor is God himself, Father, Son and Holy Spirit (Isaiah 9:6; John 14:16–17; Romans 11:33–34). However, it is of no value getting good advice if we are then unwilling to follow it.

☐ Can you find ways to listen and respond more to those you serve?

☐ Are you taking the advice of wise people and, most especially, God himself?

Bible study 3 – Counting the cost

Read Luke 14:25–33. Jesus here gives us two practical examples of the need to plan thoroughly before beginning a course of action.

☐ What might happen to the person who begins to build something without properly estimating the cost? (See verses 28–30.)

☐ What could a king do if, having considered the strength of the opposing army, he decides he is unlikely to win the war? (See verses 31–32.)

☐ Have you considered carefully all the costs, such as finance, time and other resources, that will be needed for the project you are considering?

☐ If your project seems unlikely to succeed after this analysis, do you have any other options?

Jesus uses these examples to warn us that before we begin anything we should consider fully and carefully what it is going to cost us.

☐ What does Jesus say is the cost of following him and being his disciple? (See verses 26, 27, 33.)

☐ What does this mean in our daily lives?

☐ Do you believe it is a cost worth paying?

Bible study 4 – Making good plans

What is wrong with the plans of the people in these Bible passages?

• Genesis 11:1–9, especially verse 4
• Jeremiah 22:13–17
• James 4:13–17

THE TRUTH ABOUT AIDS

☐ We may make many plans in our hearts, but whose plans take priority (Proverbs 19:21) and who needs to build the house if the labour is not to be in vain (Psalm 127:1)?

☐ How carefully have you checked that your plans are in line with God's purposes? Proverbs 16:3 says, 'Commit to the Lord whatever you do and your plans will succeed.'

☐ Have you made sure that there is no injustice in what you are doing and no exploitation of others? In Jeremiah 22:16 we read, 'He defended the cause of the poor and needy, and so all went well.'

Bible study 5 – Sharing

Read Acts 4:32–37. This passage describes a very successful 'cooperative'. Verse 34 tells us 'There were no needy people among them.' What helped it to work? Fill in the blanks:

• 'All the believers were ——' (verse 32)
• 'They shared ——' (verse 32)
• 'They testified to ——' (verse 33)
• '—— was upon them all' (verse 33)

The group is united by a common vision and their deep commitment to one another.

☐ What is the source of income here?

☐ What is the agreement between the members of the group?

In your group, your agreement and situation will be different from the one here. What is important is that everyone who is part of the group clearly knows how the group is to function and keeps to the conditions you have agreed upon.

Bible study 6 – Honesty

All members of groups need to trust one another and be honest with one another. Read Acts 5:1–11.

☐ What do Ananias and Sapphira do? (See verses 1–4, 8.)

☐ Who does Peter say Ananias and Sapphira have lied to? (See verses 3, 9.)

☐ What happens to them? (See verses 5, 10.)

☐ What impact does this have on the church and all who hear of these events? (See verses 5, 11.)

☐ Are you being open and honest in your dealings with the group you belong to?

Reflect as a group on how you can encourage each other to be more open and honest with each other.

Bible study 7 – Overcoming difficulties

Most groups will at some point face difficult times. If these situations are not handled correctly, members may become discouraged and prevent the work going ahead.

Read Nehemiah 4:1–12. This passage illustrates several things that might cause discouragement:

* Ridicule (verses 1–3)
* The size of the task (verse 10)
* Opposition and threats (verses 8, 11)
* Fear and anxiety (verse 12)

Read Nehemiah 4:13–23. How does Nehemiah deal with discouragement, spiritually and physically, caused by:

* Ridicule (verses 4, 5)
* The size of the task (verses 19–20)
* Opposition and threats (verses 9, 14, 15)
* Fear and anxiety (verse 15)

The people don't give up (verses 6, 16, 21). They work together (verses 16–18) to help one another. They design a system so that they can respond rapidly if one group needs help suddenly (verses 19–20). They are dedicated to completing the work (verses 21–23).

☐ How does your group respond when difficulties arise?

☐ Could you overcome the problems by helping one another more?

☐ Are you continually seeking God's guidance, encouragement and wisdom?

Bible study 8 – Cooperation

Read Exodus 17:11–13. These verses give examples of what can be achieved if we work together as a team. What would have happened in this situation without cooperation? Can you think of any similar situations in the present day?

Read Judges 20:11. (If you have time, read the whole of chapter 20.)

☐ What happens when people unite behind a common purpose? How can your group help to unite people in times of peace?

☐ Read Matthew 18:19–20. Why are the prayers of several people more pleasing to God than one person praying alone? How often do you discuss situations and pray about them in small groups? How could you do this more effectively?

Bible study 9 – True values

Read 1 Corinthians 3:1–15. What problem is there in this church? (See verses 3–4.) What does Paul suggest is the proper attitude to different workers? (See verses 4–9.)

Only God can make things grow (verse 9); only God can make our work prosper (Psalm 127:1). He wants us to be his 'fellow-workers' (verse 9); each achieving the part of the work he has assigned to us (verse 5), using the gifts and qualities he has given us. Compare Romans 12:4–7, which has a similar message.

Jealousy and quarrelling cause division. If a project is to succeed, we need to value every person's gifts – our own and those of other people – and work together.

Paul says he has laid a foundation (verse 10). Who is the foundation? (See verse 11.) There is no other foundation that will endure for ever. We must also be careful how we build.

☐ What will eventually happen to all our work? (See verses 12–15.)

☐ How will what you are building look in the 'light of day'? Will it survive the fire? (See verse 13.)

Bible study 10 – Good use of resources

Read Acts 6:1–7.

☐ What is the complaint of the Grecian Jews? (See verse 1.)

☐ The Twelve gather together all the disciples. What do they propose? (See verses 2–4.)

☐ What qualities do they suggest for the men who are to help in the food distribution? (See verse 3.)

☐ The apostles pray and lay their hands on the chosen men (verse 6). What is the result of the expansion in workforce? (See verse 7.)

It is good to employ people to do different tasks according to their gifts and skills and the anointing of God upon them. See also 2 Chronicles 19:11.

☐ Are you using your human resources effectively?

Bible study 11 – God's vision

Read Haggai 2:1–9 and Zechariah 4:6–10. The Lord's house is in ruins but the people have been told by the prophets to rebuild it. It must have seemed an immense task, but the people obey God's word and begin. God continues to encourage them through the prophets.

☐ What does God promise Zerubbabel? (See Zechariah 4:9.)

☐ Who will be with the workers? (See Haggai 2:4–5.)

☐ How will they succeed in such a massive project? (See Zechariah 4:6.)

☐ What does God say about the 'day of small things'? (See Zechariah 4:10.)

If something is of God, it will succeed however improbable it may seem at the outset and whatever difficulties arise during the work.

Bible study 12 – Perseverance

There is great joy in persevering until we complete what God has called us to do. Both Paul and Jesus declare at the end of their lives that they have finished the tasks they were set. (See 2 Timothy 4:6–8, John 4:34 and 19:30.)

☐ Do you know what tasks God has given you, in your family, your group, or in your community?

☐ Will you be able to echo Jesus' words – 'I have brought you glory on earth by completing the work you gave me to do' (John 17:4)?

Remember that God tells us that he is the Beginning and the End: 'It is done. I am the Alpha and the Omega, the Beginning and the End' (Revelation 21:6).

A TRAINING MANUAL FOR HIV AND AIDS – INFORMATION AND COMMUNICATION
(Africa Inland Church)

Introduction

These materials have been heavily edited from a much larger resource developed by the AIC AIDS Division, itself closely based on a manual extensively and effectively used by Family AIDS Caring Trust (FACT) in Zimbabwe. This is a wonderful example of partnership and networking, sharing expertise to get the job done. It was designed for use by people from churches and Christian groups who have a concern about HIV/AIDS, and want to see what role the church can have in this terrible epidemic. This shortened version contains useful material which should be adapted to your own specific cultural situation. Extra material which can be found in Chapters 1–16 or the other appendices has been edited from this resource to save space.

The aims of the original course were:

- To provide individuals and groups with information and materials to equip them to become HIV/AIDS information educators.
- To help individuals develop effective communication skills which will assist them in the education of others about HIV/AIDS.
- To assist groups of interested individuals in establishing their own locally based HIV/AIDS information and education units.
- To mobilise and equip the church to respond in a Christ-like way to the challenge HIV/AIDS presents.

The material was designed for use by groups of ten to twelve people. The trainer should ideally be someone with a basic knowledge of AIDS, possibly a health worker, teacher or social worker, or have attended a similar training course to this. No prior medical knowledge is assumed, though it is helpful to have an experienced person available to answer difficult questions.

The principles of adult learning
(Acknowledgement 'Violence Against Women', Musasa Project.)

Learning from experience
People have experiences and learn from them. New learning is built on what is already known. For example, people will have some idea of what other members of their communities think when someone is known to have HIV infection.

Mutual learning
Education should stress learning rather than teaching. For the educator to be effective, he or she needs to be a good listener, flexible and responsive to the learners' needs. Learners should be regarded as people with experience and valuable knowledge, and the course will be a process of sharing information with one another. For example, you may not know the group's beliefs concerning the spread of HIV, but allowing participants to discuss this enables you to learn what people from different communities know and understand.

Learning from peers
Peers are people of a similar age and background to each other. People learn best from their peers. Programmes where sex workers are used to educate their clients and other sex workers have been more effective than when these education programmes are carried out by health workers to the same groups of people. Peers identify with each other.

Relevance
Adults learn because they want to know something in order to cope with a particular situation that they have experienced. Many people have attended HIV/AIDS courses because they know someone in their community with the infection. They want to know about the disease because it is real to them.

Respect
Adults should be respected for their experience, skills, ideas, energy and creativity. Show this respect by allowing participation. Respect does not necessarily mean agreeing with everyone, but rather acknowledging that others have different views and beliefs and allowing time for these to be shared. People may have strong views about a particular custom that may not be shared by you or others in the group. It is important to listen to them, but also to share the facts and look at what the Bible says on the issue.

Discussions

Adults can share knowledge gained from their ability to observe, think and analyse their experience of life. Everybody has something to share – and something to learn by hearing it from others.

Clarity and simplicity

New information is best learned when it is given clearly and simply, not too much at a time and repeated in two or three different ways. A session may start with a brainstorming session – getting ideas from everybody – which is then followed by spending some time correcting wrong information and reinforcing the correct information, perhaps through role-plays on the same topic.

Learning through discovery

It has been discovered that we remember:

   20% of what we hear
   40% of what we hear and see
   80% of what we discover for ourselves

Because of this, as much as possible of the teaching described in this manual is done by methods that encourage 'discovery', through role-plays and discussions.

Action and reflection

Adults learn by looking at a situation, thinking about it, planning ways of improving it, carrying out the plans, then evaluating and looking at them again. This is the approach most likely to lead to an effective solution. It is often helpful to break into smaller groups to discuss a question, and then ask the groups to present their views to the whole group, for further discussion.

Cooperation

People learn best in cooperative rather than competitive situations. A group has many more ideas and skills than any one individual, and its members stimulate each other to produce yet more. In smaller groups the members all help each other to produce a good report to feed back to the whole group, or present an effective role-play by discussing together what will happen.

Enjoyment

People learn well when they feel relaxed and are enjoying themselves. It is important to have fun times. Allow people to share a joke or a funny story occasionally – so long as these do not take over the training sessions!

Transformation

The purpose of the course is to build people up, so that their creativity can make a better standard of living for their society. Learning experiences should give people an insight into what they would like that society to be. For example, in a discussion about the sexual activity of young people today, you might talk about how things are and then discuss how we would like them to be, and then how to encourage that change. People need to see that there is a way out of a difficult situation.

Training techniques

This course has been designed to assist groups with little or no existing knowledge of HIV/AIDS. The lesson material is simple and yet covers information needed to give educational talks and increase communications skills.

Straight lectures are by no means the most effective teaching method, but may be necessary at times. A participatory approach is more effective, more fun and less stressful for the facilitator (and participants). Group participation is encouraged, as it is an effective way of learning, especially when behaviour change is intended. People learn more by participating in activities.

Communication skills

Communication is a two-way process. There should be as much opportunity for exchange of information within a group of people as there would be between two people. Good communication is a dialogue where the parties are actively engaged in trying to reach a common goal.

Good communication can break down when:

• People misunderstand each other and therefore do not speak freely.
• Body language shows displeasure.
• Inappropriate methods of communication are used.
• Teaching aids are used incorrectly.

Workshops, role-playing, drama and group discussions are the most effective communication methods, from creating awareness through to behaviour change. And in HIV/AIDS education the goal is to encourage behaviour change.

Choosing participants for the course

It is important to identify suitable people for training as this affects the success of the course. Whenever possible talk with other people in your organisation or fellow workers and together discuss the following questions:

- Who are the people in your community that you think should be taught first about HIV/AIDS?
- Who are the people in a position to effectively teach others about the information that they learn?
- Should the group be mixed, only men or only women?
- At what age should people learn about AIDS? Do you want a group of all ages or the same age?
- What will be the literacy level of the group? It is easier if everyone in the group is at a reasonably equal level of understanding.
- What groups are you teaching – youth, church groups?
- Should the people all come from the same mission, village, school or whatever, or do you want to have a few people from different places?

Trainers we have worked with have identified their participants in different ways. You might issue a general invitation to interested people to attend, but you will need to ensure that the group shares a similar level of literacy (some trainers give a short test). You could discuss with superiors, workmates, workers' committees, headmasters, church leaders or hospital staff in order to identify suitable participants. Talk to village heads and counsellors to ensure that they can encourage the community members to participate.

Encouraging participants to be regular

It can be disheartening to start a course and then find that people drop out for various reasons. By identifying your group carefully this can be minimised. You can also encourage regular attendance by:

- Making sure they know from the beginning what the course is about and how it will be carried out.
- Asking your superior or some other respected person in the community or church to talk to the participants at the beginning of the first day and perhaps to distribute certificates at the end.
- Informing the participants of the serious nature of HIV/AIDS and how everybody needs to learn about this.
- Being prepared yourself, with a good understanding of the subject.
- Always arriving on time, having your materials in order and knowing the participants' names.
- Keeping the sessions lively and exciting, with lots of discussion, role-plays and group work.
- Involving participants by encouraging them to tell the stories, give feed-back after discussions and share what they have learnt.

- Telling participants that certificates are only issued to those who attend all sessions – and that also means arriving on time.
- Ensuring that participants realise what the Bible teaches on this and so see the opportunity and the necessity for the church to be involved in HIV/AIDS.
- Telling people that the course training is free of charge.
- Inviting other health workers to take part by doing some teaching, leading discussions or answering questions. (For example, doctors, nurses, family planning workers, etc.)

Principles of good teaching

- Know your subject.
- Avoid the temptation to use only lectures. It may not be in your best interest or that of your trainees.
- Try to make your sessions participatory and active. Use methods that ask questions, encourage discussion and make time for feedback.
- Support your teaching with visual aids where possible. Use other teaching aids such as the blackboard, large sheets of paper or posters. (Some groups may have access to a film or video.)
- Ensure that you are familiar with your teaching equipment: use it with confidence and take care of it, keeping it in a safe place when not in use.
- Allow for individual differences but ensure that trainees understand the material. Let them proceed at their own speed, but leave time to reinforce and summarise. Take care to avoid long debates that take up time.
- Be prepared to change your approach when necessary.
- Speak clearly, and always use language that your audience will understand.
- Watch for signs that indicate how your session is progressing.
- Make notes on each session, and file them with your handouts and other material on each subject after the lesson for future reference.

Using participatory methods of communication

Participatory activities are useful for increasing understanding of particular issues during a training session. They also allow participants to explore problems, look for answers and arrive at decisions through dialogue and information exchange.

Group discussions

Discussions are useful to highlight or develop important points in training sessions. They also help participants to get to know each other better as they share their different viewpoints, providing a positive atmosphere for the exchange of ideas and information.

You will need to get discussion started by a question, and then to accept initial contributions without too much comment – but make a careful note of them for future reference.

Watch the group and draw in the quieter members, or those who would obviously like to express an opinion but cannot find an opening. Ask them their views and thank them for sharing. Ensure that one or two people do not dominate discussions.

As people talk and share, take notes as reminders that can be useful in future discussions.

Group work is an important part of the course. Ensure that everybody has a chance to chair a group, and to report back – especially if the group is going to get involved in other activities after training, as this will give them some experience of working with groups.

Lectures

It is possible to give a good lecture. Every instructor needs to use the lecture method from time to time, so here are some tips for making a lecture session most effective.

- Gain attention from the beginning, perhaps by telling a story relevant to the lecture title.
- Make eye contact with or move among the group as you talk.
- Summarise the objectives of the session in the same order in which the information will be presented.
- Present the facts logically, simply and clearly, and keep to the subject.
- Always use some form of visual re-enforcement during a lecture.
- Vary the session by asking questions or encouraging participation.
- Summarise key points before closing the presentation.
- If possible, set an exercise, such as an essay or a project, for trainees to complete, to see if the content of the presentation has been understood.
- Be enthusiastic about your subject – and your enthusiasm will be contagious.

Using teaching aids

Visual aids are useful for attracting and focusing attention on particular issues. The following are some examples:

- Posters and wall charts come in different types: 'single glance' posters can be read and understood quickly by the observer; 'stop and study' posters require the observer to spend more time studying the message.

- Wall charts usually contain more information than posters and are therefore displayed for reference over a long period.
- A blackboard or large sheet of paper can be used to supplement a talk, emphasise important issues or words, summarise a discussion, or simply to leave a reminder for participants. It can also be used to bring participants into the learning activity by encouraging them to write on the board or paper themselves.

If you are not used to writing on a blackboard or chart, practise beforehand to ensure that your writing is of even size, you can write in a straight line, and that the words can be seen by everyone. If you are able to write your material on the board before the session, you will have more freedom to explain and point out particular items as you proceed.

Dealing with difficulties

Whenever a course is run difficulties may arise. These can range from administrative problems to difficult behaviour. (It is important that you view this as difficult 'behaviour' rather than difficult 'people' as the latter implies a judgemental attitude.) Reasons for difficult behaviour by participants may be:

- They have been sent to the course by someone else and are just not interested.
- They have had bad experiences in previous courses.
- They have no idea how people feel about their difficult behaviour.
- They feel they have no control, especially if the course is rigidly structured.
- They have other worries that are distracting them.

Understanding that there may be underlying reasons for difficult behaviour helps you to cope with it.

Different people have different ways of coping with the problems that arise in leading groups, but the following suggestions may help.

Criticism
- Don't be defensive if you are criticised, but listen to the criticism and be prepared to discuss it.
- Never put people down, even when their behaviour is very difficult. Try instead to build on contributions. When this is impossible, then simply acknowledge the contribution without comment.
- Never try to compete with a participant who tries to take the group over. Instead, give that person specific tasks to do, or try breaking into smaller groups for discussions.
- Never argue. Build on support that already exists in the group. If one

individual is causing problems, the other participants are likely to be feeling frustrated, and it may be that they can be left to sort it out among themselves.
- Don't blame yourself. Comment on any problems, and ask the group for suggestions. Simply acknowledging the problem sometimes corrects it, but always allow participants to make comments as well.
- Be sensitive to the needs and concerns of others. They may seem petty but to the person concerned they are genuine.

Silences

A silence can be felt as threatening, but it can also assist the group to gather their thoughts. However, if the discussion has ground to a halt, and silence continues too long, you could try some of the following:

- Have ready a list of relevant questions to feed into the discussion.
- Invite someone to summarise the discussion.
- Change to an alternative activity.
- Use the blackboard or a large sheet of paper to get things going again.
- Read something out for people to comment on.
- Use role play.

It may be useful for you to keep a note of anything that has created difficulties for you and discuss with your co-workers how they would handle a similar situation.

Questions

It is important to allow and encourage questions. If people do not understand clearly what is being said they are more likely to lose interest. Always tell the group that they can ask questions at any time regarding the session in progress, and that time will be set aside at the end of the session for general questions.

- If the group is large it may be helpful if they indicate they have a question by a show of hands. In a small group this is not usually necessary.
- If people have difficulty hearing the question, repeat the question out loud before giving the answer, and always answer as simply and concisely as possible.
- Use illustrations from your lesson or story when appropriate.
- Whenever possible, ask the group whether they can answer the question themselves.
- Do not be afraid to admit you do not know the answer to a question. Say that you will find out the answer for the next session, or assign a member of the group to research the answer.

Devotions

We want to learn in this programme about AIDS so that we can avoid infection and death. We want to learn, not only for ourselves, but also so that we can teach and warn others of the dangers of certain lifestyles that can result in catching HIV/AIDS.

In the Bible, Hosea tells us that people die because they ignore the law of God, and we shall see that this is very true when it comes to HIV/AIDS. Ignoring God's law has led to the rapid spread of this killer disease. God's law was given, not to deny us pleasure, but to protect us from wrong and harm, and following God's law is the way to ensure we enjoy life to the full.

This is why it is important to include, as part of the course, regular times when we can study God's law, see our need for a Saviour, and learn about his plan for our lives. You can either programme devotions into your teaching schedule, or simply ensure that some of the material is included in your introduction of a topic.

Pre-course evaluation

It is helpful to find out what knowledge of HIV/AIDS participants have, prior to the start of the training course. We therefore suggest sending out a questionnaire to each participant. Assure them that the questionnaire is anonymous, and that they should answer all questions honestly and quickly – there is no need to spend a lot of time doing this.

Collect the questionnaires in and keep them for analysing and comparing with the end-of-course evaluation. They can then be filed by the facilitators for future reference.

Sample pre- and post-course questionnaires are provided at the end of this Appendix.

Now we come to some outline sessions. Some are given in detail, others are simply suggested for you to put together in a way that will be most appropriate for the culture, age and situation of the participants in your group.

Session 1: What is AIDS?

Brainstorm

Write on a blackboard or two large sheets of paper which can be clearly seen by the participants: 'What is AIDS?' and, separately, 'What is HIV?'

Ask participants to call out what they understand by the two terms, and write up all contributions without comment.

Make sure that each participant has a chance to make at least one contribution.

Once the group has exhausted all the different viewpoints, read through the list commenting on each point and correcting it if necessary.

Lecture

(The following lecture conveys basic information about AIDS. Get someone to hold up the appropriate illustrations for all to see in order to help gain maximum understanding.)

1. The small germ that causes AIDS is called the Human Immuno-deficiency Virus or HIV. Throughout this course, this germ may also be referred to as the 'AIDS virus'. AIDS is an abbreviation for 'Acquired Immune Deficiency Syndrome'.

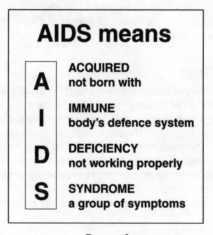

Poster 1

'Acquired' means 'not born with'. The disease is the result of an infection that comes from outside a person's body. (Some babies are born with HIV infection but it is acquired from their mother, and then they go on to develop AIDS.)

'Immune' means 'the body's defence system'. Our immune system protects us from all kinds of diseases.

'Deficiency' means 'not working properly'. A person's immune system stops working properly as a result of infection with the AIDS virus.

'Syndrome' means 'a group of signs and symptoms'. These will be described in a later session.

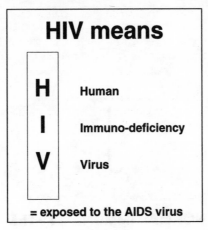

Poster 2

2. The virus that causes AIDS to develop in a person's body is called HIV or the 'Human Immuno-deficiency Virus'.

'Human' means that this particular virus will only infect and multiply in the body environment of humans.

'Immuno-deficiency' means that the virus affects the immune system by making it deficient, or unable to function properly.

'Virus' is the term given to the tiny germ. (There are other kinds of viruses that cause a wide spectrum of other diseases.)

It is important to note that there is a difference between HIV and AIDS. A person who has HIV infection does not necessarily have AIDS. It simply means that he or she has been exposed to and has the virus, and will almost certainly develop AIDS at a later stage.

3. We will now consider what it means for a person to have an acquired immune deficiency.

Everyone has an immune system. This is your body's defence against infection. It is rather like an umbrella. Right now as you are listening to this talk your immune system is working to protect you much like an umbrella would protect you from the rain. In Poster 3 the rain represents the different kinds of infection which could make you ill. Just as an umbrella protects you against the rain and stops you from feeling wet, so your immune system protects you against different infections and stops you from feeling ill.

Poster 4 represents a person who has just been infected by the AIDS virus. The small insects standing on the umbrella represent the AIDS virus. Of course, in real life it is impossible to see the tiny AIDS virus. And

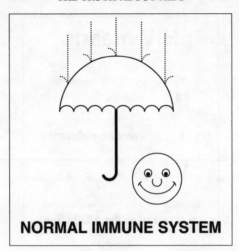

Poster 3

Poster 4

it is also impossible to tell that someone is carrying the AIDS virus just by their appearance.

The umbrella in Poster 4 is exactly the same as the one shown in Poster 3, except the person is now carrying the AIDS virus. The umbrella, however, is still working normally and the person is not getting wet.

A person who has been infected by the AIDS virus in recent months (and who is now therefore a carrier) usually displays no symptoms. Consequently they are unaware that they are carrying the AIDS virus and will continue to do so for the rest of their life. This situation means that a carrier can pass on the AIDS virus to someone else without either of them knowing it.

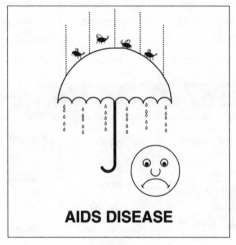

AIDS DISEASE

Poster 5

5. As time goes by, the AIDS virus multiplies in a carrier's body. It begins to damage that person's immune system and they start to fall prone to illnesses of one kind or another. In Poster 5, the person's immune system is breaking down, illustrated by the holes in the umbrella which allow the rain through, making the person wet.

It is usual for people at this stage to visit their doctor. They will be examined and informed that their condition is synonymous with the AIDS virus infection and it will be suggested that they have a blood test.

Gradually, the damage to the umbrella worsens. The person with AIDS gets severe and life threatening illnesses. The final stage of infection by the AIDS virus is known as AIDS disease, full-blown AIDS, or simply AIDS. There is no cure for AIDS. In African nations, it usually takes between five and ten years from the time of infection with the AIDS virus to the time that person gets AIDS, longer in many developed countries.

6. What happens to someone after they have been infected with the AIDS virus? We shall look at what happened to John to illustrate this point. Up to the age of 19 John had not come into contact with the AIDS virus. His immune system was therefore working normally to protect him against different infections. This is illustrated by the umbrella which has no holes in it and so keeps the rain out.

John's HIV infection

Age	Description	Symptoms	Immunity	
19	Not infected	None	Normal	
JOHN GETS INFECTED WITH HIV				
20	HIV carrier	None	Normal	
21	Swollen lymph glands	None	Getting worse	
25	AIDS-related illness	Troublesome	Poor	
28	Full-blown AIDS	Life-threatening	Very poor	

Poster 6

When John was 20 he became infected by the AIDS virus or HIV. Three months later his blood tested positive. At this time he had a 'flu-like' illness for a few days, caused by the HIV, although he did not realise the cause. For the next year or two John had no symptoms and felt completely well, even though he was now a carrier of the AIDS virus. His normal immune system is illustrated by the umbrella which still has no holes in it. But John is now carrying the AIDS virus.

In the next stage his immune system has started to weaken. To try and help him in his fight against the AIDS virus his glands have become enlarged in his neck and under his armpits. He has no other signs.

This stage is called 'Persistent Generalised Lymphadenopathy' (PGL), and may last for three to four years. John still does not know he is infected, because he feels healthy and therefore has not visited his doctor.

By the time John is 25 he has been infected with the AIDS virus for five years, and throughout this time has felt completely healthy. Only now does he start to experience the first real signs of infection.

In this stage John is experiencing AIDS related illnesses – common everyday symptoms which are becoming increasingly troublesome. His immune system is now working quite poorly and the AIDS virus is multi-plying in his body. John visits his doctor and discovers he is infected by the AIDS virus. Many people discover they have the infection during this stage of the disease.

Eight or nine years after infection, John enters the final stage of the illness. This is known as full-blown AIDS and is often marked by a severe life-threatening illness. John has recovered from his opportunistic infection but his immune system is now badly damaged by the AIDS virus so when he develops a further infection, at the age of 29, he is not strong enough to fight it off. He dies of AIDS nine years after first becoming infected.

John's infection shows a typical pattern for adults infected by the AIDS virus, and the usual time period involved. Some people, especially infected new born babies, are less fortunate. They get symptoms a few months after birth and usually die within one to five years. Others do not pass through each stage in the same way as John and may progress from no symptoms to having full-blown AIDS in a few years. Some people are able to fight the AIDS virus, keeping it under control, and are therefore still healthy ten years after infection.

Summarise

Finish the session with summarising the material and dealing with any questions that participants may have. (For more on what AIDS is, see Chapters 3 and 4.)

Session 2: Why we need to know about AIDS

Group discussion

Divide the group into groups of five or six people, and ask the groups to discuss the question, 'Why do we need to know about AIDS?'

Allow about ten minutes for group discussion, and then ask a member of each group to report briefly on their discussions.

The main reason we should know about HIV/AIDS is that in most cases it can be avoided through change in behaviour.

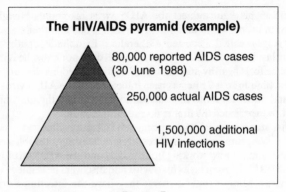

Poster 7

In this sample chart it can be seen that the reported number of AIDS cases is almost always much less than the estimated one. This is because in many cases people do not go to a clinic or there are not the tests available to confirm HIV. Also, the number of people who may be infected but still have yet to develop AIDS can be very large, depending on the rate of spread. These will develop AIDS in a few years' time.

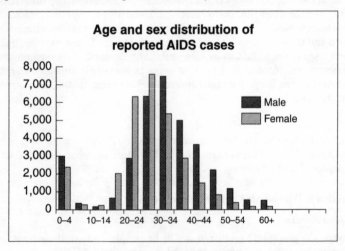

Poster 8

Poster 8 shows the proportions of AIDS cases in a typical African community by age group. Note the high numbers of people in the 20–29 and 30–39 age groups. This shows that the disease is mostly affecting the sexually active age group – the people who provide economic stability. There is a significant number in the 0–5 age group (infected from their mothers) but after that AIDS is rare in childhood. (Talk about HIV infection and the number of AIDS cases in your area. These should be available from the District AIDS Co-ordinator or MOH.)

So, it is important to learn about AIDS because:

- The number of AIDS cases is increasing.
- The economically active age group is most affected.
- HIV/AIDS is causing the death of parents, leaving children as orphans.
- Children are having to look after themselves (maybe ending up on the streets) or are being looked after by the elderly.
- AIDS puts a terrific burden on the health system.

Session 3: How HIV is spread

Brainstorm

On a blackboard or sheet of paper draw up two columns: the first should be headed 'HIV is spread by', and the second, 'HIV is not spread by'.

Record all suggestions given for each column and then discuss, correcting where necessary with the aid of the information below. Show illustrations to reinforce the information.

Lecture

AIDS is caused by a tiny germ called a virus. It is spread from one person to another only in certain ways. For a person to become infected with HIV a large amount of virus must enter his or her body. The only fluids which contain large amounts of virus are the blood and the sex fluids of men and women.

There are therefore three main ways a person can be infected with the AIDS virus. These are:

1. Unprotected sexual intercourse with someone who has the virus. The virus can spread from a man to a woman as well as from a woman to a man. The virus passes into the bloodstream of the uninfected partner, who then becomes infected. The more sexual partners a person has, the greater the risk of becoming infected with HIV.

2. Infected mothers passing it on to their babies. This may take place before or during the birth of the baby, or even through breast feeding. The chance of an infected mother passing the infection to her baby in Africa is normally around 30%, depending on the stage of the mother's infection. If she receives anti-viral medicines during pregnancy and does not breast

Fluid containing large amounts of HIV must be absorbed into another person's body.

Large amounts of HIV are found in:

Blood

The sex fluids of men and women

These are spread into other people's bodies through:

Sexual contact

Blood transfusion

Mother to unborn child

Poster 9

feed her baby, the chance of her baby being infected could be as low as 8%. If a woman becomes infected when she is already pregnant, the baby has a higher chance of being infected as there is a sudden invasion of the virus in the mother's body. The risk to the unborn child is less where conception occurs after the mother's infection and where the mother is healthy and not showing symptoms. As the mother develops symptoms, however, the chance of her baby being infected could rise as high as 50%. Some mothers may lose their babies during the course of pregnancy as a result of HIV infection. Pregnancy itself appears to speed up the progress of the infection in the mother's body.

We are unsure of the exact reason why some babies get infected and others do not. During pregnancy the baby has its own blood circulation and its food is absorbed from the uterine (womb) lining. Although the AIDS virus may not be passed to the baby, antibodies (the mother's response to HIV) for the virus are. This means almost all new-born babies test positive, as the test detects the antibodies from the infected mother which have been passed to the baby. However, if the virus has not been passed, then the antibodies will disappear from the baby over the course of a few months (even up to fifteen months) and then the baby will test negative. If the virus has passed to the baby then the test will remain positive and the child will develop AIDS. Most infected children die within the first five years, but some may survive many years.

Babies are much more likely to be infected through breast milk if the mother actually becomes infected while still breast feeding. However, unless the mother can afford formula feed, prepare it properly and ensure the sterility of bottles and teats, it is still preferable to breast feed. The risk of a baby getting diarrhoea, dehydration, chest diseases or malnutrition leading to death is greater than the risk of HIV infection from the mother's breast milk.

3. Receiving blood which is infected. Infection occurs if a person receives blood from someone who has the virus. The chances of this happening are low in countries where all donated blood is screened.

Infection can also occur during procedures which draw blood. Blood contains large amounts of the AIDS virus, and even though razor blades and medical equipment look clean, they can still contain particles of blood which are too small to see. If they are re-used without being sterilised there is a risk they could spread the AIDS virus. This is the reason that all medical equipment used in hospitals and clinics is sterilised, a procedure which kills the AIDS virus.

Sometimes equipment used by healers or at back-street clinics is not properly sterilised, and the equipment used in such practices as circumcision, scarification or ear-piercing may thus cause the spread of the AIDS virus. However, infection in these ways accounts for a very small proportion of new infections of HIV/AIDS.

The final part of this session deals with ways in which the AIDS virus is *not* spread. We want to emphasise the message that ordinary social contact with an infected person does not put people at risk.

Go back to the list on your blackboard and ensure that you mention everything there, and that you include the following as ways in which AIDS *cannot* be caught

• Sharing cups, plates, knives and forks.
• Living with a parent or relative who has AIDS.
• Shaking hands or touching people.
• Having your hair cut.

- Eating and drinking.
- Wearing second-hand clothes.
- Looking after animals.
- Sitting next to someone who is infected.
- Using the same toilet as someone who is infected.
- Playing sport with someone who is infected.
- Coughing or sneezing.
- Swimming in a pool or river.
- Having an injection with a clean needle and syringe.
- Insect bites.
- Kissing someone who is infected. Emphasise that, even though the AIDS virus is found in the saliva of a person with AIDS, it only exists in tiny quantities. And even if some infected saliva does get into an uninfected person's mouth, the virus cannot move from the mouth into the rest of the body.
- Mosquito bites. A mosquito feeds about once every twenty-four hours and the human blood it feeds on is digested by its stomach. Any virus present in this blood is destroyed. The mosquito does not become infected. When the mosquito feeds, it injects a small amount of its saliva under the skin, but no blood from its stomach. The saliva does not carry HIV (though it may carry the malaria parasites). Any blood that remains on the mosquito's proboscis (very unlikely) would not be sufficient to infect a person. If mosquitoes spread HIV there would be high numbers of children between 5 and 15 years old with HIV/AIDS – just as there are with malaria.

Ask the group 'How can we be so sure that you cannot get AIDS through some of the ways listed above?' and allow a short time of discussion.

There is one group of workers who have a slight risk of being infected by the AIDS virus as a result of their work. Some doctors and nurses have been infected, usually after accidentally injecting themselves with blood infected with the AIDS virus.

Even though health workers are at risk, this risk is very low. We need to emphasise that for every health worker who is infected in this way, there are many thousands who are not. (See Chapters 4 and 5 for more on these issues.)

Session 4: Signs and symptoms of AIDS

(For this session, it would be good to invite a local doctor to come and speak to the group. The doctor should be aware the group is made up of lay people (ie, non-medical) and can therefore adjust the lecture accordingly. If this is not possible, then continue with the following.)

Brainstorm

Ask participants to provide any information they know about the signs and symptoms of HIV infection/AIDS, and write this down on a blackboard or paper. Then go through the list, confirming or correcting the information given. Allow time for any additional questions and to clarify any misunderstandings. As much as possible, encourage the participants to answer each other's questions.

Go back to Poster 6, and the story of the young man, John, who has become infected by AIDS.

Lecture

The course of infection that we will follow will be from when John is healthy (top of poster) to when he becomes infected and his blood shows antibodies. We will talk about the different symptoms John may show and then the final stages of AIDS.

John is infected by the AIDS virus, together with another sexually transmitted disease. While it is common for this to happen, many people are also infected by HIV without ever having another STD.

Once inside John's body, the virus goes into hiding and he has no symptoms until a few weeks later. If a blood test was taken at this time there would be no evidence of infection. But the virus is there, and John is infectious, and this means he can now pass the infection on to others.

When John does develop symptoms, a few weeks after infection, it is a feverish illness that he mistakes for flu. Other minor symptoms such as skin rashes, headaches, night sweats and coughs may also occur at this time.

At the same time his blood will test positive due to the presence of antibodies. This acute stage is known as 'sero-conversion' (when the blood test converts from negative to positive) and usually occurs between six to twelve weeks after infection.

John is still healthy. He has no signs or symptoms at this time and no one can tell that he is infected unless a blood test is carried out. This stage usually continues for anything up to five years, and all during this time he could pass on the infection.

John then enters another stage known as PGL (Persistent Generalised Lymphadenopathy). This causes him to have swollen glands in his neck, armpits, and groin. This is one of the earliest signs of HIV infection and occurs in most people who have been infected with the AIDS virus for a number of years.

At first John was unaware that his glands were swollen, although if the doctor had examined him then he would have noticed them. Occasionally when John had some infection he would notice his glands were uncomfortable. These swollen glands may be the only sign John shows for the next few years or he may begin other signs and symptoms soon.

The PGL persists and, in addition, John gradually begins to experience other troublesome symptoms. His immune system is weakening and this allows AIDS-related illnesses to appear. The symptoms include loss of appetite, fever, night sweats, swollen glands, weight loss, skin rashes, diarrhoea, weakness and coughing. These are recurring often and becoming increasingly troublesome. It is during this stage that most people discover for the first time that they are HIV-positive.

John is in this stage when he is admitted to hospital with a serious chest infection. Patients with AIDS have serious, life-threatening illnesses which may start suddenly or slowly. Some people may get a sudden severe attack of diarrhoea or develop difficulty in breathing. Some others lose consciousness. For others the symptoms may be different. They may notice purple raised lumps under the skin caused by a cancer known as Kaposi's sarcoma. Or they may lose weight rapidly. Some become gradually forgetful, clumsy and confused. Not everyone follows the same course as John from stage to stage.

It is sometimes difficult for doctors to differentiate between AIDS-related illnesses and full-blown AIDS as it is a progression of the same condition.

After the development of full-blown AIDS the person usually dies within a year. New drugs may be able to extend this time but are very expensive and often unavailable. Children infected at birth usually progress more quickly to full-blown AIDS and most will have died by the age of five.

It is important to note that HIV infection can only be confirmed after a doctor has done a blood test. No one can diagnose AIDS in another person simply by looking at them and the symptoms they have.

Finish this session with a discussion on the dangers of 'diagnosing' AIDS simply on the basis of knowledge of symptoms.

(For more on these issues, see Chapter 3.)

Session 5: Sexually transmitted diseases (STDs)

Lecture

HIV/AIDS is most commonly spread through sexual activity, and is therefore categorised as a sexually transmitted disease (STD). STDs have been around for centuries, and can cause disability, illness, infertility and death.

Where an STD is present, the chances of either partner becoming infected with HIV are increased perhaps by as much as ten times or more. Women are especially at risk, because symptoms of STDs are often not noticeable for some time, and they may fail to seek treatment in the early stages. Symptoms of STDs in men are easier to detect. People may have more than one STD at a time.

STDs are relatively easy to treat and should be tackled immediately.

Recent sexual partners or contacts should also be notified as soon as possible.

The main symptoms of STDs are listed below, but even where symptoms are absent an infection may be present. People who have casual sex or have more than one partner are vulnerable to STDs or HIV.

STDs are divided into two groups: (1) those that cause ulcers or blisters, such as syphilis, chancroid, and genital herpes, and (2) those that cause a discharge, such as gonorrhoea, chlamydia, and candidiasis (thrush). Thrush is not always sexually transmitted; it can occur with the use of antibiotics, around the time of the menstrual period, or with poor hygiene.

Ulcers or sores become an opening for HIV to enter the body easily, and the discharge from them contains large quantities of the virus in people who are infected with AIDS.

Symptoms

- Pain when passing water, difficulty passing water, or the need to pass water frequently.
- Swollen glands in the groin.
- Sores and/or blisters on the genitals (may be painful).
- Genital warts.
- Itching in the genital areas.
- Flu-like symptoms/fevers.
- Discharge from penis or vagina.
- Lower stomach pains (women).
- Painful or difficult intercourse (women).
- Change in period cycle (women).

All people with STDs should be treated immediately, as should their partners. It is important if a person has an STD that they should refrain from sexual intercourse until the infection is cleared, and ideally until they have had a blood test for HIV. If the test is negative, it will be necessary to repeat it after six months, in case the person has just been infected with HIV.

Session 6: Blood testing

If there is a hospital nearby it may be possible for someone to come and talk to the group about testing, or even to take the group there for a visit.

Discussion

Divide the group into small groups and ask them to list questions that they would like answered regarding blood testing. Allow ten minutes for the groups to prepare their list of questions.

A participant from each small group should present the questions to the whole group. Discard any duplicate questions before answering the remaining ones using the information provided below. As much as possible invite the other participants to answer the questions themselves.

If there are any questions to which nobody knows the answer, then resolve to find it out later. Of course, not all the questions listed below may be asked. In that case, simply answer the ones raised.

What is the HIV test?

Most tests are done using ELISA – a very accurate test. A small sample of blood is taken and sent to the laboratory. The test looks to see if the virus has caused the body to produce antibodies in an attempt to fight off the infection. This is like looking to see if the virus has left its 'footprints' around.

The test is not a test for AIDS – most people with a positive test result do not have AIDS yet – but it does show that a person has been exposed to and has become infected by the virus (HIV) that leads to AIDS.

What is HIV blood screening?

This is a process where testing is done on large numbers of people to check the blood for HIV. Screening is done to all blood that is donated in this country, and may also be carried out as part of a survey of certain sections of the population.

How is the blood test carried out?

A small amount of blood (about 2 ml) is taken, usually from the arm, using a new syringe and needle. The blood sample is inserted into a bottle and sent to the laboratory for testing with a note specifying which test is to be carried out. The procedure does not take long and is not painful.

When a person is asked to have an HIV blood test they should be made aware of the reasons for the test and agree to have the test. Many hospitals now have facilities for 'pre-test' counselling and staff are specially trained to counsel people who are intending to have the test and those who come to collect their results.

Are there any dangers in having blood tests?

No. All the equipment used is sterile, and the staff are qualified to take samples.

Does the person's name appear on the blood test request and result forms?

Not necessarily. The doctor may have a special record book in which the patient's name is written, but the form which is sent with the blood to the laboratory only displays a number. This number corresponds to the name in the doctor's book. This ensures confidentiality. When the results are returned, the doctor can then refer to the record book to identify the person that the result belongs to. However, doctors and surgeries use different systems.

Why do a test?

- A doctor may want to know the cause of the ill-health of a patient, especially if he or she is not responding to treatment.
- Knowing one's HIV status can save money spent on seeing other doctors and healers.
- It may be helpful to know the result of an HIV test before making certain decisions in life, like marriage, expensive education or having children.
- Employers may need to know the health of a potential employee before starting an expensive training programme for that person.
- Some of the higher insurance policies insist on an HIV blood test before granting the policy.

How long does it take to get the results?

The results should be ready in a few days, but this depends a lot on available resources and manpower. Usually the results are available to the patient within one or two weeks.

If I think I am infected, should I be tested?

If a person is worried that they may have been infected with HIV, perhaps because they have led a high risk lifestyle (or their sexual partner has), it may be advisable for them to have the test so as to be in a position to make informed decisions about their future plans. It may be that the person is not infected and it will be a great relief to be informed of this. They can then change their lifestyle to ensure they remain uninfected.

Who should be tested – the man or the woman?

Both. It is always a possibility that one person is infected, and the other is not. A couple need to be aware of this so as to take precautions to avoid the other person becoming infected in the future.

Is it compulsory to be tested for HIV?

No, it is not. Some workplaces insist on a medical examination before employing someone or at certain intervals. Also, life assurance companies may insist on a test before granting a policy to someone. Some countries test everyone and other countries test couples before they get married.

Why don't we test everyone?

Mass testing is no use unless re-testing is done at regular intervals. Testing everybody would be extremely expensive and the resources are not available to do this on such a large scale. Not only is equipment and personnel needed for doing the testing but also people to do counselling before and after the results are available.

It would be against basic human rights to force people into having an HIV blood test against their will. It could lead to mass panic. Countries that have attempted to test everyone have not found it successful or useful.

Is there a charge to have a blood test?

There may be a charge for a blood test, depending on the clinic or hospital.

Is the test able to reveal the amount of virus in the blood?

No. The HIV blood test is not able to detect the quantity of virus present in the blood or how long a person has been infected. Nor can it determine when they will develop AIDS in the future.

What does the virus look like?

It is hard to describe the virus so an illustration of HIV, enlarged millions of times, is presented below.

HIV

Can the doctor determine the mode of infection?

There is no way of determining the mode of transmission by doing a blood test. Nor would it be very useful information once a person is infected. It is more important to take action to prevent further infections.

Do false results ever occur?

There are occasional false negatives and false positives but these are unusual as the ELISA test is very accurate. Where false results do occur this is generally due to the state of the patient's health, or is connected to when the person became infected rather than the fault of the equipment involved. Sometimes a negative result is a 'false negative'. This means that the person is infected with HIV but there are no 'footprints' around. A false negative result can happen when:

- The person has only been infected recently. It can take up to six months from the time of infection for antibodies to develop in the blood. This time is known as the 'window period' where the virus is present in the body but no antibodies have yet been formed.
- A different strain of the AIDS virus, such as HIV 2, is the cause of infection. HIV 2 has different antibodies and requires a different test.
- A few people who have become infected do not develop antibodies at all. As time goes by however it is more likely that these will appear. This is most common in small babies and is probably due to their immune systems being too immature to produce antibodies.
- The person is at a late stage of infection and the immune system is too weak and exhausted to produce antibodies.

A doctor who believes a person is infected, but where a negative test result is produced, will usually want to repeat the test after a few months.

There can also be the problem of a 'false positive'. There are some 'footprints' around but the person in fact has no infection. This can happen when:

- Other infections produce antibodies which look very like the 'footprints' of the AIDS virus.
- A patient has been exposed to the virus and has developed antibodies, but in fact does not have the virus. This occurs commonly in babies born to infected mothers, where the mother passes the antibodies but not the virus to the baby. The baby will test negative at a later stage.

Are patients always informed of the results?

The person must return to the doctor who requested the test in order to receive the results. However, people often do not return to collect their results for various reasons.

Who will know the result?

The doctor will only pass on the results of a test to a third party with prior consent of the patient. The doctor or counsellor will discuss with the person who they think it advisable to share the results with. A person at risk of contracting HIV may be informed by the doctor if the person infected continues to refuse to disclose this information.

Is the result written on your medical history cards?

It is important for doctors to note whether a person has had an HIV blood test, to avoid repeat tests and to indicate to other doctors the cause of illness. Results are therefore usually marked on the medical history cards which are the personal and private property of the hospital.

What happens to donated blood which is positive?

It is burned or buried. It is never used.

Is it safe to donate blood?

People are encouraged to donate blood as it is vital for hospitals in the treatment of the seriously ill or those involved in accidents. All blood donated is screened, not only for HIV, but for other contagious diseases spread through blood. If donated blood has any of these diseases the donor is notified so that they may seek counsel and medical attention.

(For more on important issues of testing, including accuracy and counselling, see Chapters 5, 7 and 14.)

Session 7: Routes for the spread of infection

Brainstorm

Ask the participants to explain what they understand by the term prostitute and who is involved in prostitution. Hold a short general discussion on the definitions given and other terms used, such as commerical sex worker.

Lecture

Sexual intercourse is the most common way of HIV transmission between both sexes in the world. AIDS is a sexually transmitted disease (STD). People infected with an STD like gonorrhoea or syphilis are at high risk of contracting HIV infection too.

HIV spreads during sexual intercourse from man to woman and woman to man. The more frequently unprotected sexual contact is made between an infected person and an uninfected person the greater the risk is of the spread of the AIDS virus to that uninfected person. In some cases, however, even after regular sexual contact with a person who is HIV infected, there are people who remain uninfected themselves, although these are in a very small minority.

In Africa, HIV often spreads in communities as a result of prostitution, which is very common in both urban and rural districts. Prostitution is the term we use when payment is asked for in return for sexual favours. There are several reasons why prostitution takes place.

- Prostitution is often the result of the breakdown of traditional moral values.
- The system of migrant labour, in which married couples spend long periods away from their partners, can influence the occurrence of prostitution, and the number of sexual partners outside marriage is then often increased.
- Poverty and destitution among women forces many into prostitution as a means of survival for themselves and their children.
- The benefit to the woman may be a gift of food or clothes or of some other kind so that neither the man nor the woman considers it a commercial relationship, even though the woman has a large number of partners on this basis.

For many women, prostitution is not a 'problem' – it is a 'solution' to the problems of poverty, unemployment and powerlessness. The majority of women who receive payment or benefits in return for sexual favours do not practise prostitution as a career, but they move in and out of the lifestyle as their economic and social circumstances dictate.

Poster 10 is an illustration of the way many people become infected with the AIDS virus. Although prostitution is a common and important method of spread in communities, people who are prostitutes are *not* the cause of AIDS. It is important to emphasise this fact. It takes two people to take part in every act of prostitution. In Africa the majority of prostitutes are (as in this illustration) women who are supplying a demand for sex by men.

In order to emphasise that the men who visit prostitutes are equally responsible for the spread of HIV, the picture starts with the man who first gives the infection to the female prostitute. He has many sexual partners each year, and during some of his sexual contacts he passed the AIDS virus to his partners.

At some time this man passes the infection on to a prostitute. She has many sexual partners each year and spreads the virus to some of her clients. Some of these men then infect other prostitutes. In this way prostitutes are often the first group of people to be largely infected by the AIDS virus. In some African cities, almost every prostitute is a carrier of HIV. This illustrates the vulnerability of a prostitute, who is at very high risk of becoming HIV infected.

One of the prostitute's clients who becomes infected is an unmarried man. He has an average of ten partners each year. This is by no means unusual, especially among men with a reasonable financial income.

One of this man's regular girlfriends is a teenage girl still at school. She becomes infected by the virus after some months of regular sexual contact. Even though she has a faithful relationship with her boyfriend,

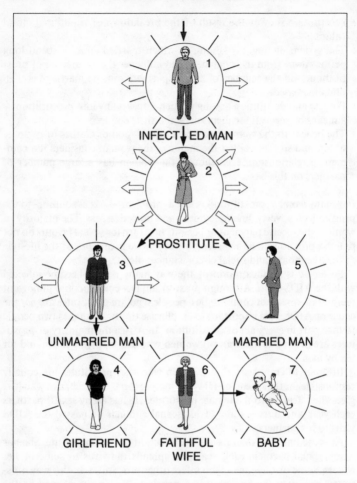

Poster 10

she still becomes infected. If she later has another boyfriend or gets married and starts having regular sex, there is a high chance that her new partner will become infected.

Another of the prostitute's clients is a married man. Even though he is only occasionally unfaithful to his wife he is unlucky enough to have become infected with HIV when he had sex with the prostitute.

The wife of this man in time also becomes infected. Her husband is the only man she has ever had sex with. Sexual faithfulness by one partner only is no defence against AIDS. He has given her one STD before, causing ulcers on her private parts, and perhaps other STDs, which in women are often not detected due to a lack of symptoms.

When the wife gives birth it is discovered that her baby has the HIV infection. A woman has a 30% chance of passing the infection on to her baby. Many married couples discover they have HIV infection only when their young baby gets sick and is diagnosed as having HIV/AIDS.

People often assume that the HIV infection spreads from a core group of highly sexually active female prostitutes, their male clients and from them on to child bearing women who are generally faithful to their partners.

But not every HIV infection in the community is acquired in this way. Some men get the infection from a regular girlfriend (4) rather than from a prostitute. Both husbands and wives are vulnerable to HIV infection as a result of unfaithfulness on the part of their partners (5 and 6).

What proportion of the adult population is at risk of being infected by the AIDS virus? Not all unmarried men have sexual contact with different girlfriends. Not all married men are unfaithful to their wives.

The answer to the question is not known. But in communities where a majority of adults have an STD at some time or other in their lives, this same majority is at high risk of becoming infected by the AIDS virus. In 1991 a survey done with people with STDs in an urban area showed that over 60% were HIV-positive. In the same area over 30% of pregnant women were HIV-positive. (For more, see Chapters 1 and 4.)

Conclusion

HIV/AIDS has caused many problems for people. For children whose parents are infected there is the prospect of becoming orphans. If the extended family cannot or will not assist them, many will end up on the streets and become involved in begging, stealing, glue sniffing, prostitution etc. and may well become infected with HIV themselves through the prostitution.

In a marriage situation, one partner will be left a widow or widower, having to try and cope with their children's welfare, their own failing health, and the prospect of their death. Those who are infected, whether ill or not, often feel unwelcomed by family, friends, workmates, employers, society and even the church. They may lose their job, and have difficulty getting another one, and yet will need to cope with increasing medical bills and the knowledge that they need to provide for their children.

God says in Psalm 146 that 'he upholds the cause of the oppressed . . . He watches over the alien and sustains the fatherless and the widow'. God's heart is for those who have no parents. He wants to show them that he is their heavenly Father and that he cares for them. His heart is for those who have lost their husbands or wives, to show them that they are not alone and that he is with them. His heart is for those who feel rejected, lonely, different, oppressed and alienated from others, to show them he is on their side to support them and strengthen them. Are people with HIV/AIDS excluded from God's love and mercy?

We can see from the life of Christ that he reached out to such people. In the Old Testament, we see provision made for such people in his laws. We see in the establishment of the early church that same love and concern for these people.

God calls us today to reach out to the orphans, widows and oppressed, even if it is as a result of HIV/AIDS. In Psalm 82:3–4, there is a challenge to help such people. In James 1:27 it says that if our faith is to be something that God sees as good and commendable then it must show itself in care for such people, yet maintaining a pure and holy life.

May we have such compassion of heart and holiness of life and so show our faith to be real and living.

Session 8: Using stories in AIDS education

Remind the group that the aim of this course is to equip them to take part in community AIDS education programmes. This practical work is very valuable in the development of relationships with local communities. In getting across information, or drawing attention to the effects of certain lifestyles, one effective means is to tell stories.

It has been found that storytelling using pictures is a simple and suitable method of AIDS education. Many people find group communication difficult but are easily able to tell a story effectively.

Pictures, which can be held up at various parts of the story, can add enormously to the impact. If you can't produce your own pictures, then find someone able to produce effective illustrations to your story.

The stories are useful to begin an AIDS education talk. They introduce subjects such as extra- and pre-marital sex, prostitution, and so on, which are embarrassing to many people.

The stories tell of someone else's problems. People may feel it is easier to discuss a problem through a character rather than relate it to themselves.

It can be difficult to stand up in front of a group of people and talk about issues such as AIDS, sex or death. With storytelling, however, people focus on the pictures and the characters, rather than the storyteller.

Storytelling using pictures creates an entertaining aspect to AIDS education. People become interested in the characters and often laugh or sigh at appropriate times in the story. This shows how people relate to the story characters.

The stories capture the interest of the audience before confronting them with the reality of HIV infection.

Stories enable the teller to talk about sexual and health matters in a way that is less embarrassing to the audience. People can identify with the characters in the story. They can then be asked to respond to the issues raised:

- What do you think he should have done?
- Why do you think people have sex outside marriage?
- What would you advise this woman to do?
- Do you think the church leader said the right thing?

Technical or scientific presentations about HIV infection can leave people feeling discouraged about how little they know of the subject. Stories can give information regarding HIV infection in a way which is socially relevant, helping people to build upon their existing knowledge.

Encourage the group to tell stories to one another, and then to discuss the storytellers and how well they did.

Section 9: Learning how to counsel

Role play

Ask two people to perform the following role play. One character is a woman, and the other an AIDS educator.

The woman's husband has just died from AIDS – thought to have been contracted through an infected blood transfusion following a road accident. She has no form of income, and has three young children. She does not yet know if she or the children have been infected.

The AIDS educator has just finished an AIDS course and is keen to teach people about AIDS. He is unaware of the woman's situation. He thinks that HIV/AIDS is always due to immoral behaviour and that in a marriage situation both partners will be infected.

> *AIDS educator*: Good morning. I don't know if you've heard much about AIDS but I want to teach you something about it today.
> *Woman*: My husband has just died of AIDS. (*She bursts into tears.*)
> *AIDS educator*: Ah, so he has been sleeping around, has he?
> *Woman*: (*Through her tears*) I thought he got it through a blood transfusion.
> *AIDS educator*: That's what they all say, but I'm sure he has been with other women. (*More tears from the woman.*) Have you been having much sickness lately? Because you will have been infected as well.
> *Woman*: (*Appalled.*) Do you think so?

AIDS educator: You are sure to have been. In fact, you could die within a year or so. (*The woman cries even harder.*) Have you any children?

Woman: (*Through her tears*) Yes, three. The youngest is less than a year old – I'm still feeding him.

AIDS educator: You probably have passed the infection to your youngest then, either in pregnancy or through breast-feeding. You'd better make some arrangements for the children who survive after you die. (*The woman collapses in floods of tears.*) Well, I'd better go and tell someone else about AIDS – there is so much to do. Would you like me to pray with you before I leave?

The woman throws a cushion at him as he makes a hurried exit.

Discussion

Divide into small groups and ask the groups to list some of the important qualities a person should have if they are to either teach or counsel about HIV/AIDS, especially on an individual or family basis.

After ten minutes, bring the groups together and get them to report back their discussions. List what they say on a blackboard or paper for all to see.

Have a general discussion about these things making sure the following are included, though there are many other qualities that could be mentioned.

- Sensitivity and approachability. We will be dealing with people who are frightened, ashamed, lonely, angry; people who are dying, or are seeing someone else die; people who have to consider a difficult future for their children; people who may (or may not) have been involved in wrong behaviour or been wronged against. (Consider Jesus' sensitivity in dealing with the woman at the well in John 4.)
- Compassion. Time and again Jesus responded to people with compassion and love (see Mark 1:41, 6:34; Luke 7:13). We must not have a judgemental attitude, but must be motivated by the love of God. We need to have compassion on those in distress, whatever the cause of infection with HIV.
- Confidentiality and trustworthiness. Some sensitive and private things may be shared with us. If we pass these on to others it may cause great hurt and greater distress for the person. It will also mean nobody will want to share such things with us again. Whereas if we are known to be trustworthy, people will feel confident sharing with us.
- Ability to listen. Although it is important to teach, it is more important to listen first to see what needs a person has, to see where they are hurting, and to help reduce the chance of saying something insensitive.

- Comfort. This word originally meant to give strength to. We need to come alongside people, to help them, and to strengthen them to go on.
- Sharing God's word and praying with people. Most people will welcome this, if done in a loving way, but we need to be sensitive to the situation to know when and how to share.
- Being willing to help in practical ways if possible, and certainly to return another time to show we are really concerned.

Session 10: Talking to dying people about God

In becoming an AIDS educator, it will be necessary to prepare to talk to people about their death. People will have many questions about what will happen to them and how they can find God. (See Chapter 9 for more on attitudes to death in churches.)

Bible study

A person is made of three parts. 1 Thessalonians 5:23 says, 'May your whole spirit, soul, and body be kept blameless at the coming of our Lord Jesus Christ.' As with the Trinity – God is Father, Son and the Holy Spirit – so with us, the spirit, soul and body are different, and yet linked closely together.

The earthly body is a shell which holds the spirit and soul. At death this is the part of us that is buried. Scripture confirms that we will still have our bodies in the life to come, but they will be spiritual bodies. Philippians 3:21 tells us that God 'will transform our lowly bodies so that they will be like his glorious body'.

The spirit and soul appear to remain together at death. The soul is recognised as being our character, our will and emotions; our spirit is the part of us that communicates with God.

While suffering on the cross, Jesus conversed with two criminals who were being crucified at the same time. One mocked him, but the other recognised his own error and Jesus' goodness. Jesus told him, 'Today you will be with me in paradise' (Luke 23:43). The other man would not be there.

In Luke 16:19–31 the death of two men is recounted. One was a rich man who ignored the poor, the other a humble beggar called Lazarus. Both men died. The poor man was carried into the presence of Abraham by the angels. The other was in hell, where he was in torment. He looked up and saw Abraham far away, with Lazarus by his side, but he was separated from them by a great chasm that could not be crossed.

Matthew 25 gives three accounts of people going before God: the ten virgins, the people with talents and the separation of the sheep and goats. Two places are spoken of for man to go to. One is a place of darkness, where there will be weeping and gnashing of teeth, and for the other, Jesus says, 'Come and share your master's happiness!' He speaks of a place where man can 'take his inheritance, the kingdom prepared for you since the creation of the world'. The last verse says, 'Then they will go away to eternal punishment, but the righteous to eternal life.'

It is clear from these teachings that different things happen to people at death according to their faith and deeds during life.

Lecture

When people are confronted by the possibility of death through hearing of their own terminal illness, or that of someone in their community, this often forces them to realise that they are not prepared for death. They have not 'made their peace', and they do not know where they are going after death. Such a person may indicate that they would like to see a priest or a hospital chaplain, or may ask you and others for spiritual help. It is important to be very sensitive to someone who has the desire to make things right with God but does not know how. We should be very careful to listen, and slow to rush in with our words. Although every situation is different the following are guidelines which should be adapted with great wisdom and compassion to suit the specific situation.

First, we need to recognise our sin. We call this *confession*. The Bible says we are all sinners. 'All have sinned and fall short of the glory of God' (Romans 3:23). In 2 Peter 3:9 it says that God does not want anyone to perish, but wants everyone to come to repentance.

Secondly, we need to turn from sin and a way of life which rejects God. We call this *repentance*. Luke 13:3 says, 'Unless you repent, you too will all perish.'

Thirdly, we need to place our faith in Jesus Christ, who died in our place and paid for our sin. That is called *faith* or *belief*. 'Believe in the Lord Jesus, and you will be saved' (Acts 16:31).

Fourthly, we need to ask God to come into our lives and take control. He does this by giving us his Spirit to dwell in our hearts, and we need to receive him. Jesus called this being born again (see John 3:3). Being born again means the Holy Spirit in us gives us the power to start living a brand new life with new values, perspectives and goals. God is now in control guiding, empowering and blessing our lives.

Having decided to turn to God, the person can be encouraged to pray, *acknowledging* his sin, that he wishes to *turn* from it, that he *believes* and *trusts* in Jesus, and *accepts* God's free gift of salvation.

'To all who received him, to those who believed in his name, he gave the right to be called children of God' (John 1:12).

To help us to do God's will we need to read the Bible (see 1 Peter 2:2: 'Crave pure spiritual milk, so that by it you may grow up in your salvation'). We should meet with other Christians (see Hebrews 10:25: 'Let us not give up meeting together'). It is said of the early Christians that they 'devoted themselves to the apostles' teaching and to fellowship, to the breaking of bread and to prayer' (Acts 2:42). This involves studying the Bible, meeting together, sharing communion (which is remembering what Jesus did for us and identifying with his sufferings) and praying.

Sharing this message is the most important and valuable thing we can do for others, including those with HIV/AIDS. How wonderful to lead them to Christ and give them a real meaningful hope in a relationship with God leading to eternal life.

But we do need to take great care that we are not imposing our own agendas on people who are sick and emotionally vulnerable, or we may rightly be accused of abusing a privileged position. So much depends on the situation. For example, it could be someone who is at church, or who is a patient in a government hospital ward with whom we have a professional caring relationship. The key is drawing alongside someone who is asking for help, recognising they may have physical, emotional, social and spiritual needs, listening to them and serving them in the way they wish. (See Appendix D.)

Conclusion

The sessions described in this Appendix are simply suggestions for your own course. There are many other subjects that could be covered:

• How to talk to men about AIDS
• How to talk to women about AIDS
• How to talk to young people about AIDS (Chapter 12)
• Recognising the strength of peer pressure (Chapter 12)
• Looking at the response of the church to AIDS (Chapters 10, 11, 15, 17)
• Discussing whether AIDS is the judgement of God (Chapter 8)
• Looking at cultural practices and changing them where necessary (Chapters 14, 15)
• Learning how to give positive messages

You can find material for sessions like these in the main text of *The Truth About AIDS* (see above). Also, use the index at the back of this book.

What now?

Some groups believe that a test should be carried out at the end of the course. A test is not included in this manual but one could easily be put together, based on the material you have used.

It is important to note, however, that an educator does not need to pass a written test to be effective. A more positive assessment might be made by observing a person's involvement and skills during the training course itself.

It is suggested that certificates be given to all the participants who complete the course rather than those who pass a test at the end. This recognises the ability of everyone to educate somebody else, whether in an informal discussion, through drama or by running a training course themselves. The facilitator should be able to identify those participants skilled in working with groups of people and involve them in educational projects where possible.

The questionnaires completed at the beginning and end of the course should be analysed carefully and any relevant points noted. For example, a participant may have suggested that certain sessions could be improved. If there is a session where several people have made similar comments, it may be necessary to make changes to that session. Notes can be made in the manual or in a separate file that would be used during future training courses.

It has been found that it is useful to keep a record of the points covered during the group discussions and then to compile a report of the workshop. This increases the reference materials available for future training programmes.

Sample questionnaires

HIV/AIDS Pre-Course Questionnaire

Please tick the answers in the appropriate boxes.

Have you ever attended an HIV/AIDS training course before?
Yes ☐   No ☐

If yes, please give some details of the course.

_____
_____

What are your reasons for attending this course?

_____
_____

Do you think HIV/AIDS is:
Not a problem ☐   A small problem ☐   A serious problem ☐
Please give the reason for your answer

_____
_____

Do you think HIV/AIDS is a church problem?
Yes ☐   No ☐
If you ticked no, why do you think that?

_____
_____

If you ticked yes, how do you think the church should be involved?

_____
_____

Do you think HIV/AIDS can be spread by the following?

		Yes	No	Maybe
a)	Kissing			
b)	Coughing and sneezing			
c)	Sex			
d)	Sharing plates, cups, spoons			
e)	Haircuts			
f)	Blood transfusions			
g)	Animals			
h)	Touching blood			
i)	Mosquitoes and other insects			
j)	Mother to her baby			
k)	Living with a person with AIDS			
l)	Injecting with a dirty needle			
m)	Sharing toilets, baths, showers			
n)	Sharing towels, clothes			

How do you think HIV/AIDS can be prevented?

_____

_____

HIV/AIDS Post-Course Questionnaire

In your view, how were the aims of the course met?
Well ☐   Almost ☐   Hardly ☐   Not at all ☐

For each of the training methods used please mark how useful you feel they were.

	Very useful	Moderately useful	Not useful
Stories			
Posters			
Group discussions			
Group feedback sessions			
Brainstorms			
Lectures/Talks			
Role plays			

Were there any other methods you feel that could have been used but were not?
Yes ☐   No ☐

If yes, please specify what other methods could have been used

_____

Were the methods used:
Easy to understand? ☐   Confusing? ☐

For each main session please mark how useful you feel they were.

	Very useful	Moderately useful	Not useful
What is AIDS?			
Why we need to know about AIDS			
How HIV/AIDS is spread			
Signs and symptoms of HIV/AIDS			
Sexually transmitted diseases			
Blood testing			

Routes for the spread of infection
Using story telling
Learning to counsel
Talking to the dying

(Include the titles of all sessions covered in your course.)

How much opportunity was given to you to participate?
A lot ☐   A little ☐   None ☐

Were the materials provided sufficient?
Yes ☐   No ☐

If no, please be specific about what you feel should have been provided.

_____
_____

How do you rate the venue (accommodation)?
Excellent ☐   Adequate ☐   Poor ☐

Comment on your answer if desired

_____

Was the timing of the course suitable for you?
Yes ☐   No ☐

If no, please specify how you feel the timing could be improved.

_____

Was there enough time to complete all the sessions?
Yes ☐   No ☐

If no, please specify which sessions were not allocated enough time.

_____

Please comment on the usefulness and value of the course to you.

_____
_____
_____

WHOLISTIC CARE TEAM TRAINING
Dr Langkham, Emmanuel Hospital Association

Editor's note: This resource from India contains useful material but needs careful adaptation to your own culture and church context since perspectives differ on the connection between physical, emotional and spiritual well-being, from medical, psychological and theological points of view.

PART ONE – Caring for the whole person

Introduction

This course was developed for EHA's work in India. Its goal is to help you learn how to care for the sick as whole people, with body, soul, spirit and living within a family. As Christian health workers, we try to help people get well by providing the physical, psychological and spiritual resources which will enable them to be restored to health. We do this in the following ways:

- Through good physical, medical care, we encourage the recovery of physical health.
- We provide emotional support and encouragement to the sick person and family.
- We gently seek to find out if the sick person has personal problems that may be affecting his health or healing.
- Where appropriate, we call on the Wholistic Care Team staff to talk with the sick person.
- Where appropriate, we minister to the sick person the healing power of Christ, through prayer, personal witness, and biblical teaching.

Lesson 1: Why this course is important

We have a serious problem in western medicine and nursing care. We believe, incorrectly, that the person is made up of three mutually exclusive parts – body, soul, and spirit – and we treat these parts separately.

When the body is ill, we assume that the problem is only physical, needing medical and nursing care. The person therefore needs a doctor and nurses.

When a person has a mental or emotional problem, we assume that the soul is ill and the person needs a counsellor or psychologist.

When the person has a spiritual problem, we send him to a pastor.

This divided approach of caring for sick people is not biblical, nor is it a complete, comprehensive approach. When a person has a physical illness, they also have emotional problems like fear, shame, remorse, or other painful feelings. They may also have a spiritual problem, such as fear of a curse or being angry with God. These emotional and spiritual problems also affect the body, making physical healing more difficult. Therefore, such a person needs care for the soul and spirit as well as for the body. So it becomes important that doctors, nurses, pastors, and counsellors work together to help the body, soul and spirit of the person in their care.

Another problem with the western approach to medical care is that we focus on diseases, and not on sick people. We want to cure the disease, but pay little attention to the person who has the disease – to his personal needs, the needs of the family and to his future life. It is important that we learn how to care for the whole person.

Exercise 1

Here is an example of how Jesus cared for the whole person. Read Mark 5:25–34. It is the story of how Jesus healed a woman who had had vaginal bleeding for twelve years.

Working together in small groups, read and discuss this story. Think about the details which Mark did *not* write about, but which were probably part of this woman's problem. Think about the following questions, discuss them and write your own notes about them.

1. What other physical problems might this woman have had as a result of her chronic bleeding? Do you suppose she had any children?
2. This woman was Jewish, and was required to live according to the laws of the Old Testament. Read Leviticus 15:19–30. It is clear from this passage that this woman had been 'unclean' for twelve years. How do you suppose that affected her life?
3. What feelings and emotions do you think she had in her heart?
4. According to Leviticus 15:31, this woman could not go to the temple to worship God. How do you think that made her feel?
5. Make a list of the likely physical, social, emotional, and spiritual problems of this woman.
6. Why did she come up behind Jesus in a crowd to touch his robe? Why did she not just go up to him and ask him to heal her?

7. After her bleeding had been healed, why did Jesus call her to come back to him?
8. How did Jesus heal her mind, soul and spirit?
9. What is it that can heal the problems in our thoughts, feelings, emotions and spirit?

Bible study 1: How God made us

Read Genesis 1 and 2.

1. Since God is spirit and has no body, what does it mean that we are made 'in his image'? In other words, what do we have that makes us like God?
2. When God took the dust of the earth and made man, what are all the things he made out of the dust?
3. After God made man out of the dust of the earth, why was man not yet alive? What was missing?
4. What does this tell us about who we are as human beings?
5. How are we different from the animals? (See Genesis 2:19.)
6. God gave eight commands to Adam and Eve. What are they? (See Genesis 1:28; 2:15; 2:16, 17.)
7. How are we to fulfil those commands?
8. What are the implications of this study for health professionals? Write down your answers on an overhead transparency and be prepared to present them to the rest of the group.

Lesson 2: Body, soul and spirit

1 Thessalonians 5:23 tells us that we have body, soul and spirit. Let's be clear on what these terms mean.

- The *body* is our physical being. It is what God made out of the dust of the earth. The Old Testament sometimes uses the word 'bones' to mean the whole body, or even the whole person. The Bible often uses the word 'flesh' to refer to the body.
- The *soul* includes our mind – our thoughts and intellect, our feelings, emotions, desires and memories.
- The *spirit* is the part of us that is in contact with God, or with other spirits.

The Bible also uses the word *heart* to mean mind, soul, and spirit. It refers to our inner self, that part of us which cannot be seen.

Body, soul and spirit are united together and we must not try to separate them: each influences the other. Emotions like fear and anger can make our body sick (high blood pressure, stomach pains, etc). Spiritual problems can cause depression or despair, can upset our emotions and can even make our body sick – through loss of appetite leading to malnutrition.

Exercise 2

Break into groups and discuss the following questions.

1. How do God and the spiritual world affect our health?
2. How can other people affect our health?
3. How can the natural world – air, water, food, land, forests – affect our health?

Lesson 3: The 'architecture of the heart'

It is important to understand what is in the heart – the inner self. Imagine that the heart is a big house, with many rooms. In each room is a different aspect of what we call 'the heart'.

- The **conscious mind** is where we have our thoughts, our reason, and our intellect. It is really a very small room because we can only think one thought at a time. Thoughts come into our conscious mind from the world around us, and we have five 'windows' that allow things to come into the room of the conscious mind:

  Our *eyes* and what we see.
  Our *ears* and what we hear.
  Our sense of *touch*.
  Our sense of *taste*.
  Our sense of *smell*.

  Ideas and thoughts come into our mind through these 'windows', and can then go out of our mind to others. Using the same imagery of a house, we can say that they go out the front door. The front door is our speech, our gestures, and the different actions we perform to express ourselves.
  When we are awake, the conscious mind is a busy place; when we are asleep it is quiet.
- The **subconscious mind** lies below the room of the conscious mind. This is a big place, for there are many things stored there. In the different rooms are our emotions and feelings, our beliefs and desires, many memories of things past, the culture we have received from our parents, friends, and country, and the basic instincts that protect our life.
  Between the conscious and subconscious mind is a door. The

thoughts in the conscious mind pass quickly into the subconscious mind to stimulate emotions, feelings and desires. They are stored there in the memory. Often things try to pass from the subconscious mind into our thoughts, words and actions. A strong emotion can burst out of the subconscious mind, go quickly through the conscious mind and make us do or say things that are perhaps not good. So the conscious mind must control the door into the subconscious mind, keeping down the bad feelings and emotions, and keeping out the bad thoughts.

- The **emotions** are our inner response to something that happens around us. We may see something or hear something, and this gives us a new thought. That thought goes down into the subconscious mind and is interpreted. If what we see or hear makes us happy, we will experience the emotion of joy. If what we see or hear is a threat, we will experience the emotion of fear, or perhaps anger.

  We can compare emotions to fire. Fire is an important part of life: it cooks our food, boils our water, and keeps us warm. On the other hand, fire can burn and destroy. The fire of joy makes us feel good and gives us the energy to do good things. The fire of anger is very strong, and if we do not control it, it can make us say harmful things or hurt other people. It is therefore important to control our emotions so that the heat and energy coming from them can help us do good, rather than harm.

  Each emotion stimulates the brain to produce a specific neurochemical that influences all the organs of the body.

- **Feelings** are the impressions we have about ourselves, and about things in the world around us. Certain things make us feel good. Other things make us feel uncomfortable. Feelings are similar to emotions, but they last longer and are not as strong. We can compare feelings, not to a fire, but to a warm glow. They also cause the brain to make neuro-chemicals that act on the organs of the body.

- We also have many **beliefs** in our heart: not just religious beliefs, but beliefs about everything. Beliefs are what we think is true, and what we think is of value. We believe different things about ourselves, our family, our country, our work and the many different things we do.

  Beliefs and values help us decide what to do and how to live. We do what we believe is good for us and of value to us. We may have beliefs about morality, about actions that are good and helpful, and about actions that are bad and harmful.

- In another room in the heart are our **desires**. We desire to be happy, to be healthy, and to be strong. Sometimes we desire to have power, to control other people, and things around us. We have sexual desires: men have strong desires to be with women; women have strong desires to be with men. Most people have a strong desire for money and to have material possessions. These desires are like an inner energy. They push us to do certain things and to behave in a certain kind of way. We do things in order to satisfy the desires of our heart.

- We have two big rooms in our heart for **memories**. Think of these rooms as being full of filing cabinets. Each filing cabinet has many drawers, and each drawer contains many files. Everything that has happened to us from the time we were born is filed in a folder and is in a drawer in one of the filing cabinets.

  Some events we can remember – recent events, and things that are important for us – and these make up our available memories: we can recall them to our thoughts. Many other events we have forgotten. We forget almost everything that happened when we were babies or small children. And we forget even more recent events, if they are not important to us.

  The memories of some events are pleasant, but the memories of other events may be painful. But even if we have forgotten a difficult event, the painful memory is still in our heart. It may not come into our thoughts, but it can still influence our feelings, emotions, and desires. These emotions can cause the brain to make neuro-chemicals, which may have a harmful effect on our body and can make us ill.

- **Culture** is a very important part of us. Culture means the collective beliefs and values of the people among whom we live. We have received thoughts, beliefs, and feelings from our parents, our friends, our group and our country. Much of what we do is because we have learned to do this from our culture. These beliefs and values influence our thoughts, feelings, and desires. They influence the decisions we make about our life.

- In a room deep in our heart are what we call **instincts**. These are deep-seated, automatic responses to life. We rarely think about these instincts, and we cannot really change them. They are for our protection: we have instincts to breathe air, to eat food, to drink water, and to sleep when we are tired. We may be able to suppress these instincts for a short while, but we cannot change or eliminate them. Nor should we try to do so.

- In this picture of the big house there is no 'room' for the spirit. This is because our spirit is everywhere. Spirit is our awareness of who we are, and it is the centre of our whole self.

It is important to remember that all these different things in the heart interact with each other. There are no real walls between them. Emotions and feelings influence our thoughts, beliefs and desires, as well as our actions. Memories affect our beliefs and values, our thoughts and feelings. In practice, we cannot separate the heart into special rooms as we have done in this exercise. The whole heart functions as a unit, responding to what takes place in the world around us and influencing the whole body.

It is very important to keep the heart in good order. If we allow ourselves to see bad things or think bad thoughts, the rooms of our heart will be full of bad things. These bad thoughts and ideas will stimulate the brain to make neuro-chemicals that, over time, can make us ill. On the other hand, if we see and hear good things, think good thoughts, and try to have good feelings and desires, our heart will be at peace, and this will in turn make our body strong.

Lesson 4: Medical science and the wholeness of the person

We now know that thoughts and emotions affect the organs of our body. Sudden fear makes the heart beat faster and the blood pressure increase. Sudden anger makes the stomach contract and produce more acid. Being nervous can cause diarrhoea or a strong desire to urinate.

If we continue to be fearful, angry or nervous, this can cause serious problems in our physical bodies. Stress due to worry or conflict stimulates the adrenal glands to produce hormones that can cause inflammation in some of our organs. Long-standing fear can cause headaches, muscle tension, and pain in the back, neck, or other places.

In Proverbs 14:30 we read: 'A heart at peace gives life to the body, but envy rots the bones.' Just as cancer destroys the body, so also can envy, jealousy, anger, fear and other harmful emotions. On the other hand, joy, peace, happiness, and laughter can make the whole body, including the immune system, stronger. We are then both healthier and happier.

Exercise 3

In small groups, discuss the following questions:

1. Can you think of a time when you had a strong fear, anger or other emotion and it seemed to make you sick? Describe your experience.
2. Have you cared for patients who have much fear, shame or sadness? Do you think those emotions affected their illness and perhaps slowed their recovery? If you know of such a person, write a brief description of the illness and how the emotional problem affected the person and the illness. Present this to the class for discussion.

As mentioned earlier the brain makes chemicals in response to our emotions and feelings. We call these 'neuro-chemicals'. These neuro-chemicals go immediately into our blood circulation and thus to all the organs of the body. They act on these organs.

For each emotion, the brain makes a specific neuro-chemical. If we feel joyful, the brain makes a neuro-chemical that makes the organs function well. The whole body will feel good. If we have other positive emotions, such as peace, love, happiness, and feelings of security, the neuro-chemicals of the brain will make our organs function better and our whole body will be strong. This is why the Bible says that peace in the heart makes the body strong.

On the other hand, if we have fear in our heart, the brain will produce another neuro-chemical, which will make the heart beat faster, the blood pressure go up, and the muscles of the stomach and intestines contract. These changes are normal and they enable us to do what is necessary to handle the problem that is causing the fear.

However, if we continue to experience fear for many days, weeks, or months, the brain will continue to make the neuro-chemical, which will keep on acting on the heart, blood vessels, stomach, and intestines. After some time the blood pressure will remain high, and problems can occur in the stomach and intestines. In other words, chronic fear can make our organs function poorly and subsequently we become ill.

The same thing is true for many of the negative emotions and feelings. Jealousy, bitterness, hatred, anger, shame, the remorse of guilt, depression, and anxiety all cause the brain to produce neuro-chemicals that act on our organs. After weeks or months, some of the organs will not function well and we will become ill.

Feelings and the immune system

The immune system is what God has put in our bodies to fight against infections, malignant tumours and other diseases, and to keep us healthy. The immune system includes our white blood cells and the antibodies which the white blood cells produce.

The neuro-chemicals the brain makes in response to our feelings and emotions affect the immune system. Positive emotions make the immune system stronger, and we remain healthy. Long-standing negative emotions such as sadness, anger, fear, and stress weaken the immune system. This is why when we are sad, fearful or under much stress, we may get colds, the flu or other infections more easily.

When we are exposed to an infection, the outcome depends on which is stronger – the immune system, or the infection. If the immune system is strong and the infection weak, we get well quickly. If the infection is strong and the immune system is weak, we become very sick and may die.

Strengthening the immune system

It is possible to make the immune system stronger. The following can help us to fight infection:

• Good nutrition. The body needs protein and vitamins in order to make white blood cells and antibodies, so a person with an infection or other serious illness needs to have plenty of good food.

- Peace of mind. If the heart is at peace, the brain will make neuro-chemicals that strengthen the immune system.
- Good medicine. Antibiotics, for example, will help to fight the cause of the infection.
- Good nursing care.
- Encouragement and good advice, to help the person get rid of negative emotions and find peace of mind.

Antibiotics attack the disease organisms causing the infections. This helps the immune system to overcome the infection, and the person can begin to get well.

If, at the same time, we can help a sick person to get rid of negative emotions and find peace of mind, this will help the immune system become stronger. The immune system can then overcome the infection and the person can get well.

Exercise 4

Discuss this question in small groups: When you are caring for a person who has a serious infection, such as typhoid fever, what can you do to help his immune system become stronger?

Lesson 5: Problems in the heart

As human beings, we experience many problems of the heart. We may call them psychological problems, but, as we have already seen, psychological problems can cause physical symptoms and illnesses. The following are some of the most common problems and how they affect our health.

- **Fear**. Many people have fear in their heart. It may be fear of failure in their studies, or their work; fear of another member of the family; fear of an evil eye, a curse, or an evil spirit; fear of losing employment or possessions, or of what another person may do to them. Fear can cause different kinds of problems:

  chronic headaches
  chronic stomach pains
  painful muscle tension or spasms
  intestinal disorders

- **Anger**. It is possible that chronic anger can enable cancer to develop by making the immune system weak. Anger can also cause or make worse:
  high blood pressure
  certain forms of arthritis

abdominal pains
frequent infections

- **Social stress or conflicts**. Conflicts, too much work, or too much uncertainty can affect the heart and blood vessels, causing high blood pressure, coronary artery disease, chronic fatigue, and headaches.
- **Guilt**. When people have done wrong, or believe they have done wrong, they will often feel guilty. This guilt can cause pain in various parts of the body, depression, loss of appetite and an inability to think clearly and accomplish good work.

Exercise 5

Break into small groups and read Matthew 18:21–35. This is a story Jesus told about a man who refused to forgive a friend who owed him a small amount of money, and how he suffered because of that. Jesus tells us that we will suffer in a similar way if we do not forgive other people the wrongs they have done to us. Many times this suffering is manifested as an illness.

1. Discuss together how the refusal to forgive someone else, and to continue to be angry and bitter, can make a person ill.
2. Have you ever cared for a person who had much bitterness in his or her heart against someone? How can you help such a person?

Bible study 2: Sin, relationships and health

Read the story of how Adam and Eve sinned against God, in Genesis 3, and then answer the following questions:

1. Why did Adam and Eve sin against God?
2. What did their sin do to their relationship with God?
3. What did their sin do to their relationship with each other?
4. What did their sin do to their relationship with nature?
5. What do you think they felt in their hearts after they had sinned?
6. How do you suppose their sin affected their health?

Exercise 6

Sin and broken relationships cause disorder and often diseases.

1. Discuss how you think good relationships can promote health.
2. How can you help sick persons who have conflicting relationships with other people?
3. If a person is sick, do you think it is the result of his sin?

Many people have conflicting beliefs in their heart. They believe in one thing, and they also believe in something else that is contrary to the first belief. This conflict takes away peace in the heart and brings tension. This can often make them sick.

Read Daniel 3 and 4. In chapter 3 is the story of King Nebuchadnezzar, a powerful king who made a huge idol. Everyone was required to worship the idol. Three men of Israel refused to worship it because they trusted in God. The king threw them into the fire, but God saved them. The king was impressed, and he accepted the God of Israel, recognising there is no God like him. But he also continued to worship his own idol.

In chapter 4 we read how King Nebuchadnezzar became mentally ill for seven years.

1. Why did he become ill?
2. When and how was he healed?
3. What lesson does this teach us about beliefs and how they influence our health?

Lesson 6: Conversion alone does not heal the heart

First discuss in the group Nebuchadnezzar's problem. Then discuss how people today can become ill if, when they take Christ into their heart, they still continue to believe in their old religion.

There is a story in the Book of Exodus that illustrates how problems in the heart cause problems in our lives. It also shows that conversion alone does not heal the problems of the heart.

Read Exodus 15:22–26. This story took place just three days after the Children of Israel had crossed the Red Sea by God's power.

The history of the Children of Israel is a symbol of our own spiritual history.

• The Children of Israel had been slaves in Egypt. They could not escape. We have been slaves of sin, and we cannot save ourselves from sin.
• God sent Moses to lead the Children of Israel out of their slavery in Egypt. God sent Jesus to lead us out of our slavery to sin.
• The Children of Israel rejoiced when they became free from the Egyptians. We also rejoice when we are saved from sin by the power of God through Christ.
• The Children of Israel soon discovered that they still had serious problems. They had only bitter water to drink. The bitterness was due to many minerals in the water of the desert spring. In the Bible, water is often a symbol of spirit. This story shows that, even after conversion, we may still have problems of bitterness, anger, fear, hatred, envy, and other negative feelings and emotions. Even though we have given our lives to Christ, these bitter problems remain.

- Neither Moses nor the Children of Israel could make the water of that spring sweet. Nor can we make our hearts pure and sweet. We cannot get rid of our own anger, fear, pride, jealousy etc.
- God showed Moses a solution to the bitter water. It was a piece of dead wood. When Moses threw the wood into the water, the water became sweet. The wood removed the bitter minerals from the water. Likewise, God has a solution for the bitterness in our hearts. It is also a piece of wood – the cross. The cross of Christ can remove or heal the problems of our heart.
- God did not put the piece of wood into the spring: Moses had to throw it in. Similarly, we have to apply the cross of Christ to our heart in order to be healed.

Lesson 7: What Christ has done for our healing

Exercise 7

Read the story of Jesus in the Garden of Gethsemane in Matthew 26:36–46.

1. Why was Jesus in such anguish of soul?
2. What was he facing that was so difficult and repulsive to him?
3. What did he actually do in the Garden of Gethsemane?

Read John 19:17–37. Normally it took between 24 and 72 hours for a crucified man to die on the cross. Death comes slowly from exhaustion and asphyxiation, because the stretched-out arms made it difficult to breathe. Jesus was nailed to the cross at 9am. He died six hours later at 3pm.

1. Why do you think he died so quickly?
2. What was the physical cause of his death?
3. What really killed him?

Read Mark 16:1–8.

1. Why is it important to know that the tomb was empty?
2. What message does Jesus' resurrection speak to our hearts?
3. Why are these stories so important for our healing?

Lesson 8: How Christ heals heart problems (emotions)

We all need a personal relationship with Jesus Christ. This means asking Jesus to come into our heart. From then on, we can talk with him, listen to him, and go to him for help. We can trust him to help us. In a sense, it is like a marriage, for we are now living with another person. Jesus is alive and a real person. We cannot see him or touch him, but he is nevertheless inside us, in our heart.

We now have a new meaning and purpose for life, and this will last for ever. We have also begun a journey which will take us to a new joy, which will bring peace into the heart, and which will make our body stronger and healthier.

We can go to Jesus with the problems in our heart and in our life. He will help us find solutions to these problems. He will also take away the pain, fear, and anxiety that come from these problems and give us peace. Over time, this will help heal the physical symptoms of illness.

Healing fear (1)

A woman has been experiencing pain in her arms, shoulders and neck for several months. No treatment has helped her. She has also had much fear in her heart – fear of her daughter-in-law, who is always angry with her. The woman describes the problem and her fear to a group of Christians. They pray for her, and ask Christ to take the fear from her heart and to replace it with peace and courage. Jesus answers their prayers, and then the woman discovers that the pain in her arms, shoulders, and neck has gone.

Here the fear in her heart caused the brain to make the neuro-chemicals of fear. These chemicals caused muscle tension in her arms, shoulders, and neck, and this muscle tension was painful. When Jesus took away her fear and replaced it with peace, the brain stopped producing the neuro-chemicals of fear. The muscles could now relax, and the painful tension went away.

Can we also help people who do not want to accept Christ? Yes we can! Jesus himself did that. We can care for them, encourage them and even pray for them. However, if we can help them come into a relationship with Jesus, his power will be able to help them even more. But we must never try to force them to accept Christ. Jesus himself never did that.

Healing fear (2)

A young man was dying from tuberculosis, in spite of good medical treatment and care. A nurse discovered that he had been cursed by his uncle and told that he would die. His heart was full of fear, and also anger against his uncle. The fear and anger suppressed his immune system so much that he could not recover from his tuberculosis.

Then the young man accepted Christ. He heard the stories of Christ's miracles, and also of his resurrection. He realised that the power of Christ is greater than the evil power of the curse. He also decided to forgive his uncle. In doing this the fear and anger in his heart was replaced by peace. This in turn strengthened his immune system so that, as he continued his medical treatment, he recovered from his tuberculosis.

Healing guilt

A man had had pain in his abdomen for some years. It began after he had an episode of gonorrhoea. Antibiotics cured this infection, but the pain remained. No cause for the pain could be found on the physical examination or laboratory tests. When the man confessed to the counsellor that he had betrayed his wife, and slept with another woman, it was clear that he had a strong feeling of guilt in his heart. The counsellor told him about Jesus and the man asked Christ to come into his heart. He then confessed the sin he had committed against his wife and asked Christ to forgive him. The counsellor assured him that, if we confess our sins to the Lord, he will forgive us and make us clean from our wrongdoing (see 1 John 1:9). When the man heard this assurance of forgiveness, his guilt was healed, and his abdominal pain went away.

In this case the pain was caused by muscle tension, or by inflammation in his muscles or ligaments. This came from the neuro-chemicals produced by the brain because of his feelings of guilt.

Healing anger

A school headmaster came to the hospital because of severe vomiting, diarrhoea, and weight loss, which he had experienced over a period of four months. The doctors found no cause for these symptoms. A counsellor talked with the man and discovered that he was very angry with the superintendent of the school. The counsellor suggested that he forgive the superintendent, but the anger in his heart was so great that he refused to do that.

Then the sick man asked Christ to come into his heart. When he realised how much Christ had forgiven him, he asked Christ to give him the courage to forgive the other man. When he was finally able to forgive the superintendent, his vomiting and diarrhoea stopped, and he recovered completely.

Healing bad behaviour

Certain habits are very difficult to change: for example, smoking, taking drugs, and immoral sexual activity. A young woman had been having sex with many men. She knew this was wrong and that it was bad for her health but she could not stop. She talked with a Christian counsellor, who introduced her to Jesus. She asked Jesus to come into her heart. She heard what Jesus did in Gethsemane and on the cross. She realised that Jesus took her sins into himself along with the evil powers of lust and immorality. He rose from the dead because his power is greater than the powers of sin, lust, and immorality.

The young woman asked Jesus to take away from her the desire for sexual immorality and replace it with a desire to know him and to study the Bible. She also asked him to help her stay away from all places where she would be tempted to be immoral, and God answered her prayer and helped her.

Exercise 8

These are stories of how Jesus can resolve problems of the heart, habits and bad behaviour. When these are taken away, physical health improves, and illness may be healed.

Do you know of a similar story? If so write down the story and be prepared to share it in class. Be sure you do not name the person you are describing.

PART TWO – Methods of caring for the whole person

Establishing a caring relationship

The qualities of a Christian caregiver

- A close personal relationship with Jesus Christ. Caring for sick people is difficult. If you have Jesus in your heart, he can give you wisdom, courage, and patience to do this difficult work.
- A good knowledge of the Bible. There are many passages in the Bible that can give encouragement to people and help them find answers to their problems. Even with those who may not want to hear the Bible, you can share encouraging thoughts with them without having to tell them where those thoughts come from.
- A willingness to help people with problems in their lives.

The attitudes of a Christian caregiver

- Compassion. This means to try to feel what another person is feeling. When someone is suffering, we must try to understand and empathise with what they are feeling.
- Acceptance. Sick people may be weak, very poor, have a bad odour, or come from a different caste. But we must accept each one as a real person and affirm him or her as a person of great value. Jesus did that. He even touched people with leprosy. We must have the same attitude.
- Gentleness. This means always speaking softly, kindly, and without criticism or judgement. Often we may hear sick people describe something bad they have done. We can ask them how they feel about this, but should not tell them that it is bad or wrong. They must come to recognise that for themselves.
- Sincerity. We must show genuine interest in what a person is telling us and express a willingness to help them. We cannot simply pretend to be

interested, for the sick person will realise this quickly and will have no confidence in us.

- Keeping confidence. When sick people tell us their problems, we have no right to tell those problems to someone else, except when disclosure is on a professional basis and in the person's best interests. If you do need to seek advice, do not use the person's name or give other information that will allow others to know whom you are describing, unless you are talking to a trained health care professional to whom you are accountable in your work.
- Politeness. You must never be brutal, abrupt, or rude to a sick person. Words can harm the soul and spirit, so be careful what you say. Always speak gently and kindly.

Exercise

Each of you think of a person – teacher, tutor, nurse, doctor, or someone else – who has been especially good to you. What is it about that person that has been good and helpful?

Then think about someone who has been harmful to you and made you feel bad. Describe to the others what that person did. And why it hurt you.

The purpose of this exercise is that you learn to be like those who are good and avoid being like those who are difficult and harmful.

Getting acquainted with a sick person

- Learn the name of each person you care for. If you can call them by name, this will help them trust in you.
- Begin by asking easy questions to find out about them, questions that do not make them embarrassed or uncomfortable.

    Where do you live?
    How many people are in your family?
    What do you do?
    How long have you been sick?

- Always listen carefully to what people say. If you do not understand clearly, you can ask them to explain further. If people see you listening, their confidence in you will increase.
- When you have become acquainted, then you can ask the more difficult questions.

    How are things going in your life?
    Are there worries that you have?

Do certain people in your life bother you?
Are there certain things that make you afraid?

- As you listen, try to determine what the real problems and true concerns of the person are.
- If it is a simple problem, you can offer a word of help or encouragement.
- If it is a serious problem, ask if the person would like to talk with the chaplain or pastoral counsellor about it. If so, go to the chaplain or counsellor and ask him or her to come and see the person.
- Remember that whatever the person tells you, you must not tell this to someone else without their permission, unless in very exceptional circumstances in the person's own interests, or to save the life of another, and then only to a trained professional health care worker.

Talking to sick people about faith

You will care for persons from different faiths. Some will be Christian, some may be Hindu, Muslim or Buddhist, and others may follow traditional tribal religions. You must respect the faith of every person.

A relationship with Christ does help sick people find solutions to their problems and sometimes even to find healing. However, you must never impose your faith on others, or put pressure on them to change their faith.

What you can do is to tell a sick person how faith in Christ has helped you in the context of a discussion about spirituality that is being driven by the person who is looking to you for help and for answers to ultimate questions. If the person asks you to tell them more about this, you can do so. If the person is very interested and wants to become a Christian, you can then explain how he can ask Christ to come into his heart.

However, if a sick person is not interested in the Christian faith, then do not continue to talk about it. Continue the rest of your care with compassion, and pray for wisdom in knowing how to care well.

To find out the faith of a sick person, do not ask outright about their religion. Here are the sorts of things you could say, depending on the culture and situation:

- Tell me about your faith.
- Has your faith been of help to you in this sickness?
- Has God been of help to you?
- Have you prayed for help and for healing?

When it is appropriate, there may be an occasion to talk to a sick person about your faith in Christ and the strength and help Christ gives you. This is simply sharing your faith, as they may wish to do with you. It is not proselytising.

For those who do not know about the Christian faith but want to know about it, use the following points:

- God created the world and he made men and women. Everything God made is good.
- God loves us, knows each of us by name and wants us to love him, trust him, and to obey the instructions and commands he has given us.
- However, we have a lot of pride in our heart and do not want to obey God. We want to follow our own desires, and so we refuse God and sin against him.
- Sin is very serious, for it separates us from God and we die spiritually. Sin also causes much disorder between people, and can even make us sick.
- But God still loves us. He does not want us to die in our sin, and he wants us to come back to him.
- So he came to us as a man, to live among us. This man is Jesus Christ. We call him the Son of God because he is, indeed, God living as a man.
- Because sin is serious and leads to death, either we die because of our sin or else someone else must die in our place.
- Jesus did die in our place, on the cross, and so he has paid the penalty for our sin. Then Jesus came back to life by rising from the dead. If we believe in Jesus and ask him to come into our heart so that we can obey him, we will not die because of sin, for he has already died for us.
- When Jesus comes into our heart, he shows us how to live a good life and gives us the wisdom, courage and power to be good and not to do evil.
- He also can help us solve our problems and even give healing when we are ill.

If a person does want to ask Jesus to come into his heart, help him to pray this prayer:

Jesus, I realise that I am a sinner, and that you died in my place. I ask you to come into my heart now and live with me. Please forgive me my sins, and help me to live as I should live. Help me to love you as you love me.

If a person does accept Christ, he will need help in growing in faith. He will also need a Bible and instruction in the faith. Ask the chaplain or counsellor to talk with him.

As you continue to care for him, tell him stories from the Bible about

God and about Jesus. If he asks you questions you cannot answer, ask the chaplain for help.

Now the person can ask Christ for healing of any worries, anxieties, fear or other negative emotions in his heart. He can also ask help from Christ for resolving any conflicts between him and others in his family. And you can pray with him for the healing of his illness.

The healing power of forgiveness

When someone does something to us that hurts us, we feel angry and upset. If we hold on to this anger and keep on being angry or bitter for a long time, this can make us sick. So it is important for us to forgive the offending person.

Unfortunately, this is not easy. Often we enjoy being angry against the other person. It makes us feel good. Yet this anger is harmful. We must therefore make a decision in our mind that we will forgive the other person.

What happens when someone offends us?

• We hurt. What the person did is painful and upsets us.
• We become angry and want to take revenge.
• We condemn the other person before God and even before other people. We tell other people: 'See what that horrible person did to me. Isn't that terrible?'
• Our heart becomes full of resentment and bitterness. This can make us ill.
• We must now decide whether we want to go on being bitter and angry, or want to be free from this anger and be healed.
• When we forgive the other person, we are released from anger and our heart is healed.

Why should I forgive someone who has done me wrong?

• God requires it. (See Matthew 6:12–15; 21:21–35; Mark 11:24,25; Ephesians 4:32.)
• Revenge is bad. It only makes the problem worse.
• When we forgive, we are healed of anger and bitterness. We can forgive the other person even if he does not ask for forgiveness, or has gone away or died. Jesus forgave those who crucified him, even though they did not ask him to.
• If we forgive, it may then be possible to re-establish a good relationship with the other person. We call this reconciliation.

Forgiveness does not mean that we condone the other person or the wrong thing he did. It does mean that we now put that person in God's hands. We agree before God to stop judging or condemning. We recognise God as the only righteous judge. We release that person from our own judgement and let God be the only judge.

We can then ask Christ to take away the anger from our heart, to heal the pain of the hurt and the anger, and to give us peace and joy.

If we fail to forgive another person, this may be one reason why our prayers to God are not answered (see Mark 11:24,25).

How can we help someone to forgive?

- Ask the person to describe what the other person did to him and how it hurts.
- Ask him how he feels about it and about the other person.
- Explain the danger of continuing to be angry and bitter.
- Ask him if he would like to forgive the other person and be set free from anger.
- A person who does not know Jesus may have difficulty with this. Explain how Jesus can help him forgive someone else. It is because Jesus has forgiven us.
- If the person does want to forgive the other person have him pray like this:

> Lord, I release —— into your hands. I forgive him and will no longer judge or condemn him. Please take away my anger and heal my heart. Give me your peace and joy, and help me no longer to remember the hurt that has been done.

Praying for a sick person

Prayer is entering into a relationship with God in order to cooperate with him in accomplishing his purposes. It is a real and active power passing between God, the intercessor and the person or request for which prayer is being made.

Some diseases respond more quickly to prayer. This is especially true for acute infections. Other diseases require more prayer. This includes many malignancies, chronic infections and diseases of long duration.

Prayer is hard work and can be exhausting. We need to pray with our mind, our soul and our spirit.

- **Mind**. Our thoughts should be focused on the person and the particular disease or aspects of the illness. We should be specific in our prayer. This is why knowing about the person's illness, worries, concerns, and problems is important. We can pray for coronary arteries, for the liver or kidneys, for the white blood cells and antibodies. We can ask God to help the person with the specific needs, like a good night's sleep, a better appetite, freedom from pain. We are bringing these matters to God and consulting with him about them.

- **Soul**. Our feelings and emotions need to be involved. We can express them to God – our worry, concern and even anger. 'The prayer of a righteous man is powerful and effective' (James 5:16).
- **Spirit**. In real prayer, we enter into the presence of the Almighty God. We are doing business with him. We are offering ourselves to him as a channel through which his power can flow into the one for whom we are praying.

Prayer is not manipulation of God. There is no magical formula that will require God to act as we want him to act. Rather, prayer is entering into the work that we believe God wants to do and may already be doing, and working with God to accomplish his will.

Prayer is listening. On occasion, as we pray, God will impress on our spirit a message we need to hear and obey. As our relationship with God deepens, we will be increasingly able to discern which of the thoughts that come to us are from God himself and which are simply our own thoughts.

Praying 'in the will of God'

God wants us to be healthy (see John 10:10; Psalm 91:14–16; Deuteronomy 28). God tells us in Jeremiah 29:11–13: '"For I know the plans I have for you," declares the Lord, "plans to prosper you and not to harm you, plans to give you hope and a future. Then you will call upon me and come and pray to me, and I will listen to you. You will seek me and find me when you seek me with all your heart."'

Physical healing does not always come. Nevertheless, God is at work in our circumstances (illness) for our good (see Romans 8:28).

The healing of the heart can always come, for Christ can heal the fear, worry, guilt, or other negative feelings in the heart of anyone, no matter how sick he or she may be.

Heart healing, with its consequent peace and joy, can strengthen the body and enable it to cope better with whatever the disease is. In other words, heart healing creates a favourable environment for the person in the struggle with disease.

So we can ask God to heal this person 'in his time and according to his plan'.

Prayer should be specific

- We can pray about the disease and affected organs.
- We can pray about specific symptoms, that God will relieve them.
- We can pray for the family and the personal life of the sick person.
- We can pray for the care-givers and the various treatments.

Bringing problems into the presence of the Lord

When a person wants prayer and has specific problems, ask him or her to be quiet for a moment and focus their attention on the real concerns of the heart – the disease, or symptoms, or a particular worry, concern, or painful feeling.

Now ask them to take these concerns, problems, or feelings and offer them to God, placing them in his hands, and asking him to take them away. Have them try to imagine God doing this.

Now they can listen for any word the Lord may say. If God does speak, they may want to share it with you.

Then, after a moment, pray out loud yourself, bringing these concerns to the Lord.

(See Chapter 9 of *The Truth About AIDS* for further discussion on why the church often finds it hard to cope when people are not healed, and how we should respond in such situations.)

Talking to a person about death and dying

Most of us are uncomfortable in this area. Since some people you will be trying to help will be facing death from disease, it is important that you first face up to the reality of your own mortality. What will happen to you when you die?

The Christian understanding of death

Death is a transition from our life here on earth, in a space/time world, to another life beyond this world. It is like moving from one town to another better one. It is like going on a journey to a place we have not yet seen, but that we know is a good place. In the new life, we keep our personality and our personal characteristics.

Death is like a journey

When we are going on a journey, we must prepare for it. If we travel to another country we need a passport. Without that passport we cannot enter into the new country. To enter into eternity with God, into God's country – heaven – we need a 'passport'. That passport is faith in Christ. Before we make any long journey, we must prepare other matters as well. We arrange our personal affairs; make sure that what we leave behind is in order, and say goodbye to our family and friends.

When we face the final journey to heaven, we should do the same. Many arrangements need to be made – wills, property, money, possessions. Taking care of these things brings peace of mind to us and to those who remain behind.

We also need to make sure our relationships with others are in good order. Time spent in resolving conflicts, settling grievances, and restoring friendships can be beneficial both to us and to those who remain behind.

Many people facing serious illness want to talk about death and dying, but are afraid to raise the subject. If you care for a dying person and are hesitant to talk about dying yourself, you can ask the person if he would like to talk to someone else about it, like the hospital pastor or a counsellor.

A gentle question or two can offer the sick person the opportunity to discuss the concerns and fears they have about death if they wish to. You can ask, 'Do you think you might die from this disease? How do you feel about that?' Then comparing dying with a journey can be helpful in allowing practical issues to be discussed.

We can reassure people that discussing death does not mean we are going to die right away. On the contrary, it can help to resolve worries and fears and bring a sense of peace and preparation for closure whenever the time may come.

(See Chapter 9 for more on this.)

APPENDIX E

FRIENDS IN NEED
by Marion and Les Derbyshire
(VIVA Network)

Editor's note: Although written to assist development of programmes to help orphans, this excellent resource contains many useful lessons that can be applied to many different kinds of project.

A Handbook for the Care of Orphans in the Community

Suggestions for using this handbook

- Work through it thoughtfully and prayerfully.
- Consider your own situation. Circumstances and cultures differ.
- Compare and contrast what you find here with your own situation and learn from what is relevant.
- Make notes where you may agree or disagree, or add useful comments and ideas. Others may benefit from these, either by using the same material or as discussion points.
- Use for training sessions, perhaps taking one section at each session, and expanding the ideas in your own way according to your needs.
- Use for each leader and worker to study and re-read as an individual guide as required.
- Use as a basic manual, adding extra notes for your particular ministry.
- You may want to use this material to help you to discern your vocation.
- Refer to this book when you have particular questions or difficulties.
- If you have found it useful, please recommend it to others.
- Your comments would be welcome for our further handbooks.

Acronyms

CBOC   Community-Based Orphan Care
HIV   Human Immuno-deficiency Virus
AIDS   Acquired Immune Deficiency Syndrome
CEDC   Children in Especially Difficult Circumstances
CWC   Child Welfare Committee
IGP   Income Generating Project

Introduction

How this book was written

The field research for this handbook was carried out in Zimbabwe by Marion and Les Derbyshire in March and April 2001. We visited three projects selected as examples of good practice in the field of community-based care for AIDS orphans and children affected by AIDS. We interviewed the founders and leaders, observed each programme at first hand over a short period and spoke to volunteers and children involved with the projects. This handbook contains material gleaned in this way together with some edited from existing documentation kindly copied for us by project staff and additional comments from our own experience and background reading.

Problems faced by orphaned children and their carers

There is a high incidence of HIV/AIDS in Zimbabwe. This has been escalating since the first reported case of AIDS in 1985, and has left a huge number of orphaned children. This situation of poverty and illness is self-perpetuating. Families affected by AIDS lose their independence and dignity. They lack employment, income, education and guidance. They have often lost their rights to land and property and may lack basic necessities such as food, shelter and clothing. This creates high dependence on others, which leads to sexual abuse and exploitation and high-risk promiscuous activity. Poverty exacerbates the spread of AIDS and vice versa. In addition, in spite of the high incidence of HIV/AIDS, much of the population remains ignorant about the subject.

Surveys have shown that

- Zimbabwe has the third highest HIV incidence rate in the world
- 25% of the sexually active group aged between 15 and 49 was estimated to be HIV positive (now estimated to be nearer 33%)

- there are more than 900,000 orphans in Zimbabwe, mainly due to HIV/AIDS
- over 25% of the children less than 15 years of age have lost a mother and/or father
- HIV levels in Mutare and Manicaland are very high
- in 1997, HIV incidence in antenatal mothers was 37% in the city of Mutare and 51% in rural Manicaland (Buhera District)
- over two thirds of medical admissions to hospitals in Manicaland are HIV-related.

The projects define an orphan as being a child under the age of 18 years who has lost one or both parents. The traditional system whereby the extended family took care of orphaned children has become over-stretched and ineffective. Many children are being cared for by a remaining parent who is sick or dying. There are many elderly grandparents trying to care for their late children's children. These grandparents are often themselves in need of care and support. Generally they:

- are unable to work and have no or extremely little income
- are coping with the grief of multiple bereavement
- would in normal circumstances be supported by their children.

An increasing number of orphaned children are looking after themselves, with the eldest child taking responsibility as the head of the household. Where children are looking after children, they often

- have no means of generating an income
- have no one to love them or give parental guidance and nurture
- are unable to go to school and gain a basic education
- are hungry
- are lonely and withdrawn
- feel confused and guilty about the death of their parents.

Community-based orphan care

It is important that children remain in their own environment where they can learn essential community values and skills. A child who is taken away from his or her own community for a short period may find it very diffi-cult to reintegrate on returning. In Zimbabwe, as in many other countries, there has been significant change in the culture of the rural communities. Due largely to the breakdown of the economy, there is greater mobility and many families have become separated. Protection of the children is now more difficult.

The concept of community care for orphans is simple. Where children no longer have adequate carers within their own families, members of the community are appointed as volunteers to visit them and help them to care for themselves or otherwise cater for their basic needs. The aim is to train whole communities in the care and support of orphaned families so that children are able to remain living in the community rather than being placed in institutions. This approach is more viable economically, and gives the children a more normal upbringing.

All three projects that we visited for the purposes of research for this handbook work on this basic model. FACT in Mutare initiated the idea and has continued to develop it over the years. Its FOCUS team works primarily through traditional leaders and members of local communities. The Bethany Project in Zvishavane originally copied the FOCUS plan, adapting it to suit the local situation. Jean Webster, who founded ZOE, also learnt from the experience of FACT, but works primarily through church leaders and members throughout the country.

Examples of Good Practice in CBOC Ministry

This chapter gives an outline of each of the three community-based orphan care projects studied for the purposes of this handbook. It describes the process by which each was founded, how it is structured and the ongoing work of the organisation.

FACT

Background information

The Family AIDS Caring Trust (FACT) is a Christian-based AIDS service organisation, founded in 1987 by Dr Geoff Foster, an Englishman. It is based in the city of Mutare, the provincial capital of Manicaland, in the Eastern Highlands of Zimbabwe. Mutare, which has a population of 200,000, comprises a central city area and the high-density township areas of Sakubva, Chikanga and Dangamvura. The 1.6 million inhabitants of Manicaland live mainly in the rural areas and practise subsistence agriculture, though there are also major industries of forestry and commercial farming.

The foundation of FACT

FACT began as a small group of volunteers from various churches who recognised the impact of HIV/AIDS on their community. They were keen to build a church-based and community-based response to the problem. Initially, churches formed a rota of volunteers to counsel people affected by AIDS. They then developed further programmes in response to the needs. These included home-based care, support for people living with HIV/AIDS, testing, training, youth HIV-prevention programmes and support for children on the streets.

FOCUS

Foundation of the FOCUS programme

Dr Geoff Foster works as a paediatrician at the Provincial Hospital in Mutare. In the late 1980s, he began to notice how many children attending the hospital had parents with terminal illness or were brought by their relatives because the parents were dead or too sick to accompany their children. At the same time, FACT home care providers were becoming concerned that, after their patients died, many children were being left orphaned and untended. In 1991, this growing awareness led to a survey of orphans being added to an existing maternal and child health survey in Manicaland.

Survey results

Surveys showed that

- 6.8% of children under 15 years were orphaned by loss of their father or mother
- there were about 47,000 orphans in the province. In 1992, this had risen to 50,000
- over 99.5% of the orphans were being cared for by their extended family
- only 170 (0.4%) were being cared for in children's homes.

In 1991, a study suggested that one in every 15 children under 15 years of age was orphaned (i.e. had lost at least one parent) and that nearly all orphans were cared for by the extended family. In 1992, FACT carried out a second enumeration, this time in one urban and one rural site. This study also aimed to discover how the extended families and the local community were coping with the ever-increasing number of orphans.

In 1993, following these research studies and observations from practitioners, FACT decided to establish a programme to care for orphans within the community. Named 'FOCUS' (Families, Orphans and Children Under Stress), this programme was established by Dr Foster and at the time of our research was being supervised by Choice Makufa, Deputy Director of FACT. The initial focus of the programme was on orphan enumeration, needs assessment and prioritisation, regular visiting, provision of material support and record-keeping.

Activities of FOCUS

The main activity of FOCUS is to work with communities to assist them to look after orphans. At the first site it set up a pilot project in the church. It recruited volunteers and sensitised other churches to give support to extended families to care for children in especially difficult circumstances. In response to the need, FOCUS recruited 25 women volunteers from 18 villages throughout the programme area. They operated in a communal farming area of approximately 200 square kilometres with a population of 10,611 people.

Dedicated volunteers

Although volunteers receive minimal financial incentives, very few have dropped out of programmes, even those established several years ago. New forms of support to volunteers have been developed, such as the supply of uniform T-shirts, annual Christmas monetary gifts and the provision of training through exchange visits to other FOCUS programmes.

Development of the FOCUS programme

From one pilot site in 1993, FOCUS now works closely with seven community groups that together provide regular support to around 9,000 orphaned children. The programme expanded to include income generation projects, micro-credit schemes, advocacy, and psychological assessment and support. FOCUS also undertakes to raise public awareness of sexual abuse and child rights. Carefully established record systems have enabled communities and programme directors to identify and study emerging issues such as the stigmatisation of orphans, child-headed households and the increasing vulnerability to HIV of orphaned children.

Integration of FACT's programmes

FACT's Home Care Programme, which began in 1992, also offered counselling and guidance. It linked into the Orphan Programme for resources and some people were referred to other programmes. Orphans only came into the programme after their parents had died, but it was realised that their needs begin sooner, when one or both parents are sick. In 2001, the separate programmes in FACT were integrated so that all team members now offer holistic care and counselling for sick and bereaved people and their children. Volunteers caring for sick adults bond with their children and when the parents die, the same volunteers can continue to care for the children with whom they have already built a relationship. If you ask the kids, 'Who do you turn to in time of need?' they say that they trust the volunteers.

Replication of the FOCUS programme

The FOCUS programme has influenced a range of Zimbabwean orphan projects as well as those from other countries in the region. It has attracted interest and visits from local, national, regional and international groups. In 1995, the Bethany Project in Zvishavane, Midlands Province was formed on a similar model. Orphan programmes were also established in Zambia, Kenya and Malawi following visits to FOCUS sites as part of FACT'S Regional Training Programme.

Spreading the word

The programme has led to the establishment of partnerships between government and non-governmental organisations, and between international, local and community-based NGOs. FOCUS stresses the importance of using research as the basis for developing local programmes, techniques designed to mobilise the whole community and the value of regular reporting systems.

Bethany Project

Background information

The Bethany Project is a Christian orphan care programme registered as a Social Welfare Organisation operating in the Zvishavane District of the Midlands Province, Zimbabwe. It helps to mobilise holistic care and support for the neediest orphan children and families within the district and for children whose wellbeing and normal development are at risk due to the difficult nature of their social circumstances. The project aims to raise awareness of such children's rights and to advocate on their behalf.

Foundation of the Bethany Project

Susie Howe, from England, started the Bethany Project in July 1995 with a small group of local Christian women who were concerned about the plight of destitute orphans. According to national statistics, Zvishavane District had the highest prevalence of HIV/AIDS in the country. Both national and local newspapers were constantly reporting on the increasing number of orphans in the district. However, no one appeared to be doing anything about it.

The women felt that the Christian church should be caring for these children. They met with church leaders to pray and thus the Bethany Project was formed. First, they carried out research with a local group of mothers and caregivers to find out what their problems were. Through the church, they called together people in the locality to sensitise them about the issues. A small number of women in the church, directly managed by the Bethany Project, reported on the needs. With much faith and no finance, they started training a group of local villages in community-based orphan care. As the first ward[1] was a large one, adjacent to the town, it was split into two groups.

Resources

After six to nine months, the community wanted the Bethany Project to provide material support such as clothing and food for the orphaned children. The women themselves provided for their emotional needs. Susie Howe built relationships with local town people to obtain provision for the families' needs. These included payment of school fees. Social Welfare paid tuition fees, but Bethany provided funds for obligatory building fund and sports fees. These funds were coming from UK churches and individuals.

Sustained development

In the second ward, also adjacent to the town, they trained in the same basic way, using local church leadership and community volunteers. This ward being large was also split into two groups. It also reported needs to the Bethany Project.

At that time, only a few women were involved. Susie, Heather and several other women, including a local councillor, steered the work. However, they soon realised that the model was not sustainable because they had worked only through the churches and the other members of the community did not recognise it as being their programme. They began to work with traditional leaders to involve the wider community, rather than exclusively with churches. They held a training workshop, which resulted in the formation of a group that elected its own leaders to carry the programme forward.

Mission statement

- To help meet the mental, physical and spiritual needs of the neediest orphan children in the Zvishavane District and of Children living in Especially Difficult Circumstances (CEDC).
- To help mobilise local communities and churches to care for such children.
- To raise awareness of the rights of children.

Purpose

The main concerns of the Bethany Project staff members and executive are to enable orphans to lead lives like other children and to mobilise

---

[1] Each ward comprises five to seven village development committees, known as 'Vidcos'. Each Vidco consists of approximately seven villages; each village has several homesteads.

the community and train them in community-based orphan care. They source funds for material assistance to the families and for awareness in HIV/AIDS. They aim to improve the quality of life of orphans and other especially vulnerable children through emotional, practical and spiritual support in the community. They work in the field of HIV prevention in children and youth and in advocacy and awareness-raising. The spiritual nurture of the children is a high priority, with staff and volunteers believing that they are 'the hands and feet of Jesus' to his children.

Establishing local community care

The Bethany Project holds workshops for leaders and representative members of each community to discuss how to care for its children. Through structured group work, participants learn how to establish and manage their own orphan care programmes, which they then continue with the ongoing support and monitoring of the Bethany Project. Each site forms its own committee and people volunteer to become childcare workers within their locality.

The volunteers carry out a survey to enumerate the total number of orphans within their catchment area, and then do a simple assessment in order to identify those in greatest need. They visit these families on a regular basis to give practical, emotional and pastoral care and support. They also give loving care and support to children within their communities who may not be orphaned but who are at risk due to the difficult nature of their social circumstances.

Management of the Bethany Project

An Executive Committee of eight members oversees the work of the project. Four members of staff undertake the management, training, monitoring and administrative aspects and there are about 650 community volunteers. At the time of our visit, Gill Grant had been Director of the Bethany Project for two years.

Development of the Bethany Project

The Bethany Project has now helped to establish 22 CBOC programmes, in all 16 rural wards within the Zvishavane District and one urban location. Over 8,200 of the neediest orphans and vulnerable children are now registered with the project. Many have the burden of responsibility and care of their siblings and other children, often with no means of generating income and no one to love or care for them. Many are unable to go to school and gain a basic education. Some are hungry, some lonely and withdrawn, grieving for lost parents and a lost childhood.

Other activities of the Bethany Project
- Empowering the extended family to cope by reinforcing its natural and traditional ways of coping.
- Identifying ways in which orphan families may become self-sufficient.
- Ensuring that material assistance given to orphan families and CEDC is relevant and being used responsibly.
- Providing a model for community-based care of orphans and CEDC.
- Promoting co-ordinated childcare services locally.
- Promoting the rights of children through teaching and example.
- Teaching HIV prevention and awareness among youth.

ZOE

Background information

Having been in Zimbabwe throughout the 1970s, Jean Webster was concerned about the plight of the orphans there. In 1992, she was challenged by God while reading a letter from Dr Foster, the Director of FACT. This mentioned the research survey carried out in Manicaland, showing that there were 47,000 orphaned children in Manicaland alone in 1991 and 50,000 in 1992. The number of children bereaved due to HIV/AIDS-related deaths was enormous and rising fast. FACT was working with people with AIDS but had not yet started their FOCUS programme for orphans. During six months' experience with FACT, Jean began to share and talk over her vision at Rusitu, Chimanimani. She spent six months back in England, then returned to Zimbabwe. She worked in a children's home and at the same time started talking to pastors about the role of the church in caring for orphans.

Consulting others

Matabeleland AIDS council told Jean that it was not planning to work with AIDS orphans because the numbers were too large. Jean became aware that little was being done for these children. She spoke with three national church leaders to test the reality of her perception of the situation. Each confirmed it with facts and recent events. They all knew that they would be answerable to God for what happened to the orphans and realised the need and felt called to help. Jean talked to the Deputy Director of Social Welfare and the Head of Child Welfare in Zimbabwe. She also spoke with a friend working with Tearfund, to make sure that she was not alone in her opinions. Everyone endorsed her views. Although her response to God seemed a simple matter at the time, she was aware of the responsibility involved when initiating new work. Much later she realised that she had started something big.

National vision

Jean had already lived in Zimbabwe, known as Rhodesia before independence. She had worked as a nurse in charge of a hospital at Rusitu, Chimanimani, then nationally with a prayer movement, so she knew of the issues. Her vision was not just local but national, working through already established relationships with local church overseers and leaders. She says she began this totally new venture by means of 'trial and error' but the strategy has emerged as something that works, though varying from place to place. She has mobilised churches to work with orphans throughout the country of Zimbabwe.

Extended hands

Jean's ministry has recently been given the title 'ZOE', which stands for 'Zimbabwe Orphans through Extended hands'. The Greek word *zoe* signifies eternal life, as in John's gospel (chapter 10, verse 10): 'I am come that they might have life, and have it to the full.'

Mission statement

ZOE is committed to the total wellbeing of orphans.

Vision

To raise awareness in the church about the importance of ministering to the spiritual, emotional and physical needs of orphans, so that they grow whole and in good stature.

Aims and objectives

1. To introduce churches to orphans in their local community, to take care of their spiritual and material wellbeing.
2. To fully address their physical, emotional and spiritual needs.
3. To introduce orphans and their families to Christianity and the Christian way of life.
4. To facilitate and give advice on access to education, training and employment.
5. To offer rehabilitation services.
6. To offer counselling to guardians on the proper care of children.
7. To assist the orphans in starting self-help projects.
8. To equip orphans with life skills and morals.
9. To bring awareness on AIDS and AIDS-related issues.
10. To promote and emphasise the importance of the family unit.
11. To encourage orphans that have been ministered to, in their turn to minister to others.

The purpose of the ministry

The main purpose of the ZOE programme is to bring children to Jesus. To succeed, orphan ministry must be an active part of the life of every church.

The purpose of the ministry is also to facilitate churches nationally to fulfil their mandate to care for orphans.

ZOE strategy for orphan ministry

- Share the vision with church leaders.
- Share intentions with local community leaders and government officials. Get to know them.
- Share with the body of the church.
- Establish a heart-concerned central steering group.
- Involve those who have a heart for orphans to be volunteer visitors.
- Hold training days with church leaders and with volunteers.
- Make a list of destitute orphans and their carers within the church. Volunteers visit these to take the love and strength of Jesus.
- Use questionnaires to assess vital needs.
- Extend visiting into the community, using church volunteers, especially the women, and often able widows. Make enquiries in the community, visit the homes of those mentioned and assess their needs. Record those with little or no emotional/material support. Don't promise anything too soon!
- Go in the name of and with the love of Jesus, praying and believing that God will strengthen and use the volunteers.
- With a core group, construct a map of the area. Divide the list of destitute families according to existing church, administrative or geographical areas. Share among church volunteers, with one co-ordinator per area and no more than six to eight families to each volunteer.
- Volunteers take monthly reports to the central group for discussion.
- Where necessary, volunteers encourage families to visit the local hospital or clinic to get a councillor's letter for free medicine.

Caring for children

This Christian ministry is not concerned with building orphanages, but with caring for the family: with no houses to build, no staff to pay, simply volunteers fulfilling God's mandate to the church. Even in cases where children have no family to care for them and who need residential care, the community is encouraged to build a homestead like the other local homes, appointing a widow to provide a home for just a few children, in their natural surroundings.

Jean Webster's role in this programme

- Jean is a promoter and facilitator. She acts as consultant to church groups.
- She shares with church leaders in different areas the vision that God's solution for the care of orphans lies in the church.
- She initiates new ministries, making herself available for training, first with pastors then with volunteers from their churches.
- She maintains ongoing contact with these church-based programmes.
- She seeks out resources to kick-start income generation projects to sustain the church programmes.
- She spends time every day in prayer and intercession for the work.
- She networks with other Christian groups, finding solutions to problems.

Spiritual Foundation and Motivation

Spiritual needs of children

In all the projects we visited, leaders were committed to promoting the spiritual as well as the physical wellbeing of orphans and children in especially difficult circumstances. They believe that children need to know they are loved by their heavenly Father and that Jesus Christ died for them because of his love for them, so that they too may belong to the kingdom of God. They all subscribe to the biblical statement on which FOCUS has based its motto:

- Religion that God our Father accepts as pure and faultless is this: to look after orphans and widows in their distress and to keep oneself from being polluted by the world (James 1:27).

Biblical mandate

Children are precious to Jesus. He was indignant when his own disciples tried to keep children away from him. He calls us to take up our responsibility to look after the vulnerable ones, to love and care for them and to speak up on their behalf. Since God has given us this mandate to look after orphans, we must respond in obedience and love. In the Bible, there are numerous references to orphans (or 'the fatherless') and widows, as well as the weak, the poor and the destitute. From this we can see how God commands us to look after orphans and widows.

Jesus said: 'Let the children come to me, and do not hinder them, for the Kingdom of God belongs to such as these' (Mark 10:14; Luke 18:16). Jean

Webster and a friend both pictured this as hordes of them running freely to Jesus. Another friend saw an image of masses of kids who had fallen into a ditch. Christians were pulling them out. They saw Jesus reaching down from the cross and drawing children to him. Another said she had a vivid dream of hordes of children falling headlong into a ditch, unable to move in the mud. The Lord had shown her that they were pulling them out one by one, cleaning them up, and setting them free in Jesus' name.

Jesus also said: 'Whoever receives such a child in my name receives me; but whoever causes one of these little ones who believe in me to stumble, it is better for him that a heavy millstone be hung around his neck, and that he be drowned in the depth of the sea' (Matthew 18:3–6).

God's concern for widows and orphans

The Bible leaves us in no doubt as to God's concern for widows and orphans.

- I will not leave you as orphans: I will come to you (John 4:18).
- He defends the cause of the fatherless and the widow, and loves the alien, giving him food and clothing (Deuteronomy 10:17–18).
- You hear, O Lord, the desire of the afflicted; you encourage them and you listen to their cry, defending the fatherless and the oppressed (Psalm 10:17–18).
- A father to the fatherless, a defender of the widows, is God in his holy dwelling (Psalm 68:5).
- The Lord watches over the alien and sustains the fatherless and the widow, but frustrates the ways of the wicked (Psalm 146:9).

Biblical commands regarding widows and orphans

- Defend the cause of the weak and fatherless; maintain the rights of the poor and oppressed (Psalm 82:3–4).
- Do not take advantage of a widow or an orphan (Exodus 22:23–24).
- Do not move an ancient boundary stone or encroach on the fields of the fatherless, for their Defender is strong; he will take up their case against you (Proverbs 23:10–11).
- Seek justice, encourage the oppressed. Defend the cause of the fatherless, plead the case of the widow (Isaiah 1:17).
- Woe to those who make unjust laws, to those who issue oppressive decrees, to deprive the poor of their rights and withhold justice from the oppressed of my people, making widows their prey and robbing the fatherless (Isaiah 10:1–2).
- Do what is just and right. Rescue from the hand of his oppressor the

one who has been robbed. Do no wrong or violence to the alien, the fatherless or the widow, and do not shed innocent blood in this place (Jeremiah 22:3).

- Administer true justice; show mercy and compassion to one another. Do not oppress the widow or the fatherless, the alien or the poor. In your hearts do not think evil of each other (Zechariah 7:9–10).
- Cursed is the man who withholds justice from the alien, the fatherless or the widow (Deuteronomy 27:19).

Biblical references to the poor, weak and defenceless

- 'Because of the oppression of the weak and the groaning of the needy, I will now arise,' says the Lord. 'I will protect them from those who malign them' (Psalm 12:5).
- I command you to be open-handed towards your brothers and towards the poor and needy in your land (Deuteronomy 15:11).
- I know that the Lord secures justice for the poor and upholds the cause of the needy (Psalm 140:12).
- He who despises his neighbour sins, but blessed is he who is kind to the needy (Proverbs 14:21).
- He who oppresses the poor shows contempt for their Maker, but whoever is kind to the needy honours God (Proverbs 14:31).
- Speak up for those who cannot speak for themselves, for the rights of all who are destitute. Speak up and judge fairly; defend the rights of the poor and needy (Proverbs 31:8–9).
- Is this not the kind of fasting I have chosen: is it not to share your food with the hungry and to provide the poor wanderer with shelter – when you see the naked to clothe him, and not to turn away from your flesh and blood? (Isaiah 58:7).

God's commands to his people

- Cease to do evil; learn to do good; seek justice; reprove the ruthless; defend the orphan. Plead for the widow, though your sins are as scarlet they shall be white as snow (Isaiah 1:16–18).
- Show justice for the orphan and the widow. Show love to one another by giving food and clothing (Deuteronomy 10:18).
- In the statutes and judgements to Israel, when they are instructed about their tithes, they are told to give to the Levite in their town at the end of every third year. The Levite, alien, orphan and widow come and eat and are satisfied. Then the Lord will bless them. So it is at the time of the festival of weeks; the freewill offering goes to the orphan and the widow and they rejoice! (Deuteronomy 14:29; 16:11, 14; 26:12).

Further warnings and commands

- Cursed is the one who distorts justice to the orphan (Deuteronomy 24:17).
- When you are reaping the harvest, if you forget a sheaf it is for the orphan and the widow, so that the Lord will bless you (Deuteronomy 24:19, 20).
- Do not go into the fields of the fatherless, because their Redeemer is strong. He will plead their case against you (Proverbs 23:10).
- Amend your ways, and you shall dwell in the land. Do not oppress the widow or the orphan (Jeremiah 7:6; 22:3).
- Woe to those who deprive the needy of justice, rob the poor and plunder orphans (Isaiah 10:2).
- Do not afflict any widow or fatherless child. If you afflict him, I will hear his cry, and my anger will come against you and I will kill. Then your wives will be widows and your children fatherless (Exodus 22:22–24).

A biblical model

Jean Webster says, 'I asked the Lord how to pray. He directed me to the book of Nehemiah, and as I prayed through that book, I realised why he had directed me there. I saw that God's plan for Nehemiah in rebuilding the broken down walls of Jerusalem was for each local family to rebuild the bit of wall next to itself, having the resources for their own portion though not the entire wall. Everywhere in Zimbabwe there is a local church with local Christians. God's mandate to us more than 40 times in the Bible is to care for orphans. So his answer for these orphans with broken down family walls and a growing number of parent deaths is for the local Christians to know and care for their own local community orphans.'

Understanding God's will

1. God said we should take care of orphans and widows.
2. The world we're living in is cruel. If political leaders don't care for children, we must advocate for them.
3. God wants children to be restored through relationship with him so that they can be the people he intends.
4. Children should be able to live free of AIDS and death, not be robbed of the life God has ordained for them.
5. We must end the injustice of child abuse.
6. As adults we should give guidance to children.

7. As Christians we must demonstrate love and service to him through love and service to his children in their desperate plight.

Spiritual values

The Bethany Project is founded strongly on the biblical facts of hope and restoration through Christ. All staff and long-term volunteers must be Christians. The work is based on prayer and relationship with Christ, encouraging openness to spiritual matters.

The African traditional model of community is compatible with God's will that children should be protected and cared for. Unfortunately, that model is being eroded. Village ownership of children is being destroyed by HIV/AIDS deaths. However, therein lies an opportunity for the gospel and a turnaround in spiritual values. The church must take up the challenge. Raising awareness in the community makes people realise that they have neglected their own flesh and blood, that they must return what they have taken away from the children and that they have a responsibility to care for all the children affected by AIDS.

Motivation of Christian staff

Staff in the three projects gave the following reasons for their continued motivation for this ministry.

- Obedience to God.
- Having a natural love for children.
- Being concerned for children affected by AIDS.
- Seeing children in great need of love.
- Desiring to alleviate suffering and give light and hope to children.
- Realising that, though we cannot take care of all children, we can care for some.
- Seeing children smiling again after losing parents, aunts and uncles.
- Seeing children who had dropped out being enrolled back into school.
- Having started the work, wanting to see it continue and to support it.
- Wishing to combat the spread of HIV and its effects.

Essential Steps before You Start a Programme

Careful preparation is vital to the ultimate success of any programme. This section combines advice from leaders in all three programmes researched.

1. Research

Purposes of research

In order to define your ministry, you will need to do some basic research. You will want to find answers to questions, such as:

- Where are the areas of most need?
- What are our goals?
- What are the real needs of the children?
- How can we best respond to them?
- What resources are needed and available?
- Who will work with us?

Investigate established provision

Go out and see what others are doing in their ministries, or better still work with them for a while and learn from them. Talk with leaders in the local and umbrella Christian movements in the country. Find out where the gaps are. Networking is vital to avoid duplication. When the programme leaders conducted their research, they found that provision for the orphans was patchy and those who were trying to help had little in the way of resources or support.

Study your locality

Find out what data is available about the area and record your findings. Possible sources of information include: local council officials, the social welfare department, workers in existing programmes, school teachers, traditional leaders, church leaders, shop keepers and clinic/hospital staff. Questions could include:

- What is the population?
- How many people are HIV-positive?
- Is there evidence of large numbers of orphans?
- What are the main languages spoken?
- Are there any successful community-owned projects already operating in the area?
- Is there a large refugee population?
- Are the churches strong and active?
- Who are the community leaders?
- Is there strong leadership?
- Do good relations exist between leaders and the people?
- What is the nature of the geography and infrastructure of the area? Is it a settled rural area or a more mobile urban district?
- What are the strengths and weaknesses of the area?

Relate to the people

Identify your target area. Get to know this area well and spend time building relationships. Talk to the families and destitute children: find out their names, schedule, needs, educational attainment, livelihood, desires and family situations. Use the collected data to develop and plan the ministry into which God is leading you and your team.

Research resources

Investigate possible resources in the community and the church, nationally and possibly internationally. Resources include finance, manpower, material resources, prayer backing and expertise. Help may be available from government officials, village chiefs, businesses, police, other agencies and churches. Income-generation projects have been found to be successful socially but not very profitable for fundraising. They are excellent for raising awareness because they provide a setting in which to discuss the issues.

Network with other agencies

Make contact with any established community-based programmes already operating in the area and find out what they are doing. Enquire whether there are any church-based initiatives. Where possible, it makes sense to work with established infrastructures and programmes that share the goal of developing and empowering the community. Consider whether you could co-ordinate activities such as home-based care programmes with others. If you are able to forge links with churches and agencies who have an established ministry, these may be useful for referring clients who do not fall within your own parameters. Your staff can also learn from more experienced workers.

Assess the sense of community

Community-based care relies upon there being a community in the first place! This may seem obvious, but you should reflect upon it. Find out the community dynamics of your area. Is there a strong sense of community? Is there a sense of unity? Are there tribal divisions? Some places, as in the rural areas, have a better sense of community involvement than others do. Programmes work better where people share community involvement. In high-density urban areas and temporary housing such as squatters' camps, there may be little sense of belonging to a community. A geographical area may not define the 'community': it could be a church or school or other organisation.

Find out the legal framework regarding orphans

All staff members must become familiar with childcare laws, which will vary in different countries. In addition, there will be regulations attached to creating an NGO. You may need to form a board, appoint Trustees and elect an Executive Committee, as FOCUS and the Bethany Project have done. The process of deciding on a name, aims, objectives and mission statement is useful in itself as it helps everyone to discuss and define the vision, objectives and direction.

Consider alternative forms of childcare

Community-based care may not be appropriate for every child. There is no blanket solution for all circumstances. In some child-headed households, the carer may be very young, perhaps a 10-year-old girl looking after three siblings. Teenagers sometimes confide in leaders about their missed childhood due to the burdens placed on them. Care in an institution has its own disadvantages. In some, children are treated as individuals, but most are overcrowded. In such cases, a better solution may be to foster or seek adoption for the children. You can empower communities to support orphan children. The ideal would be to encourage fostering: a local family who could take in all the children of a family until they were old enough to care for themselves in their own home. However, take care that these children do not lose their rights.

2. Clarifying the vision

Vision is the ability to see what God wants to accomplish through the ministry. Vision changes the future and drives people into action. It is an inward and invisible reason for the ministry that God gives.

Listen to God

Using this handbook, pray through the material to see what fits your own culture and structure. Let people know that you are following what you hear from God. Get good prayer backing. Never depend on your own wisdom; place everything in God's hands.

Form a mission statement

A mission statement will address the question 'Why are you doing this?' You must be able to answer that question precisely before deciding what you will do or how you will do it. A clear mission statement will help the team to stay focused and guard against the danger of over-stretching your financial, manpower and time resources. You can be very busy but not accomplish what God really intends for you. A good mission statement will reflect the God-given vision and strategy. It will be brief enough to be remembered but long enough to be complete and broad enough to be comprehensive for the entire ministry. Both insiders and outsiders will understand it.

Define your objectives

Have a goal. Know your objectives and stick to them. Projects get requests for many kinds of ministry but if they do not fit the parameters they should not be taken on. They are accepted only if they comply with the mission statement.

Decide your strategy

In order for a vision to be fulfilled, it needs a strategy that is practical, detailed, clearly defined and well reasoned. Then it must be communicated to others who will grasp and carry out the planned vision when they start seeing the results. At this point, others will start owning the vision too. Allow criticism: it helps you to realise your mistakes and strengthens you.

3. Preparation

Find the right people to back the work

Find ways to spread awareness of the need and share the vision. Talk to key people at the highest level in national government and other organisations, so that they know where you are coming from and what you are doing. Speak at meetings, sharing the issues and asking, 'Where shall we go from here?'

Involve all the community

Those who live in the community must own the work. Your role is to ensure that they see the need, think of solutions and define the process. This will help to make the programme sustainable and able to continue even in your absence. Build on what is being done already. For instance, before the programmes started, church members were already visiting the sick and caring for some orphans in the area.

Work out your finances

This sometimes includes financial help. You cannot visit and pray with a hungry child and not bring food sometimes. Balance the need to give with the need to avoid creating dependency. There will be a need for financial support so you must consider how best to finance the programme.

4. Recruitment

It is generally accepted that community-based programmes can only be promoted by someone who has been living and working in the area for a long time. You will need national workers if your organisation is to be trusted by the indigenous people. Other points of advice include:

- Advertise in churches and through a Christian organisation such as the Viva Network (using the Internet to reach nationals of your country who may be abroad).
- Have a child protection policy to help guard against paedophiles.
- Send an application form, requiring three references. If possible, these should be from a church pastor, previous employment and a personal acquaintance.
- References should always be followed up, if possible before interview.
- Interview those who seem suitable (conducted by the project leader and two committee members).
- Have a three-month probationary period of employment.

Care for your workers

Set up regular supervision and weekly staff meetings. Value everyone involved: many staff members work without salary but they need to feel valued. Listen to staff views when appointing new members to the team. Maintain confidentiality. Realise that it takes time to build confidence and trust. Team co-operation can be problematic in a culture where subordinate employee relationships are the norm. When there are conflicts within the team, talk and pray together. You may have to teach staff members to respect authority. Commit to talking through issues with one another during the course of the day or in supervision sessions.

Provide training

Staff training can be set up internally, or you can make use of workshops provided by others. FACT invites workers from other African countries to spend two weeks with its programme to learn and experience orphan care. This two-week period has a wider syllabus than its Regional Training Course.

Personal advice for expatriate leaders

- Learn the local language.
- Strive to understand the history from background reading.
- Learn about the national culture and traditions.
- Set up a spiritual covering for yourself (people praying for protection for you as you cope with the impact of different practices).
- Look to your own needs, e.g. personal space, maybe your own home.
- Train yourself to switch off from work, enjoy leisure activities, make friends, have a social life and relax.
- As a Christian, you need to spend personal time with God.
- Attend church, but if you are not gaining much, obtain materials such as cassette tapes to help you to listen to the gospel and hear good teaching and worship God.

- Maintain personal discipline.
- The prayerful support of family/friends is essential. Keep in touch with them by means of regular newsletters.
- Build good relationships with all members of your staff.
- You need your own level of support, e.g. an Executive Committee.
- Cultivate local friends and church members to give you personal support.

How to Involve the Whole Community

1. Relationships

Arrange a meeting with the community leaders in order to gain their perceptions of the orphan problem in their area. Start by talking to key people and community leaders, discussing with them the needs of orphans in their area. These may include heads of local government, education and health and, in rural communities, heads and chiefs. The local churches should also be involved at this early stage. Get everyone's understanding and backing and create a sense of working together. Good relationships make for good programmes.

2. Ownership

The aim is that, when you have built good relationships and the leaders begin to appreciate the problems confronting them, they will invite you in to help them to do something. Approach the community leaders to see whether their community would be interested in discussing community-based orphan care. This is better than beginning by suggesting you have the solution and offering to help them. It encourages them to take ownership, and avoids potential jealousy. People in later groups might be envious if you find yourself able to do less for them than you did for previous communities.

3. Workshop

Respond to this invitation by offering to facilitate a workshop to discuss the issues and decide on further action. Representatives from every part of their community should be invited to attend, e.g. traditional leaders, village/urban community workers, school teachers, church leaders, representatives from other projects, grass-roots men *and women and children*. Agree times and details such as the venue, whether food will be provided by you or whether participants are expected to bring their own, and who is going to invite the potential participants (usually the community leaders).

The components of the workshop will be:

* raising awareness of the issues
* looking at problems and solutions
* motivating the community to take action.

Advice from project leaders

1. Be seen as non-political.
2. Be open about your Christian ethos.
3. Research what the needs are in each specific area, as these may not be the same as other places. Encourage local participation in this: those involved can identify and own the issues. Children can also participate at this stage.
4. Start small, where you are, with what you have. Aim for a good quality programme before scaling up.
5. Establish who the beneficiaries are to be.
6. Define your geographical area.
7. Sensitise the whole community, leading them to agree that all volunteers should meet certain criteria. The whole community must own the programme and support the volunteers.
8. The community should find volunteers who love God.
9. Involve everyone in the community.
10. Do not make promises, especially to volunteers.
11. Enable people to see how the problem of AIDS and orphans affects them and understand the value of children in the community. This will encourage them to get involved.

Planning a workshop

Questions to consider and act upon:

* What is the best way to elicit and impart information in the workshop? For example, participatory approach (recommended), role-play, brainstorming, discussion groups.
* How can children participate in both the planning and the workshops? Bearing in mind the service is for their benefit, who better to ask exactly what service is wanted and needed than the children themselves?
* Who will facilitate the workshops?
* Will the task be shared with others, e.g. other agencies, social welfare, church leaders or key people from the community?
* Which main language will be used?
* Will an interpreter be needed?
* What materials will be necessary, e.g. pens and paper/exercise books for participants, flip charts, marker pens, something to stick paper to walls,

etc? Remember materials should be appropriate to the venue and environment. For example, an overhead projector would be of little use if the workshop is to be conducted under a tree or in an area with no electricity!

• If you are providing a meal or refreshments, who is going to cook the food, and who will provide pots, pans, cups and plates?
• Is the venue suitable for any weather? Does it have a wall, a large tree trunk or another suitable place to stick up large flip chart paper?
• Obtain global HIV/AIDS statistics.

Hint: Gather everything you need to take with you for the workshops in advance. If you leave it to the last minute you might discover something is missing or not working!

Organising a workshop

Community leaders and representative community members attend the workshop in order to discuss how children can be cared for in the community. Through structured group work, they learn how to establish and run their own orphan care programmes. It is essential to encourage a participatory approach from the start, in order to achieve full community participation in the programme.

Although most of Bethany Project's workshops such as those indicated below take one day, some communities may need more time to address all the topics sufficiently. Flexibility is important as different people absorb information and learn at different rates. The syllabus for the workshop is included in full, the first part below and the second in the following chapter.

Bethany Project: Workshop 1

An introduction to community-based orphan care

Introduction

1. Registration of participants. (Have enough blank forms with you.)
2. Welcome, prayers and Bible reading.
3. Setting 'ground rules' for the workshop. These should come from the participants, e.g. women have an equal right to hold opinions and to express them as men, equality of every person within the group regardless of community status, confidentiality, etc. (It is unlikely that participants will include in their ground rules that children should be encouraged to attend, to contribute and have the right to express their opinions. You may have to add and explain this one so that participants agree to it.)

4. Elicit what participants expect from the workshop.
5. Give aims of the workshop (identified and written down beforehand).
6. The theology of orphan care – an outline of biblical references relating to God's mandate that we should care for orphans and widows, and how this relates to the community. Prayer and the biblical basis should be an integral part of each workshop.

Topic 1 – What problems are you currently experiencing in your community?

List the problems the participants raise (somewhere visible to all, e.g. flip charts, blackboard), and discuss. Inevitably, this will highlight the problem of the increase in numbers of deaths and of orphans.

Topic 2 – To what do you attribute the increase in deaths and orphans in your community?

List participants' answers and discuss. Some communities may be reluctant to talk about HIV/AIDS and the facilitator will need to exercise sensitivity and skill in guiding and opening up the discussions.

Topic 3 – HIV/AIDS and orphan statistics – global, national and local

The reality of the problem can be highlighted, and the fact that it affects not only their particular town/village, but is a global issue. Figures can be written up for all to see. At this stage it may be useful to acknowledge that we *all* know and love someone who is a member of our family, a friend, a church or community member who is either living with HIV disease, or who has died of AIDS.

Topic 4 – How is HIV virus passed on?

Since this topic could easily fill a whole day's workshop or more it can only be touched on briefly. It is often appropriate and important to hold a separate workshop later to cover this topic in adequate depth. It is important to dispel any myths or misunderstandings that participants mention, and to teach them the truth about how the virus can and cannot be spread, and to overcome any prejudice towards people who are HIV-positive or who are sick with AIDS. To elicit information from the participants, they should be asked their understanding of the various issues. This will establish their level of knowledge, and this method can be used later to review the amount they have learnt.

Topic 5 – What is our definition of an orphan?

Some may say that a child only becomes an orphan when the mother dies; others that an orphan is a child who has lost either one or both parents. Some may say it is children who are 15 years and under, and others that it is children up to 18 years. If your programme is working in an area with other orphan agencies, you may need to acknowledge the validity of their definitions, but dictate *your own project's* working definition, for the sake of rationalised statistics.

Topic 6–What problems do the neediest orphans in your community face?

This works well if participants are split into groups to discuss the question and come up with a list (group work). Write up their answers and discuss. It is important to include the following question for discussion within this topic: What is the community already doing to help these children? The participants are sometimes surprised that they are already doing something as part of their daily life and routines. For instance, they may already be helping an orphan family to plough and plant maize seed.

Topic 7–What other children in your community are experiencing similar problems and difficulties, even if their parents are alive?

This could be group work. If children are present, they can contribute. List and discuss responses, e.g. neglected children, abused children, etc. State your project's definition of children in especially difficult circumstances (CEDC). Often participants will not be willing to help such families, because they blame the parents for their own situation. They may have to be led to realise that these children also should be helped and that they cannot be blamed for their parents' behaviour.

Topic 8–Whose responsibility is it to care for orphans and CEDC, and how can they best be cared for?

List and discuss responses. Some may say that the government should care for the children, and others may say that they should be placed in orphanages. Get participants to highlight the strengths and weaknesses of each approach suggested. If necessary, remind them of appropriate Bible verses to help them to conclude that it is 'our' responsibility to care for such children.

Topic 9–What is community-based orphan care? (CBOC)

Explain the CBOC approach and get participants to discuss what they think may be the advantages and disadvantages of this approach.

Topic 10–What practical help and support can the whole community give to its neediest orphan children and CEDC using only the resources that it has readily available within the community?

This works well if done as a group work exercise. List and discuss responses. At this point it is generally a revelation to participants just how much they could do to assist their needy children. Someone may suggest recruiting volunteer childcare workers from within the community, but if not then this idea could be thrown in by the facilitator and discussed by participants.

Topic 11 – What existing community structures could work together in your community to promote care of orphans and needy children?

List responses and discuss e.g. churches, schools, recognised community workers, local businesses, etc.

Topic 12 – How do you want to proceed from here?

At this point, it is useful to get participants to discuss whether they want to go ahead with establishing a CBOC programme in their community. If they do, it could be suggested (if it hasn't already come up) that they could form a committee (e.g. a Child Welfare Committee (CWC)) to help with the planning and implementation of their programme. Emphasis needs to be placed on the fact *they* will own and run the programme, but that you will offer ongoing training, support and encouragement.

Participants may decide to elect a CWC immediately, or may choose to go and discuss what they have learned with the rest of their community first before choosing a committee. Allow plenty of time for participants to decide on their course of action. If participants do want to go ahead with setting up their own CBOC programme, set a date, time and venue for the next workshop. Get participants to discuss who they think should be present, and explain that it is their responsibility to invite others. (The next workshop should be as soon as possible.) Explain that the workshop will go over the introduction to CBOC again, but that it will also concentrate on the more practical steps that need to be considered when setting up a programme.

Topic 13 – Evaluation of workshop

Refer back to participants' expectations. Have their expectations been met? How do participants think the workshop could have been improved upon? Was the approach too easy/hard, etc?

Close the workshop

Ask a participant to pray. Dismiss the participants. Keep all the flip charts written on, for use at the next workshop.

ZOE

When initiating a ministry in a new area, Jean Webster goes there for two or three days, training pastors in the local churches. She lives and works alongside them and gets to know them. Jean responds to all requests for teaching on the subject of community-based orphan care. She has devised the following syllabus for this purpose.

Teaching programme for pastors and volunteers

1. Why the church and community?

(a) Orphan theology. This is God's mandate for his church, following the 40 Scripture references to the fatherless and orphans.

(b) Look at Jesus' lifestyle. He did not sit behind a desk with an appointment diary but walked the streets and rural roads, reaching out to the poor and needy. He went to one little girl after he heard she was dead and even though a woman first drained strength from him, he said to her, 'Little girl, arise.' That is what he intends for church life and for his children.

(c) The vision and calling: Luke 18 and the example of Nehemiah. Jesus said, 'Let the little children come unto me.' Children are top of his list. They come to Jesus through what they see of us in their times of need.

2. What is an orphan?

(a) Traditional/modern definitions. Traditionally, an orphan is someone who has lost both parents by death. The World Health Organisation, however, include all who have lost one or both by death. When one parent dies, the other is often sick or runs away, or remarries and the new partner doesn't care, so even with one parent still alive, the child lives like an orphan.

(b) We discuss queries regarding definitions in this ministry. Some tend to say, 'But what about the blind/handicapped/mentally ill, etc?' We talk about the need to clearly define our parameters. This is an orphan programme, in which we cannot care for all. Of course the church should be caring for all, but we are just looking at the proliferation of orphans. I am sure God was aware that a deluge of orphans was on its way, hence he raised up bodies such as ZOE, Bethany Project and FACT.

(c) Sometimes there is a very desperate situation although neither parent has died. To include these, we define the client group as VCO (Vulnerable Children and Orphans).

3. How to find and list the destitute families

(a) Characteristics of a 'destitute family'. Unable to function in life without help. Unable to help themselves and no one at all to help them in one or more dimensions of life, i.e. emotionally, materially, physically, mentally or spiritually.

(b) In establishing whether a family is destitute, be transparent with questions, not afraid to be direct and yet sensitive in approach.

4. *The evaluation chart*

The last column of the chart used for assessment bears the question 'Are other relatives helping?' If someone is noted in this column, then this family may well not be a priority. Emphasise the need for the last question to be laboured if necessary. Ask who is helping the family and persist until you are certain that there is no one at all. Chart only those who have no assistance.

5. *Local record-keeping*

Explain that when you have the list of destitute orphan families, you appoint one or two volunteers to every six to eight families, to visit them weekly or twice a month. The volunteer should write details of the families in her exercise books. She keeps two books, submitting them alternately to the committee, co-ordinators or steering group, who keep a central register. At each monthly report meeting, the books are exchanged, so that the volunteer always has one to use whilst the other is held centrally.

6. *Essential needs of families*

- Spiritual, emotional, physical, practical.
- Assess physical health: look for signs of protein, vitamin or mineral deficiencies, coughing or diarrhoea.
- Basic material needs are sufficient food and clean water, household utensils, suitable clothing and adequate housing. In addition, school fees when the family, government or church has not been able to provide them.
- Advice, including that available in the community through local government.
- Advocacy.
- Help to generate income. Micro-enterprise for each individual family, in the urban areas through seed money loans. Growing maize in rural areas without ploughing. Other small community projects to generate income in rural areas, e.g. sunflower seed oil, peanut butter, a grinding mill.

7. *What have we ourselves that we can give?*

With reference to children's perceived needs, we can offer love, Jesus, acceptance, touch, skills, advice, time, counsel, clothing, seeds and food. Changing the mindset as to the essential needs of an orphan makes people more willing and eager to help. We have established that God has called us to this ministry. If he has called us, he has equipped us (Hebrews 13:21;

2 Timothy 3:17). He says to us as to Moses, 'What is that in your hand?' (Exodus 4:2). One of the reasons the extended family has opted out is that they are struggling to put their own children through school and the care of orphans in their minds means material needs, so they stay away. For this same reason the church, though it knows and wants to care, has been paralysed.

My feelings are:

- God has made me with a heart of love and enabled me to love with the love of Jesus: agape.
- He has made me with eyes to see: the soft brown hair, the swollen hands, feet and belly of Kwashiorkor, the abuse spoken silently through the eyes of a child.
- He has made me with ears to hear: spiritually, God's word for this family; to hear physically the old grandfather who has been sitting all year with no one to listen, knowing that another son is sick and when he dies he will take in those children also.
- He has made me with a mouth to speak the words of God: that advice or word of encouragement or those words of advocacy on behalf of the voiceless.
- He has made me with a mind to think: to reason, to discover what is available for this family in the community and in God.
- He has made me with hands: to prepare the thatch where there is a hole and the rains are coming soon; to prepare the land so those children who live can then sow and reap for themselves.
- He has made me with feet: to collect that letter from the local council-lor to exempt that grandmother from having to pay for medicines for her little ones.

This discussion releases people to realise they can begin without waiting for anything else to come their way. Material goods can come later, when the church can begin to provide. Even this is much less painful when the children are becoming your own children. Care immediately available includes:

- friendship, giving families and individuals self-worth
- some legal and social advice or help to obtain the same
- advice about local assets, and maybe help to access them. For example: letter from a councillor to obtain free medicine, secondary school fees from social welfare, free milk when a mother has left a breast-fed baby
- advice about generating personal or group income
- fellowship with others.

8. Involving existing community structures

What are these structures and facilities? Their relevance to the orphan and destitute scene, e.g. Social Welfare, schools, clinics, the District Administrator, chiefs, headmen, councillors or police. We do not have to apologise for our involvement or to ask permission, but to build relationships and keep people informed of what we are doing. See where we can flow together, yet not compromise! Talk about how to approach and relate to officials: inviting them to a Christmas party, for example.

9. Generating income and other resources

Do not look at the matter of income-generating projects until the local church has established relationships with the families in the visiting programmes, otherwise the project, rather than the family, becomes the focal point of the ministry.

- Avoid the dependency syndrome.
- Describe various individual and group situations.
- Ask local leaders what is appropriate in the area.
- Discuss what local women do to generate personal income.
- Talk about group work.
- The local area committee will brainstorm together as to which ideas are locally viable, marketable, manageable and sustainable.

On a flip chart, give a local example and emphasise the importance of mapping

- to plan area strategy and to quickly find the gaps
- for visitors coming in or for people taking over.

Get the local people to write on paper where they are and a major local landmark and then indicate where the families in the programme live. The ensuing gaps are pertinent and indicate the need to do some research in those areas to find families missed there.

10. Working together

Unity, networking, locally and nationally (example of a local scheme). When churches work together they release more prayer and a stronger human resource.

11. HIV awareness

- Bacteria/germs or virus.
- The HIV virus and the path to full-blown AIDS.

- How to stay healthy and prolong life. Early treatment of opportunist diseases.
- How AIDS can be acquired. How it is not acquired: you can hug a child!
- Protection precautions for volunteers.

12. Child abuse

Types of abuse: physical, verbal, sexual, exploitation, e.g. child labour. No one should keep quiet when aware of abuse. Workers must follow through any suspicion – not alone, but in conjunction with committee leaders. They will liaise with social welfare and local government to seek to see justice carried out and to ensure safety for the children concerned. Emphasise the need for advocacy for the voiceless.

   Encourage the church in each area to have a 'safe house'. An approved family would be on immediate standby for any abused or abandoned child, or where the sole carer of a baby dies, to take in children overnight or for a few days while things are sorted out.

13. Child counselling

Using the expertise of Christian child psychologists to train them in the basic skills and truths, Jean is planning workshops on the psychosocial support of children during the coming year.

14. Character building and discipline

Volunteers must

- have a heart for children
- have a commitment to God and his church
- not have selfish motives
- be physically active
- be able to read and write, or to work with someone who can.

Setting up a Care Programme

This chapter shows how to set up a community-based care programme for orphaned children. It describes the process undertaken by FACT in setting up the FOCUS programme, then proceeds with recommendations and the relevant workshop syllabus from the Bethany Project.

FOCUS takes great care to establish each local care programme in response to the felt needs of the particular community. After initiating the work, FOCUS is not directly involved but is available for support and training and to pay school fees. The community identifies the needs and those who most need help.

Recommendations for establishing a local programme

- Only community-based groups can implement programmes, though NGOs have a supportive role.
- Carry out careful mapping, define each catchment area and identify the community where the local programme will operate.
- Do some research: the programme is more likely to succeed if it is based on and develops existing activities.
- Community chiefs, councillors and other community members must all own the work before it can move forward. This releases resources; for example, a chief may give a field where food can be grown for orphans.
- Take great care how you select, train, support and motivate the volunteers. They are the key human resources within the programme.
- Use paid staff members to co-ordinate the various programmes.
- Define your target group by means of enumeration, registration, needs assessment and prioritisation.
- Establish a record system and train volunteers in its use.
- Wherever possible, avoid giving material support to families until committee members have shown they are able to prioritise those in greatest need of such support and monitor their activities.
- Set up ways in which you can monitor and evaluate the programme, identifying and objectively measuring processes and outcomes.

Training the committee

FACT works with six sites and other communities who request help are referred to the nearest of these existing sites. FACT encourages visits to community programmes in other areas so that leaders can learn from them and share problems and expertise with pastors and community leaders. *All* are welcome to learn from FACT's 'training without walls' and hear from other workers.

Aims and objectives

Each programme has the following objectives:

- To identify all orphaned children in each programme's catchment area and prioritise those households with the greatest needs.
- To visit all prioritised households at least twice per month.
- To identify households where children's basic needs are not met and to

provide these households with limited development-oriented material support.

- To liaise with other community groups, leaders and organisations concerning the operation of the programme.
- To enable community members to own each FOCUS programme and over time reduce their dependence on FACT.
- To identify new or emerging problems affecting orphaned children.

Volunteers

Volunteers are recruited on the basis of their concern for orphans; most are already caring for orphaned relatives. As a community visitor, each becomes responsible for identifying and visiting orphan households within two kilometres of her own home. These women ascertain the parental status of families living nearby and place the names of orphan households on a register. The most needy families (approximately half of those identified) are placed on a priority register. As the programme becomes known, concerned neighbours or school authorities refer unregistered orphan households to the community visitors.

Training volunteers

1. Projects provide volunteers with basic training so that they are able to identify and register all orphans in the community. Trainers show them how to write records and explain how these are used.
2. They teach them what to observe and how to assess needs. For example: 'How do you know there's no food without asking directly? Arrive after lunchtime and see whether there is any sign of a fire used for cooking. Children may be crying. Look at their clothing. Record your observations so that the FOCUS team knows what is happening.'
3. Volunteers have one week's initial training, then monthly reviews to address issues arising from their work. Communities appoint their own trainers. When visiting, FOCUS workers ask questions, to learn themselves and to reinforce teaching.
4. Volunteers meet as a group, give reports, discuss how to help the families, share with one another and give advice and support.

Prioritising needs

The accurate identification of orphans and prioritisation of their needs is vital for the successful operation of the programme. This process seems natural and obvious to the volunteers, for whom it involves a mixture of intuition and objective criteria. The committee of community leaders then reviews their judgements, verifying the needs of the targeted households.

This practice ensures transparency and fairness in the selection of beneficiaries. The involvement of the community in selecting orphans for assistance contributes to the confidence that the community and its leaders place in the programme.

Examples of practical criteria used to identify children in need of care

- Living on their own with no adult supervision or guidance.
- Living with a terminally ill parent.
- In households where multiple families are looked after by an elderly grandparent (over 70 years).
- Children dirty or in rags.
- Withdrawn appearance.
- Hut in poor state of repair.
- Lack of chickens or farm animals, no crops.
- No food in the hut and no sign of a recent fire for cooking.

Visiting families

Volunteers are given the responsibility of looking after the orphan households that have been selected. They aim to visit each household twice per month, with those in greatest need such as child-headed households being visited weekly. Each volunteer is allocated families whose homes surround her own so she knows the circumstances of illness and bereavement. The volunteer creates a bond with the family. She is always within easy reach because she lives locally. This also makes the scheme more cost effective. FOCUS does not allocate a set number of families to each volunteer; each is given what she can cope with.

What happens during a visit

Volunteers who visit orphans may undertake bereavement counselling and talk to young boys and girls about issues concerned with growing up. They teach home management, mending and domestic skills to young household heads. They take sick children to the nearest clinic, clean the house, fetch water and bath the younger children. They help to plough the orphans' field and encourage the children by singing, sharing the gospel and praying with them.

Supporting caregivers

The volunteer gives support and advice to the caregivers in the household. This is culturally acceptable and ensures that they complement existing community coping mechanisms, rather than undermining or displacing them. The need to strike the appropriate balance between the needs of caregivers and the needs of children calls for initiative and understanding from the volunteer.

Counselling children

Sometimes volunteers visit in pairs, one to look at issues in the home, the other to talk to the children and offer counselling. Children may be traumatised by sickness or death of loved ones, and may have been forced to move home or split from siblings. They may be HIV-positive or sick or affected by the sickness in the family, or afraid that a sibling might die or that they themselves might catch a fatal disease. It is generally better for children to remain in their own home environment so that something in their lives stays constant and stable.

Protecting vulnerable children

The project does not encourage children to break with their families, but in rural areas there may be a problem of exploitation. Visits by volunteers who are known in the community discourage abuse (even if relatives look after children) as abusers are scared of someone finding out. They are deterred from physical and sexual abuse if they know the community cares and is watching. Volunteers are trained to approach social welfare or the chief if they notice signs of abuse. Because the community has selected the volunteers, it has to listen to them. Sometimes children may sleep in the vatete's hut for protection at night.

Wider role of volunteers

Volunteers are responsible for referring children to social welfare, other NGOs, churches, legal advice projects (donor-funded lawyers). They work in conjunction with the police, schools and churches.

Bethany Project: Workshop 2

Setting up a CBOC programme

Introduction (as for Workshop 1)

As part of the registration, identify how many newcomers are present. This will help decide what depth of revision is required.

Topic 1 – Recap of last workshop

1. Get participants to highlight what they learnt at the last workshop.
2. Put up the flip charts of the work they did at the previous workshop.
3. Go over any areas that need covering again and answer any questions.
4. Particularly re-emphasise the problems that orphans face, as high-lighted by participants in the previous workshop, and the practical ways they felt as a community they could help to support their needy children (Topics 5, 6 and 9).

Topic 2 – What role would your Child Welfare Committee (CWC) play in your programme, and what qualities should members of this committee possess? How can they be elected?

This can be a brainstorming session. List and discuss responses. Encourage the participants to consider electing a responsible child on the CWC.

Topic 3 – What role would your volunteer childcare workers play in supporting needy children and their families? What qualities should volunteers possess? How and when can they be elected? Who will monitor their work and encourage them?

This could be done working in small groups with feedback. List responses and discuss.

Topic 4 – What role would the whole community play in the support of its needy children and their families?

This again can be done working in small groups. List responses and discuss. Although this topic may have been partly covered in the previous workshop, it was more hypothetical then, so it is good to go over it again in the light of the reality of their own programme being set up.

Encourage the groups to consider how children in the community can support the orphaned children. If children are present, they could form one group and contribute their own ideas of how they could help and be involved.

Topic 5 – What are your definitions of destitution and what criteria would need to be present in order for a family to be termed destitute?

This could be a brainstorming session. List and discuss responses. Signs of destitution could include:

- children in rags
- children dirty
- children appear withdrawn
- children appear malnourished
- children sick

- hut falling down
- no chickens or animals
- no crops or food
- no sign of recent fire, therefore no food to cook or eat
- no or few pots, plates, etc
- lack of blankets
- lack of clothes
- children not at school

Topic 6 – What would be the advantages of conducting a survey and enumerating the total numbers of orphans in your community, and identifying and registering the neediest?

Explain how the survey could be done, giving an overview of the process of enumerating and registering. List responses and discuss. Bring out the importance of keeping statistics in order that we can (a) get an idea of the extent of the problem, and (b) direct help and resources to the neediest.

Topic 7 – Design a questionnaire (enumeration survey form) which will help you to identify all orphans and CEDC in your area, and which will identify those who are the neediest

Participants can be asked to list what points they think would need to be on such a questionnaire. At this point, facilitators may need to teach the use of an already established form if the training is part of a larger programme, in order for the approach to be rationalised. The established form can be compared to the participants' suggestions and the differences highlighted and discussed. Give plenty of time for participants to discuss each question on the form, and to understand how to fill it in clearly and correctly. Participants could get into groups or pairs and fill in an example form.

Topic 8 – Points participants should consider when undertaking an enumeration of orphans and CEDC in their area

- What is the catchment area to be surveyed?
- Who will undertake the survey?
- When will they do it?
- What materials will they need?
- Who will provide the materials, e.g. forms/books/pens?
- Sensitise the *whole* community as to the purpose of the survey and answer their questions about it *in advance* of doing the survey, in order to maximise co-operation. Who will do this, and how?
- Approaches which help/hinder effective communication – the need for sensitivity and confidentiality when conducting the survey.

Topic 9–Registers

(You may consider that this topic should be covered at another meeting after the surveys have been completed.) The information collected through the surveys can be used by the communities to draw up registers of their neediest children. Participants should discuss the following points:

- What might be the value of keeping registers of their neediest children?
- The importance of keeping them up-to-date (e.g. new children will be orphaned, other children may move away to relatives in other areas, situations and circumstances may change).
- Who will keep the registers and update them?
- Should there be separate registers for different geographical areas and then a 'master register' for the whole area held by the committee?

N.B. The Bethany Project currently teaches programmes to maintain three registers as follows:

1. A high-priority orphan register, giving details of the neediest orphaned children who are deprived and at risk.
2. A low-priority orphan register, giving the details of children who are orphaned, but whose circumstances are good and do not put them at risk.
3. A register of all CEDC in the area, giving details of children who are not orphaned, but whose circumstances put them at risk.

Put up flip charts showing the required details and suggested layout of the registers, so that participants can copy this down if desired.

Topic 10–What is your next step forward?

Participants should be given time to discuss when, where and how they will identify volunteer childcare workers and the Child Welfare Committee and conduct the orphan survey. All outcomes and decisions should be documented and a record kept.

Set a date, time and venue to review the outcome of the survey and registration exercise. Discuss and agree who should be present at this review.

Topic 11–Evaluation of workshop

Refer back to participants' expectations. How do participants think the workshop could have been improved?

Close the workshop

Ask a participant to pray. Dismiss the participants. Keep all the flip charts written on, for use at the next review meeting.

NB: The content of Workshops 1 and 2 may need to be extended over three workshops, depending on the 'pace' of the individual community. Flexibility is the key.

Review meeting

Community survey and registration

Each programme forms its own committee. Men and women who volunteer carry out a survey to enumerate the orphans within their locality, then do a simple assessment in order to identify the neediest families. The elected committee, volunteer childcare workers and community leaders meet together to review this assessment. The framework of this meeting is outlined below.

Review of enumeration and registration exercise

The review meeting should be attended by the elected CWC, the volunteer childcare workers and representatives from community leaders. Certainly, those who actually performed the survey will need to be present. In most communities the volunteers carry out the survey with members of the CWC. The following issues need to be addressed at this meeting.

How easy/difficult was the survey?

- What were the problems encountered? For example, there may have been pressure on those doing the survey to falsely register a non-needy family, if people thought they might receive 'handouts' as a result of being registered.
- How co-operative was the community? Was there any opposition?
- How were problems handled?
- What did they learn from doing the survey?
- How could the exercise have been improved?

Review of the surveys and registers

- Are they complete?
- Are they clear and readable?
- What information is still missing?
- How can they be improved?
- How can the group now use these registers effectively?
- What do these registers teach us?

Often it takes a while for communities to complete their registers, and patience, encouragement and guidance may be needed as they learn to improve them. Probably this will be the first time that they have ever undertaken such an exercise. It may be necessary to give them extra time to complete or improve the registers and to arrange a second review meeting.

Further discussions

Participants are often shocked at some of the situations uncovered during the survey, such as the extent of hardship of some families, or the suffering of some children. Take time to discuss these things, and how the community and volunteers may be able to help. Always emphasise what can be done to help, rather than what cannot be done. Not every problem can be solved, but situations can be alleviated by small, practical expressions of love and concern.

Who will visit which families?

- How will the volunteers organise themselves? Will they visit the neediest families in their villages in pairs or individually?
- How many families will they each visit, and how often will they visit?
- Are there enough volunteers to cover all the neediest families, or do they need to recruit and train more?
- Will they divide the families according to geographical proximity or in some other way?
- What will be their priorities when they first visit, e.g. relationship building with the children and their caregivers?
- How will they keep records of their visits? An easy record book may need to be designed by the volunteers, e.g. including date and details of visit.

What is the role of the CWC?

This may need to be discussed again, as well as lines of accountability and communication, and what procedures the community wishes to establish to address grievances and disciplinary issues.

Support of the volunteers

- To whom are they accountable?
- How often will they meet with the CWC?
- How can the CWC and the wider community support them in their work?
- To whom should they turn in a crisis or with problems?

How can the support of the whole community be maintained?

Emphasise the importance of them meeting regularly with their wider community to feed back information (e.g. results of survey) and to discuss problems, progress and issues with them, and to elicit their continued support.

Close the meeting

Ask a participant to pray. Dismiss the participants. Keep records of all that has taken place and been decided.

The role of the volunteers

The volunteers, known as vatetes, visit the selected families regularly to give practical, emotional and pastoral care and support. Some children on their list may not be orphaned but are at risk due to the difficult nature of their social circumstances. If vatetes are reluctant to visit children when they cannot give material help, they have to be convinced that it is equally valuable to give time and attention, love and prayers. Every sector of the community is encouraged to engage in the support of its needy children. Each community manages its own programme with the ongoing support and monitoring of the Bethany Project.

Working with the children

The range of activities undertaken with the children includes:

- fetching firewood and water
- helping to clean the homestead
- sharing food and clothing
- providing blankets and soap
- washing and mending clothing
- washing the children
- playing with the children
- loving them
- teaching them skills
- teaching them spiritual values
- helping to plough fields
- caring for sick children
- taking them to a clinic or hospital
- helping to pay school fees
- providing seed
- creating vegetable gardens and growing vegetables for the children
- helping to rebuild or repair their huts
- getting local school children involved in the support of their orphaned peers
- praying with the children and sharing Scripture with them
- teaching the children about their culture, history and traditions

Other activities undertaken by the community for the children

- Advocacy on behalf of individual children and families.
- Raising awareness of the rights of orphans and children in need.
- Enumeration and registration of orphans and CEDC.
- Establishing income-generation projects to involve and benefit orphan families and other children.
- Celebrating with children and their families at Easter and Christmas.
- Anti-AIDS clubs for young people.

Recommendations

- Stick to your objectives and resist attempts from those who ask you to take on other tasks. For instance, a councillor of a ward might want you to pay fees for more children (not within parameters of the programme), in order to make the councillor popular.
- Remember that you are working with human beings: you have to use your judgement and be firm.
- You have to draw a line because if you take other children on to the register, all the community may ask for help.
- Don't try to cover a large area immediately. Go bit by bit and make sure you set up the programme in a way that will last.
- Take note of the political climate when deciding whom to approach first.
- Never promise anything, e.g. finances or material.
- Be aware that cultural traditions are very important.
- Note the existing community structures and consider how you can work together as a team.
- Try to learn from mistakes and avoid repeating them.
- Focus on one thing at a time, e.g. CBOC first then AIDS clubs.

Personal advice

- Be prepared for the fact that when dealing with needy children, you may find that you get involved in their problems.
- Try to listen to the children's truth.
- Live by Christian principles. Be good stewards.
- Ensure that you have the right motivation for this ministry.
- To win the war against AIDS, you must teach by example. Children will take notice of what you do, not just what you say.
- Pray for children. It makes a difference.
- Remember that God will give you what you need and deserve.
- When feeling discouraged – maybe others criticise the programme – good teamwork is essential. Plan things together. Don't keep quiet; share your feelings.

- Expect to experience emotional stress when you see children hungry, exploited and even dying. Some vatetes are also HIV-positive. At review meetings, you will be told of volunteers who are sick and sometimes some who have died.
- Take encouragement from your leader or other supportive people, e.g. your church pastor. Set up a personal support structure, ensuring that you have someone promise to pray specifically for you on a regular basis.
- Expect conflicts to arise within the team sometimes. Learn to listen to everyone and deal fairly, kindly and firmly with disagreements.

Ongoing Encouragement and Support

FOCUS

Development of the FOCUS programme

The FOCUS programme originally began with 22 volunteers but, by the time of our research in 2001, children were being cared for by 140 volunteer visitors. These were based at five separate rural sites (with an estimated total catchment area population of 50,000) and a low-income high-density area in the city of Mutare where a large number of dwellings are wooden shacks.

To motivate volunteers

FOCUS tries to encourage and motivate its volunteers by giving them status, emotional support and tokens of appreciation. To this end, it

- provides uniforms (T-shirts with the FOCUS motto on the back)
- gives occasional small gifts, such as soap
- brings visitors from other community programmes
- invites them to workshops on children's issues
- gives words of encouragement in bi-monthly meetings.

Development of programmes

New features have been introduced into community care programmes, often initiated by community members in response to felt needs, or following research indicating new or emerging problems affecting orphaned children. Developments include the following:

1. *Voluntary effort from within the community*

Local people who are not volunteers within the programme have given their time and materials to help orphaned families. Activities include ploughing fields, repairing broken-down housing and giving advice about agriculture, health care, childcare and income supplementation.

2. *Income-generating activities*

They have also contributed to community-based projects, such as poultry farming and vegetable gardens. Income from these projects is used to support destitute families and to raise money for use by the community group.

3. *Micro-credit schemes*

These schemes operate to train individuals in family-based income-generating skills and simple money management.

4. *Psychosocial support*

Members of the community hold crafts, agricultural, cultural or sporting activities for the benefit of older orphaned children.

5. *Awareness raising and advocacy*

Volunteers connected with programmes have advocated with political and traditional leaders, headmasters and health workers in order to improve the situations of orphans and children in difficult circumstances.

6. *Protecting from abuse*

The presence of a group of community members concerned about children acts as a reference body. Volunteers have reported incidents of sexual and physical abuse and because of such supervision it is likely that instances of abuse have reduced. In 1998, a child psychologist conducted training with volunteers and teachers within communities with FOCUS programmes, teaching them how to identify and manage cases of abuse.

7. *Regional Training Programme*

FACT's Regional Training Programme was established in 1994. By August 1998, 63 participants had attended the two-week field-based training course, exposing them to FACT's Prevention and Care programmes.

8. *Confidentiality*

Throughout its work, FOCUS takes care to protect the confidentiality of people affected by HIV/AIDS. Although the project does not directly address HIV/AIDS issues, it conveys a positive, non-discriminating approach to awareness raising and care. It emphasises prioritisation of those in greatest need and regular visits and material support to the most needy households. This strategy supports children's rights to protection, health, education, non-discrimination and freedom from exploitative labour.

Case study 1
Our meeting with a FOCUS community programme committee and volunteers at Marange, near Mutare. (A personal report by Marion Derbyshire)

At Marange Methodist Church, Les and I were warmly greeted with singing and handshakes by nine lady volunteers dressed in blue FOCUS T-shirts (with the words of James 1:27 printed on the back). We were introduced to the Chairman and clerk of the committee, together with three more gentlemen involved in the home-based care programme.

Volunteers from different churches introduced themselves: they came from Methodist, UBC, Anglican UMC and AFU. They began to report on their progress and, through an interpreter, to answer our questions.

What do the volunteers do?

They support orphans at home, teach them to plough fields and offer guidance. They give practical help, such as fetching firewood. They get land to help them grow food and, when there are problems, they go to the chief. He can help them to obtain food, arrange for sick children to attend hospital or trace extended families. Volunteers visit children in hospital. They go to the homes of child-headed households and train them in essential skills, such as household chores and vegetable growing, to help them to become independent. They teach those who have money how to use it and encourage them to go to school. They monitor schoolwork.

What does the committee do?

The committee is expected to recommend the 15 neediest children in each catchment area for FACT to support in school. This is problematic as there are many more. Paying school fees reduces stress and helps to ease the children's minds but it is also important for children to be supported in their life and work at school. At Christmas, they hold a party with poetry, drama and games for the children.

What is the hardest difficulty to cope with in a family?

Shortage of money poses a great problem, particularly when children have no food, clothing or other necessities. Some volunteers have nothing to offer; others go home to get mealy-meal of their own or go to the chief to ask for help. Sometimes they can do nothing materially, but they show love to the kids and share Jesus. They help in a practical way, such as cleaning the house, but cannot give food.

How do you make everyone in the community aware of what children are facing?

Through community leaders: for example, the chief calls the whole community together and addresses the meeting. They also invite others to speak about health and orphan matters and sensitise the whole community to the issues.

Does this approach work?

A man answers, 'Yes, all the community members take responsibility for the children and their problems, but sometimes it seems that they are not helping because they have nothing.' We heard that in 1995 24 people went round the village each week with soap, food and other provisions. Now resources are so low in Zimbabwe that they are forced to go with nothing. However, FACT used to pay only primary school fees; now they pay secondary school fees too.

What can you tell us about child safety and protection?

They used to have vulnerable child-headed households, but now the community has been sensitised to the issues, they find that families have taken them in. Through the teaching of the FOCUS programme, relatives have learnt to care for the kids.

Are orphaned children kept in their village or removed from it?

It depends where the extended family lives. If they are in the village the children stay, but if from afar they take the children away because they are their guardians. The men say that in their community they care for the children. Orphans stay in the village and the vulnerable are protected. In other places they leave for towns and cities and take up bad habits.

What about the children's property?

The chief becomes the custodian of the children's field. It is his responsibility to give and take land. It is kept until the children are grown up, then they can come back and take their father's land. The field can be ploughed by the villagers, but food grown on it must be given only to the orphans. A former chief used to give money to orphanages and left some to help them when he died. FOCUS has taken up the support but chiefs encourage and motivate the volunteers because they care about the children.

How do you counsel orphaned children?

Due to the high incidence of HIV/AIDS, many children are left without parents. Volunteers say they support them in their bereavement by remaining true and by praying with them and they comfort them by sharing from the Bible. Care starts when the parents are sick and continues with the bereaved family. They organise times when the orphans can integrate with other children to play soccer and other sports. They provide physical exercise and activities, such as Bible study and games, to stimulate their minds. They want the orphans to experience love and normal life with other children.

How do you raise funds for this programme?

(a) The committee members contribute a little money of their own to plant maize, to grow vegetables to sell and to raise chickens. This church donated a chicken run but they sold the chickens to pay school fees.
(b) They set up a mushroom project, using spores given them by the African University. This group have had three batches, but some were unsuccessful owing to cold weather. They say they need extra training.
(c) They used to have a drama group that charged for its performance, raising school fees for one child, but now people say they are too tired to walk to watch the drama.
(d) They have established a garden in the church grounds. In this they grow yams and rice to sell.

As a farewell, the ladies from this devoted group sang a song of their own composition, in English, for us.

Case study 2
Our meeting with a FOCUS community programme committee and volunteers at St Augustin Diocese (A personal report by Marion Derbyshire)

Here we were shown a training centre where orphans learn dressmaking, carpentry, bricklaying and agriculture – including mushroom growing and chicken rearing. Although at an early stage of development, it was nonetheless impressive. Trainees made their own benches for seating and the carpentry benches. They built the chicken shed and plan to build accommodation for boarders too.

We then met with vatetes from the surrounding district, asked questions and listened to their reports. By now, much of it was familiar, repeating what we had learnt from others, but we gained a new perspective on some of the work.

Home care

A typical visit to a sick patient at home involves helping to feed, wash, give medication, take to a clinic or collect medicine. A doctor does not visit people at home, but home nursing sisters do, or sometimes the doctor visits the clinic.

Orphan care

Volunteers:

- encourage self-respect and teach orphans how to be self-reliant, e.g. sewing own clothes, working in fields, attending church
- teach them to behave well in the community, study hard at school and do things for themselves
- pray and read the Scriptures with families
- teach them hygiene and how to prevent further infection
- sometimes visit orphans to socialise, entertain, integrate with other kids, help with lessons, talk and listen to help them survive their bereavement
- get help from others, such as asking for land or seeds, and encourage neighbours and church community to give
- present problems to church, e.g. the need for clothing and school fees
- build good working relationships with other support groups and officials, hospital staff, chiefs and political councillors so that they work well together
- take some of their own food, if children have none

Difficulties

- They have few problems with the very young children, but adolescents won't always listen to the volunteers, as they think they know it all.
- Sometimes children do not attend school and volunteers have to watch carefully to make sure they get there.
- Sometimes visits are made to homes at a long walking distance, or even a bus journey, from their own.
- They encountered mistrust when families stopped getting material help from FACT. Some thought that maybe the volunteers kept things for themselves.

Motivation of volunteers

- Initially women who used to visit poor families before the programme started felt that they wanted to help. With training, the work became lighter, because they knew how to ease suffering and were enabled to help sick people.
- They understand that their efforts are part of Christian service in the church.

- They meet together as a group once a month. It can be a great relief to share problems and benefit from the experience of others. They encourage one another in practical ways of solving problems.

How they measure the effectiveness of their work

- Observation that young people who have finished school have been able to support their families.
- Orphans no longer hide when volunteers come because they recognise and value them.
- Recording in notebooks what has been seen and done and what needs remain, as well as the number of orphans and families they look after.
- Now independent of FACT, two co-ordinators in the Anglican diocese supervise the programme. These two men always know what is going on.

Advice from volunteers

- Dedication is essential. We were impressed and touched by the love and dedication shown by all the volunteers we met.
- Must have love for all children. Without that, this work would be impossible.
- Remember one day you may need care yourself!
- Never make promises, as you may not be able to keep them. If you can bring something, it will be a surprise.
- When helping families, always involve them. Avoid doing anything that would make them too dependent.
- When visiting orphan families, talk to the children – not just about them to their guardians.
- Community care only works where there is a strong sense of community.
- If children are difficult, volunteer should refer them to the church pastor, who goes to counsel them and reports back.

Bethany Project

Local community commitment

It is encouraging to see and hear of the commitment and dedication of the volunteers in the CBOC groups. Many of the vatetes visit their neediest orphan families daily and encourage the wider community to help by repairing huts, helping to plough and raising money for school fees. In spite of little or no recompense, the vatetes continue to give of their time, energy, love, advice and food. When asked what motivates them to continue caring and nurturing the orphans, the most common reply is along the lines of: 'We see the children change from being withdrawn, sad, shy, rejected and confused to become smiling, happy and more confident with hope.'

Supporting the community programmes

The Bethany Project provides ongoing training and support to these programmes. Heather Mkandawire is the project co-ordinator. Her role is to train the communities in orphan care and to monitor the 22 programmes in the Zvishavane District which are under the BP umbrella. She undertakes reviews with each community in order to support and encourage them. She also visits the families, especially the child-headed households in order to pray with them and to listen to their problems personally. Her support encourages the vatetes and the community at large, making them feel they are not alone in the work. She also pays the children's school fees and takes them to church and advocates for them with the social welfare office.

Case study 1

Emily, a vatete, visits her ten families at least once or twice a week, but one child-headed household she visits daily and makes sure they have eaten, or cooks for them. She might help practically by washing the children's clothes and teaching them how to keep themselves and their homestead clean. She plays with them, reads to them from the Bible, prays with them and encourages them, showing them love.

This family is an example of many that go through similar problems, and that the Bethany Project is trying to help. The number of child-headed households is growing at an alarming rate.

Case study 2

Tadiwa is an 11-year-old girl doing Grade 6. Her parents both died of AIDS in the course of three days, and as a girl child Tadiwa is looking after her brothers, Takudwa aged 12 and Tapiwa aged 4, who is also HIV-positive. When going to school, they leave Tapiwa with a Bethany Project volunteer, and after school Taku remains with Tapi, while Tadiwa works in the neighbour's field for income in order to obtain food and keep herself and the siblings in school. Sometimes she has sleepless nights because Tapiwa is so sick, and this makes her miss school. The volunteer sees them regularly and shares with Tadiwa the practical and emotional burdens of nurturing the children.

Material assistance

The Bethany Project assists communities to establish income-generating projects, which help to support the children. In this way sewing, knitting and peanut butter making projects have been established. Although Bethany is not a relief organisation, it provides a little in the way of material assistance to families and children experiencing particularly difficult circumstances. This takes the form of food, seed, soap, clothing and school fees.

Workshops for children

Once a quarter, a different group of children who are heads of households are offered a week long camp/workshop where they are trained in life skills. Activities include simple things that adults take for granted such as budgeting time and resources and taking care of children. These workshops also give these hardworking children an opportunity for experiential learning and relaxation, and time for bereavement counselling.

Good relationships

The Bethany Project places emphasis on the need to create awareness about caring for children affected by AIDS. The project leaders give priority to their relationship with all the stakeholders in the district. They know they must light the fire in the hearts of the communities of the district. In the first two wards that they trained, they say they went there with the aim of helping the orphans rather than really making those two communities own the project. Now it is difficult to wean them because they became accustomed to being spoon-fed.

Recommendations for working with volunteers

- You will always need to motivate and encourage volunteers to sustain their efforts. Where there is general poverty, there may even be a good case for financial incentives.
- Even acquiring knowledge empowers. If volunteers attend workshops, their status in the community improves: chiefs, kids and school staff take notice of them.
- In some areas, the extent of the HIV problem can be overwhelming for volunteers, who could suffer burnout. In other areas, where there are few orphans, the volunteers may lack status. Remember that the work is emotionally and spiritually draining, as well as physically tiring. Volunteers need spiritual input, prayer and teaching, to constantly renew and equip them.
- Some volunteers did not go to school. Be very patient and use simple, relevant concepts. You may need to explore and discuss issues in detail, going over the same area more than once.

- Never give them solutions to their problems. Let the community suggest what they could do to solve them.
- Never try to give the community the impression that you are superior, or they will resent you.
- Listen to them when they tell you problems, give them time and never rush your meetings.
- When they suffer bereavement, sit with them and really show that you care for them.
- Always pray with them and encourage them too.

ZOE

Education

Jean Webster teaches co-ordinators about the spread of AIDS and in particular how it is not spread. These in turn teach the volunteers, who can then pass on relevant information to the rural families in ways that they can understand.

Training

In the year 2002, ZOE began training workshops in such matters as administration, micro-enterprise and psychosocial support. They are encouraging the area co-ordinators to do more of the training in their localities and in surrounding areas. Exchange visits are planned to encourage people to visit and learn from other projects. The project encourages income-generation projects for groups in the rural areas and micro-enterprise schemes for individual families in the urban areas.

Children's camps

Using Salvation Army Masiye Camp in the south and Life Explosion camps in the north of the country they seek to systematically take groups of children to camp during the year. Priority will be given to the heads of child-headed households.

Visiting the sick

Jean is pursuing funding for training 'barefoot doctors': lay people in each area for whom she will seek a supply of essential basic medicines.

Christians working together

- Some areas have developed a monthly fellowship group for widows and orphans. These are positive times of sharing testimonies such as how each has managed through struggles, God's provision and income-generating successes.
- Community and church leaders share together in an area with the view to working together.
- Leaders from an area that is commencing a ministry can visit another area to see how it works for them.

Administration and Finance

Efficient administration is vital to the success of any childcare programme. This section explains how leaders in each of the projects deal with administration and finance. A study of the similarities and differences could help you to determine the best model for your own project.

Focus

Record-keeping and research

It is important to establish clear record systems at every stage of setting up and implementing a programme. This enables communities and programme directors to identify and study emerging issues such as stigmatisation of orphans, child-headed households and the increasing vulnerability of orphaned children to HIV. In the case of the FOCUS programme, this research led to features being added to programmes to meet recognised needs. These include income generation, micro-credit, advocacy, psychological needs assessment and support, and raising awareness about sexual abuse and child rights.

Financial expenditure

In 1999, the cost of the FOCUS programme was approximately US$1,150 per month, plus another 20% incorporated in FACT's administrative costs. Of the direct FOCUS expenditure, 56% was spent on material assistance to needy families and support for volunteers. Assistance was mainly in the form of maize seed and fertiliser, primary school fees, blankets and food. Allowances to volunteers included bus fares to support meetings, a T-shirt, a skirt, a scarf and a pair of training shoes each, plus a Christmas bonus of US$10. Some who look after orphans in their own homes received small amounts of material support (average US$11 per year). The remainder was used to pay a Co-ordinator and Assistant Co-ordinator, for travel costs and for administrative expenses such as office and computer rental, telephone, stationery and photocopying.

Plan International (Mutare) has been the principal donor to the programme. Donations have been received from NORAD and UNICEF and smaller donations in cash and kind have gone through FACT. In addition, people visiting the programmes have made gifts directly to community groups.

Sustainability

There has been a low turnover of volunteer staff with only one leaving the programmes, some of which have been established for nearly five years. Some community members have even applied to programme supervisors to be allowed to become FOCUS visitors. Volunteers receive initial and monthly training and some visit other programmes through an exchange scheme.

The project has maintained its funding resources by keeping to a low-cost programme. However, applications for future funding will include research as part of ongoing programme activities. The FOCUS initiative has led to policy changes by the Department of Social Welfare, which is now a strong advocate of community-based orphan support.

Meeting the needs

FOCUS is keen to meet children's needs but at the same time to discourage local communities from depending upon external donations. With this in mind, material gifts are distributed in small quantities and only at certain times of the year. In general, maize seed is given in the planting season, and blankets are given in the winter. In Zimbabwe, rural primary schooling is free but each school charges a levy of US$2 to US$4 per year. To ensure that they can remain at school, FOCUS supports about 1,000 needy children by paying their levies.

Contributions from the community

Initially, ownership of the project rested largely with FACT but the care programmes have been owned increasingly by community organisations. Community members who are not family visitors have given their time and materials to help orphaned families. Their contributions include ploughing fields, repairing broken-down housing and giving advice on agriculture, health care, child care and income supplementation. Others have given time, money or material gifts in order to set up community-based fundraising initiatives, which are encouraged by FOCUS. Self-help projects, such as chicken rearing, mushroom growing, sewing and gardening are encouraged. These projects generate income for site activities, promote community involvement and help to teach children skills they can use to be self-reliant. Some micro-credit schemes also operate to benefit individual volunteers, who thereby learn family-based income-generating skills and simple money management.

Cost of the programme

FACT leaders say that the FOCUS programme is a cost-effective method of caring for children. It is a process whereby the Lord multiplies the small quantity of bread and fish available in order to feed the multitude. All it takes is commitment from the Christian community to work for the cause of orphans.

The cost of the programme in a four-year period is shown in the table below. Notice that the total cost is reduced as the number of volunteers and orphans increases. When there are more volunteers, travel costs are reduced and resources can be shared with many more families. All amounts are in US$.

Average cost per	1996	1997	1998	1999
Volunteer	373.8	204.2	150.4	68.2
Visit	1.8	1.3	0.4	0.1
Family	37.9	24.0	9.5	4.4

Bethany Project

Organisational structure

The Bethany Project has a simple organisational structure. At first there was a voluntary steering committee, a prayer group of local volunteers and a few staff workers. Then an Advisory Board was formed, which in turn gave place to an Executive Committee. In order to comply with conditions required for registration, this committee must not contain volunteers. Registration is a lengthy process, progressing from district to provincial and then to national level; it involves visits, changes and approval at each stage. It took three years for the Bethany Project to achieve registration. The Executive Committee consists of a chairman, vice-chairman, treasurer, secretary, vice-secretary and three other members. At the time of our visit, the staff team comprised the Director, Project Co-ordinator, Administrator and Youth Co-ordinator. Volunteers and other members of the local community assisted them.

Office administration

Patience Msipa undertakes most of the administrative tasks in the office. Her training included a secretarial course comprising business English, shorthand, computers and accounts. Patience pays the bills and books venues and accommodation. She has given names to different accounts, e.g. transport, and watches expenditure on each account. She also helps the Director to set budgets and write proposals to funders.

Funding dilemma

It can be much more difficult to obtain funding for administration than for direct support to families because it does not have the same emotional appeal. Administration, however, is the vital link between a child and a donor. Transport and fuel are also essential components in the tasks of distributing food and paying school fees.

Administrative role of the Director

The Director also has a part to play in the administration of a project. At Bethany Project, Gill Grant:

- supervises and manages the staff team
- writes budget proposals for funding and resources
- initiates policy changes: the next will be to establish a child protection policy
- has hands-on involvement: accompanies the Project Co-ordinator on visits to some community programmes and families
- types her own letters and documents
- promotes the work of the project, e.g. forms partnerships with funders
- represents the project on local and national multi-disciplinary committees.

Recommendations from the Administrator

- Set up clear and legal procedures for receiving donations.
- It is best to start with only a few children until you become established.
- It is preferable to give material goods, such as children's clothes, in small amounts rather than many at once.
- Rather than give to people who come to the office and ask for aid, pass on the requests to the review meetings so that everyone can see that things are given to the community to distribute. This makes them more accountable. If families come to the office for help, tell them they must talk to their vatete.
- Do not register anyone in the programme at the office. The onus is on the community programme committee to assess, register and provide names. The community is trained to identify 'children in especially difficult circumstances'. After a funeral, someone must do an assessment.
- Try to train them to look for their own solutions from the start, rather than run to the project for help every time. Bethany Project does not pay school fees unless the committee contributes something too.

- Be sure that new people in your organisation are good stewards, training them if necessary.
- Set up procedures to protect the organisation and its assets. Define these in writing and make them available on a long-term basis to all staff members.
- You need a strong Executive Committee to control the organisation and to contribute both finance and time. Choose people who are interested in seeing the work develop and who will exercise control and support. Not those who just want to see their names on the letterhead but have no time to help.
- When you start, remember that you are all learning; support one another.
- If you start with unqualified workers, you can show what you are doing in order to obtain funding. However, if those who start the project as volunteers are not employed later, someone who has given time for free may feel left out. If your organisation can afford it, it may be better to define roles and to employ qualified people for each section of the work from the start. When Bethany Project procured funds and started employing educated people, some accused them of not working for God now they had money.
- Stand firm where budget decisions are involved. Whatever staff members want, even if they get emotional, you cannot give money if it is not in your budget. As Administrator you are accountable to the Executive Committee and you must be strong. Everyone thinks his/her own department is a priority, but if you keep the books you know what can be afforded.
- Always try to get information on the aims, objectives and motives of potential partners or funding agencies. Sometimes the Bethany Project feels constrained to decline offers from potential funders who have an incompatible agenda.

Handing over

If you have set up your organisation under expatriate leadership, you may find it difficult to find a suitable replacement. A national person is preferable but it will not be easy to get someone suitably qualified and experienced. In addition you may have a problem with the low level of trust given to nationals, even in their own community. Local businesses trust a foreigner more than they trust a national because of the general level of corruption. A good national leader will take time to build trust but it can be difficult to get funding. It may be a long time before you can relinquish complete control and you will need to institute a high level of accountability and support.

Funding

The Bethany Project has good support from local businesses as well as one or two formal donor organisations. Some donations received by the project are from churches and individuals in Zimbabwe and overseas. External auditors audit the accounts every year. NGOs must submit audited accounts to the government, otherwise registration can be withdrawn.

ZOE

Administration

Jean Webster spends about two half days a week doing administrative tasks such as answering letters and emails, generally networking, collating surveys, dealing with statistics and keeping simple accounts. She aims to keep records of those to whom she has spoken and who have come back to her, following them up closely rather than relying on them to take the initiative and be self-starting. Jean is working to strengthen the administrative, structural base of ZOE to make room for growth. To this end, she aims to hold an annual conference for most of the co-ordinators.

Local support

Once a programme is operating with volunteers, the leaders consider material provision. The principle is that local churches must draw from their own resources and those of the local community. The main needs are food, clothes and housing. Many districts have a 'giving box' in the church for items of food and clothing that members want to give. It is worth approaching more affluent churches in the cities, especially those where there are existing relationships. Churches are encouraged to talk to local businesses, seeking donations with no strings attached. Food, particularly lacking in drought time, is distributed according to family need, as determined by the volunteers' records. Church members who are willing and available help to build or repair housing.

Resources for the orphan ministry

Support comes from several concerned church groups overseas who make a long-standing commitment to a specific area. These connections have been made through established links with the church in Zimbabwe or through the Children Alone Trust (CAT), which is given gifts to pass on to the ministry. CAT opened an account in Jean's name and she is accountable for the expenditure. She keeps a triplicate receipt book and an income/expenditure cash book, which she sends to CAT for accounting purposes.

Group income-generating projects

In rural areas, projects are usually teamwork and play a vital part, although they rarely raise enough to sustain the work, especially in the current economy. A group of Christian farmers in Bindura are now training people in 'Farming God's Way' and sharing this vision with the churches. IGPs are often 'kick-started' with a small contribution from Jean's funding sources.

In the urban ministry in Bulawayo, materialism is more apparent, but the need is still great. Mrs Manceda, wife of the Bulawayo Co-ordinator, has previously worked in micro-enterprise. With an assistant, she has provided skilful training, and churches have received initial funding for a pilot scheme to enable each family to set up in a small business.

Personal finance

Jean's personal funding comes from her home church in Britain. She originally shared the whole process with the members and with other Christians. The Baptist Church commissioned her, and church members write about Jean's work in their magazine. She receives a regular gift each month and further gifts that come in from contacts. When Jean's supporters realised that she was using public transport, they collected enough to buy her a pick-up truck. The church pays for the diesel and major servicing.

Friend raising

Jean sends out one or two newsletters a year and tries to keep up personal correspondence. She recommends using short airletters, saying it is best to keep within bounds of what you know you can do, as one can easily get behind with correspondence. CAT gives her the names and addresses of those who have sent gifts, so she can respond with letters of thanks. When Jean goes home every three years she tries to visit those who give regularly and holds a get-together to keep in touch with them.

AIDS: Education and Prevention

This section is based mainly on the work of the Bethany Project, which places particular emphasis on this aspect of the ministry. It ends with a section based on an article in a recent journal.

HIV awareness and prevention youth programme

At the time of our research, Darlington Changara had been working as Youth Co-ordinator with the Bethany Project for three months. He co-ordinated all the youth activities within the Bethany Project, setting up AIDS Action Clubs in schools and Out-of-School Youth Clubs. He had established five In-School Anti-AIDS Clubs for 10- to 14-year-old orphan children, and two Out-of-School Youth AIDS Awareness Groups. Within the year, 23 In-School Clubs have been formed. There are 63 schools in the area and these are being incorporated into the programme over a period of three years.

Aims

The aim of these clubs is to teach children and youth HIV prevention within a broad context of lifeskills, choices and values that are more likely to lead to their health and wellbeing. Young people learn how to live in a way that will reduce their chances of becoming HIV-positive. The teaching approach is fun and participatory and it is hoped that the children will eventually become peer educators within their communities. The Bethany Project hopes to develop further its youth training programme in the future.

Purpose of the programme

The specific purpose of the youth programme is to build up good moral values and Christian principles. Based on biblical teaching, abstinence is advocated in preference to protection or 'safe sex' (the approach adopted by the Health Ministry). When the Bethany Project works alongside a Ministry programme, it backs up the 'official' approach with its own message based on biblical principles. Children need to develop good attitudes and behaviour, and learn to live God's way. Programmes teach them to live to their full potential – not just as 'good kids' but becoming 'God's kids'.

The In-School Clubs programme

This programme is aimed at AIDS education and social support and is present in both primary and secondary schools. A typical number in a group would be 50 and it is considered important that this contains a large proportion of orphans and children in especially difficult circumstances as well as children of better off families. Activities include quizzes, drama and music – all with an AIDS-educative theme – and may incorporate competitions.

AIDS education is a part of the national curriculum and the voluntary clubs, held in the period following lunch, complement this formal teaching. Two teachers run each school group and receive special training. They work to a prepared syllabus and progress is reviewed weekly. Head teachers are supportive and teachers are selected from those who volunteer, with regard to their particular ability and suitability for this type of work.

Darlington finds people with appropriate knowledge and skills to train the teachers. Trainers may come from bodies such as the Child Protection Agency, Education Authority, Social Welfare Department or Health Department. Darlington is attending a one-year course to learn counselling and social support skills.

Since he was appointed as Youth Co-ordinator there have been many improvements.

(a) Children are running the clubs themselves, with support from trained teachers, known as 'club patrons'.
(b) Clubs include children who are not orphans.
(c) They have recreation facilities.
(d) There is a measure of psychosocial support.
(e) They are setting up IGP training.

Recommendations for organising In-School Clubs

1. It is essential to hold a sensitisation programme, to make people aware of what you want to do. Explain this at a higher level. Go with the regional education officer to encourage head teachers and others in the schools.
2. Team work is essential, in order to cover many schools, and it is more economical to involve others.
3. Fit sensitively within the school timetable. For example, hold the club when other children are also in club activities, such as after lessons, not instead of, but not when others are going home.
4. Network with other organisations. Don't duplicate efforts within the same school, and don't clash with other groups.

Bethany Project hopes in the future to organise a retreat for children in their final year of school. They will invite representatives from the police, health ministry and education department, a college principal and local pastors to talk to the young people.

Out-of-School Youth Groups

Out-of-School Youth Groups cater for the 16- to 25-year age group, those who have left school or perhaps never attended. Two of these groups have so far been established. The focus of these groups is AIDS education and also what the young people can do for the orphan children. The groups are awaiting funding but have started by discussing problems and solutions to relevant life problems. They are using some Bible-based periodicals covering health and social issues, e.g. 'About HIV/AIDS', 'About love and relationships', 'About STDs' and 'About faithfulness'.

Recommendations for organising Out-of-School Youth Groups

1. In most areas people have one day off per week. It is best to choose that day for activities.
2. Work with local area leaders. Inform them of what you are planning and doing or they may accuse you of negative teaching. If young people misbehave, you may get the blame.
3. Darlington considers that it is vital to give youth enough time to be together in appropriate activities, for example at a centre with TV/ video facilities for videos on AIDS, and how people grow in different cultures. They also need libraries that contain books on health education. They need to be able easily to visit the project's offices, which should be open and accessible to young people. A larger office to include these facilities would be ideal.

KAOS

KAOS is a youth group that had just started when we visited the Bethany Project. Darlington provides guidelines for the group. Ideas come from the young people themselves. They submit them to him to agree their viability.

The aims and purposes of the youth group (from the constitution)

The club's objective is to help young people to have upright morals and to meet their spiritual and psychosocial needs. The club aims to help those who are depressed and indulging in alcohol and sexual laxity.

The activities of the club

1. To identify ways in which young people can enjoy their youth without involving themselves in sexual activities and alcohol abuse that can lead to loose morals.
2. To participate in entertainment activities that benefit the youth members without causing offence to any other party involved, e.g. owners of a venue for a specific event may stipulate that there will be no alcohol.
3. To enable the members to take part in fundraising activities for the benefit of vulnerable children.
4. To train youth in health education and any other information felt to be helpful or necessary.
5. Promoting the rights of young people.

Constitution

1. The club name to be used in all cases shall be Kicking AIDS Out of Shabanie and the abbreviation to be used will be KAOS and that no other club in Zvishavane shall use that same name in any way.

2. The club shall be an affiliate of Bethany Project.
3. The club shall engage in fundraising activities with the aim of helping vulnerable children not registered by Bethany.
4. The club shall engage in entertainment activities that will benefit the entire group and at the same time promote social interaction with the community.
5. All club members are to be governed by the constitution.

One of the young founder members also gave us the following information.

- The aims and purposes of the group are to educate families about AIDS and its prevention, to raise funds to help people with AIDS and to improve young people's relations with their parents.
- Activities include sweeping the streets and pavements in a town clean-up (already done) and a sponsored walk and other fundraising activities (planned).
- The club has membership conditions, an executive committee, democratic decisions, an AGM and disciplinary procedures for misconduct.
- The club is looking for a space to set up training and sports activities in order to divert teenagers from sexual activities which often lead to HIV/AIDS. Also, sports training could lead to a career and encourage young people to consider physical health and fitness rather than drug or alcohol abuse.
- The club wants to set up a library accessible to youth and others. It would provide access to books on AIDS prevention and related matters.

Prevention of the problems of AIDS orphans

The following was inspired by a study of SAFAIDS News. Although perhaps not strictly relevant to a handbook on community care, it is included here as a valuable insight into practical ways in which it might be possible for the health of women to be improved, and in consequence for the numbers of orphan children to be reduced.

Poverty

Likely causes of immuno-suppression in rural African women, which hastens the conversion to full-blown AIDS, are fundamentally due to poverty, traditionally based inequality and the drudgery of farming. These can be summarised as:

Malnutrition, poor diet
Exposure to other infections

Successive pregnancies
Re-infection with STIs and HIV
Exposure to organophosphate pesticides
Fatigue due to hard labour
Anxiety due to poverty and family rejection

In order to promote the increased health and survival of mothers in rural areas, we need innovative approaches to addressing their needs, as both a care and a development strategy.

Appropriate information

This must be geared to the level of illiterate and semi-literate people in rural areas. It should include teaching about a healthy lifestyle, such as the need for clean water, a nutritious diet and nutrient supplements as well as safe sexual practices. It would also be useful for them to know how to prevent infection, how to recognise the first signs of HIV infection in themselves and others and how to live positively with HIV.

Counselling and HIV testing

If tests for HIV status were widely available and women were encouraged to take advantage of them, early diagnosis would be possible. This would enable women to have suitable counselling and treatment, including dietary supplements.

Nutrient supplements

There is a need to make nutrient supplements widely available for HIV-positive people. They are presently available in parts of Africa in World Health Organisation care packs, for people who are dying of AIDS. If they were also given to those at an earlier stage of the disease, particularly those who have extremely poor diets, many early deaths could be prevented.

Supply of clean water

Contaminated water can cause intestinal infections and diarrhoea. These can lead to extreme dehydration, which can itself be fatal.

Outlaw the use of dangerous pesticides

Research has shown that exposure to organophosphates and carbonates can suppress immunity capacity in humans (Sharma and Tomar (1992) and Rodgers et al (1992)). This reduces their resistance to bacterial infections, viruses and parasitic diseases. In many African countries, women and children apply toxic chemicals, generally without any form of protection. In addition, many of the vegetables consumed by people in the rural areas contain harmful pesticide residues.

Advocacy

What is advocacy in the context of community-based orphan care?

Advocacy entails pleading in support of others and speaking for those who are powerless to speak for themselves. Orphan children are low in social status and do not know their rights. They need people with more knowledge and power to lobby for them. Advocacy will help children to access legal advice and assert their rights, and to get social and medical assistance.

How can adults advocate for children?

During training, volunteers must learn what children's rights are and then they must be willing to stand up for them. Volunteers and others in the community can advocate for children, but they also need to be educated. At grass-roots level more information and understanding is needed. Partnership with the media can help to disseminate information and change attitudes.

Avoid labelling

Calling children 'AIDS orphans' labels them and can lead to them becoming withdrawn or teased by the other children. It is preferable to call them children. They should be able to play with other children and not be constantly reminded that their parents died of AIDS.

Protect children's rights

Children should be taught their rights, for example regarding sexual, physical and emotional abuse. If a child is being abused, ask the social worker to visit and monitor the situation. In Zimbabwe, for instance, there is now a law against taking children's belongings, so if anyone takes things from widows and children it can be reported to the police. Legally, every child has the right to shelter and education, though in practice this is not happening.

Liaise with social welfare

It is vital to build a good relationship with the social worker. Many people do not know what funds are available from the social services, especially if an old person or a child is looking after the family. Talk to a social worker about the needs of the children and find out how to apply for assistance.

Represent children at the local level

There are many ways in which interested adults can advocate for children.

- Report cases of child abuse or child labour to social welfare and police.
- If a case goes to court, insist on the use of child-friendly courts.
- Deal with injustice and abject poverty by talking to village leaders or urban councillors.
- Talk to staff in the schools, if necessary begging teachers not to send children away but to give them time to pay their fees.
- Look at each child's background to see whether help can be obtained from another source.

Educate children

Lobby for free education, so that poor children are better able to look after the family if their parents die. Educated children are less vulnerable and therefore have greater life expectancy. Girls who stay at home, rather than going to school, are more likely to have early sex and get HIV. Teach children to be open with trusted adults. In clubs, children should be encouraged to tell their problems to staff, who can take the matter to the police and relevant authorities.

Obtain certificates

An easier process to obtain birth certificates, when achieved, will solve future problems. Many children fail to get places in secondary school because they have no birth certificates. When they are adults, without birth certificates they will be unable to obtain identity cards or passports and will not be entitled to vote.

Lobby for change

Project workers can advocate for children by lobbying for change at government level, together with other NGOs and through other agencies. In Zimbabwe, members of the AIDS Network join together to try to influence government policy. They work with the Child Protection Society to get birth certificates for children. NANGO (National Association of NGOs) lobbies the Ministry of Finance for a child-friendly national budget. They form childcare forums so that together they can work out the best care for destitute children.

Influence international law

The projects we researched have limited influence with the government in Zimbabwe, but the Bethany Project did sign up to a UN document on child rights. Since a Child Protection Act has been passed, cases of abuse can be taken to a higher level.

Network for the cause of children's well-being

- Liaise with town people, other organisations, local authorities, government ministries and churches.
- Represent your organisation at workshops in town. Sit on relevant committees.
- Attend local council meetings and meetings of the Ministry and social welfare.
- Liaise with other governmental services and NGOs.
- Attend meetings of other organisations that have similar problems to yours and work together to lobby for change.
- Become members of district and provincial child welfare forums and national associations of NGOs and other bodies.
- Exchange visits with other orphan care programmes.

Note: A full explanation of the use of networking in community care programmes can be found in the following section, written by Chloe Elkin.

Networking for child rights – a guide for NGOs

This is a new report by the NGO Group for the Convention on the Rights of the Child. It is available online at: http:www.crin.org/docs/resources/publications/NGOCRC-a-guide-for-NGOs.pdf Aimed at national child rights coalitions, it uses the convention on the rights of the child as a basis. It is a practical guide for NGOs that are in the process of forming coalitions and for existing coalitions who want to develop their work. The sections are:

- Developing a framework for action
- Organising for impact
- Methods and approaches for advocacy
- Monitoring and reporting.

This report would be useful for networks involved in advocacy or working with large rights-based organisations.

Networking
by Chloe Elkin

Chloe Elkin is currently working for Viva Network in the Network Development Department. She read Development Studies at the University of Leeds and is studying for a Master's Degree in the same subject from Middlesex University. She has had first-hand experience of community development in Brazil and Zimbabwe. She completed a three-year period facilitating and co-ordinating a local network for Christians reaching 'children at risk' in Harare, Zimbabwe, connected to the Viva Network movement. In this section Chloe gives advice and recommendations based on her experience of working with projects that had initiated community-based programmes in Zimbabwe.

Paul Starkey in his book *Networking for Development* (1998) says, 'Networking involves making contacts and encouraging reciprocal information exchange and voluntary collaboration.' In other words, networking is about getting to know others working in the same field to share useful information and potentially work together to help realise common goals.

The aim here is to talk about what networking involves, how it can be of use, and to look at ways in which individuals and groups working with children affected by AIDS can start to work together.

Why don't we network?

Often in a local area a number of Christians from various churches and Christian organisations are helping 'children at risk'. Sometimes these groups work together well, but often they don't. Here are three possible reasons why they don't.

Reason 1: Lack of awareness of one another

Often projects just don't know who is working in the same field as them, not because they don't want to know them, but because they don't interact with others on a day-to-day basis outside of their project. Working with children affected by AIDS is more than a full-time occupation, so project leaders and workers simply do not have the time or energy to look beyond their programmes to gather information about who is doing what, where and who could help them.

Reason 2: Lack of awareness of the benefits of working together

Sometimes when given the opportunity to get to know others in the same field, projects do not take it because they are not aware of the benefits to their project, other projects and to children affected by AIDS generally if they do. As networking is therefore not a high priority for them, they do not take given opportunities. Later we will talk more about these benefits.

Reason 3: Lack of desire

Often projects are competing for limited resources, particularly funding, and must justify what they are doing to donors in order to win more funding to continue their programmes. There is a popular misconception that in order to justify what they are doing they must be the only ones in the field doing it! Projects may also compete for relationships with local professionals, politicians, church leaders and others who may be able to help their programmes. Such individuals may have limited time and therefore may only be able to invest in one project. All these factors create a sense of competition between projects and fear that getting to know others too closely may threaten their own standing. Again, this demonstrates a lack of understanding about the benefits of working together, which far outweigh these perceived drawbacks.

Why should we network?

Let us now look a little more closely at the benefits that may come out of networking, for your specific project, for children affected by AIDS in your area and for the community at large.

1. Less duplication

Projects working together will lead to a more co-ordinated, integrated response to children affected by AIDS in your local area, meaning that more children are reached with care that is appropriate for them.

2. Improved standards of care

As projects build relationships with one another, shared experience, ideas, expertise and models of care will help them to learn new things and improve overall standards. This will be like iron sharpening iron.

3. More information

As projects build relationships with one another, they will share information such as where to buy the cheapest rice, the best person to talk to in the Ministry of Health, the best book to read on Project Management or the latest HIV therapy, and therefore help one another to increase knowledge and contacts.

4. Effective referrals

There may be a particular group of children that you do not reach out to but that come up in your dealings with children affected by AIDS. For example, you may come into contact with street children and be ill equipped to help them. Knowing others in the field will allow you to refer these children to the right place, knowing that they will receive the care that you cannot provide.

5. Shared opportunities

Some opportunities can best be maximised on a large scale, such as the opportunity to use a building, a training course or a bulk purchase. We can best use economies of scale when there is more than one of us. Other opportunities may come your way that you cannot use now, such as a volunteer or a bag of material. Other projects that you know may be able to use this service, so you can pass it on and therefore the opportunity is not wasted.

6. One voice

Christians together can shout more loudly on behalf of the 'children at risk' in their care. A louder shout is much more likely to be heard and acted upon in our churches, government agencies and secular institutions. We can therefore have a far greater influence on behalf of the children in our care.

7. Encouragement for workers

Working with children affected by AIDS can be quite lonesome. There are unique burdens associated with this work that others may not appreciate. There is therefore great encouragement from having fellowship with others working in the same field. With such encouragement, we are much more likely to continue in our work long term.

8. We receive God's blessing

God loves unity. In Psalm 133 it says, 'How good and pleasant it is when brothers live together in unity! ... For there the Lord bestows his blessing, even life for evermore.' This is perhaps the greatest benefit of all.

Three steps to begin networking

Step 1: Introspection

It is sometimes necessary to sit back and take a look at where your project is before you are able to reach out and start networking. Ask yourself: 'What can I as a project and as an individual give to someone else working with children affected by AIDS?' Consider what the strengths of your project are, such as your experience, your model of care, the skills of your staff, the ability to pray, a venue or a useful contact and consider how these may help another project in the same field.

Then ask yourself: 'What does my project need?' Consider which areas you need assistance with, such as training for your staff in a specific area, particular resources, a contact in a government ministry or the use of a car. Now consider who you and your project could get to know that might be able to help. Knowing why you are networking will help you to be targeted in your approach and will help you to get the most out of the relationships that you build.

Step 2: Building relationships in your local area

The next step is to start building relationships with others in your local area. There are several steps you may go through to do this:

(a) Is there already a local network to link in with? There may already be a network for Christians reaching children at risk in your local area. Many of these will be affiliated to the Viva Network movement. If you do not know if a network exists near you, then contact Viva Network and find out. If there is a local network near you, this will be a great place for you to gather information about who else is working with children affected by AIDS. Go and meet someone from the network to find out how you can get involved.

(b) Is there no network? If no formalised children at risk network exists in your area, then look at whom you already know working with children affected by AIDS and make an effort to start communicating. At some point a group of you could consider if you would like to establish a network formally to help you work together long term. If so, then contact Viva Network, who will equip you with information to help you do so.

(c) Building relationships. Relationships are the foundation for any effective networking. The better your relationships are, the more likely you are to work together. Focus then on becoming friends with others working in your field. Listen to each other's problems, learn from each other's strengths and focus on the things that you have in common. At first it may seem that you have more differences than common ground, but as your friendship grows you will be surprised at how similar your experiences may be. Pray for each other and even take communion together to remind yourselves of how you are part of one body.

(d) Useful links. When you have something to give or something that you need, think about those you are building relationships with and consider whether you can link to see either a need met or a gift transferred. The more you know one another, the more you will be able to do this. If there is a network in your area, you could use the central contact point to do this if you do not know the right person to contact yourself.

(e) Forming partnerships. As you get to know others in the field well, you can start to look at what you are doing to help children affected by AIDS and what others are doing and see if there are any ways in which working together will enable you to help the children more effectively. Consider whether a partnership can be created to address a specific area of need in the long term, such as buying in bulk or a joint programme for AIDS testing, in order to share resources. You will of course all maintain

your own identity as individual projects, but will become more effective in what you do. The opportunities are endless!

Step 3: Building relationships beyond your local area

(a) Networking country-wide. As you start to network in your local area, you will see the immense benefits from working together. There may come a time when you need to think beyond your local area to what is going on in other regions of your country. There may be some really important work going on that could impact what you are doing, or there may be others out there who could learn from you.

You can use the same processes suggested in Step 2 to work out if there are networks operating in other parts of your country that you could link up with. If there are none, then perhaps you could think about starting to communicate with others yourself. Once you know others beyond your local area, you could even think about setting up regular communication and information on areas concerning work with children affected by AIDS. Think about perhaps phoning each other regularly, emailing, writing letters or even the occasional visit to get good communication going.

(b) And even further afield... Further even than this, you can begin to communicate with others working with children affected by AIDS outside of your country. Viva Network facilitates a discussion forum on this subject. This may be of great interest to you. Again, do get in touch with Viva Network to find out how you can be a part of this. There is also information on how to link with other information at the international level on the Viva Network website. If you do not have access to the Internet, then write a letter to Viva Network and the information can be sent to you by post. There is a whole world of information out there. So let's get networking!

Evaluation

What is evaluation?

Evaluation is an exercise that is carried out in order to assess or appraise the adequacy, effectiveness and worth of what is being done. It is a way of looking objectively at a programme to assess what progress has been made and to determine its value.[2]

---

[2] The first page of this section has been quoted from the Viva Network Handbook 'Body, Mind & Soul', by the same author.

The purpose of evaluation

It is essential to monitor and evaluate all aspects of a project in order to:

- give everyone a chance to pause and review what has been happening
- highlight what is working well and be encouraged to continue
- see what activities and methods are worth repeating
- find out what is not successful and prevent its repetition
- discover what mistakes have been made and avoid making them again
- allow all staff members a chance to express their views and opinions
- appraise the personal and job satisfaction of workers
- obtain feedback from clients and participants
- examine whether everyone in the team is working effectively
- give a sound basis on which to make changes where necessary
- establish whether the aims and purposes of a programme are being fulfilled
- see how the project is viewed internally and by those outside
- improve communications
- provide input to the training curriculum
- continue developing the programme on ethical and professional lines
- document and pass on to others the experience and knowledge gained.

The process of evaluation

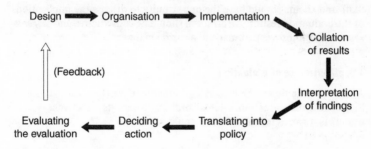

Criteria for evaluation

- It should address the same issues as the aims and goals of the project.
- It should develop and change as the programme develops and changes.
- It should be comprehensive and continuous.
- Everyone involved in the project should be included in the evaluation process.
- Everyone should be briefed as to the purpose of the evaluation.

- As far as possible, workers and clients should agree the design of the evaluation exercise.
- It must be done in a non-threatening way to achieve honest answers.
- Ground rules on confidentiality should be agreed in advance.

Methods of evaluation in CBOC programmes

The projects we studied were using a mixture of evaluation methods.

- Record keeping and feedback.
- Bi-monthly reviews.
- Return visits to monitor and follow up local programmes.
- Questionnaires and surveys.
- Formal and informal interviews and discussion.
- Anecdotal evidence gathered in workshops and elsewhere.

External evaluation

It can be valuable to appoint an external evaluator to undertake a full assessment at less frequent intervals. This person is likely to view the project more objectively and should be able to give guidance for the future.

After the evaluation

Staff and clients should have the opportunity to discuss the implications of the evaluation results. All criticism should be constructive and any suggestions for improvement made in a caring manner.

The effectiveness of evaluation

At appropriate times, the leaders and other staff workers should discuss the process of evaluation itself in order to assess its effectiveness. Is it useful? Is it worth repeating? How could it be improved?

What aspects of community-based care can be evaluated?

1. Relevance
2. Effectiveness and impact
3. Efficiency
4. Ability to replicate programmes
5. Implications for future development
6. The value of training

FOCUS

Record keeping and feedback

Volunteers record when they visit each household, to whom they talk, what they do, what needs they observe and what action is needed for that particular household. The supervisor collates this information and sends it to FACT, where the team uses it to establish the effectiveness and impact of the programme and decide how to develop the project. The same data is used to collate statistics and to report to donors.

Bi-monthly reviews

Volunteers report monthly to the supervisor at a site meeting, which community leaders are encouraged to attend. FOCUS staff members attend these meetings every two months to give support and encouragement. Regular reporting of their activity to their peers and community leaders is a way of motivating volunteers and ensuring that they understand that their efforts are recognised and appreciated. It also helps the supervisor to compare the level of support given to individual households and, if necessary, to discuss with the volunteers where visiting is erratic or insufficient.

Formal evaluation exercises

FACT also conducts formal evaluation on a regular basis. The following sections outline the conclusions FACT drew from the evaluation exercise carried out in 1999.

1. Relevance

- The goals and objectives of the programme were being achieved.
- The goals of the initiative were relevant and realisable given the resources and capacity of the community.
- The objectives were relevant to the assessed needs and resources of the community.
- New needs had been identified and responded to since the start of FOCUS.
- The strategies were relevant to existing social, cultural and political contexts.
- The programme challenged existing structures. Advocacy for children is a new concept among many of the community members and participation in AIDS-related activities through working with orphans had been a challenge for some churches involved.

2. Effectiveness and impact

- FOCUS had identified a large proportion of orphans in the catchment area and prioritised the most needy orphan households.
- It had succeeded in identifying, training and mobilising village-based volunteers to regularly visit orphan households.
- Members of the rural community owned the programme and some had initiated new activities in response to perceived needs.
- The four rural programmes had developed successful levels of programme activities, but the model was less effective at urban level.
- Material support had been targeted to the most needy households.
- The total numbers of visits by volunteers during the first four years were:
  - 1996: 12, 000
  - 1997: 20, 000
  - 1998: 54, 000
  - 1999: 93, 000

3. Efficiency

(a) The available resources were used to the maximum.

(b) Resources were mobilised efficiently, though sometimes disbursements were delayed or donors placed limitations or conditions on expenditure.

(c) The programme could be made more efficient by redesigning the strategy so that support was offered to families affected by HIV/AIDS during parental illness rather than after parental death. This could be done through a combination of the two programmes (Homecare and Children Affected by HIV/AIDS) and by combining prevention activities with care provision.

(d) Human resources could be used more efficiently by encouraging greater involvement of other agencies, e.g. health workers, teachers, police and political and traditional leaders.

(e) The particular skills and commitment of volunteers were crucial to the efficient management of the initiative. The experience gained by FACT in the management of volunteers could be valuable to other organisations.

(f) Expectations raised by the community regarding financial commitments were often not provided through the programme. This decision was based only partly on limited funding availability. The main reason for limiting material support was due to concerns about programme sustainability.

(g) The use of resources was monitored reasonably, though with so many small gifts of material support to programme beneficiaries, it is difficult to monitor how these are targeted. FACT closely monitors its own use of resources and relies on community groups to monitor use of those provided by FACT.

(h) There was fair co-ordination with other partners.

4. Replication of programmes

(a) Following the successful evaluation of the first FOCUS programme, it was replicated in four further rural sites and one urban site.

(b) In 1995, the Bethany Project in Zvishavane, Midlands Province, was set up following visits to the FOCUS programme.

(c) The strategy had been found useful and adaptable for other countries in southern and eastern Africa.

5. Implications for future development

The research and evaluation activities of the FOCUS programme also identified some newly emerging problems. These included:

- Psychosocial needs of orphans. Focus group discussions were held with groups of orphaned children to identify their perceptions concerning effects of loss of parenting, discrimination, exploitation and abuse.
- Child-headed households. A study of the surveys completed by community-based volunteers revealed why such households were occurring. Households were interviewed. Feedback from this research led to greater awareness of the needs of children in especially difficult circumstances.
- HIV prevention needs in orphaned girls and needs of HIV-infected orphaned children and mothers. FACT programme researchers are continuing to study problems that have been identified by community members.

The value of training

- Training had been provided wherever possible. FACT had been able to help community organisations to develop their own project proposals.
- The recruitment and training of volunteers matched their skills to the needs of the initiative. Incentives were provided to keep volunteers motivated.
- The regional training programme was assessed by means of questionnaires plus visits to African countries from which most participants had come. Three NGOs in Zambia, Kenya and Malawi had set up orphan programmes following training with FOCUS. Two further NGOs had initiated CBOC programmes.

Bethany Project

Regular reviews

When a member of the Bethany Project staff attends review meetings, along with vatetes and the local committee members, she monitors the work by talking to them, especially about difficult cases, and hearing their reports on current issues. She notes whether the community is able to meet its needs, if there are new issues or where training is needed. The staff member enters data on a form, from which she compiles a report for the Director and together they decide what action can be taken. In the income-generation projects, progress is monitored each month and reports are prepared for the donors who fund the projects.

Assessment of the AIDS Prevention programme

In the Youth Programme, Darlington tests the children regularly to see what they have grasped. He writes monthly reports and checks back to measure performance against his plans. In the clubs, lessons are reinforced with writing and teachers assess learning of previous work. Teachers expect to see changes in behaviour but this is more difficult to evaluate. A good indicator, and an encouraging one, would be to see a reduction in reported new cases of STDs. (HIV/AIDS statistics are not recorded separately but are likely to follow trends for STDs.)

Results of workshop evaluation

It is always good to look at what has been achieved before considering changes and improvements. During a workshop, Bethany Project staff members were invited to discuss their perceived successes and failures and to identify problem areas. Their comments included the following:

1. They have mobilised and equipped all 16 rural wards and one urban district. Communities are accepting that the orphans are their children and this is their problem, not the government's or due to a curse.
2. Voluntary work is unusual in Zimbabwean culture but Bethany has inspired people to care about the children and changed their attitudes. The vatetes are motivated by the smiles re-appearing on the faces of the children, and people saying, 'The children are our country's future.'
3. In anti-AIDS clubs, they have trained children in HIV awareness (biblically based).
4. They have managed to pay over 1,500 children's school fees and sent some for A-levels. Children have gained good examination results.

5. They have organised community income-generating projects to raise funds for children.
6. They have secured employment for some school leavers, especially those responsible for other children.
7. The children are becoming a part of the community again.
8. They have met some basic needs for the neediest children, e.g. food, seeds and clothing.
9. Before the Bethany Project worked in the district, there were small kids roaming the streets of Zvishavane. Now you will find that most street kids are not local but from other districts. Something is clearly being achieved in Zvishavane District.
10. They have gained support in the urban community, e.g. local businesses. Shopkeepers give them food nearing its expiry date. Charities such as local Lions Clubs raise funds or give various items.

Problem areas

1. The project leaders felt that the first wards where they set up programmes became donor dependent. Now they take a different approach.
2. They have had limited success in gaining the support of bank managers, town council leaders and heads of government ministries.
3. The HIV/AIDS awareness programme did not sufficiently involve teachers. Some groups only met when Bethany staff came, not regularly. Of 50 people trained to lead out-of-school youth groups, only six continued. The others did not take ownership of the programme. Since Darlington was appointed as Youth Co-ordinator, there have been many improvements.
4. Some of the income-generating projects failed, probably because they were equipped with materials but not business skills or knowledge. They also needed more support and monitoring.
5. The Bethany Project has not yet been able to reach out to street kids, due to a lack of resources.
6. The project has so far failed to mobilise residents of squatter camps to care for orphans within their communities. Some of these groups of 'temporary housing' created by the government resettlement programmes have existed for 10 to 20 years. Sanitation levels and housing are poor, the children are dirty and do not go to school and there is a high rate of HIV/AIDS in these camps. Different cultures co-exist within the camp, making for difficulties with establishing community-based care. Maybe a different approach is needed and staff should take advice from those who work in such camps.
7. The project does not always get support and understanding from some authorities, for example regarding school fees.

8. They would like to create more awareness of children's issues among the business community.

Implications for the future at the Bethany Project

- Community-based orphan care must continue.
- There is a longing to see a God-fearing AIDS-free nation.
- They wish to be used as a resource to train other organisations that want to start similar programmes. However, they must take care to keep the major focus on the children.
- The AIDS awareness lifeskills programme must aim for more effectiveness rather than just bigger numbers.
- While it is necessary to discourage over-dependency, hungry children and adults need money to buy essentials such as food and baby milk. The solution may be to set up more income-generation projects in communities, youth groups and individual households. Bethany Project could be more proactive and provide adequate training, and maybe even obtain funding for a salaried IGP supervisor.
- There is a need to recruit and train more staff, including an assistant to help with family co-ordination and an assistant administrator.
- The Bethany Children's Trust UK is recommending an external audit-style evaluation soon to ensure that they are on track.

ZOE

Informal and anecdotal evidence

In the Zimbabwe Orphans through Extended hands programme, Jean Webster says that she finds it difficult to document and do formal evaluation when busy working, but that she hears others ask questions and show approval. She invites constructive criticism from visitors from other ministries and takes positive encouragement from their comments. The number of orphans being cared for is growing and sick children are getting better.

When Jean shares her experience in pastors' fraternal meetings, she is thrilled to find that pastors and volunteers catch the vision and invite her to come back for training. That generally happens and works well. Occasionally, however, she has not heard again from a group she has spoken to and regrets that she has been too busy, working alone, to follow up the contact.

Return visits to monitor and follow up local programmes

When Jean pays return visits to monitor and obtain feedback, she experiences the obvious integrity and zeal of co-ordinators and committees in different areas. Very few volunteers drop out. She sees that the community-based orphan care works and that it is what is needed. Because the ministry primarily offers care and encouragement rather than 'hand-outs', it can be owned and in some measure sustained by local churches. She also sees, however, that expansion and development would be a question of resources, requiring more promoters with area co-ordinators who know the people well.

A Final Word from the Authors

There is no doubt that whatever the difficulties faced by the three projects we studied, they are all making a difference in the lives of children. In the course of our research for this handbook, we visited households in which older siblings and elderly grandparents struggle to meet the needs of orphaned children in extremely difficult circumstances. Nevertheless, the lives of these families are being transformed by the care of the volunteers who bring them reassurance of the love of God as well as emotional comfort and practical help. Although life remains a daily challenge for the children, most are now back at school or soon to be involved in income-generating schemes. Through the patient work of all those involved in community-based orphan care, the families are encouraged to persevere and children regain their lives. Volunteers visit them regularly, pray for them and, by being available to give holistic care, prove that they are indeed 'friends in need'.

Les and Marion Derbyshire can be contacted at:
mj.derbyshire@ntlworld.com or les.derbyshire@ntlworld.com.
Your questions, comments and feedback are always welcome.

Viva Network is an international association of Christian work among children at risk.

PO Box 633, Oxford OX2 OXZ, England.

Tel: +44 1865 320100
Fax: +44 1865 20356
Email: info@viva.org
Website: www.viva.org

Viva Network resource services

In order to help project workers find suitable resources for their needs, the Viva Network offers a personalised resources directory. It itemises appropriate written, audio and training resources along with information about how to obtain them and the likely cost. Contact Sally Clarke on: resources@viva.org The resource directory is available on the web at www.viva.org

In addition, resource libraries are being developed in regional offices, from which items can be borrowed.

APPENDIX F

SERMON/TALK OUTLINE AND OTHER RESOURCES (WORLD VISION)

Outline of a talk based on Luke 5:12–16

Introduction

- AIDS affects millions of people in the world, including many church-going Christians.
- AIDS isn't about numbers but real people – people who are sick, people who have lost close friends and relatives, children who have lost parents (you could refer to or use the Monologues here).
- AIDS is having a devastating impact on the lives of families, communities and nations, especially in Africa. Many of those affected suffer terrible ostracism.
- Christians have responded to the HIV/AIDS pandemic in different ways. Some see it as the judgement of God, others as an opportunity to express compassion and care.
- How should we respond?

Jesus and the man suffering from leprosy

- Like HIV and AIDS, leprosy caused its sufferers to be ostracised, usually out of fear or ignorance.
- Like HIV and AIDS, some believed leprosy was caused by God's judgement on the individual (see Numbers 12:10ff; 2 Kings 5:26–27).
- Confronted with a man suffering from leprosy, Jesus reacted in an unexpected way:
  - He touched the man (v. 13a) – the importance of human contact for someone living in isolation.
  - He healed the man (v. 13b) – his healing was physical, social and spiritual.
  - He encouraged the man to rejoin his community (v. 14) – being part of a community is an important part of being human.

A Christian response to HIV and AIDS

Any response to the AIDS epidemic needs to address three major issues:

1. Prevention – ensuring that anyone at risk of catching the disease (and that means *everyone*) knows how to prevent infection. The church is the world's largest 'grass-roots' organisation and has the reach and the moral authority to play a major part in education programmes. Since most people are infected through sexual intercourse, many Christian agencies (including World Vision) adopt the ABC message:

A Abstain from sex outside of marriage.
B Be faithful to your partner within marriage (known in Africa as 'zero grazing').
C If in any doubt about the HIV status of yourself or your partner, use a condom.

2. Care of those living with AIDS – ensuring that everyone who is infected is treated with dignity and receives all the medical, practical and spiritual help possible. Compassion not condemnation is essential. Jesus' example in treating the man with leprosy is particularly relevant here.

3. Support for everyone else who is affected – including partners, carers, widows, widowers, children, orphans. The Bible's teaching about care for widows and orphans is particularly relevant here (e.g. James 1:27).

Why Christians should be concerned
- Although the number of people in some countries who are HIV-positive is small, the body of Christ, especially in Africa, is suffering (1 Corinthians 12:26) in various ways:
  - Christians have died or lost partners, parents or friends.
  - Christians are caring for the sick, often at great personal cost.
  - Christian leaders are carrying a huge pastoral burden.
- In some places the church has added to the stigma by condemning or ostracising those who are affected, contrary to the example of Jesus.
- Christ's example shows us that we should care for the suffering, particularly those who are stigmatised by their community. Note also Jesus' treatment of 'sinners' such as Zacchaeus (Luke 19:7).

What we can do
- *Pray* regularly for people whose lives are affected by AIDS, including medical staff, carers, young people, the elderly, the sick, widows, widowers and orphans.
- *Ask* your church, denomination or aid agency for more information

about what they are doing to prevent the spread of AIDS and care for those who are suffering.
* *Support* efforts by Christians or others to make a difference.

Quick quotes for AIDS talks or sermons

As pastors we are called to walk with those who are affected by this disease, to offer support and compassion and bring the Christian message of love, forgiveness and hope to the world. We are inspired and guided by the example of our Lord Jesus Christ, who ministered to all without fear or discrimination. *Statement of Anglican Primates, 2002*

Every day lost is a day when ten thousand more people become infected with HIV. We can beat this disease, and we must. *Kofi Annan – United Nations Secretary General*

Every human being is created in God's image ... Accordingly, all persons have worth and dignity, rooted simply in who they are (and not in what they do or achieve). This conviction about the preciousness of every life grounds the Church's teachings about HIV/AIDS. *US National Catholic AIDS Network*

Following the example of Jesus, the Church has long cared for the sick. The global spread of HIV/AIDS and the serious suffering that marks this disease challenged and renewed this ministry, especially in developing countries where health care resources are so severely limited. *US National Catholic AIDS Network*

Jesus redefined the meaning and activities of holiness. In Jesus, holiness included entry into the lives of others: holiness became an act of engagement, not a state of separation. In Jesus, holiness took on the suffering of others; holiness associated with what was meek, lowly, despised. In Jesus, holiness' healing touch was the touch of inclusion and participation; the touch that said 'you belong'. *Cathie Lyons of the United Methodist Church of America*

People living and dying with AIDS have spiritual and emotional as well as medical needs. They ask questions related to God and the soul, life and death, condemnation and forgiveness, eternity and transcendence, forgiveness and salvation. They are looking for pastoral counselling, consolation and acceptance. In some places, pastors and churches are the nearest or only resources available in times of crisis and need. *World Council of Churches*

Sadly, there have been many people infected by HIV who come from a church background. Even more tragic, most of them have been ostracised, neglected and ignored by the church. The time has come to say no to our fears and yes to embracing the dying. *Mennonite Brethren Church in Canada*

There can be no doubt that the heart of our Lord is broken by what is happening in Africa, even now. If nothing else, our hearts should burn within us as we face the fact that 13 million children in Africa have been orphaned because of AIDS, and that for each of them Jesus sheds his tears. *Tony Campolo*

We need to remind ourselves that God will not accept our acceptance of lives made wretched by geographical accident of latitude and longitude. We must wake up the sleeping giant of the Church; we must set up alarm clocks to rouse our politicians who also slumber. The choice is there before each and every one of us: to stop and tend to the distant pilgrim sick on the side of the road, or, a nervous glance, and we turn away ... away from the pilgrim, away from God's grace. *Bono – rock singer with U2.*

Monologues

These monologues (adapted from original interviews by Paul Birch and Paul Burbridge of the Riding Lights Theatre Company) are designed to be read out as part of an event or service to encourage Christian action on AIDS. They aim to bring out the ways in which HIV/AIDS affects the lives of ordinary people. Each monologue should be read by a different person. If you do not have time for all five, pick those that you think are most appropriate.

John's story (Tanzania)

It is my biggest regret that I did what I did. That I was unfaithful to my wife. Through what I did we both became HIV-positive. I cannot be sorry enough and it is an amazing thing that she has stuck by me. My children are HIV-negative, thank God, and I am able to keep them in school.

It's hard, though, because I cannot work at the moment – I have problems with my chest because of TB. If it hadn't been for the TB, I would never have gone for the AIDS tests. Counsellors persuaded me to have the test and I found out that I was positive. It was too late for my wife.

Now my biggest fear is for my children. They may not have the disease, but when I die, they will have to live with the consequences. I am very worried for their future. We are out in the country here and things are very hard. I am raising a cow and growing crops. So far we have managed, but when I die ... well, I don't know what will happen then, especially if my wife becomes sick too.

The counsellors wanted me to warn others before it was too late, but at first I was embarrassed. No one wants to talk about AIDS. I soon realised that things have to change, and if talking spares people's lives, it has to be worth it. The message for everyone is that prevention is better than cure and that a man should be with his wife – only one wife, not two.

Pauline's story (Kenya)

My name is Pauline Wanjiru Kamau. It took 13 years before I realised that I had AIDS. I had often suffered from sexually transmitted diseases before I separated from my husband, who used to work far from home. But I could not believe that I had suffered from HIV for all those years. It was even worse when I found out that my last born son, who is 13, also has the illness. Things have been very bad, but then I realised that you can go one of two ways. You can decide to spread the virus, as many AIDS sufferers do when they say that at least they will not die alone. Or you can decide to be positive. I decided not to spread the virus, even though things were very hard.

I lost my business and several jobs, through being too sick or for revealing that I had AIDS. I could not pay school fees either, but I was determined to buy food and shelter for my four children. I went to the local World Vision office and got referred to the Kariobangoi HIV/AIDS programme, where I received counselling. One of my children is now being sponsored through school. If they can get a good education and a career, they will be able to support themselves when my time to rest comes.

I am determined not to give up. I have set up a group, 'Wise Women and Children Living with AIDS', which tries to help us all live positively and to be educated about the disease. Explaining this condition to my children was very important so that I could prepare them for every eventuality.

If you asked me where this power to live comes from, I would have to say from God. For though many people have abandoned me, God is always close and will never do the same. I know that I have hope for now ... and beyond the grave in eternal life.

Duncan's story (Kenya)

My name is now important to people. My name is known. My name was not always important to people. It was irrelevant because I am an AIDS orphan.

My parents died of the disease when I was very young. It took them a long time to die and it was hard for me just to watch and not be able to do anything. They became very thin and were covered in sores and were sick for a long time. Everyone knew they had AIDS and so people avoided them. It was then that their names were forgotten. When they died, everyone watched me too, from a distance, to see if I was going to die. I became a thing to avoid rather than a boy called Duncan. And so I was left to fend for myself with the other AIDS orphans.

At least I wasn't alone – many others had lost their parents. Some of them were sick and some of them, like me, were not. But all of us were avoided. It was then that Spiriana took us in. She has two houses in the slums of Nairobi and we all live there. Each house has two rooms and each room sleeps eight of us on two mattresses. It's very cramped, but at least it's a roof.

World Vision are helping her to look after us, by sponsoring our education. I am training to be a mechanic. If I do well, I will give Mama Spiriana a gift. She has always called me Duncan.

Man Pich's story (Cambodia)

My son is dead. He was a soldier and when he came back to us he had AIDS. My daughter-in-law is also dead. She got the disease from my son. She worked very hard to look after him as well as my three grandchildren. In the end, when my son died, she could not even pay for his funeral.

None of us can afford much to pay for anything. She then came to live with me, and though I am 57 I have to work in the fields. I used to do this while my daughter-in-law was alive, and now she has passed away I still have to work because of the children. Sun Sophy is the youngest – only three. She is HIV-positive too.

Sun Sophy always asks me a few times a day for a hundred riels to buy the same kind of cake – the one she likes most. She points to her stomach and then says, 'I am hungry! I am hungry!' One day I did not give her the money because we were short. She pulled out a knife to threaten me to give her the money. A knife in the hands of my three-year-old grandchild!

Sun Sophy is very miserable. She has a skin infection on her head and because of her wounds, she smells. Most children won't play with her. It's a good job that her sisters do. They are very good and Sun Thai, who is the oldest, often says, 'I wish that happiness is with me and my two sisters in this life.' I wish for that too. I wish an end to the sickness that has killed so many and I wish for money to buy a little more food and medicine.

It is not a grandmother's job to see her family suffer so much and die before her own life is over.

Muni's story (Bangladesh)

This place is called Banishanta, but it has changed very much since the people came to teach us.

Many women come here to work as prostitutes. I came here after I was raped by the master of the house I worked at. I was his maid. After he did that, I was considered an embarrassment to my family and so they threw me out. I worked at a rice mill, but I was raped there also. I had nowhere else to go and so I came here to work as a prostitute. Many girls here were abused or raped before they ended up in this village.

AIDS is spreading more and more, and everyone is afraid of it. Once someone gets it there is no way they can live. A man came to talk to us about it and we used to tease him, 'AIDS is coming!' But he and others like him kept coming back to teach us. Now we make sure condoms are used and we understand about prevention. But not only that, we now have a pre-school for our children and I am being taught to read and write. There is talk of businesses being set up so that we can live another way. I am even thinking about becoming a volunteer to help tell others about the dangers of AIDS.

Yes, Banishanta has changed very much. It is more a place of hope these days.

Prayers

Prayer topics

- Pray for all those living with AIDS who face discrimination on a daily basis because of their condition.
- Pray for those who care for people who are sick as a result of HIV/ AIDS.
- Pray for the millions of children who have lost one or both parents to HIV/AIDS – and pray for those who are caring for them.
- Pray for all that is being done to inform and educate those who are vulnerable to HIV/AIDS.
- Pray for efforts to develop cheaper and more effective drugs to treat the symptoms of HIV/AIDS.
- Pray that the church around the world will play a major part in caring for those whose lives have been affected by HIV/AIDS.

A prayer for World AIDS Day

Almighty God, who enabled your servant Job to go victoriously through pain without denying your name, stretch your healing hand on individuals, families, communities, institutions and nations suffering under the weight of the AIDS epidemic. Strengthen and comfort the sick, widows, orphans and the bereaved. Send your Holy Spirit to renew us and to rekindle in us a sense of hope and victory. Grant wisdom, knowledge and perseverance to all those involved in research, policy making, funding and prevention, care, and treatment projects. And help us to understand better how we can defeat this disease. Amen. (*Written by Canon Gideon*

Byamugisha of the Church of Uganda, a leading champion in the fight against HIV/AIDS, who is himself HIV-positive.)

A prayer for people living with AIDS

Dear Father, we pray for all those people in the world today who are living with AIDS. We pray they will receive understanding, compassion and care from those who are close to them. We pray especially that the church worldwide will take a lead in this. We pray too for every effort to raise awareness of the disease and its devastating impact on the lives of individuals and families. We ask that around the world, people will be willing to change attitudes and lifestyles so that they and others might live. For Jesus' sake. Amen.

A prayer for orphans

Almighty God, full of compassion, remember the orphans of the world; children who have had their parents torn away by death or separation. Orphans who have to wait in misery and hunger for someone to plead their cause or come to their aid.

Almighty God, Father of the fatherless, let the cries of the innocent pierce the armour of heartless men and women, and teach them love, understanding and compassion. Amen.

APPENDIX G

ANTIRETROVIRAL THERAPY AND THE WHO 3 BY 5 INITIATIVE

Free medicine for 3 million people by 2005

Note by Dr Patrick Dixon: After long delays and political fights, the wealthiest nations have woken up to the fact that the majority affected cannot afford antiretroviral treatment, even though it prolongs life of most with HIV, and can prevent up to 66% of all infections in babies born to infected mothers. A new initiative aims to get free antiviral tablets to at least 3 million people in developing countries. This will also encourage people to be tested, because there is treatment available. Testing is a powerful way to prevent spread: those who are negative are motivated to stay that way, and those who are positive are more likely to change behaviour if they know they could infect someone else.

This is the system (still being developed at time of writing):

- WHO provides Department of Health in the country with medicines.
- Organisations apply in-country to partner with WHO and the government – usually by contacting the AIDS Control Programme or equivalent.
- Supply is given (probably in boxes containing enough for one person for one month).
- Other resources are provided, eg instant testing equipment, together with training of a nurse or nurses (no doctor is needed).
- Local population is encouraged by organisation to be tested, after counselling.
- Those who are positive, and have clearly defined patterns of ill health, or are pregnant, are started on treatment after a simple blood test, repeated every two weeks.
- Therapy is usually taken for the rest of the person's life unless stopped to allow the blood test to return to more normal levels.

- Careful records are kept of how the drug supplies have been used.
- Records are shown to the distribution centre, to get further supplies.

Smaller organisations and churches will need to partner with larger groups to get access. WHO will be monitoring each country to ensure good flow of medicine to organisations, and welcomes information about problems on the ground in making this work. See http://www.who.org – and adapted WHO material which follows. WHO/UNAIDS/Global Fund are very unlikely to achieve the 3 by 5 target without effective partnerships with churches and Christian organisations, particularly in Africa where the faith-based community provides such a significant proportion of care. A major challenge both for WHO and the church will be to find new models for partnership fast enough to get the job done.

This appendix has been edited from WHO publicly available material. Inclusion of this adapted material should not be taken as endorsement by WHO of any aspect of this book.

Treating 3 Million by 2005
Making It Happen: The WHO Strategy

Summary

'Lack of access to antiretroviral treatment is a global health emergency ... To deliver antiretroviral treatment to the millions who need it, we must change the way we think and change the way we act.'

LEE Jong-wook, Director-General, World Health Organization

'We must meet the challenge of expanding access to HIV treatment. This requires overcoming the formidable barrier of creating sufficient operational capacity – a key area where UNAIDS Cosponsor WHO must play a critical role. We have adopted a target of 3 million people on antiretroviral treatment by 2005 – a massive challenge, but one we cannot afford to miss.'

Peter Piot, Executive Director, Joint United Nations Programme on HIV/AIDS (UNAIDS)

This WHO strategy aims to set out how life-long antiretroviral treatment can be provided to 3 million people living with HIV/AIDS in poor countries by the end of 2005. HIV/AIDS has devastated the populations and health services of many developing countries. We must act now. Further, since this magnitude of scaling up HIV/AIDS treatment has never been attempted before, we must learn by doing.

To ensure that no time is lost, WHO-led emergency missions have already been sent to several of the countries with the highest burden. Detailed and measurable national targets are being set to track progress. Long-term WHO teams will be sent to key countries and health and community workers trained to deliver antiretroviral therapy. Simple, standardized guidelines are needed for testing, treatment, monitoring and evaluation. These are already being developed. An AIDS Medicines and Diagnostics Service (AMDS) has been established to ensure that countries have access to good quality medicines and diagnostic tests at the best prices.

Each of these measures requires rapid action and great flexibility. To achieve this, funding needs have been calculated, requiring resource mobilization on an international level. The strategy will continue to be adapted as it is implemented and as new evidence emerges. A global partnership is being designed and built, action is underway. This may be the toughest health assignment the world has ever faced, but it is also the most urgent. The lives of millions of people are at stake. Everyone involved must find new ways of working together and new ways of learning from what they do. This strategy is a step towards achieving that aim.

The crisis

Of the 6 million people who currently urgently need antiretroviral therapy in developing countries, fewer than 8% are receiving it. Without rapid access to properly managed treatment, these millions of women, children and men will die.

This human toll and the accompanying social and economic devastation can be averted. The delivery of antiretroviral therapy in resource-poor settings, once thought impossible, has been shown to be feasible. The prices of antiretroviral drugs, which until recently put them far beyond the reach of low-income countries, have dropped sharply.

COVERAGE OF ADULTS IN DEVELOPING COUNTRIES WITH ANTIRETROVIRAL THERAPY, BY WHO REGION, 2003

Region	Number of people on treatment	Estimated need	Coverage
Africa	100 000	4 400 000	2%
Americas	210 000	250 000	84%
Europe (Eastern Europe, Central Asia)	15 000	80 000	19%
Eastern Mediterranean	5 000	100 000	5%
South-East Asia	60 000	900 000	7%
Western Pacific	10 000	170 000	6%
ALL WHO REGIONS	400 000	5 900 000	7%

In 2001, partners within the Joint United Nations Programme on HIV/AIDS (UNAIDS) and other organizations along with scientists at WHO calculated that, under optimal conditions, 3 million people living in developing countries could be provided with antiretroviral therapy and access to medical services by the end of 2005. Nevertheless, treatment enrolment in afflicted countries continued to lag. On 22 September 2003, LEE Jong-wook, Director-General of WHO, joined with Peter Piot, Executive Director of UNAIDS, and Richard Feachem, Executive Director of the Global Fund to Fight AIDS, Tuberculosis and Malaria, to declare the lack of access to antiretroviral drugs to be a global health emergency. In response, WHO and its partners launched the 'Treat 3 Million by 2005' (3 by 5) Initiative. Given the proven feasibility of treating people living with HIV/AIDS in industrialized and developing countries, a *global target of treating 3 million people with antiretroviral therapy by the end of 2005* is a necessary, achievable target on the way to the ultimate goal of universal access to antiretrovirals for everyone who requires such therapy.

A health emergency propels action and upends 'business as usual' attitudes where they may exist. Reaching the 3 by 5 target demands new commitment and a new way of working across the global health community. Countries are on the front lines of the struggle, but they cannot succeed alone. Intensive, collaborative mobilization linking countries, multilateral organizations, bilateral agencies, communities and the non-state sector is required.

Prevention will remain central to all HIV interventions. Universal access to antiretroviral therapy for everyone who requires it according to medical criteria opens up ways to accelerate prevention in communities in which more people will know their HIV status – and, critically, will *want* to know their status. As HIV/AIDS becomes a disease that can be both prevented and treated, attitudes will change, and denial, stigma and discrimination will rapidly be reduced. Rolling out effective HIV/AIDS treatment is the single activity that can most effectively energize and accelerate the uptake and impact of prevention. Under 3 by 5, this will occur as part of a comprehensive strategy linking treatment, prevention, care and full social support for people affected by HIV/AIDS. Such support is critical – both to adherence to antiretroviral therapy and to reinforce prevention.

The fight against HIV/AIDS has implications for the entire health sector. The impact of HIV/AIDS both directly and indirectly undermines the performance of national health systems. Effectively countering this impact requires both a core response from within health systems and a broader societal response. As more health workers die from AIDS, health systems falter in delivering basic services. As workers across an economy die, revenues available for health systems fall, compounding damage to the health system. Increased access to integrated HIV treatment, prevention and care services is needed to reverse this pattern.

In addressing the needs of health systems in support of 3 by 5, the Initiative will consider both common and unique attributes of national and local health systems. The challenge of addressing these concerns across varied settings will entail the involvement of multiple stakeholders within health systems. Major new investment in countries' health systems will also be needed. New financial inputs must be carefully co-ordinated with existing resource and budgeting frameworks, including countries' Poverty Reduction Strategy Papers (PRSPs) and sector-wide approaches (SWAPs). Successful implementation of 3 by 5 will accelerate the attainment of Millennium Development Goals (MDG) for HIV/AIDS, as well as associated health and development MDGs. WHO is consulting intensively with national authorities and relevant international partners, including the World Bank, to ensure the coordination of efforts.

The strategic framework will continue to evolve through dialogue with partners as treatment programmes roll out and knowledge grows. The urgency of the crisis means it is vital to get started, creating channels to share evidence and make necessary changes as the work proceeds.

The goal

The goal of the Initiative is for WHO and its partners to make the greatest possible contribution to prolonging the survival and restoring the quality of life of individuals with HIV/AIDS, advancing toward the ultimate goal of universal access to antiretroviral therapy for those in need of care, as a human right and within the context of a comprehensive response to HIV/AIDS.

The target

By the end of 2005, 3 million eligible people in developing countries who need antiretroviral therapy will be receiving effective antiretroviral therapy.

Guiding principles

- *Urgency.* Immediate action is required to avert millions of needless deaths. The HIV/AIDS treatment emergency demands new resources, swift redeployment of resources, streamlining of institutional procedures and a new spirit of goal-focused teamwork.
- *The centrality of people living with HIV/AIDS.* The Initiative clearly

places the needs and involvement of people living with HIV/AIDS at the centre of all of its programming.

* *Life-long care.* Once started, antiretroviral therapy is for life. The world community has a responsibility to ensure uninterrupted medicine supply once antiretroviral therapy has been started.
* *Country ownership.* Country ownership of the programme and its activities is essential. The Initiative will strive to avoid duplicating existing country-level coordination mechanisms and to build a sustained response.
* *Treatment and human rights.* The Initiative will advance the United Nations goals of promoting human rights as codified in the Universal Declaration of Human Rights, as expressed in the WHO Constitution in seeking the attainment of the highest possible standards of health, and clarified in the Declaration of Commitment of the United Nations General Assembly Special Session on HIV/AIDS in 2001. Under 3 by 5, special attention will be given to protecting and serving vulnerable groups in prevention and treatment programmes.
* *Partnership and plurality.* The Initiative and its activities are centred on developing and strengthening partnerships and networks that maximize the contribution of all stakeholders in a given country.
* *Complementarity.* The Initiative will strive to ensure complementarity by integrating planning and funding with existing programmes and activities.
* *Learning, innovation and sharing.* Capturing and disseminating lessons across countries and regions in a rapid manner is essential to effectively and rapidly scaling up.
* *Ethical standards.* The Initiative will identify options for an ethical approach to meeting 3 by 5 targets.
* *Equity.* The Initiative will make special efforts to ensure access to antiretroviral therapy for people who risk exclusion because of economic, social, geographical or other barriers.
* *Accountability.* The Initiative will support the development of national accountability among policy-makers, providers, people receiving therapy and all stakeholders.

The strategic framework

Treating 3 million people by the end of 2005 will require concerted, sustained action by many partners. To chart the direction and to show what WHO itself will be doing to accelerate action, WHO has developed an initial strategic framework. WHO's 3 by 5 team assembled and refined the framework in intensive consultation with partners. This consultation will continue, and the framework itself will continue to evolve. The framework is complex, because scaling up antiretroviral therapy delivery in developing countries is a multidimensional challenge. Although such challenges are daunting, they can be met, as WHO and its partners have shown. The expansion of tuberculosis control and the roll-out of programmes for the Integrated Management of Childhood Illness (IMCI) are just two recent examples.

WHO's strategic framework for emergency scaling up of antiretroviral therapy contains 14 key strategic elements. These elements fall into five categories – the pillars of the 3 by 5 campaign:

* global leadership, strong partnership and advocacy
* urgent, sustained country support
* simplified, standardized tools for delivering antiretroviral therapy
* effective, reliable supply of medicines and diagnostics
* rapidly identifying and reapplying new knowledge and successes.

Pillar 1: Global leadership, alliances and advocacy

The most vital work towards the 3 by 5 target will happen in countries and communities, but global alliances and advocacy will be crucial enablers. UNAIDS has driven the global advocacy effort and catalysed growing international determination to respond to the HIV/AIDS crisis, including in the area of treatment access. Working within UNAIDS and alongside other partners, WHO will step forward and fully exercise its specific responsibility for the health sector – above all in advocating treatment.

WHO is committed to work in all global forums to spur urgent action towards universal access to antiretroviral therapy for everyone who needs it according to medical criteria. This is reflected in WHO's budget, which will commit additional resources to 3 by 5, while maintaining full support for HIV prevention. The foundations for global advocacy are equity, human rights and the evidence base for treatment and prevention. WHO, UNAIDS and partners will develop principles and approaches for implementing antiretroviral therapy programmes that: promote gender equality; include children and marginalized groups; maintain explicit promotion of antiretroviral therapy among the poor; and ensure comprehensive, community-driven treatment, care, prevention and support for all affected people.

WHO and its international partners are moving swiftly to identify roles and responsibilities among all stakeholders in the antiretroviral therapy scale up process and to establish mechanisms for ongoing collaborative action with all partners. Meanwhile, WHO will work closely with other multilateral organizations and international partners to ensure that the 3 by 5 effort is integrated into the broader global development agenda. International resources committed to 3 by 5 should be additional to the support for countries' efforts to achieve targets such as the internationally agreed Millennium Development Goals. WHO will support all national antiretroviral therapy programmes while focusing particular efforts on the high-burden countries in greatest need.

Key WHO actions and deliverables under Pillar 1 include

- establishing a WHO 3 by 5 budget committing hundreds of WHO personnel to be deployed at the country level;
- agreeing with all partners and stakeholders on their specific roles in 3 by 5;
- publishing with UNAIDS ethical guidelines promoting equity in antiretroviral therapy; and
- with UNAIDS, identifying the global funding gap and developing plans to close it.

Pillar 2: Urgent, sustained country support

The success of antiretroviral therapy programmes depends on coordinated, scaled-up country action. Countries must drive the process of expanding HIV/AIDS treatment, and countries' specific needs and capacities will shape the strategies and determine the scaling-up activities. WHO has significant opportunities to lend concrete support to these processes. WHO will provide implementers with essential technical and policy advice and tools and will cooperate with countries at every stage in designing and implementing national plans for scaling up antiretroviral therapy. Countries have demonstrated their demand for active collaboration from WHO by responding to the declaration of the global health emergency on 22 September 2003. Immediately following the declaration, more than 20 countries aligned their national goal to the global emergency and requested collaboration with WHO and partners, including visits by WHO 3 by 5 emergency missions.

WHO will use its leadership and advocacy position to encourage national political commitment to the 3 by 5 process within a comprehensive programme including HIV/AIDS prevention, treatment and long-term care. The Organization will support the preparation of coordinated national plans for scaling up with clearly defined roles and will also work to broker additional finances where these are required for scaling up in accordance with 3 by 5. WHO will support national operational capacity for scaling up antiretroviral therapy programmes, for example, by publishing simplified facility-level operational guidelines. The Organization will also use innovative strategies for quality assurance, such as certifying service delivery points. WHO will work with countries to ensure that scaling up antiretroviral therapy catalyses the strengthening of health systems.

The crisis in the health workforce facing many countries has implications both for the 3 by 5 Initiative and for the viability of health systems. Expansion of human resources for health is a critical need. WHO and 3 by 5 partners will work with countries to find and implement solutions that can quickly fill gaps while laying the groundwork for long-term sustainability. Key actions would include: intensified recruitment for specific tasks; overcoming fiscal constraints related to public sector hiring; recruiting both young people and experienced people into health work; increasing community input; initiating large-scale in-service training focused on antiretroviral therapy; and expanding pre-service training. Issues of recruitment, funding, training, appropriate incentives and retention of health workers will require a broader cross-sector dialogue, involving health and non-health ministries, trade unions and the private sector. The health workforce administration should include the various service levels (local and regional) and sources of services (public and private). WHO will develop a range of policy options and tools to assist countries, including standardized training packages for all cadres involved in delivering antiretroviral therapy.

WHO is committed to supporting the expansion of community involvement in planning and delivering antiretroviral therapy programmes. It will advocate for the engagement of people living with HIV/AIDS in all stages of the planning and roll-out of national treatment programmes and will work to expand resources and capacity for involving community-based organizations in national advocacy, planning and delivery.

Key WHO actions and deliverables under Pillar 2 include

- securing commitment to 3 by 5 targets and processes from all participating countries;
- agreeing on national 3 by 5 implementation plans with all stakeholders in each country;
- deploying WHO teams with appropriate skills to each country;
- training health and community workers in delivering antiretroviral therapy; and
- strengthening physical resources (laboratories and testing equipment) in each country by collaborating with funders.

The 3 by 5 Initiative and strengthening health systems

In many countries, the impact of HIV/AIDS is severely distorting health systems. AIDS death tolls are rising among health workers. Hospital wards overflow with HIV-positive people for whom no effective therapy is available. The 3 by 5 Initiative has the potential to reduce these burdens and strengthen health systems through mechanisms including: attracting resources to the health system in addition to those required for antiretroviral therapy; improving physical infrastructure; reducing morbidity and mortality among health workers; improving procurement and distribution systems; and promoting community empowerment. 3 by 5 programmes should be designed to strengthen the capacity of health systems to reach broader health goals, for example by promoting training and education that can expand a national health workforce for overall primary care.

LEADERSHIP. 3 by 5 creates a set of health system leadership challenges and opportunities that will require both strong central coordination and encouragement of local innovation and participation. To build and sustain momentum on 3 by 5, health and non-health ministries alike will need systems and skills to build coalitions and link their 3 by 5 activities.

FINANCING. Many high-burden countries are already engaged in policies to mobilize additional domestic resources for health, whether through fiscal policy or health systems financing, such as various forms of insurance. The aim will be to create sustainable financing mechanisms that ensure that poor people are exempt from co-payments. This issue is important for successful HIV/AIDS therapy because of evidence that co-payments reduce adherence to treatment regimens. Successful therapeutic outcomes depend directly on financing mechanisms that do not burden poor people. On the macroeconomic level, coordinating monetary and fiscal policies with foreign assistance could yield substantial benefits for 3 by 5 and health systems by overcoming bottlenecks or better aligning policies.

DELIVERY SYSTEMS. The mix of providers could change significantly as 3 by 5 scaling up proceeds. The public sector health programme could be expected to become more prominent among providers, but private sector efforts will remain substantial. As antiretroviral therapy expands, the demands on several essential delivery system capacities such as drug supply, laboratory facilities, patient monitoring and referral systems will increase dramatically. The operations of delivery system components must be coordinated to maximize impact.

MOBILIZING DEMAND. Uptake of antiretroviral therapy has been lower than anticipated in some high-prevalence settings, suggesting that, in addition to making antiretroviral therapy services available, physically accessible and affordable, demand must also be stimulated. Appropriate interventions include providing education on antiretroviral therapy and the availability of community-based services; reducing HIV/AIDS stigma and discrimination; strengthening entry points to HIV care; and improving referral from entry points to antiretroviral therapy. Community mobilization will be key to the process. The active involvement of community workers – especially to support uptake and adherence – will be a hallmark of the 3 by 5 strategy. Such community mobilization around the uptake of antiretroviral therapy will dramatically accelerate HIV prevention and catalyse wider public health benefits.

HEALTH INFORMATION SYSTEMS. Timely and accurate health information forms the essential foundation for making policy on, planning, implementing and evaluating all health programmes. The investments and innovation in monitoring and evaluating 3 by 5 will provide an opportunity to support the long-overdue strengthening and reform of country health information systems. WHO is working to strengthen health information systems and to advance a health metrics initiative that will contribute to monitoring and evaluating antiretroviral therapy.

Pillar 3: Simplified, standardized tools for delivering antiretroviral therapy

Rapidly scaling up antiretroviral therapy requires user-friendly guidelines to help health workers identify and enrol people living with HIV/AIDS, deliver therapy and monitor results. Providing these guidelines and updating them as new information comes in, is a central part of WHO's role.

Most people who have HIV/AIDS have no idea of their HIV status or the need to be evaluated for treatment. To help speed up the identification and enrolment of people needing antiretroviral therapy, WHO will simplify guidelines for HIV testing and counselling and for the referral of individuals at high risk of HIV disease. Guidelines will be developed for better use of multiple 'entry points' to identify people who need antiretroviral therapy and to start or refer for therapy. Such entry points include: tuberculosis clinics; acute medical clinics; programmes for the prevention of mother-to-child transmission of HIV; sexually transmitted infection and other reproductive health services; and services for injecting drug users. WHO will provide operational models for effective ways in which entry points can link with antiretroviral therapy programmes without compromising their own core activities.

WHO will also simplify and standardize clinical protocols for delivering antiretroviral therapy. It will revise antiretroviral therapy guidelines to include recommendations for standard first- and second-line regimens. Guidelines for adherence support will be developed for use by facilities, those monitoring treatment and those receiving therapy. WHO will publish guidelines on the requirements for laboratory monitoring of antiretroviral therapy. WHO, UNAIDS and their partners will make guidelines available for the nutritional support of adults and children on antiretroviral therapy. In addition, to enable programmes to be effectively monitored and ongoing performance improved, WHO will develop simple, standard, easy-to-use indicators for monitoring and evaluating antiretroviral therapy programmes. The Organization will publish guidelines and foster networks for the surveillance of antiretroviral drug resistance.

Key WHO actions and deliverables under Pillar 3 include

• using multiple entry points to identify people needing antiretroviral therapy;
• publishing and implementing simple, standard testing procedures;
• publishing and implementing simple, standard technical guidelines; and
• publishing and implementing simple, standard monitoring and evaluation systems at the country level.

Pillar 4: Effective, reliable supply of medicines and diagnostics

The viability of antiretroviral therapy programmes and the lives of people living with HIV/AIDS depend on a reliable, efficiently managed supply of quality medicines and diagnostics procured at a sustainable cost. WHO recognizes the importance of drug procurement and supply management for scaling up antiretroviral therapy and of the challenges many countries and providers face in this area. For this reason, a key component of the WHO 3 by 5 strategy is the establishment of an AIDS Medicines and Diagnostics Service (AMDS).

The AMDS will be a network hub, helping to coordinate the many ongoing efforts to improve access to medicines and diagnostics for treating HIV/AIDS. Accordingly, whenever possible the AMDS will seek to use and strengthen the capacity of partners already at work in this area.

The AMDS will not directly purchase medicine. However, such a service can do much to assist national authorities and programme implementers, drawing on the expertise of WHO and its partners in medicine policy and supply management. AMDS will provide an information clearinghouse for all market participants. It will give manufacturers, procurement agents and treatment programmes Web access to up-to-date demand forecasts, information on prices and sources and information on patent, customs and regulatory matters.

The AMDS will also build or disseminate technical tools to help programmes improve every step of the supply cycle. It will back these tools with a global network of experts who can be deployed in teams to help individual countries or programmes to improve their procurement and drug management. As a key part of this work, the AMDS will seek to improve security in the supply chain. To ensure quality, the AMDS will link with the WHO Procurement, Quality and Sourcing Project (prequalification), which assesses products and manufacturers according to stringent standards. The AMDS will work to strengthen the Project and increase manufacturers' participation. Finally, the AMDS will establish global and/or regional networks of buyers to help them share information and coordinate their purchases. In a later phase, the AMDS may facilitate the procurement of essential medicines and diagnostics by aggregating demand on behalf of buyers and supporting joint competitive and open negotiations or tenders.

Key WHO actions and deliverables under Pillar 4 include

- continuously updating demand forecasts and information on legal issues, prices and sources and making them available on the Web;
- disseminating technical tools for forecasting, procurement and management;
- supporting countries in all aspects of procurement, management and distribution through WHO teams;
- accelerating the pre-qualification of manufacturers, products, procurement agencies and laboratories;
- establishing global and/or regional networks of buyers; and
- deploying integrated monitoring and quality improvement teams.

Pillar 5: Rapidly identifying and reapplying new knowledge and successes

The most successful organizations are those that have valued and applied experimentation, innovation and real-time learning with rapid diffusion. The many challenges surrounding the scaling up of antiretroviral therapy require a robust programme to consistently learn, document, share and act.

Recognizing and building on success is key. WHO will document experiences and lessons from successful antiretroviral therapy programmes, such as those in Botswana, Brazil, Senegal and Thailand and projects elsewhere supported by nongovernmental organizations. It will document experiences and draw lessons from successful programmes addressing other diseases, such as Stop TB, the Global Polio Eradication Initiative and the fight against SARS (severe acute respiratory syndrome). These will be used to develop learning and advocacy materials for scaling up antiretroviral therapy in accordance with 3 by 5. WHO will seek ways to support learning networks – especially among and between developing country partners – to rapidly disseminate successful strategies and innovative approaches among programmes on the ground.

The foundation of scaling up antiretroviral therapy is urgency. We must learn by doing. Although lessons can be drawn from previous health programmes, the effort to expand HIV/AIDS treatment is unprecedented in many ways. We do not have pre-set solutions to the problems that will arise. For this reason, mechanisms for ongoing evaluation and analysis of programme performance and a focused agenda for operations research are crucial. WHO will coordinate and help to develop an appropriate agenda for operations research relevant to the needs of antiretroviral therapy programmes and will seek to ensure that data and new knowledge are rapidly incorporated back into the policy and practice of antiretroviral therapy programmes. Research priorities will include: identifying ways of measuring the externalities of scaling up antiretroviral therapy for the wider performance of health systems; monitoring resistance; and monitoring the impact of scaling up antiretroviral therapy on accelerating prevention programmes. WHO will carefully measure the impact of treatment programmes on prevention and then rapidly disseminate successful models to other countries.

Key WHO actions and deliverables under Pillar 5 include

- establishing global collaboration and communication systems and processes to enable sharing and reapplication;
- tracking progress towards the milestones established for measuring project success at the country, regional and global levels;
- quickly documenting and disseminating successful models from early country experiences;
- identifying and funding specific operations' research needs; and
- documenting and monitoring the impact of treatment programmes on prevention.

The next steps, timetables and tracking

WHO's 3 by 5 strategy is a work in progress motivated by the antiretroviral treatment gap emergency. During December 2003 and early 2004, detailed plans for each element of the strategy will be developed in collaboration with all stakeholders, including countries, funding organizations, multilateral partners, implementers of treatment programmes and community-based organizations. Specific detailed timelines and action plans for each deliverable will be established, along with measurement and review processes to monitor progress. Risks will be identified and plans to mitigate them developed.

A set of major milestones has already been developed by which progress can be judged and assessed. Regular, transparent reviews of progress will help drive the Initiative forward. A situation room will be set up at WHO headquarters for tracking progress towards the targets.

The budget required for WHO to implement this strategy estimates a need of US$ 350 million for the 2004–2005 biennium. Of this amount, 84% is allocated to fund staffing and activities in countries and regions. The budget also calls for several hundred WHO staff to be sent to work in countries and regions. It is further anticipated that 3 by 5 countries' efforts will be supported not only by WHO resources but also by important contributions from various partner organizations active in each country.

Global funding needs for the 3 by 5 Initiative

Based on current assumptions,[1] the total cost of achieving the target of 3 million people on ARV treatment by the end of 2005 is estimated to be at least US $5.5 billion, some of which has already been pledged.

Making it happen: changes at WHO

In response to appeals from countries, WHO and partners have begun deploying emergency response teams to countries to assess their specific situations in antiretroviral therapy and to identify how WHO and other partners can help accelerate the provision of treatment. By 12 December 2003, six country emergency missions will have been undertaken and a further 15 are planned. Each country is different, but common practical issues faced by all have enabled WHO to develop a broad-based country support strategy. The strategy is compatible with a wide variety of national programmes for accelerating the scaling up of antiretroviral therapy in accordance with the 3 by 5 target.

The 3 by 5 Initiative places the country at the centre of implementation. WHO is realigning its structures and redeploying resources to be optimally prepared to convert commitment into action. The changes will equip WHO country offices to better support national scaling-up efforts, to make use of the country-based resources of UNAIDS and the UNITED NATIONS at large, and to coordinate activities with other partners. Initial WHO country assessment missions will be followed by long-term teams to support antiretroviral therapy expansion in countries. The first long-term country-based 3 by 5 team will be on the ground in at least one country by the end of January 2004.

Each WHO regional office will have a team whose sole task is to support the implementation of the Initiative. Properly staffed and supported, the regional offices will play a critical facilitating and coordinating role, enabled by their close working relationship with countries.

At WHO headquarters, the 3 by 5 team is within the HIV/AIDS Department, in the new HIV/AIDS, Tuberculosis and Malaria cluster, which will coordinate its planning and actions across WHO's clusters, regional and country offices. This will ensure linkage of all available expertise that contributes to antiretroviral therapy scale-up and health

---

[1] WHO 3 by 5 technical paper 'Estimated cost to reach the target of 3 million with access to antiretroviral drugs'.

THE TRUTH ABOUT AIDS

systems strengthening. This team is supported and complemented by a high-level WHO 3 by 5 Task Force that will coordinate the inputs of the Director-General and Assistant Directors-General.

The HIV/AIDS Department sponsors ten working groups focused on specific issues that relate to:

- country support
- partnerships
- community involvement
- entry points to treatment
- treatment guidelines
- accelerating prevention
- monitoring, evaluation and surveillance
- capacity development
- operations research
- the AIDS Medicines and Diagnostics Service.

Each working group has developed a technical brief explaining its activities. These briefs are available. The working groups will be reviewed after six months; new groups may be established as the needs of antiretroviral therapy programmes evolve, and existing groups may be reformulated in the light of progress and experience. In addition, specific working groups in the HIV/AIDS, Tuberculosis and Malaria cluster will ensure effective sharing, lesson learning and problem solving across the cluster and Organization along certain themes. These include a working group on strengthening health systems and on access to medicines and diagnostics.

Working with partners

No single agency can achieve the target of 3 million people receiving antiretroviral therapy by the end of 2005. It could not be realized without the firm commitment to treatment already shown by many countries, the increased funding pledged or flowing from a variety of sources and the treatment centres already established in many settings with the help of numerous partners. There is significant activity on which to build in scaling up antiretroviral therapy.

This comprehensive Initiative requires the development and maintenance of a wide range of relationships. The alliances and partnerships necessary for 3 by 5 to succeed are extremely broad: national and local governments, civil society, bilateral donors, multilateral organizations, foundations, the private sector (as employers and as treatment implementers), trade unions, traditional authorities, faith-based organizations, nongovernmental organizations (international and national) and community-based organizations.

People living with HIV/AIDS and the activist community are indispensable partners at all levels of WHO's activities.

Establishing and maintaining effective alliances and partnerships takes time and resources. Coordination and collaboration are critical to fill gaps while avoiding duplication of effort – from the level of district-led initiatives right up to the international level and the United Nations system.

A 3 by 5 partners group has been formed, open to all who have been active in and committed to scaling up antiretroviral therapy in resource-constrained settings. The strategic framework presented here was discussed in draft form with the group, and the rich feedback and comments have helped shape the final framework and text of this document.

At the country level, particular attention will be paid to strengthening the stewardship role of government while enabling constructive dialogue between the state and non-state sectors. Both the private health care sector and the wider business community will be crucial in expanding the availability of antiretroviral therapy.

At the international level, WHO is involved in close and ongoing consultation with major bilateral initiatives and donors. WHO will coordinate with all other United Nations agencies to harness each organization's comparative advantage. Among the specific resources that can be brought to bear for maximum impact are: UNICEF (United Nations International Children Emergency Fund) on issues involving AIDS and children, and in procurement; the International Labour Organization on work with the public-private interface, workplace and labour; the United Nations Development Programme on capacity-building; the United Nations World Food Programme on nutrition and food issues; the United Nations Population Fund on reproductive health; and the UNAIDS Secretariat on country coordination, advocacy and leadership for all activities related to HIV/AIDS. The active involvement of the World Bank and the Global Fund to Fight AIDS, Tuberculosis and Malaria is vital to ensure that financial resources flow quickly to countries and programmes that show commitment to scaling up.

Beyond 2005

This Initiative does not end in 2005. Antiretroviral therapy does not cure HIV infection and must be taken for life. When properly managed, it can transform AIDS into a chronic disease similar in many ways to diabetes or hypertension. Nevertheless, withdrawing or ending treatment will lead to the recurrences of illness and with it the inevitability of premature death. Lifelong provision of therapy must be guaranteed to everyone who has started antiretroviral therapy. Thus, 3 by 5 is just the beginning of antiretroviral therapy scale-up and strengthening of health systems.

Further, although achieving the target of 3 million people on anti-retroviral therapy will test the capability of the global health community, the target covers only half the global HIV/AIDS treatment gap. It will leave another 3 million people in urgent need of antiretroviral therapy. Progress achieved in scaling up access to antiretroviral medicines by 2005 must rapidly be extended to people who are still deprived.

Eventually, almost all of the more than 40 million people now infected with HIV worldwide will require access to therapy. Looking beyond 2005, WHO and its partners will be developing a new strategic approach to maintain the gains of 3 by 5 and to extend them, using sustainable financing and delivery mechanisms, so that antiretroviral therapy becomes part of the primary healthcare package provided at every health centre and clinic.

Mobilizing Communities to Achieve '3 by 5'
The WHO '3 by 5' Community Mobilization Plan

Background

WHO and UNAIDS have identified the global HIV treatment gap as a public health emergency. In setting the target of 3 million people on anti-retroviral treatment in developing countries by the end of 2005 (the '3 by 5' target), the aim is to mobilize the many stakeholders globally, regionally and locally who all need to play a part in rapidly expanding access to antiretroviral therapy (ART) in resource-constrained countries.

Affected communities, vulnerable groups living with HIV/AIDS and faith-based organizations have been a driving force in the response to the HIV/AIDS epidemic in many countries, performing a critical role in advocating for access to antiretroviral therapy (ART) as a human right, as well as filling gaps in health sector capacity through the direct provision of services. These responses have been highly successful in many countries, even though the resources made available to support community-based activities are often limited and stigma and discrimination remain pervasive.

There is strong consensus that the '3 by 5' target can only be reached if the capacity of community- and faith-based organizations – including vulnerable groups living with HIV/AIDS – is further legitimized and greatly expanded.[2] The full engagement of civil society, where necessary in part-

---

[2] For the purposes of this section, 'community' refers broadly to all of the individuals and groups of individuals affected by HIV/AIDS. These include people living with HIV/AIDS who are and who are not taking ART, their

nership with the public and private sectors, is essential if HIV/AIDS treatment and care is to be provided to the millions who need it. It is also a necessary prerequisite to the full realization of the human rights of all people living with HIV/AIDS, including their rights to the highest attainable standard of health and to freedom from stigma and discrimination.

Objective

In accordance with the overall '3 by 5' strategic framework, the objective of this '3 by 5' Community Mobilization Plan is to strengthen the capacity of community- and faith-based organizations to be fully involved at all levels of the planning and implementation of ART programmes. This involvement can and should range from participation in the design of national ART scale-up plans to acting as treatment supporters for family members and friends living with HIV/AIDS and the evaluation of ART programmes, including quality assurance and operational research.

The plan was developed in consultation with community-based treatment advocates, practitioners and other experts in the community sector, as well as individuals within and outside the UN system.

The key elements of the '3 by 5' Community Mobilization Plan are:

- capacity-building grants for community-based organizations to strengthen their role in national HIV/AIDS treatment advocacy and education;
- promotion of community-driven approaches to HIV/AIDS treatment and care;
- facilitating stronger linkages and partnerships between the public sector and civil society through WHO technical support to governments;
- standardized training for community HIV/AIDS treatment supporters and educators;
- operational recommendations and policy guidance for ART implementers on involving communities in ART scale up at service delivery/ health facility level;

---

families and friends, community health workers including treatment supporters, and community leaders (including religious leaders and traditional healers). 'Community organizations' include community-based AIDS organizations, community-based organizations representing marginalized populations (e.g. sex workers, injection drug users, men who have sex with men), faith-based organizations, associations of people living with HIV/AIDS and their advocates, and other non-governmental organizations, including trades unions and other employee or employer associations.

- identifying and elaborating the key ethical principles for fair and equitable distribution of ART;
- promotion of community-based operational research and quality assurance, through partnerships with academic and other institutions;
- strengthening the performance, legitimacy, and accountability of the community sector through support for the establishment of guiding principles and minimum standards of good practice;
- increasing the capacity of WHO offices in regions and countries, and at headquarters, to provide effective technical support to and liaison with people living with HIV/AIDS, affected communities and their organizations;
- ensuring access to the necessary treatment, care and support for WHO staff living with HIV/AIDS, including adequate insurance coverage and reimbursement mechanisms for ART and other medical expenses.

Further input will be necessary to refine and implement this plan. In January 2004, WHO will call for nominations to an international '3 by 5' Community Advisory Committee (CAC), including ART expertise from people living with HIV/AIDS, community-based HIV/AIDS organizations and those representing marginalized communities, faith-based organizations and international development NGOs. The CAC will provide ongoing guidance to WHO on the implementation of the '3 by 5' strategy.

For '3 by 5' to be realized, the bulk of activities described in this plan must be undertaken within regions and countries. Accordingly, a series of regional workshops for people living with HIV/AIDS, community- and faith-based organizations will take place in 2004, beginning with Eastern Europe and Central Asia (the EURO region) in January. These workshops will focus on detailed work planning for the implementation of the plan and its deliverables.

The '3 by 5' initiative will necessarily involve increasing the number, capacity and competence of WHO staff. This will specifically include increasing the number of staff responsible for liaison with and technical support for civil society, including, where possible, increasing the number of WHO staff who are themselves living with HIV/AIDS. The focus of this expanded WHO capacity will be on building strong civil society participation in scaling up ART at regional level and in high burden countries and on strengthening the role of WHO as a facilitator of linkages between the public sector and civil society.

Detailed plan components

Capacity-building for national HIV/AIDS treatment advocacy

Increased technical and financial support for community-based organizations in resource-limited countries is essential to strengthen their capacity to advocate at a national level for scale up of ART and to promote community-based responses to the HIV/AIDS epidemic. WHO will work with partners to establish a fund to provide grants to support national treatment advocacy activities. These activities may include mobilizing political and financial support; promoting treatment literacy, such as information and education campaigns aimed at communities; work to combat stigma and discrimination, and participation in ART programme planning processes, such as Country Coordinating Mechanisms, National AIDS Commissions and other multi-stakeholder fora. Regional workshops will inform the development of the review process for grants and provide guidance to prospective applicants.

Initially, the Tides Foundation will be contracted to provide specialized technical support to WHO to work with community-based advocacy organizations, facilitate regional workshops and develop mechanisms for grants review and evaluation with community-based organizations in each region.

Milestones:
31 December 2003: Tides Foundation contracted to develop grants review process and organize regional workshops
January and February 2004: Regional workshops in EURO and Asia Pacific
March 2004: Capacity building fund established and call for proposals distributed
May 2004: Regional workshops completed
June 2004: First capacity building grants distributed

Promoting community-driven approaches to HIV/AIDS treatment and care

Enhancing the role of the community sector as a provider of health care services is essential to expanding overall human resource capacity to deliver ART and to ensuring that HIV testing and treatment become available in a manner that is socially equitable, acceptable and sustainable. In addition, the community sector has a key role to play in developing innovative campaigns to raise awareness of HIV testing, counselling and treatment. WHO is committed to supporting, evaluating and promoting community-driven approaches to HIV/AIDS testing, treatment and care, including fostering partnerships between community-based providers and the public and private sectors.

As diverse a range of approaches and partnerships as possible will be promoted and supported, including ART programmes driven by community- and faith-based organizations, PLWHA associations, large national and international NGO programmes, and community components of private and public sector initiatives. Drawing upon the expertise and infrastructure of UN, NGO and civil society partners, WHO will promote close collaboration between civil society and governments in the provision of HIV/AIDS treatment and care, offer technical support to community-driven service providers, evaluate the outcomes and impact of these programmes and document the lessons learned. A key objective of this initiative will be to strengthen links and referral systems between different fields, including, for example, sharing information and lessons learned about community-driven approaches to HIV/AIDS, TB, substance use, maternal and child care and family planning. Opportunities to work with traditional healers in AIDS treatment and care will also be explored.

Milestones:
April 2004: Civil Society Technical Officers in all WHO Regional Offices
*June 2004: Civil Society Technical Officers in WHO offices in 10 high
    burden countries*

These technical officers will also play a key role in facilitating stronger linkages between the public sector and civil society through WHO technical support to governments and the health sector.

Standardized training for community HIV/AIDS treatment supporters and educators

Family members, friends, people living with HIV/AIDS, FBOs, other peers and community members have a key role to play in helping individual patients adhere to long-term therapy, as well as educating others in the community about the benefits and limitations of HIV/AIDS treatment and promoting HIV/AIDS prevention. As part of its '3 by 5' training and human resources development programme, WHO will work with its partners to develop dedicated training modules for community- and peer-based treatment supporters and educators, including, where appropriate, a certification scheme for trainees and an inventory and referrals service for training.

The initiative will also support collaboration, exchanges of personnel and adaptation of training and education materials between grassroots peer education and treatment support programmes in developing countries, with a particular emphasis on promoting 'south-south' collaboration.

Milestones:
April 2004: Analysis of existing models of community treatment support
May 2004: Standardized training module for ARV treatment supporters
May 2004 onwards: Technical support for implementation of training

Operational and policy recommendations on community involvement in ARV programmes

Technical and operational guidance is required at health centre/facility level to guide implementers of ART programmes. WHO is working with many partners to develop initial operational and policy guidance for ART delivery at facility level, including specific recommendations on the basic package of care needed to support ART, human resource requirements, drug supply management and monitoring and evaluation. In addition, the document will make recommendations on the involvement of communities at service delivery points in the areas of advocacy and education; direct service provision; ethical decision making and the protection of human rights; operational research and quality assurance.

Milestone:
1 December 2003: Preliminary operational and policy recommendations on involving communities in ART implementation at service delivery/health facility level

Identifying and elaborating the key ethical principles for fair and equitable distribution of ART

Universal access to HIV treatment will not be achieved immediately in many resource-limited settings. Guidelines are therefore needed to help ensure an ethical roll-out and fair distribution of HIV treatment services in such settings. In the absence of such standards and procedures, decision-making about who receives ART is open to arbitrariness, corrupt practices, and even discrimination based on race, religion, ethnicity, gender, and sexual or political orientation.

WHO and UNAIDS are developing a guidance document for countries in this complex and sensitive area which will elaborate upon options that are both ethically sound and contextually and practically useful to national, local and institutional policy makers in countries. Topics that may need to be addressed include the extent to which patient eligibility criteria be determined on scientific, medical grounds alone; whether selection criteria that favour a particular set of patients are ethically sound and defensible; what categories or groups of people (e.g. women, women with children, pregnant women, young people and children, civil servants, trained human resources such as health workers and teachers, the sickest or according to other concomitant medical conditions, the poorest) should be considered priorities for ART services, and upon what grounds, and what procedural mechanisms should be established to ensure fair distribution of ART services.

Milestone:
31 January 2004: Preliminary draft guidance document

Promotion of community-based operational research and quality assurance, through partnerships with academic and other institutions

Service users, their families and communities have an important role to play in assessing the quality of health services, including HIV testing and treatment, and in shaping and implementing operational research programmes to improve service delivery. WHO will work to ensure that all community- and faith-based organizations involved in the provision of ART programmes develop partnerships with academic or other institutions with expertise in programme evaluation, operational research and quality assurance. This activity will be led by regional and country-based technical officers with a focus on high burden countries and those with highly concentrated epidemics.

Results of community-based research will be documented, disseminated and incorporated into all WHO HIV/AIDS programme and policy development.

Milestone:
June 2004: 10 CEO/academic partnerships in AFRO; 10 in SEARO and WPRO; 5 in EURO; 5 in AMRO; 3 in EMRO

Strengthening the performance, legitimacy, and accountability of the community sector through support for the establishment of guiding principles and minimum standards of good practice

As resources for ART are scaled up in resource-limited countries, community organizations will be subject to increased scrutiny and accountability. The community sector can consolidate its role and protect itself from illegitimate competition by adhering to agreed-upon guiding principles and minimum standards in the provision of HIV-related services.

WHO will support both new and ongoing processes to develop voluntary standards of practice in the community sector and strengthen them with further resources, particularly as they relate to the provision of HIV/AIDS treatment, care and support.

INDEX

553

ACET INTERNATIONAL ALLIANCE

The ACET International Alliance is a growing family of independent programmes in many parts of the world, all of which have a significant AIDS/sexual health component to their work. It began in the UK under the ACET name in 1988. ACET stands for AIDS Care Education and Training and was founded by Dr Patrick Dixon. Alliance members are united in a common aim to see an effective Christian response to AIDS:

* Unconditional, compassionate care for all affected by HIV/AIDS
* Life-saving prevention, respecting and upholding the historic teachings of the church
* Effective training with a holistic approach to personal and community development

Among other things, working together, ACET International Alliance has educated more than a million school students, reached over 100,000 health care workers, provided community care for over 4,000 people and distributed over 1.5 million booklets and 100,000 books. Other projects include in-patient care, orphan support, income generation, targeted prevention programmes and so on.

The Alliance consists of

* National Resource Centres: centres of excellence that are actively seeking to be an encouragement and resource to others in different countries who share the same values and vision
* Partner Programmes: organisations providing HIV-related services
* Development Partners: international organisations which act as resources to different parts of the Alliance

The Alliance is a network of organisations co-operating together, rather than a funding organisation. It does not have a big central administration and does not make central grants, so funding applications to ACET International Alliance will always result in disappointment.

The main work of the Alliance is carried out by programmes based in countries such as Uganda, Nigeria, Zimbabwe, Thailand, India, the Czech Republic, Slovakia, Ukraine, Croatia, England, Scotland, Ireland and Russia.

In almost every case, these independent initiatives are run by citizens of the same country. All projects aim to work in close partnership with local churches, with a strong emphasis on sustainability and reproduceability. Many of these programmes have project partnerships of their own, providing support, encouragement and technical expertise to other organisations and nations, usually in the same region, encouraging best practice, capacity building and effective, culturally appropriate programme development.

New Programme Partners join the Alliance on the recommendation of an existing National Resource Centre, after a period of working together. Members commit themselves to effective Christian action in the AIDS field, and to sharing/networking expertise, experience and resources as they are able.

Further information about ACET International Partners near you, up-to-date lists of countries with projects linked to ACET, more about what the Alliance does, as well as latest news about HIV, action packs and many other useful materials, is all available on the website:

http://www.acet-international.org
e-mail: isdixon@dircon.co.uk

Free copies of this book, as well as the shortened version, *AIDS and You*, can be ordered in bulk for distribution by Christian organisations in the poorest nations. *AIDS and You* is also available in French, Spanish, Russian and other languages.

Please send us any comments or suggestions about factual errors or omissions, and ways we can improve this book.

Please tell us about any programmes started as a result of reading the book. It is a great encouragement to our sponsors.

OPERATION MOBILISATION

Operation Mobilisation is pleased to co-publish and sponsor this edition, and is totally committed to seeing churches everywhere make a compassionate, caring and practical response to all those affected by HIV and AIDS, as well as helping to save lives.

OM was founded by George Verwer, whose energy, originality and challenge to discipleship and world evangelism touched many people. Emphasis on 'training through doing' was a central feature of the many teams that went out, in different parts of the world. The vision and eventual purchase of OM's mercy ships probably put OM on the map more than any other single factor.

Today, OM is a dynamic, global ministry with almost 3,000 full-time staff working in over 80 countries. It is committed to working in partnership with churches and other Christian organisations for the purpose of world mission. The different ministries of OM provide speakers for churches, conferences and seminars, experienced training in all forms of evangelism, leadership and pastoral care and a wealth of resources, including videos, books, presentation materials and prayer cards.

http://www.om.org
http://www.ombooks. org

TEARFUND

Tearfund is an evangelical Christian relief and development organisation. It was established in 1968 to enable churches in the United Kingdom to respond to the needs of poor people around the world. It works in partnership with local organisations and churches that share Tearfund's Christian beliefs, to bring help and hope to communities in need in over eighty countries. Tearfund also has a trading branch, Tearcraft, which markets products made by producer groups around the world.

Tearfund's approach to partnership is based on capacity building: working with organisations to strengthen them and to enhance their effectiveness. Tearfund also works through its own operational disaster response teams. Tearfund's main approaches are in the areas of community development, disaster management, advocacy and pro-poor economic development.

Our focus is on four key areas:

- HIV/AIDS
- Health, water and sanitation
- Basic education and literacy
- Disaster management

Tearfund supports a wide range of different community development, trading and training projects around the world, which:

- build on local initiatives, knowledge and capabilities
- encourage project ownership by local communities
- focus on the poorest in the community
- address the root causes of poverty and influence decision-makers
- recognise that people have a range of needs, including physical, spiritual, social, emotional and environmental

- allow the development of a two-way partnership with Tearfund
- are willing to evaluate the effectiveness of their work regularly

Tearfund produces a range of information publications, including PILLARS guides (see Appendices A and B), and *Footsteps*, a quarterly magazine for development workers, which shares best practice and learning.

Contact details

Head Office

100 Church Road, Teddington, Middlesex TW11 8QE
Tel: +44 845 355 8355
Fax: +44 20 8943 3594
Email: *enquiry@tearfund.org*
Website: www.tearfund.org

Resources Development – International publications

PO Box 200, Bridgnorth, Shropshire WV16 4WQ
Tel: +44 1746 768750
Fax +44 1746 764594
Email:pillars@tearfund.org
Website:www.info.tilz

WORLD VISION

World Vision is a Christian organisation and one of the world's leading relief and development agencies, currently helping over 85 million people in nearly 100 countries in their struggle against poverty, hunger and injustice, irrespective of their religious beliefs.

World Vision's Hope Initiative, launched in December 2000, is its global response to alleviate the worldwide impact of HIV/AIDS. This will be achieved through the enhancement and expansion of World Vision programmes focused on HIV/AIDS prevention, care and advocacy.

World Vision UK
Opal Drive
Fox Milne
Milton Keynes MK15 OZR

Tel: 01908 841000

EMMANUEL HOSPITAL ASSOCIATION

EHA, with a vision of 'Fellowship for Transformation through Caring' is a federation of Christian institutions and individuals that exists to transform communities through caring, with primary emphasis on the poor and the marginalised.

Working across thirteen states of North India, EHA provides appropriate and affordable clinical services through a network of nineteen hospitals to more than half a million patients every year. Besides basic health care, EHA is also committed to working with the communities to help achieve community health and development. This includes involvement in preventive health care, literacy training, establishment of income-generation projects and co-operative banking schemes. EHA also serves through spiritual ministries and leadership development.

Some of EHA's special focus areas of work include reproductive health, disaster management and HIV/AIDS.

EHA's vision for HIV/AIDS action

Emmanuel Hospital Association is firmly convinced that beyond the appalling figures and estimates of HIV's spread in India lies the reality that HIV/AIDS is a concrete set of challenges faced by real people in our communities. Any response to HIV/AIDS must therefore focus on the people themselves. EHA's response to HIV/AIDS in India is guided by the following people-oriented principles:

- Every individual should have the opportunity to explore and evaluate information, attitudes and behaviours.
- Relationships between people matter and they can be strengthened and empowered.

- It is possible to provide substantial healing of the whole person in the context of the family.
- 'Positive life' is within the reach of all, including people infected or affected by HIV/AIDS.

EHA's work in the field of HIV

One of the most important contributions EHA has made to the national health services is its pioneering work in HIV/AIDS management, especially among injecting drug users. Starting with Manipur HIV/AIDS Care and Prevention Project, EHA is positioning itself to be a major player in addressing the growing epidemic of HIV/AIDS among injecting drug users and commercial sex workers in the northeastern states of Manipur, Mizoram and Nagaland. EHA's other activities include prevention, care and support in the states of Bihar, Jharkhand, Uttar Pradesh, Uttranchal, Delhi, Madhya Pradesh and Maharashtra. The EHA AIDS Resource Team provides training and consultancy services within and outside its organisation.

Emmanuel Hospital Association (EHA)
808/92 Deepali Building
Nehru Place
New Delhi   11 0019 India

Tel: 00 91 11 26432055, 26461487
Email: Info@eha-health.org
Website: http://www.eha-health.org

AFRICA INLAND MISSION

Working across Africa and with African peoples around the world, AIM is an international and interdenominational evangelical Christian organisation with over 750 personnel. Personnel are drawn from Africa, North and South America, Europe, Asia and Australasia.

The main focus of AIM International is on planting churches and helping churches to grow across Africa and within African communities elsewhere in the world. Besides evangelism and theological training at all levels, there are significant activities in medical care, HIV/AIDS, education, literacy and agriculture.

AIM seeks at all times to serve the local church and partner in shared objectives, often in the most needy and challenging of situations. These include work among street children and refugees and in areas of conflict.

AIM has recognised for some time that HIV/AIDS impacts all of its work and is seeking to be strategic in its response as partner to African Christians, seeking to learn together effective responses and proclaiming a hope in Jesus Christ.

Opportunities to serve with AIM are numerous and varied.

AIM International
3 Halifax Place
Nottingham
NG1 1QN
UK

Tel: 0115 983 8120
Email: *enquiries@aimeurope.net*